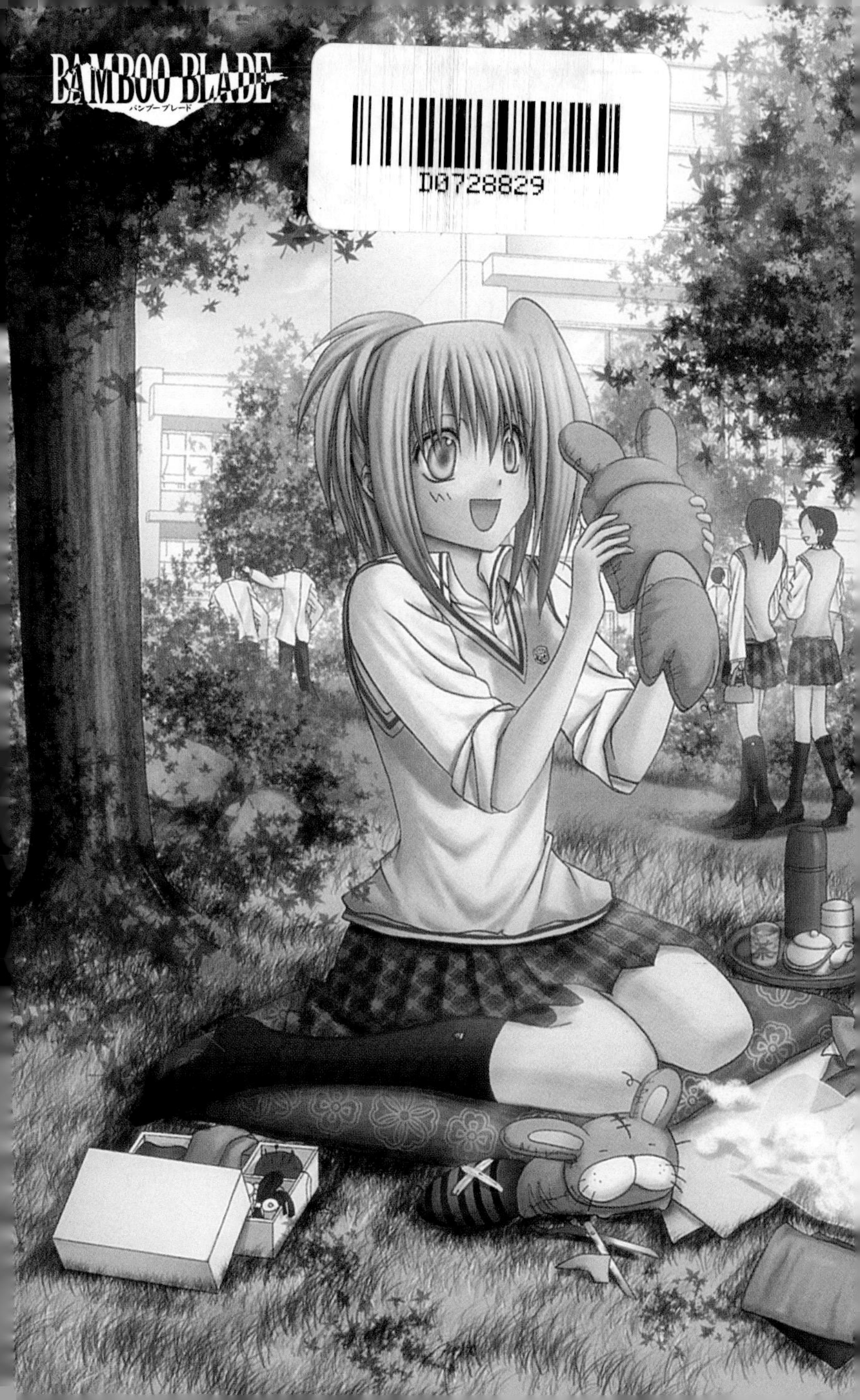
BAMBOO BLADE
バンブーブレード

BAMBOO BLADE 2
CONTENTS

Story: Masahiro Totsuka / Art: Aguri Igarashi

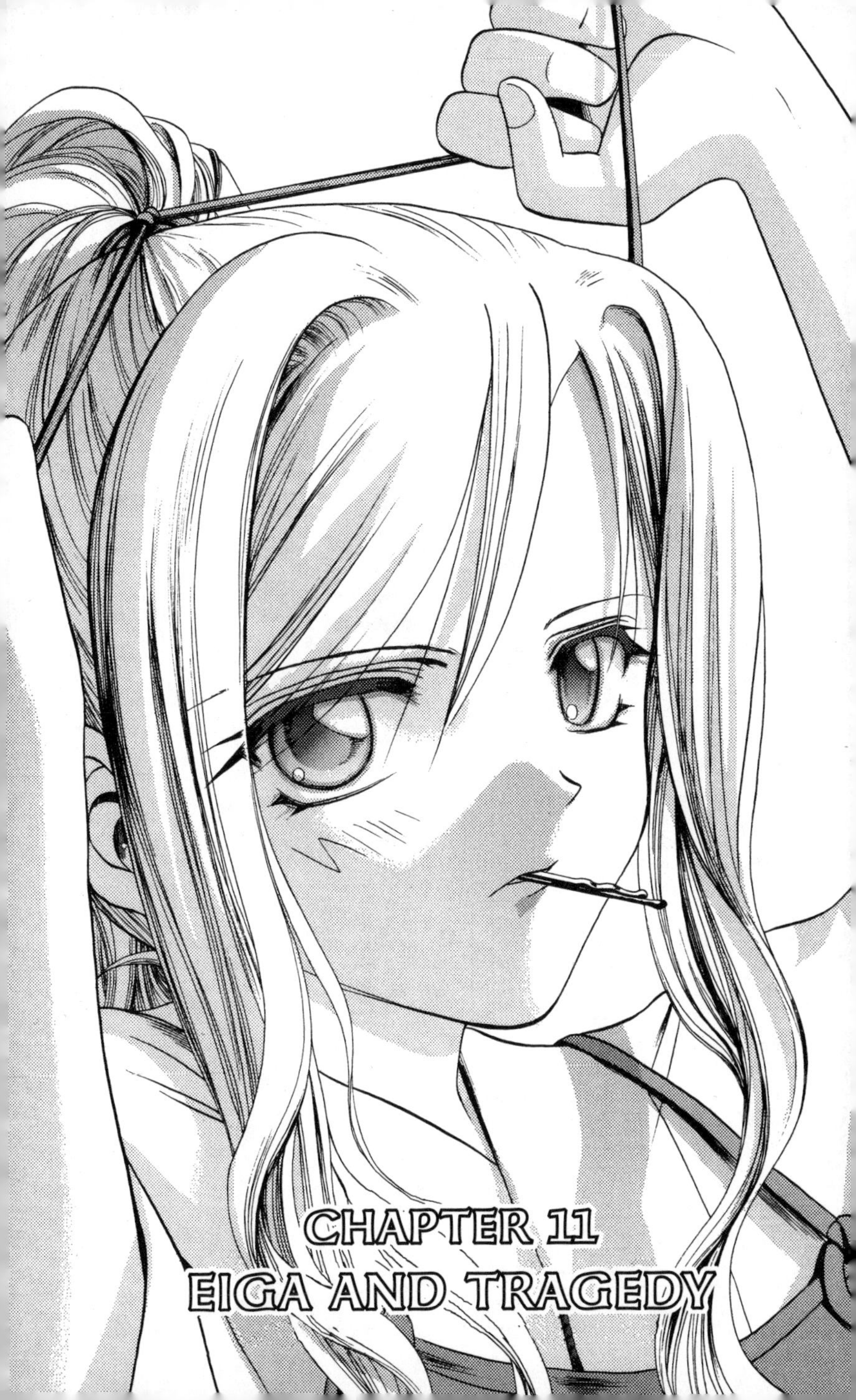
CHAPTER 11
EIGA AND TRAGEDY

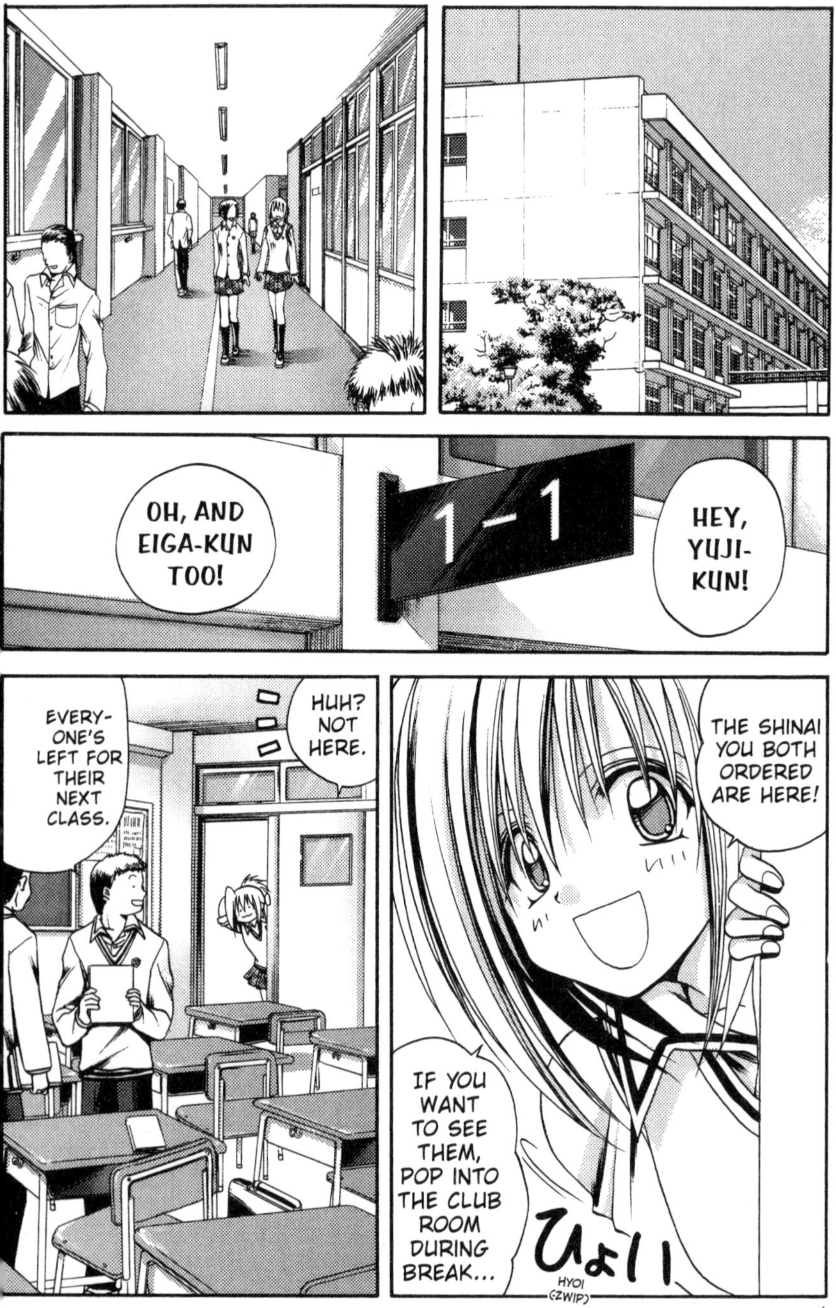
HEY, YUJI-KUN!
OH, AND EIGA-KUN TOO!
THE SHINAI YOU BOTH ORDERED ARE HERE!
IF YOU WANT TO SEE THEM, POP INTO THE CLUB ROOM DURING BREAK...
ひょい
HYOI (ZWIP)
HUH? NOT HERE.
EVERYONE'S LEFT FOR THEIR NEXT CLASS.

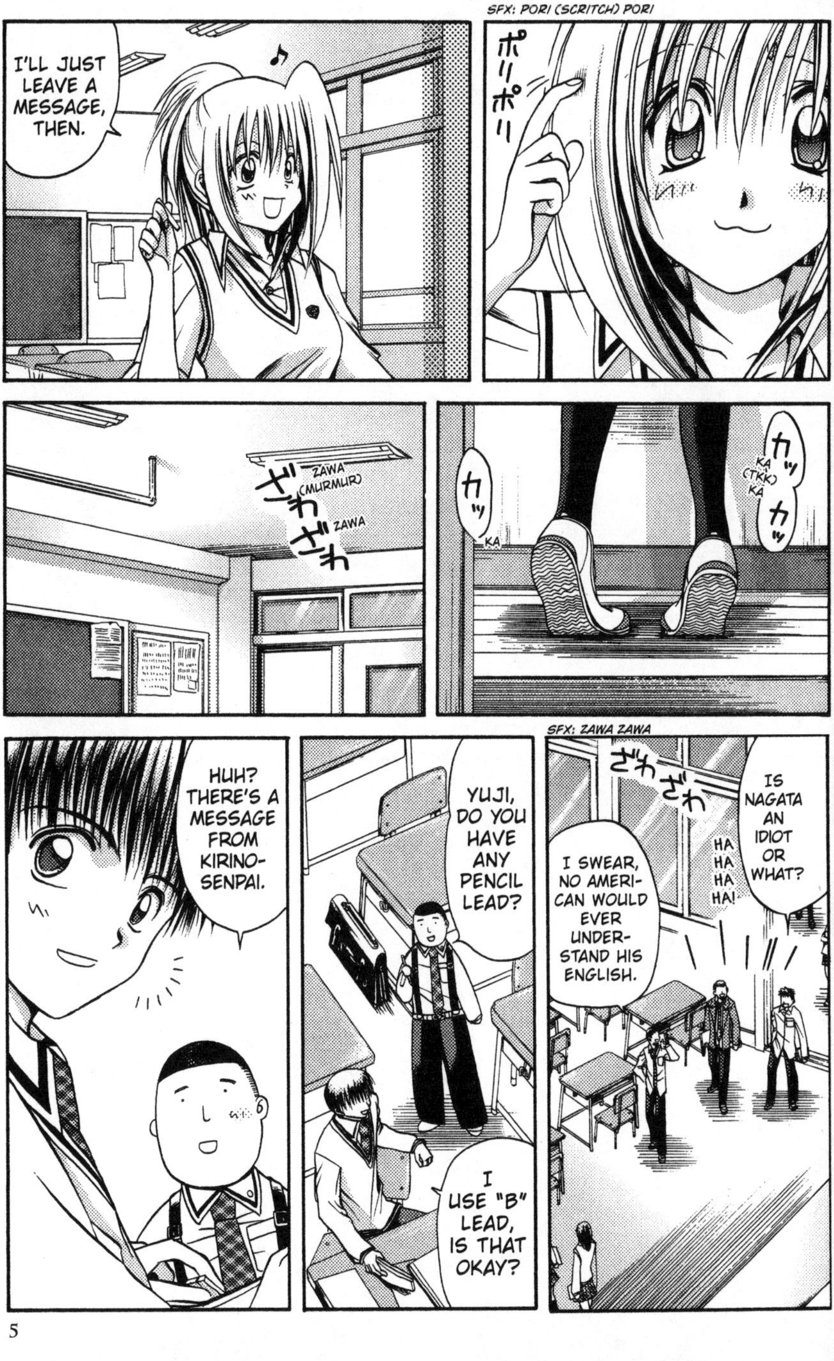
SFX: PORI (SCRITCH) PORI
ポリポリ
I'LL JUST LEAVE A MESSAGE, THEN.
カッ
KA (TKK) KA
カッ
カッ
KA
ざわざわ
ZAWA (MURMUR) ZAWA
SFX: ZAWA ZAWA
ざわざわ
IS NAGATA AN IDIOT OR WHAT?
HA HA HA HA!
I SWEAR, NO AMERICAN WOULD EVER UNDERSTAND HIS ENGLISH.
YUJI, DO YOU HAVE ANY PENCIL LEAD?
I USE "B" LEAD, IS THAT OKAY?
HUH? THERE'S A MESSAGE FROM KIRINO-SENPAI.

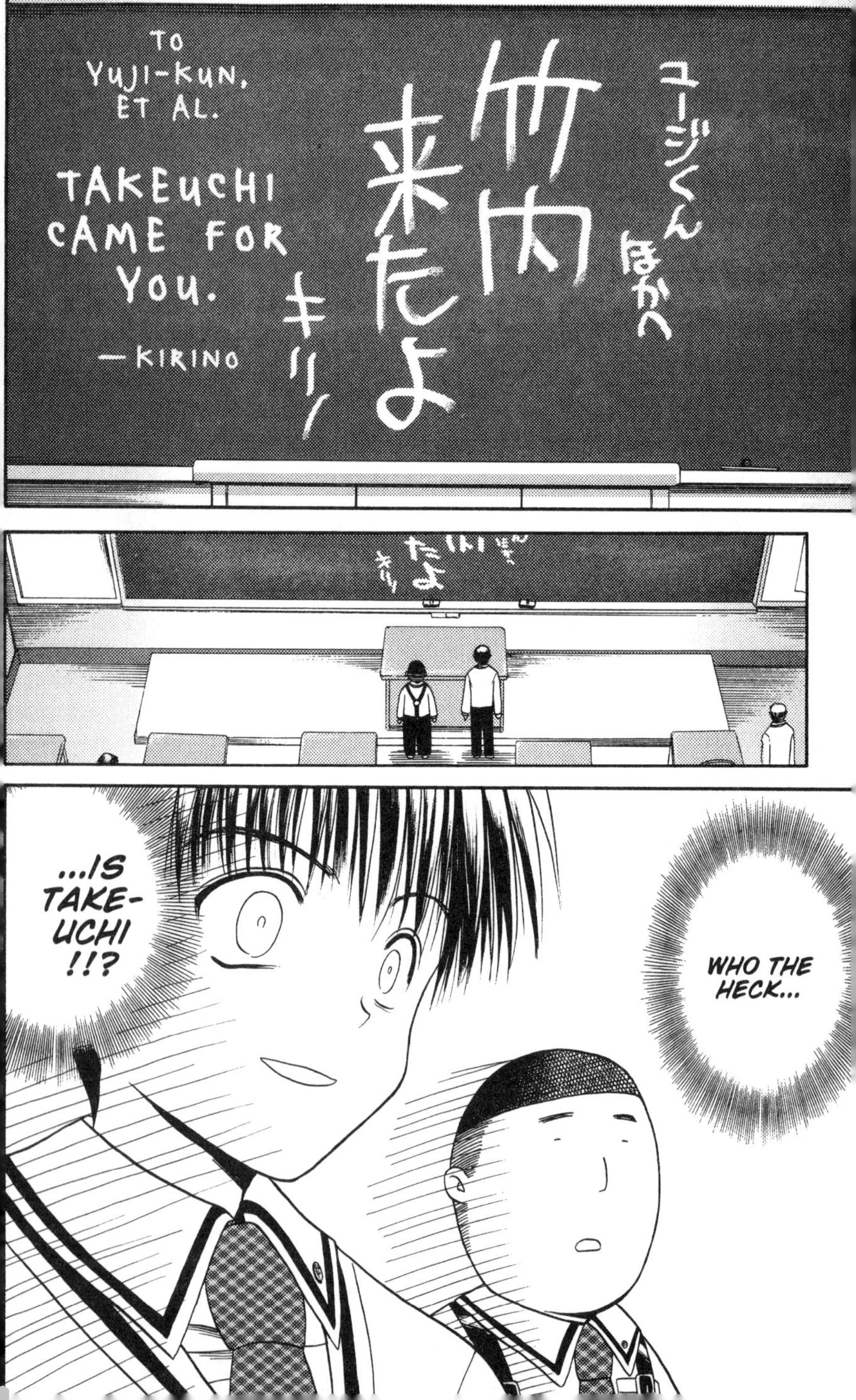
ユージくんほかへ
竹内来たよ
キリノ
TO YUJI-KUN, ET AL.
TAKEUCHI CAME FOR YOU.
—KIRINO
WHO THE HECK...
...IS TAKE-UCHI!!?

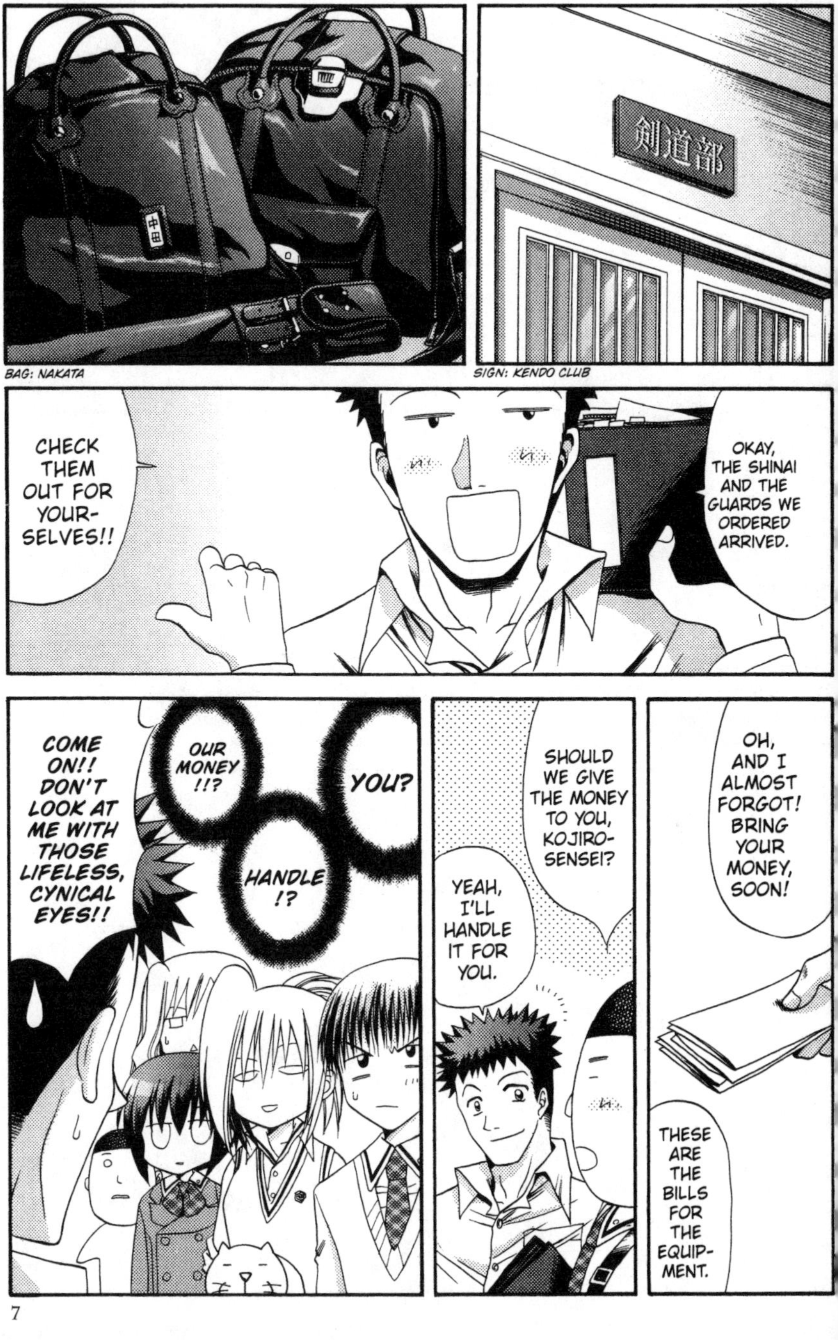
SIGN: KENDO CLUB
BAG: NAKATA
OKAY, THE SHINAI AND THE GUARDS WE ORDERED ARRIVED.
CHECK THEM OUT FOR YOUR-SELVES!!
OH, AND I ALMOST FORGOT! BRING YOUR MONEY, SOON!
THESE ARE THE BILLS FOR THE EQUIP-MENT.
SHOULD WE GIVE THE MONEY TO YOU, KOJIRO-SENSEI?
YEAH, I'LL HANDLE IT FOR YOU.
YOU?
OUR MONEY!!?
HANDLE!?
COME ON!! DON'T LOOK AT ME WITH THOSE LIFELESS, CYNICAL EYES!!

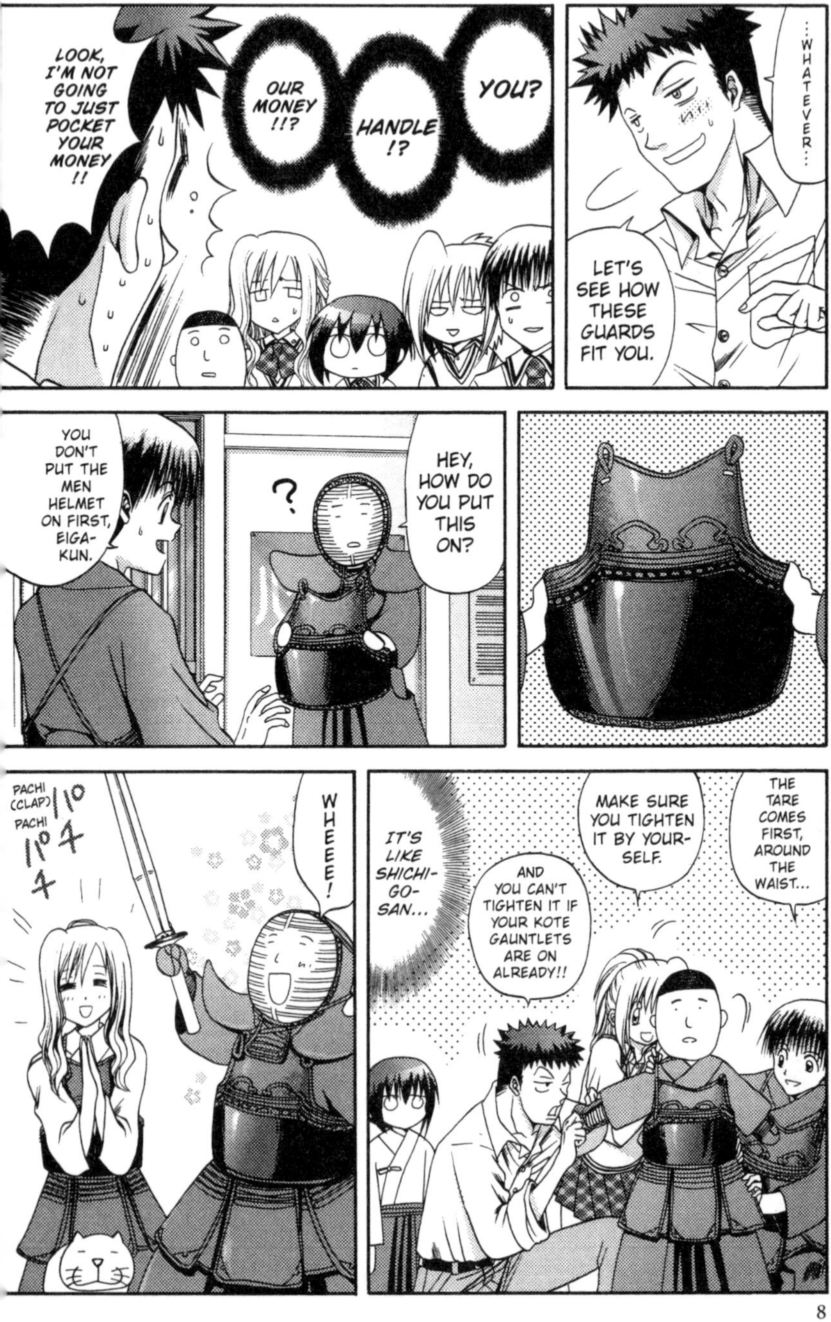

...WHATEVER...
LET'S SEE HOW THESE GUARDS FIT YOU.
YOU?
HANDLE!?
OUR MONEY!!?
LOOK, I'M NOT GOING TO JUST POCKET YOUR MONEY!!
HEY, HOW DO YOU PUT THIS ON?
YOU DON'T PUT THE MEN HELMET ON FIRST, EIGA-KUN.
THE TARE COMES FIRST, AROUND THE WAIST...
MAKE SURE YOU TIGHTEN IT BY YOUR-SELF.
IT'S LIKE SHICHI-GO-SAN...
AND YOU CAN'T TIGHTEN IT IF YOUR KOTE GAUNTLETS ARE ON ALREADY!!
WHEEEE!
PACHI (CLAP) PACHI

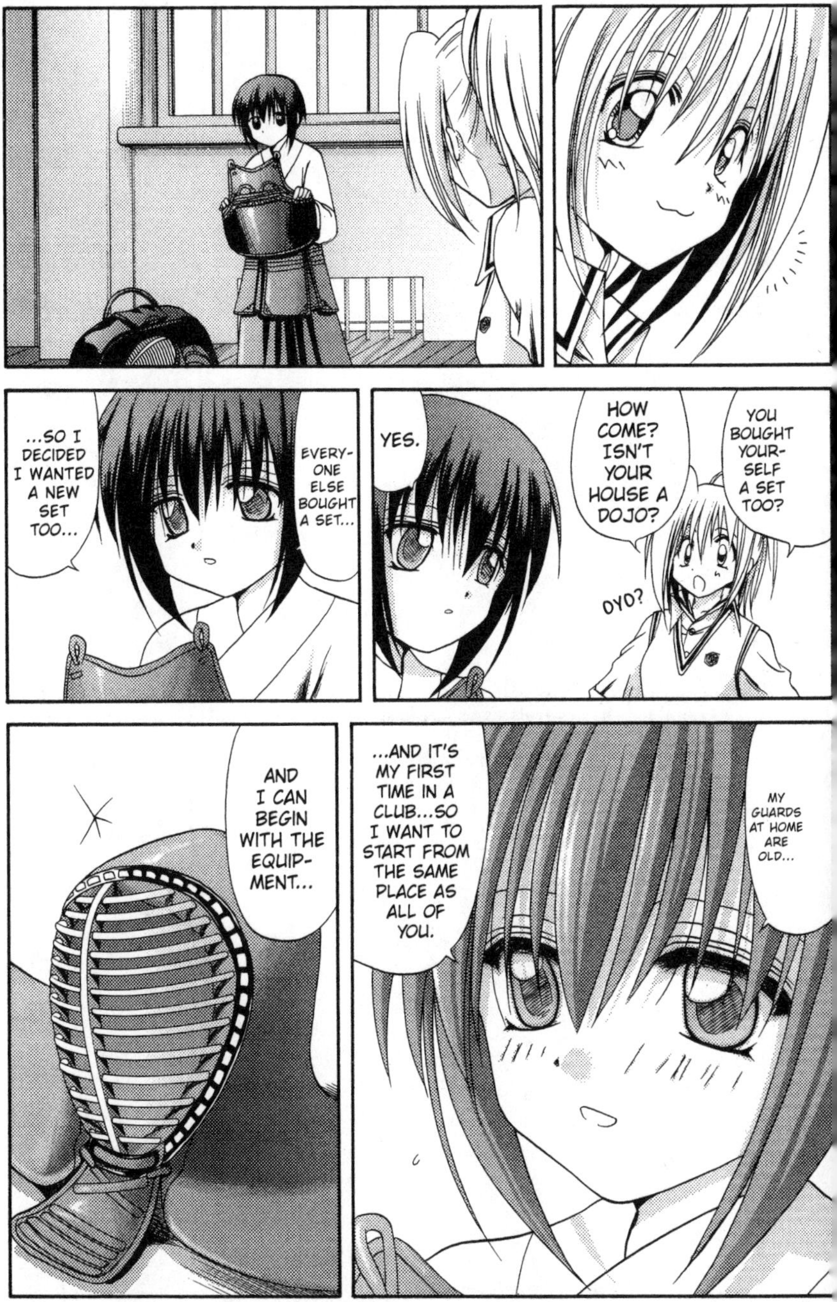

YOU BOUGHT YOURSELF A SET TOO?
HOW COME? ISN'T YOUR HOUSE A DOJO?
YES.
OYO?
EVERYONE ELSE BOUGHT A SET...
...SO I DECIDED I WANTED A NEW SET TOO...
MY GUARDS AT HOME ARE OLD...
...AND IT'S MY FIRST TIME IN A CLUB...SO I WANT TO START FROM THE SAME PLACE AS ALL OF YOU.
AND I CAN BEGIN WITH THE EQUIPMENT...

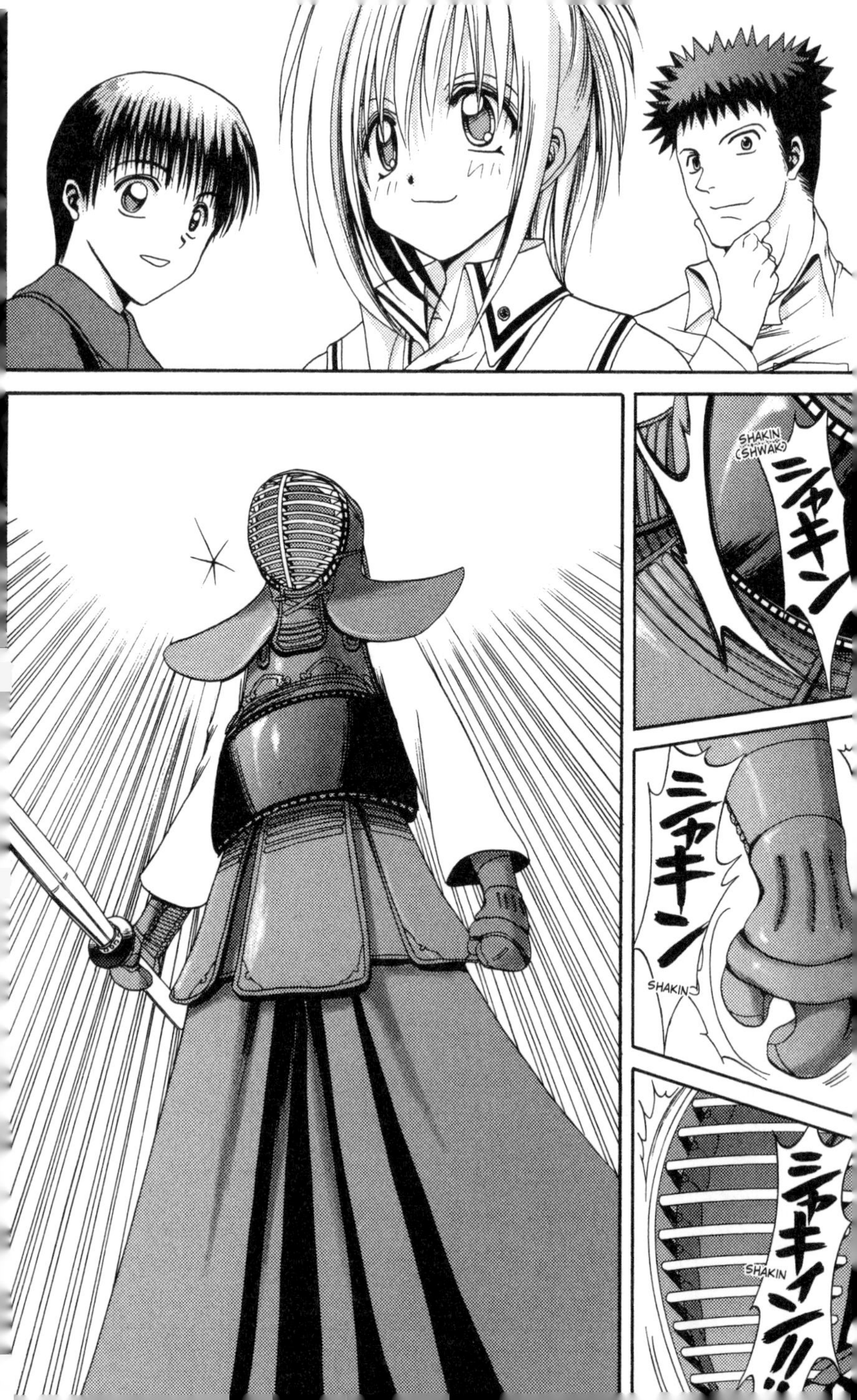
SHAKIN (SHWAK)
シャキン
シャキン
SHAKIN
シャキイン!!
SHAKIN

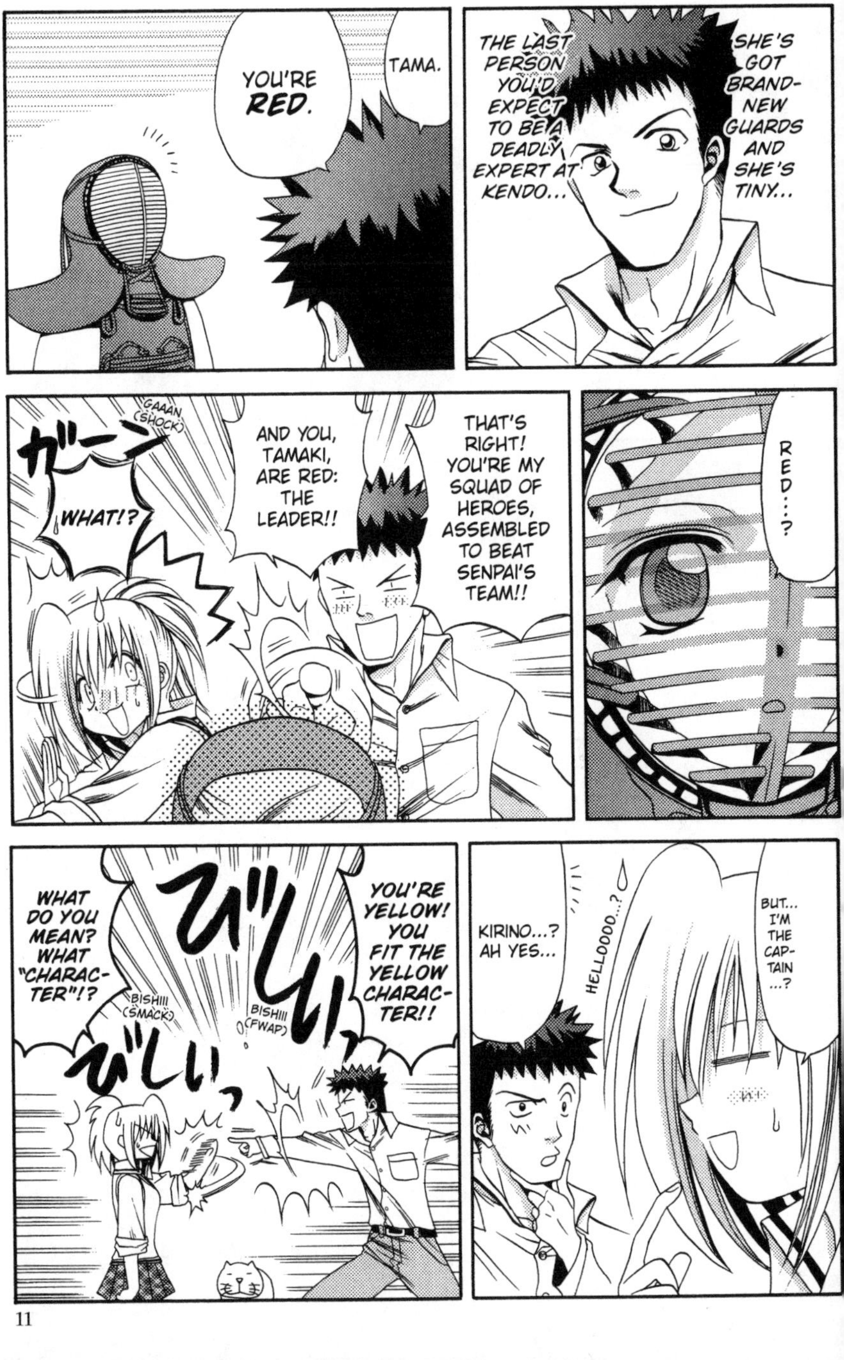
SHE'S GOT BRAND-NEW GUARDS AND SHE'S TINY...
THE LAST PERSON YOU'D EXPECT TO BE A DEADLY EXPERT AT KENDO...
TAMA.
YOU'RE RED.
RED...?
THAT'S RIGHT! YOU'RE MY SQUAD OF HEROES, ASSEMBLED TO BEAT SENPAI'S TEAM!!
AND YOU, TAMAKI, ARE RED: THE LEADER!!
GAAAN (SHOCK)
ガーン
WHAT!?
BUT... I'M THE CAPTAIN...?
HELLOOOO...?
KIRINO...? AH YES...
YOU'RE YELLOW! YOU FIT THE YELLOW CHARACTER!!
びしぃっ
BISHIII (FWAP)
WHAT DO YOU MEAN? WHAT "CHARACTER"!?
BISHIII (SMACK)
びしぃっ

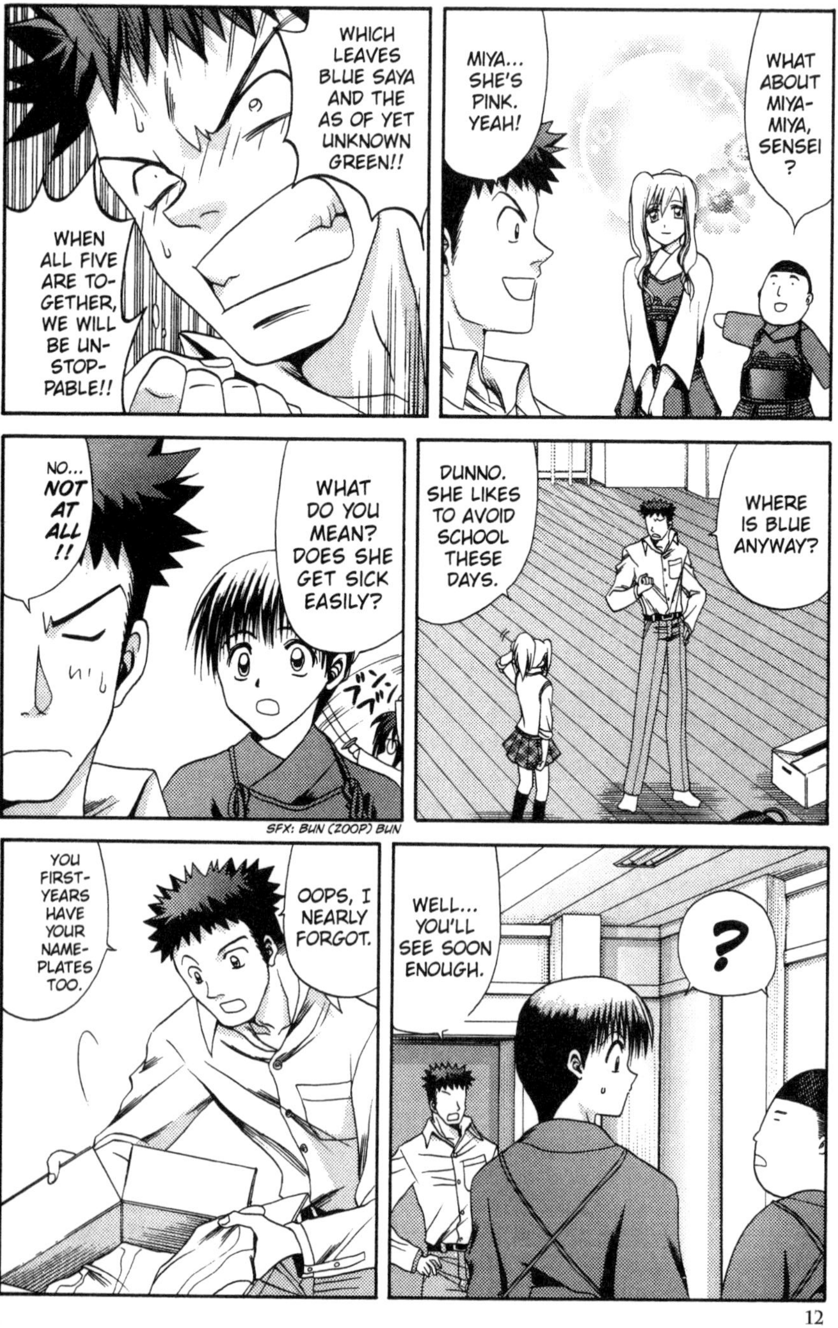
WHAT ABOUT MIYA-MIYA, SENSEI?
MIYA... SHE'S PINK. YEAH!
WHICH LEAVES BLUE SAYA AND THE AS OF YET UNKNOWN GREEN!!
WHEN ALL FIVE ARE TOGETHER, WE WILL BE UNSTOPPABLE!!
WHERE IS BLUE ANYWAY?
DUNNO. SHE LIKES TO AVOID SCHOOL THESE DAYS.
WHAT DO YOU MEAN? DOES SHE GET SICK EASILY?
NO... *NOT AT ALL!!*
SFX: BUN (ZOOP) BUN
?
WELL... YOU'LL SEE SOON ENOUGH.
OOPS, I NEARLY FORGOT.
YOU FIRST-YEARS HAVE YOUR NAMEPLATES TOO.

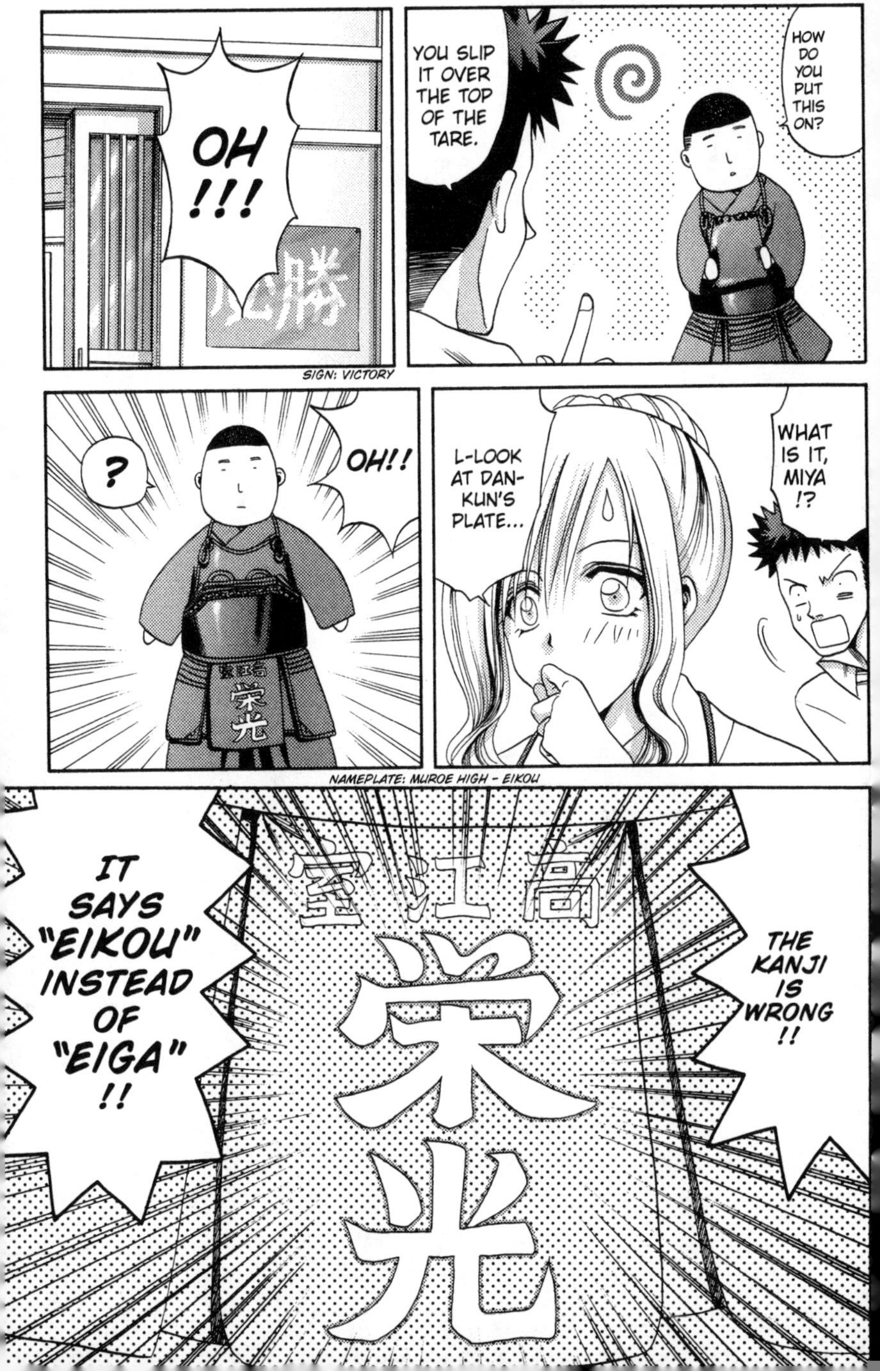
HOW DO YOU PUT THIS ON?
YOU SLIP IT OVER THE TOP OF THE TARE.
OH!!!
SIGN: VICTORY
WHAT IS IT, MIYA!?
L-LOOK AT DAN-KUN'S PLATE...
OH!!
?
NAMEPLATE: MUROE HIGH - EIKOU
THE KANJI IS WRONG!!
IT SAYS "EIKOU" INSTEAD OF "EIGA"!!
室江高
栄光

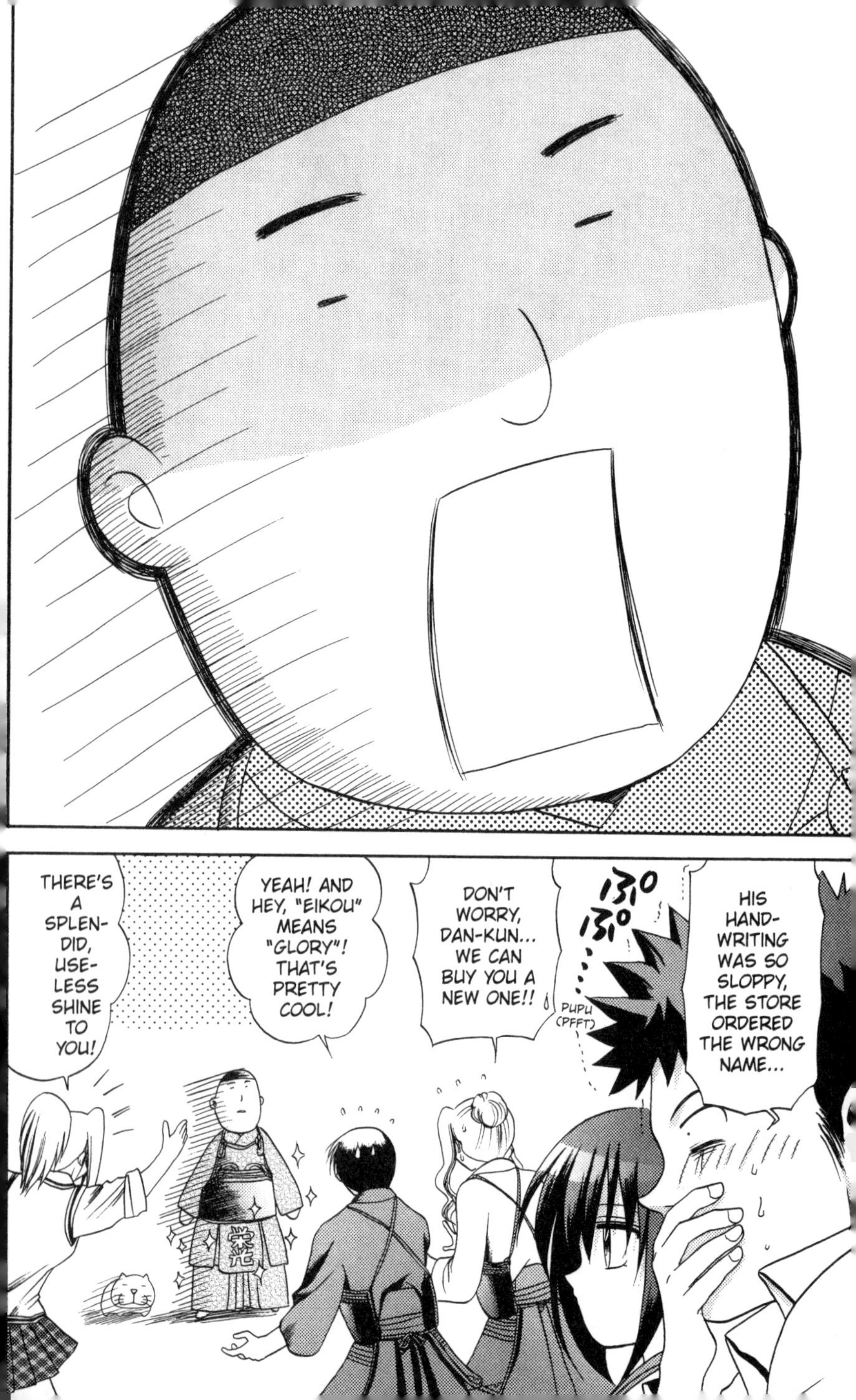
HIS HANDWRITING WAS SO SLOPPY, THE STORE ORDERED THE WRONG NAME...
PUPU (PFFT)
DON'T WORRY, DAN-KUN... WE CAN BUY YOU A NEW ONE!!
YEAH! AND HEY, "EIKOU" MEANS "GLORY"! THAT'S PRETTY COOL!
栄光
THERE'S A SPLENDID, USELESS SHINE TO YOU!

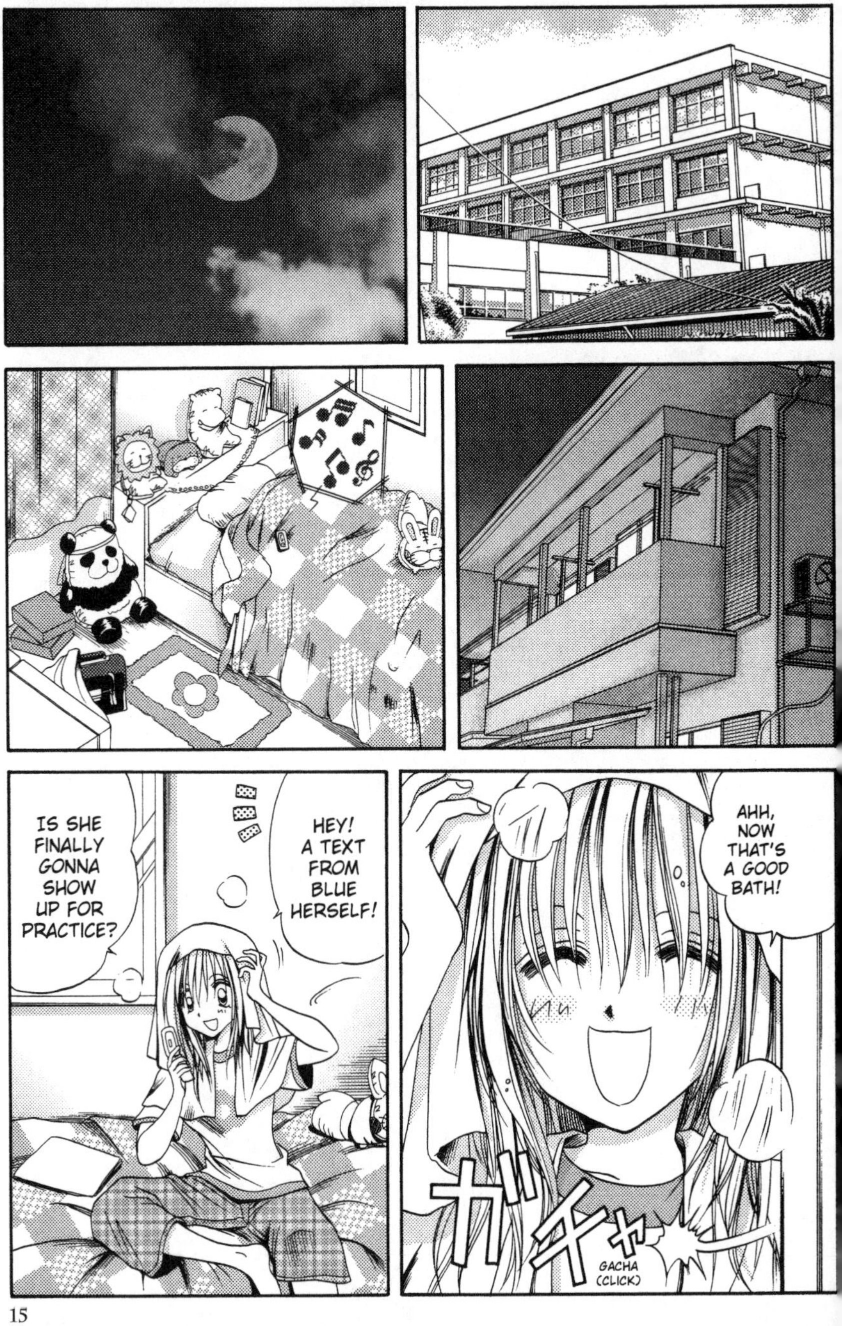
AHH, NOW THAT'S A GOOD BATH!
ガチャ
GACHA (CLICK)
HEY! A TEXT FROM BLUE HERSELF!
IS SHE FINALLY GONNA SHOW UP FOR PRACTICE?

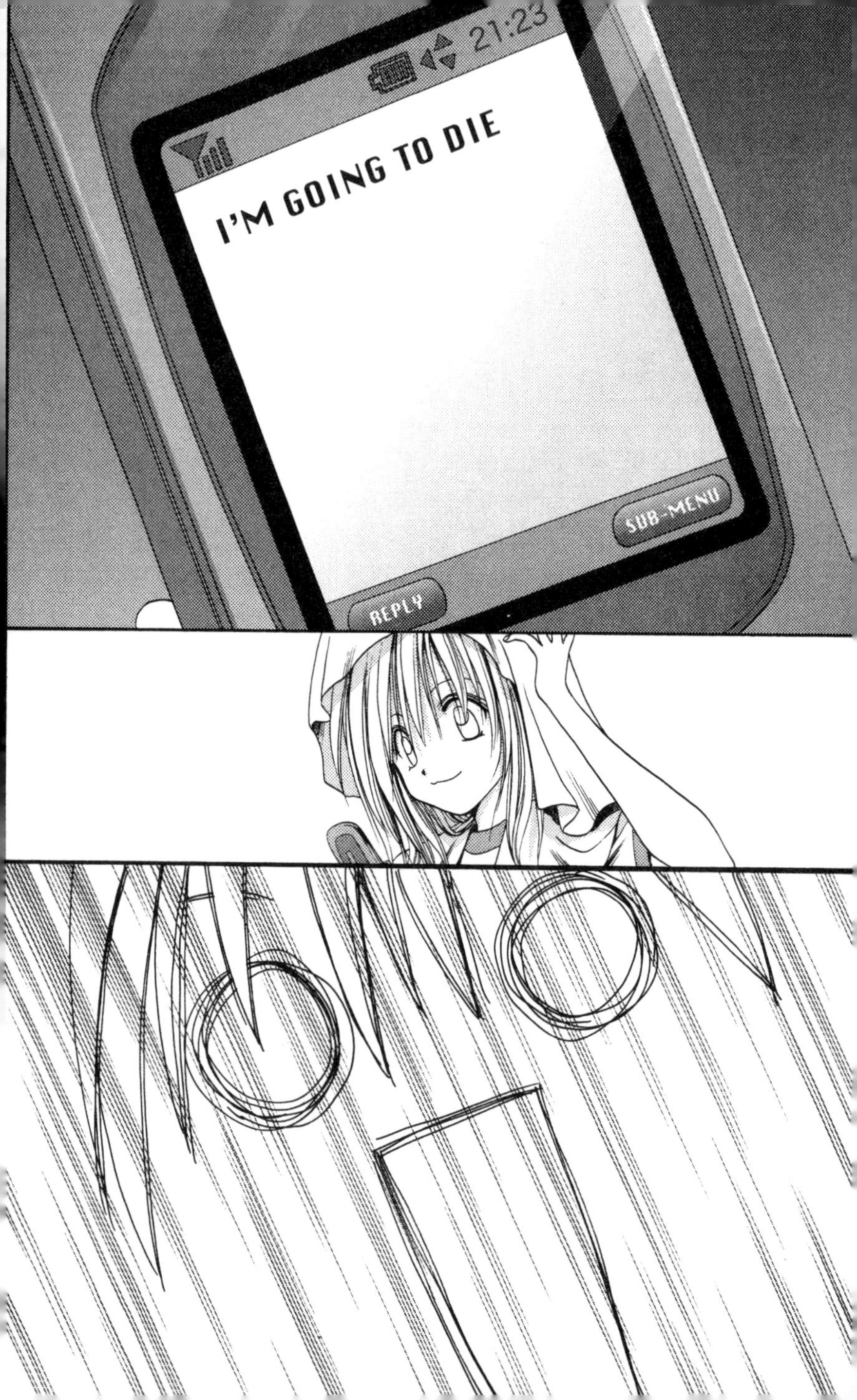
21:23
I'M GOING TO DIE
SUB-MENU
REPLY

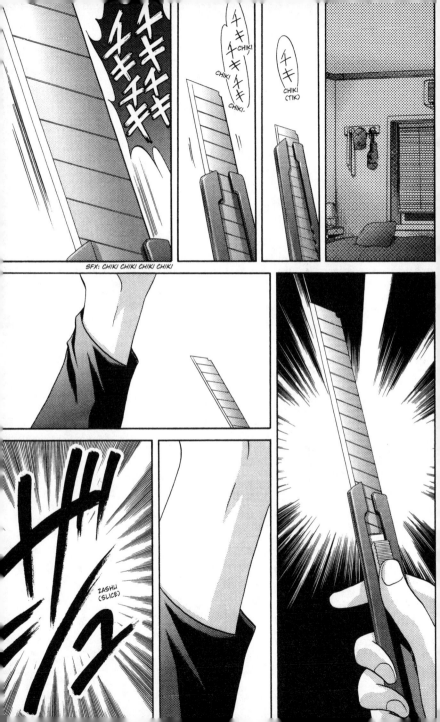

SFX: CHIKI CHIKI CHIKI CHIKI!

CHIKI!
CHIKI!
CHIKI!
CHIKI-

CHIKI
(TIK)

ZASHU
(SLICE)

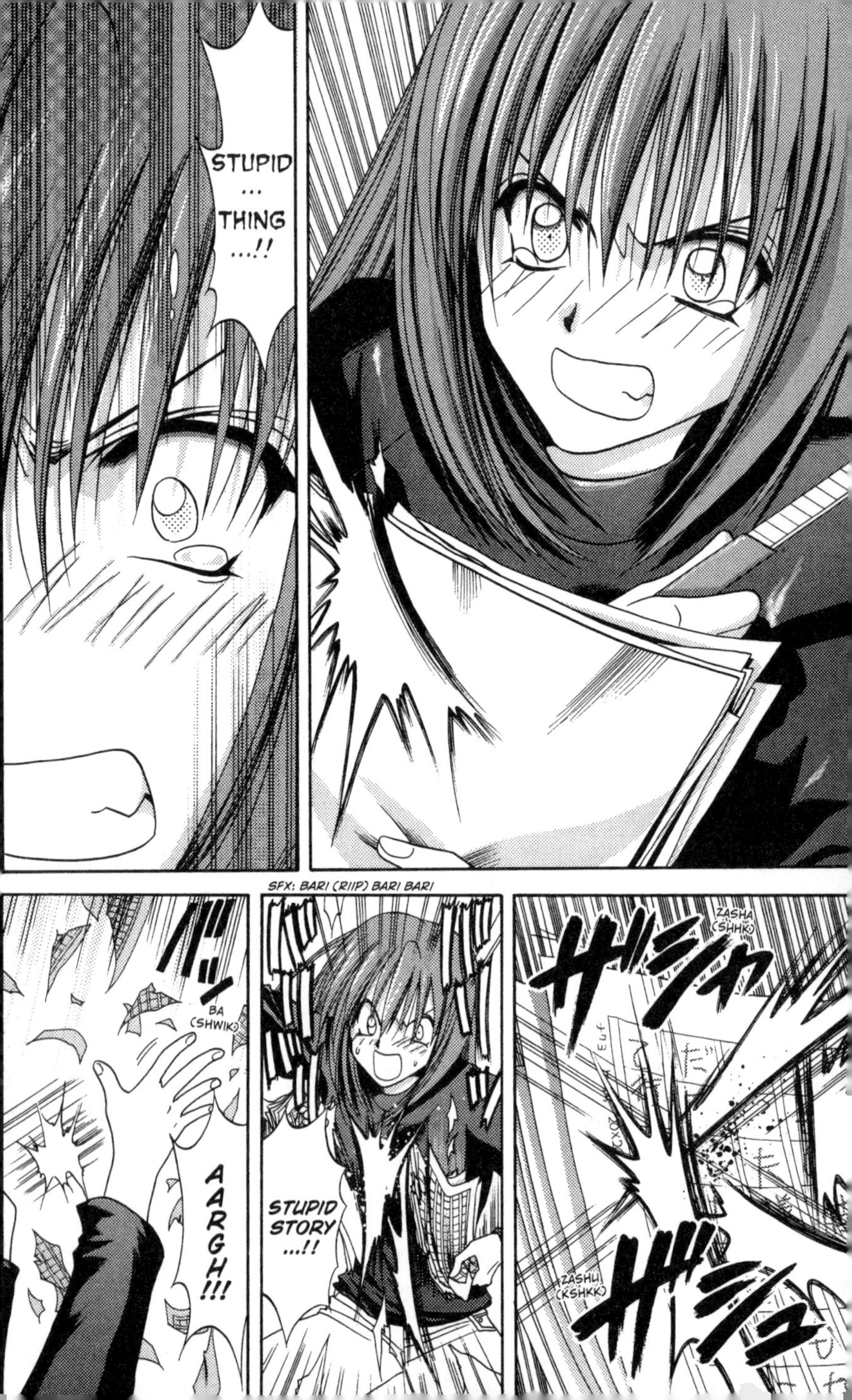
STUPID ... THING ...!!
SFX: BARI (RIIP) BARI BARI
ZASHA (SHHK)
ZASHU (KSHKK)
STUPID STORY ...!!
BA (SHWIK)
AARGH!!!

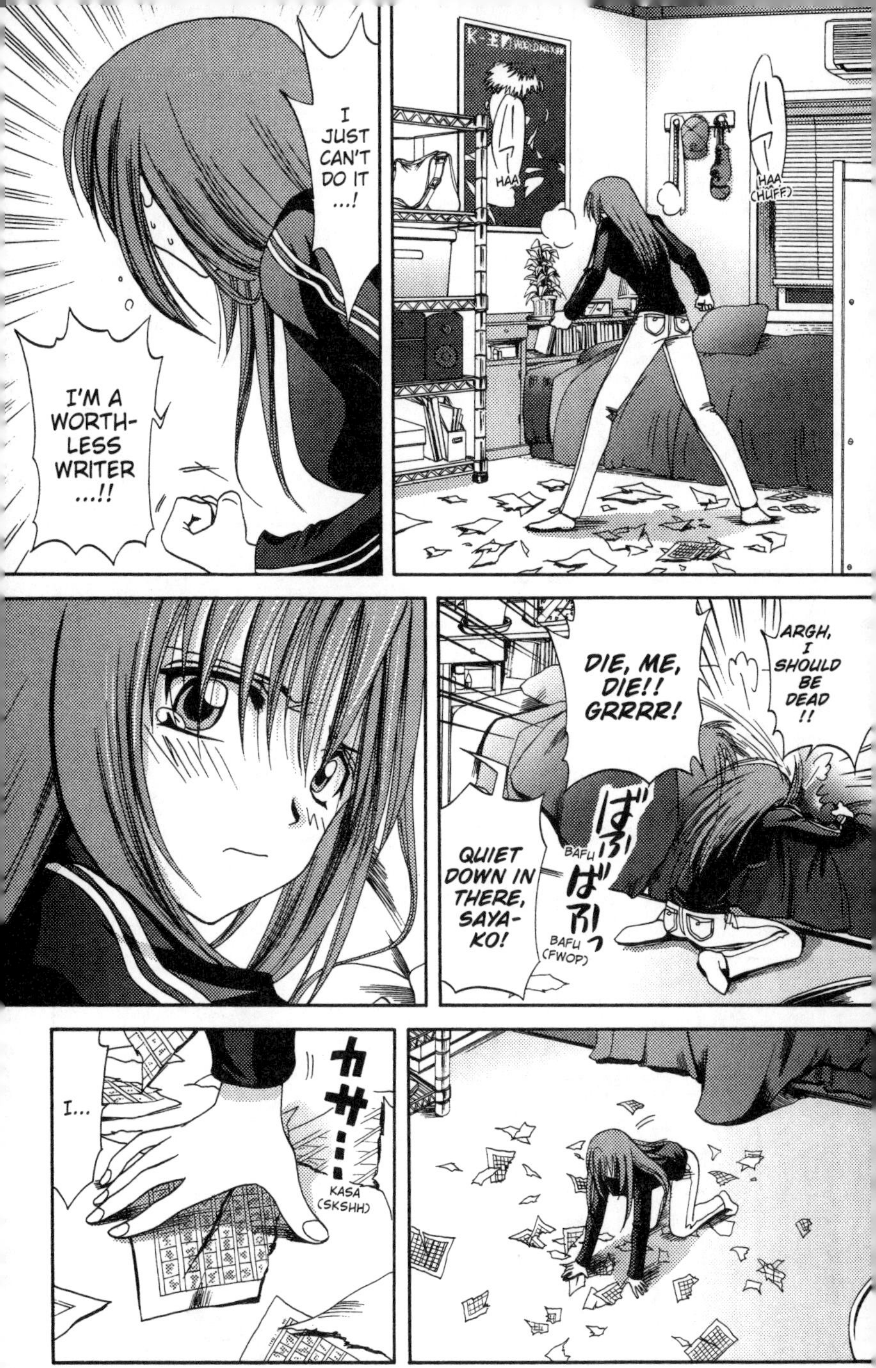
HAA
HAA (HUFF)
I JUST CAN'T DO IT ...!
I'M A WORTH-LESS WRITER ...!!
ARGH, I SHOULD BE DEAD !!
DIE, ME, DIE!! GRRRR!
ばふ
BAFU
ばふっ
BAFU (FWOP)
QUIET DOWN IN THERE, SAYA-KO!
カサ…
KASA (SKSHH)
I...

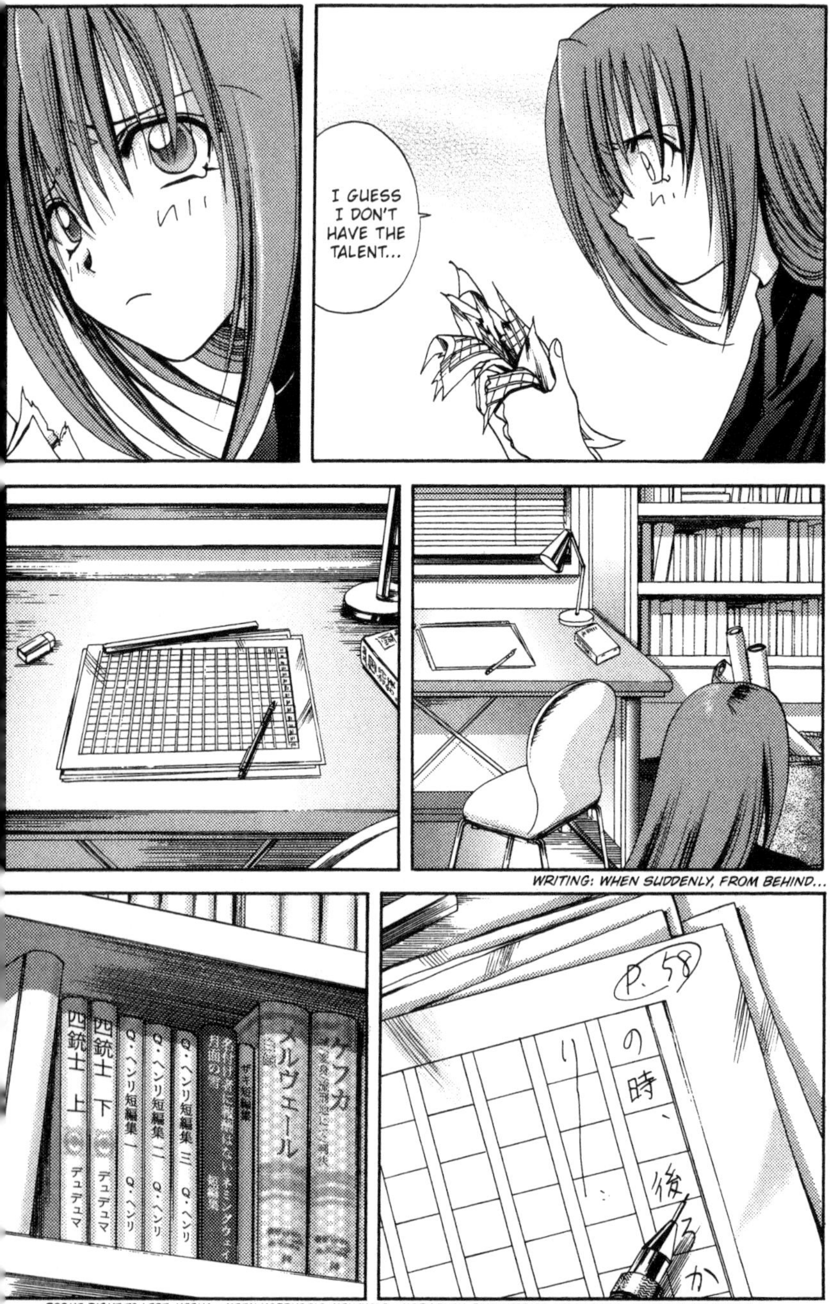
I GUESS I DON'T HAVE THE TALENT...
WRITING: WHEN SUDDENLY, FROM BEHIND...

BOOKS RIGHT TO LEFT: KEFKA - METALMORPHOSIS, MELVHALE - MOBY DUCK, ZAKI STORIES, NAMINGWAY - NAMER TAKE NOTHING / THE SNOWS OF THE MOON, Q. HENRY - Q. HENRY'S SHORT STORIES, VOL. 1, Q. HENRY - Q. HENRY'S SHORT STORIES, VOL. 2, Q. HENRY - Q. HENRY'S SHORT STORIES, VOL. 3, DUDUMAS - THE FOUR MUSKETEERS, PART 1, DUDUMAS - THE FOUR MUSKETEERS, PART 2

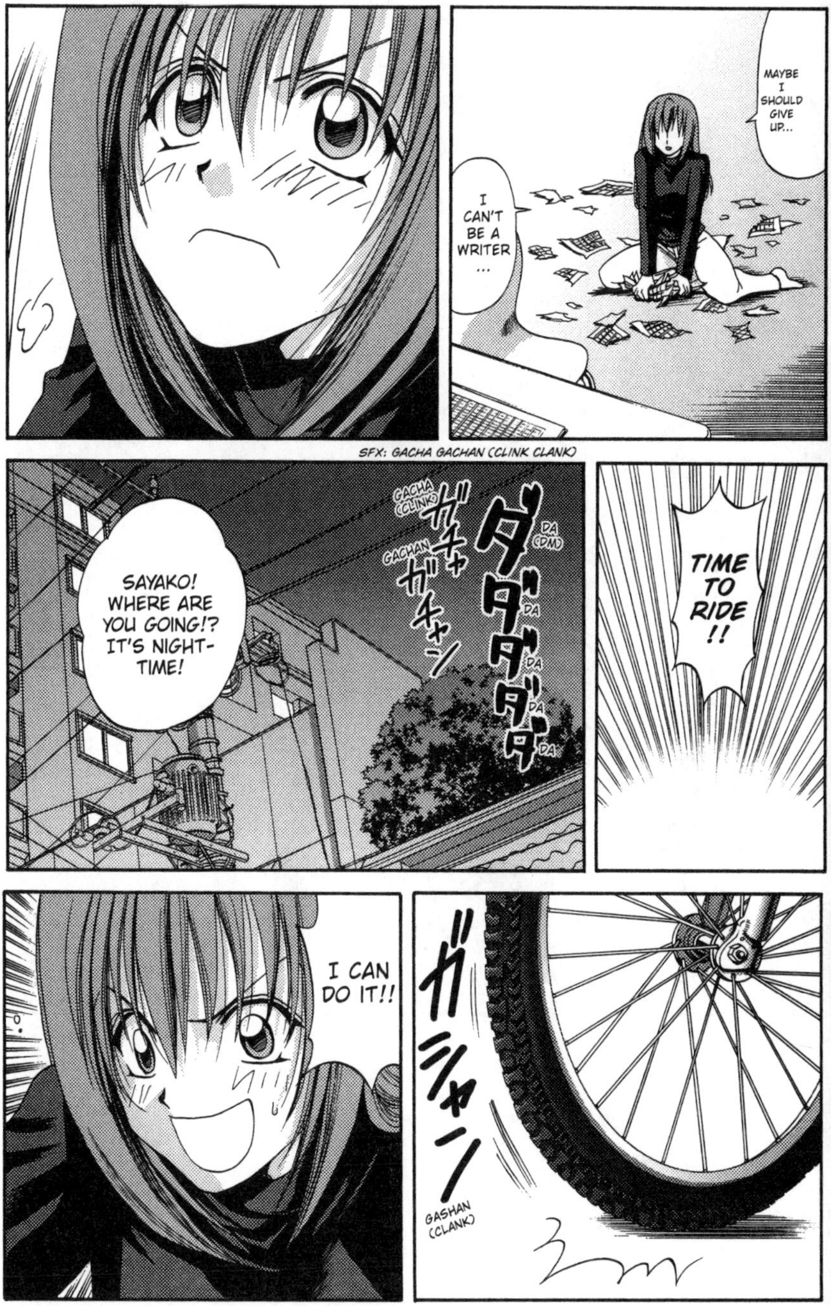
MAYBE I SHOULD GIVE UP...
I CAN'T BE A WRITER...
SFX: GACHA GACHAN (CLINK CLANK)
TIME TO RIDE!!
DA (DM) DA DA DA DA
GACHA (CLINK) GACHAN
SAYAKO! WHERE ARE YOU GOING!? IT'S NIGHT-TIME!
GASHAN (CLANK)
I CAN DO IT!!

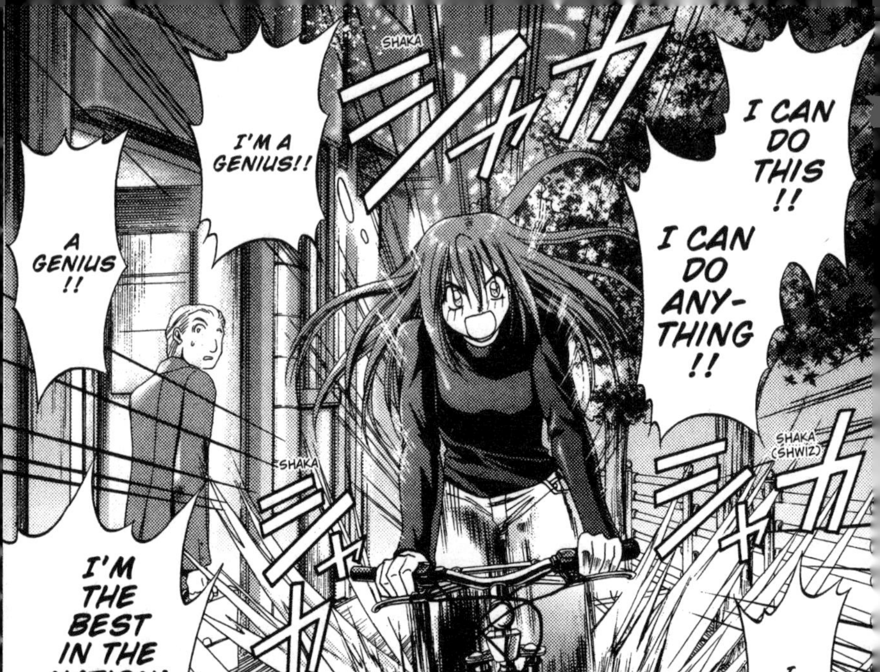
SHAKA
I CAN DO THIS!!
I CAN DO ANY-THING!!
SHAKA (SHWIZ)
I'M A GENIUS!!
A GENIUS!!
I REALLY CAN!
SHAKA
SHAKA
I'M THE BEST IN THE NATION! I CAN DO ANY-THING! WHY? 'COS I'M A GENIUS-SSSS!

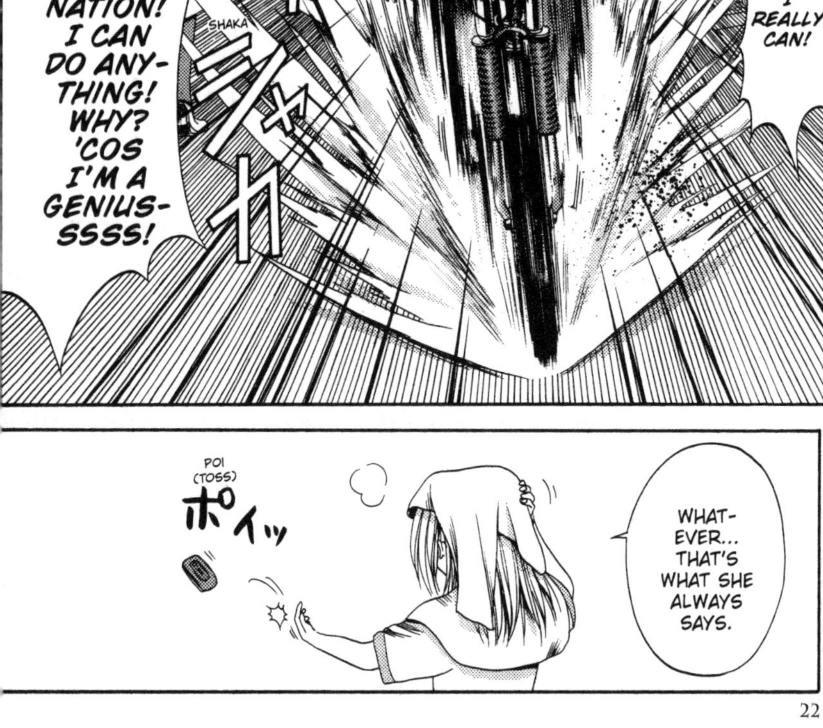
WHAT-EVER... THAT'S WHAT SHE ALWAYS SAYS.
POI (TOSS)
ポイッ

BAMBOO BLADE

Illustration:Aguri Igarashi

Illustration:Masahiro Totsuka

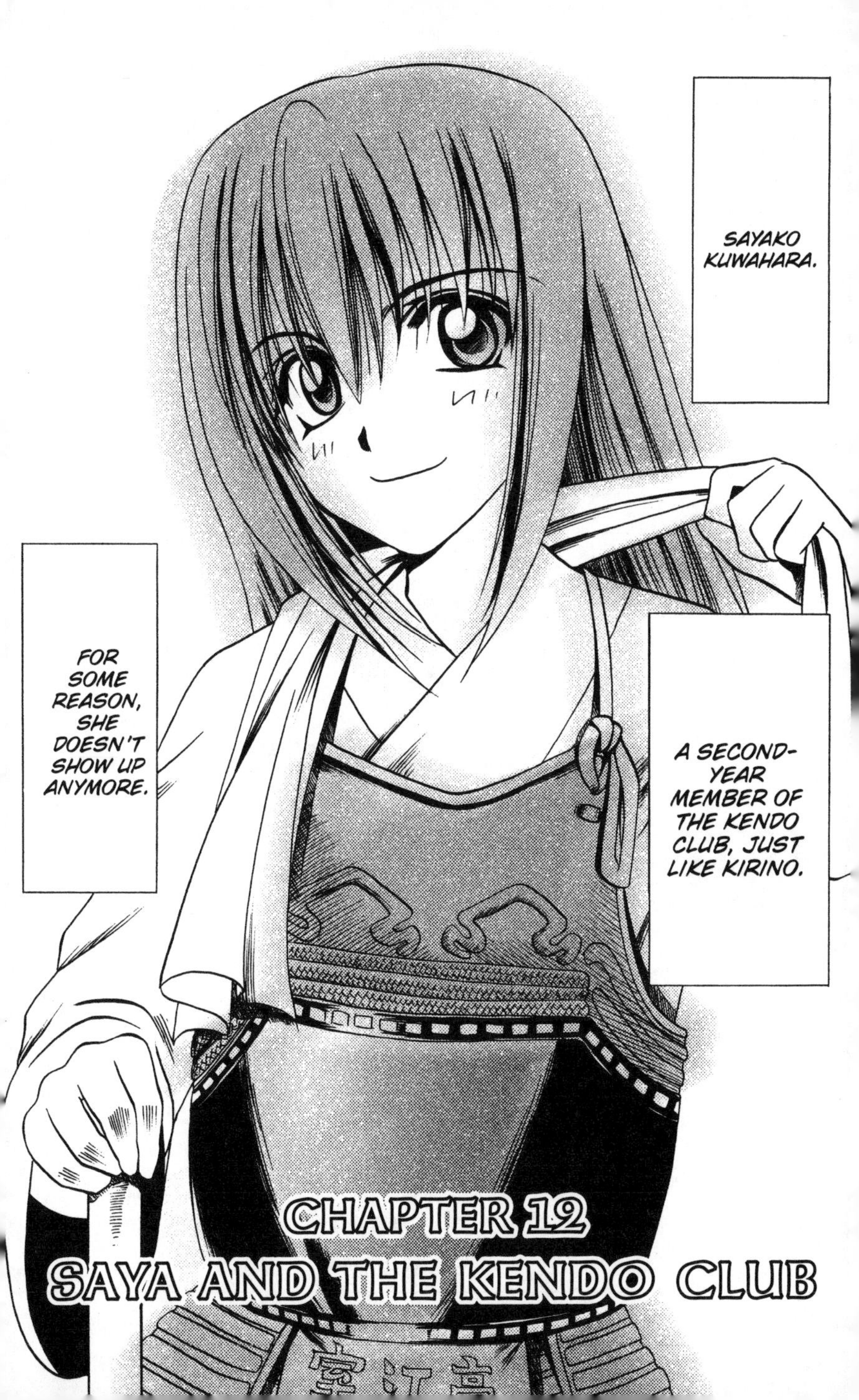
SAYAKO KUWAHARA.
A SECOND-YEAR MEMBER OF THE KENDO CLUB, JUST LIKE KIRINO.
FOR SOME REASON, SHE DOESN'T SHOW UP ANYMORE.
CHAPTER 12
SAYA AND THE KENDO CLUB

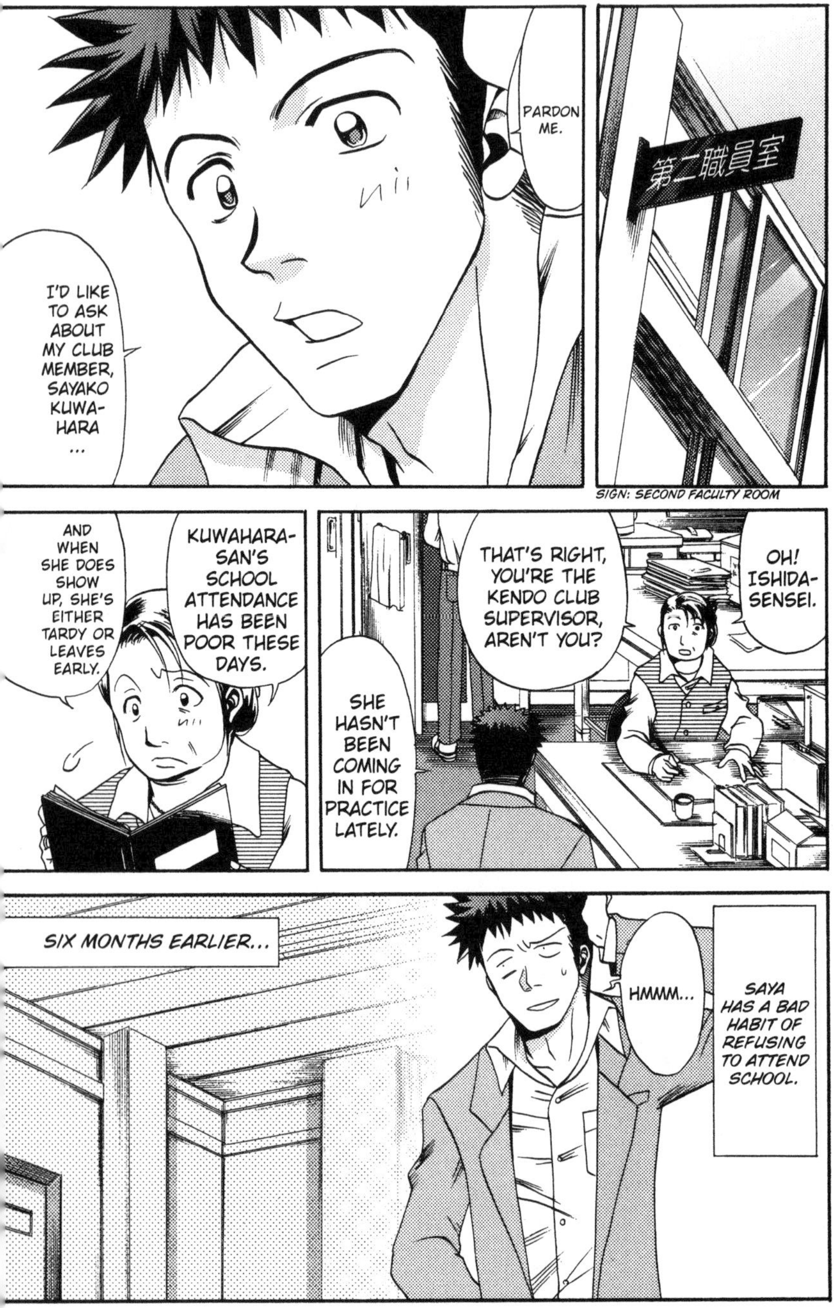
第二職員室
SIGN: SECOND FACULTY ROOM
PARDON ME.
I'D LIKE TO ASK ABOUT MY CLUB MEMBER, SAYAKO KUWA-HARA ...
OH! ISHIDA-SENSEI.
THAT'S RIGHT, YOU'RE THE KENDO CLUB SUPERVISOR, AREN'T YOU?
SHE HASN'T BEEN COMING IN FOR PRACTICE LATELY.
KUWAHARA-SAN'S SCHOOL ATTENDANCE HAS BEEN POOR THESE DAYS.
AND WHEN SHE DOES SHOW UP, SHE'S EITHER TARDY OR LEAVES EARLY.
SAYA HAS A BAD HABIT OF REFUSING TO ATTEND SCHOOL.
HMMM...
SIX MONTHS EARLIER...

BYU
(ZWIP)

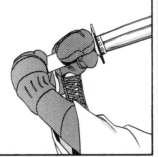

OOH...

BYUON
(ZWOP)

YOU WERE SWINGING SO HARD, I THOUGHT YOU WERE ONE OF THE BOYS, KUWAHARA.

YOU THINK I LOOK LIKE A BOY BECAUSE I'M SO HUGE!?

UH, I DIDN'T SAY THAT.

WHAT WAS THAT?

27

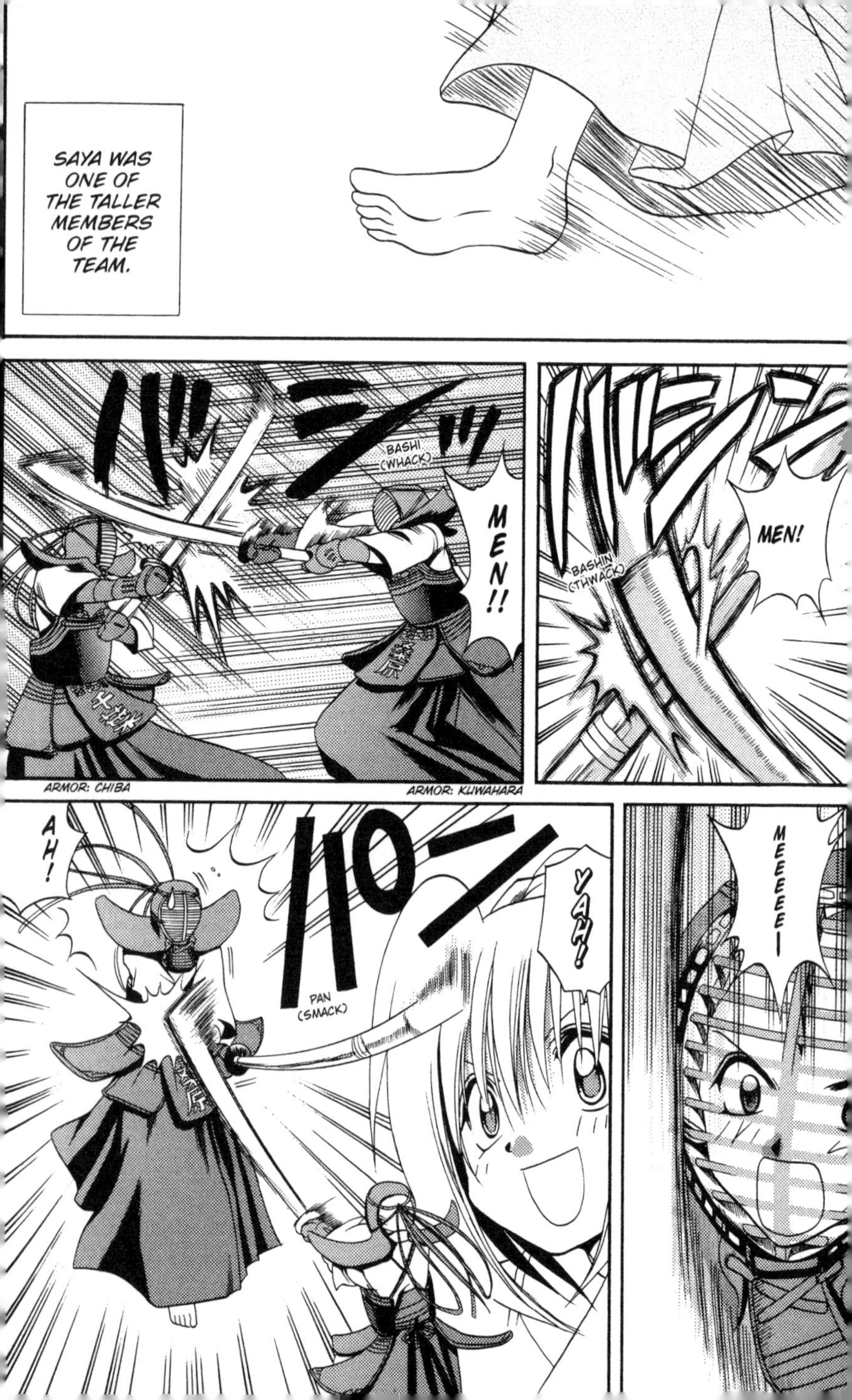
SAYA WAS ONE OF THE TALLER MEMBERS OF THE TEAM.
MEN!
BASHIN (THWACK)
MEN!!
BASHI (WHACK)
ARMOR: KUWAHARA
ARMOR: CHIBA
MEEEEEI
YAH!
PAN (SMACK)
AH!

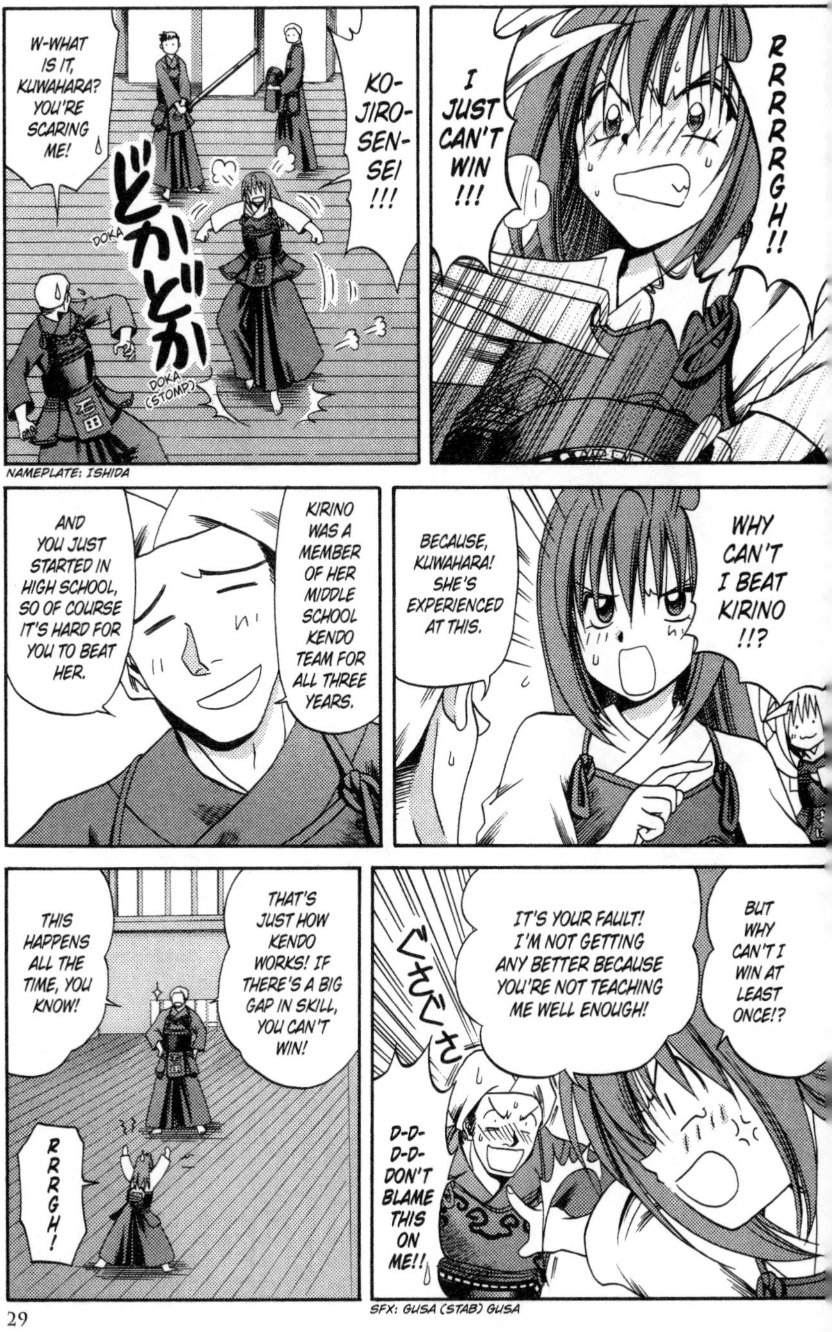
RRRRRGH!!
I JUST CAN'T WIN!!!
KO-JIRO-SEN-SEI!!!
W-WHAT IS IT, KUWAHARA? YOU'RE SCARING ME!
どかどか
DOKA
DOKA (STOMP)
WHY CAN'T I BEAT KIRINO!!?
BECAUSE, KUWAHARA! SHE'S EXPERIENCED AT THIS.
KIRINO WAS A MEMBER OF HER MIDDLE SCHOOL KENDO TEAM FOR ALL THREE YEARS.
AND YOU JUST STARTED IN HIGH SCHOOL, SO OF COURSE IT'S HARD FOR YOU TO BEAT HER.
BUT WHY CAN'T I WIN AT LEAST ONCE!?
IT'S YOUR FAULT! I'M NOT GETTING ANY BETTER BECAUSE YOU'RE NOT TEACHING ME WELL ENOUGH!
ぐさぐさ
D-D-D-D-DON'T BLAME THIS ON ME!!
THAT'S JUST HOW KENDO WORKS! IF THERE'S A BIG GAP IN SKILL, YOU CAN'T WIN!
THIS HAPPENS ALL THE TIME, YOU KNOW!
RRRGH!

NAMEPLATE: ISHIDA

SFX: GUSA (STAB) GUSA

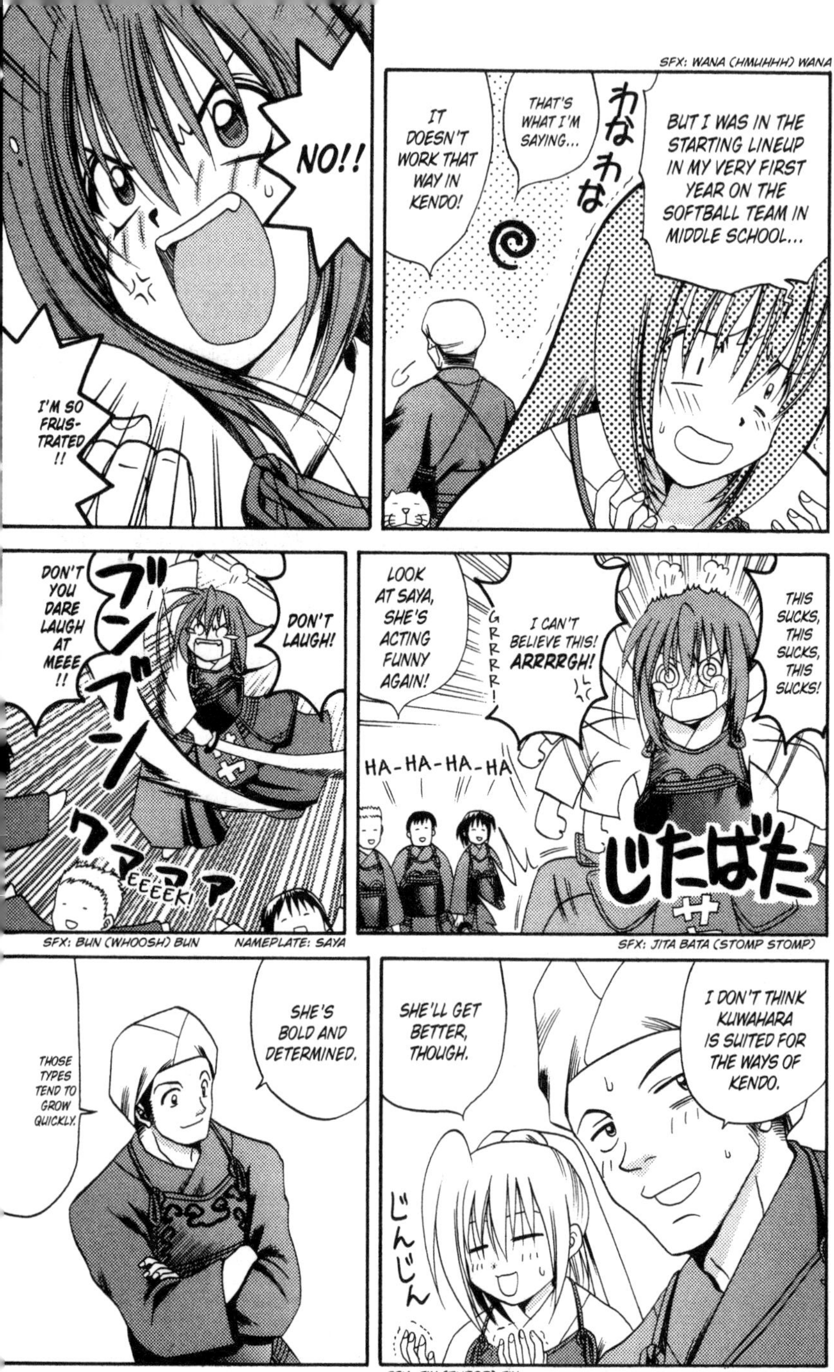
SFX: WANA (HMUHHH) WANA
BUT I WAS IN THE STARTING LINEUP IN MY VERY FIRST YEAR ON THE SOFTBALL TEAM IN MIDDLE SCHOOL...
わなわな
THAT'S WHAT I'M SAYING...
IT DOESN'T WORK THAT WAY IN KENDO!
NO!!
I'M SO FRUS-TRATED!!
THIS SUCKS, THIS SUCKS, THIS SUCKS!
I CAN'T BELIEVE THIS! ARRRRGH!
GRRRR!
LOOK AT SAYA, SHE'S ACTING FUNNY AGAIN!
HA-HA-HA-HA
じたばた
SFX: JITA BATA (STOMP STOMP)
DON'T LAUGH!
DON'T YOU DARE LAUGH AT MEEE!!
ブンブン
ワァァァ
EEEEK!
SFX: BUN (WHOOSH) BUN
NAMEPLATE: SAYA
I DON'T THINK KUWAHARA IS SUITED FOR THE WAYS OF KENDO.
SHE'LL GET BETTER, THOUGH.
じんじん
SHE'S BOLD AND DETERMINED.
THOSE TYPES TEND TO GROW QUICKLY.
SFX: JIN (THROB) JIN

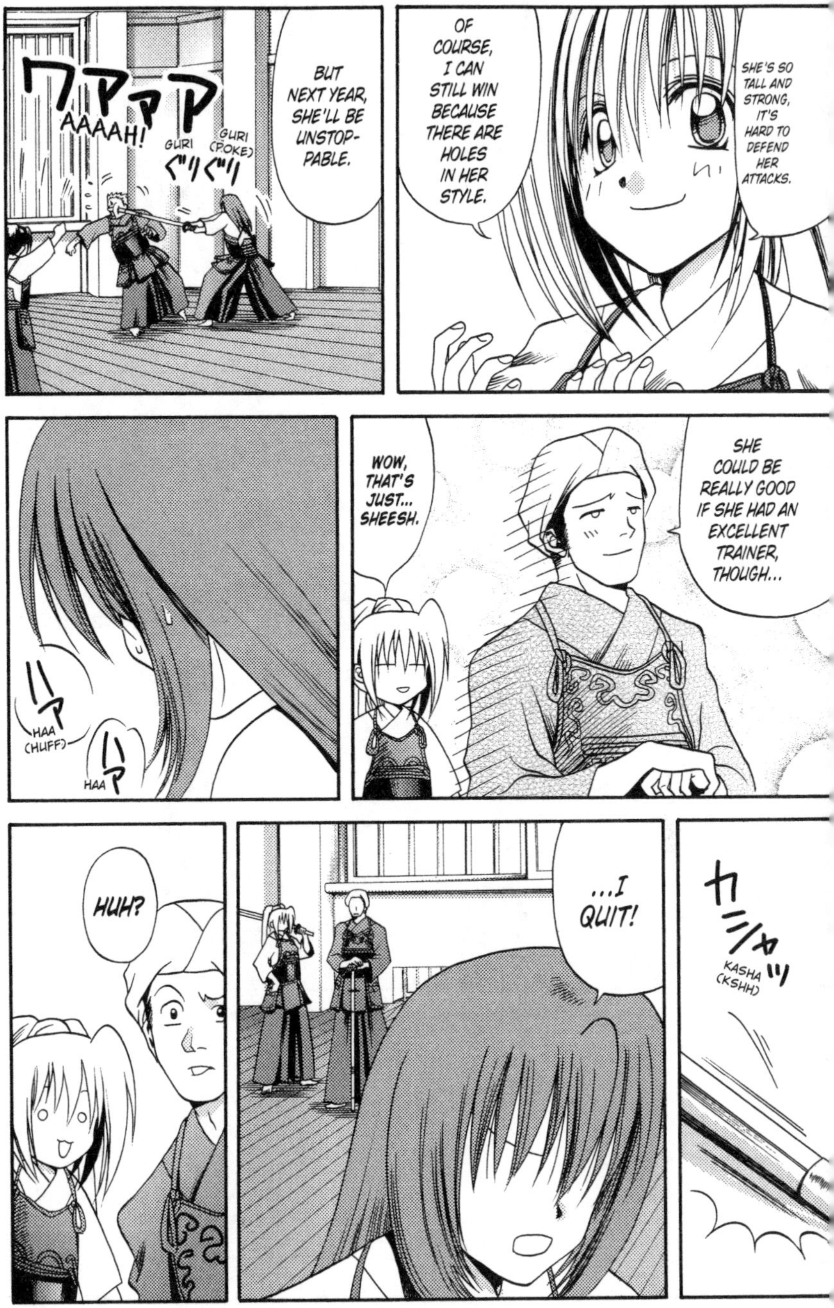
SHE'S SO TALL AND STRONG, IT'S HARD TO DEFEND HER ATTACKS.
OF COURSE, I CAN STILL WIN BECAUSE THERE ARE HOLES IN HER STYLE.
BUT NEXT YEAR, SHE'LL BE UNSTOP-PABLE.
GURI (POKE) ぐりぐり GURI
ワァァァ AAAAH!
SHE COULD BE REALLY GOOD IF SHE HAD AN EXCELLENT TRAINER, THOUGH...
WOW, THAT'S JUST... SHEESH.
ハァ HAA (HUFF)
ハァ HAA
カシャッ KASHA (KSHH)
...I QUIT!
HUH?

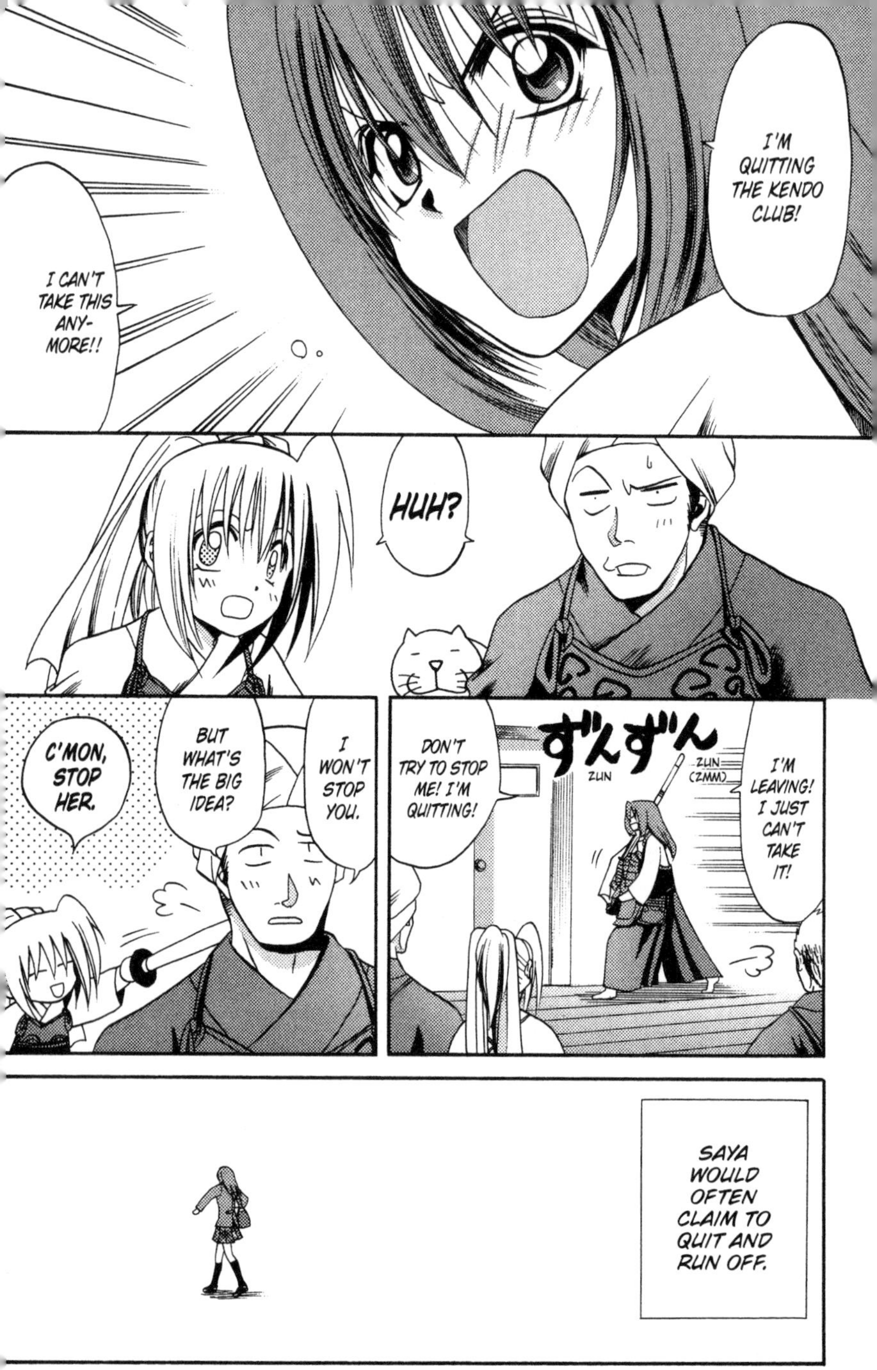
I'M QUITTING THE KENDO CLUB!
I CAN'T TAKE THIS ANY-MORE!!
HUH?
I'M LEAVING! I JUST CAN'T TAKE IT!
ずんずん
ZUN (ZMM)
ZUN
DON'T TRY TO STOP ME! I'M QUITTING!
I WON'T STOP YOU.
BUT WHAT'S THE BIG IDEA?
C'MON, STOP HER.
SAYA WOULD OFTEN CLAIM TO QUIT AND RUN OFF.

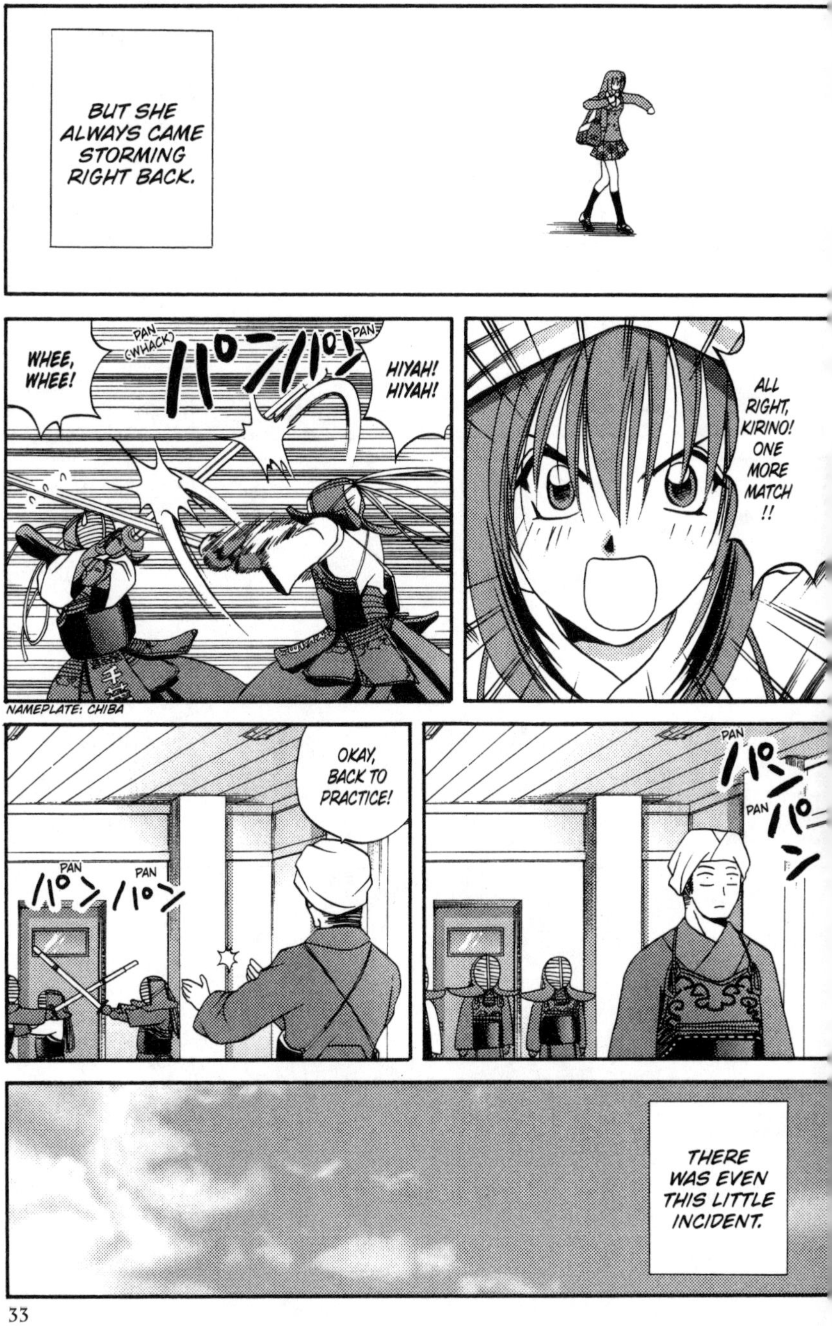
BUT SHE ALWAYS CAME STORMING RIGHT BACK.
ALL RIGHT, KIRINO! ONE MORE MATCH!!
HIYAH! HIYAH!
PAN
PAN (WHACK)
WHEE, WHEE!
NAMEPLATE: CHIBA
PAN
PAN
OKAY, BACK TO PRACTICE!
PAN
PAN
THERE WAS EVEN THIS LITTLE INCIDENT.

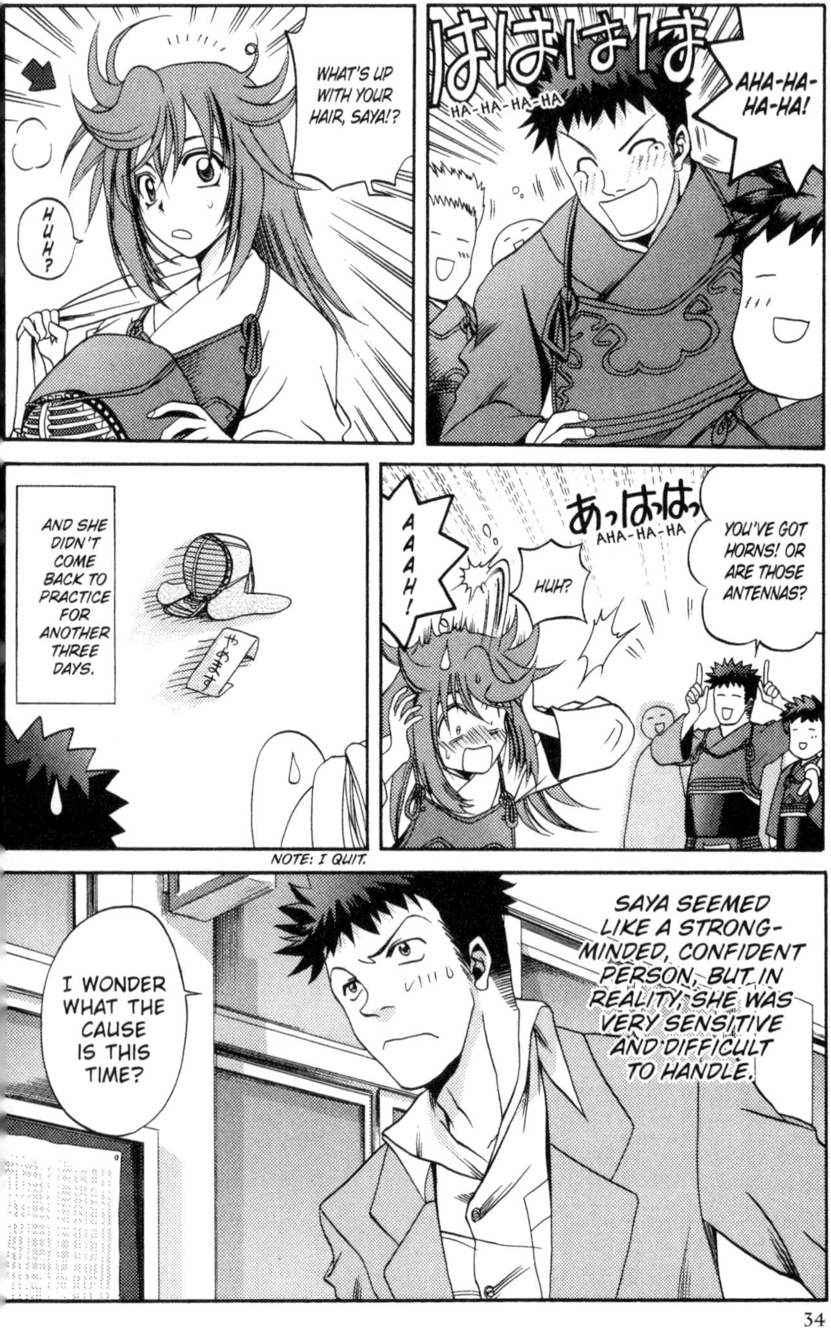
AHA-HA-HA-HA!
はははは
HA-HA-HA-HA
WHAT'S UP WITH YOUR HAIR, SAYA!?
HUH?
YOU'VE GOT HORNS! OR ARE THOSE ANTENNAS?
あっはっはっ
AHA-HA-HA
HUH?
AAAAH!
AND SHE DIDN'T COME BACK TO PRACTICE FOR ANOTHER THREE DAYS.
やめます
NOTE: I QUIT.
SAYA SEEMED LIKE A STRONG-MINDED, CONFIDENT PERSON, BUT IN REALITY, SHE WAS VERY SENSITIVE AND DIFFICULT TO HANDLE.
I WONDER WHAT THE CAUSE IS THIS TIME?

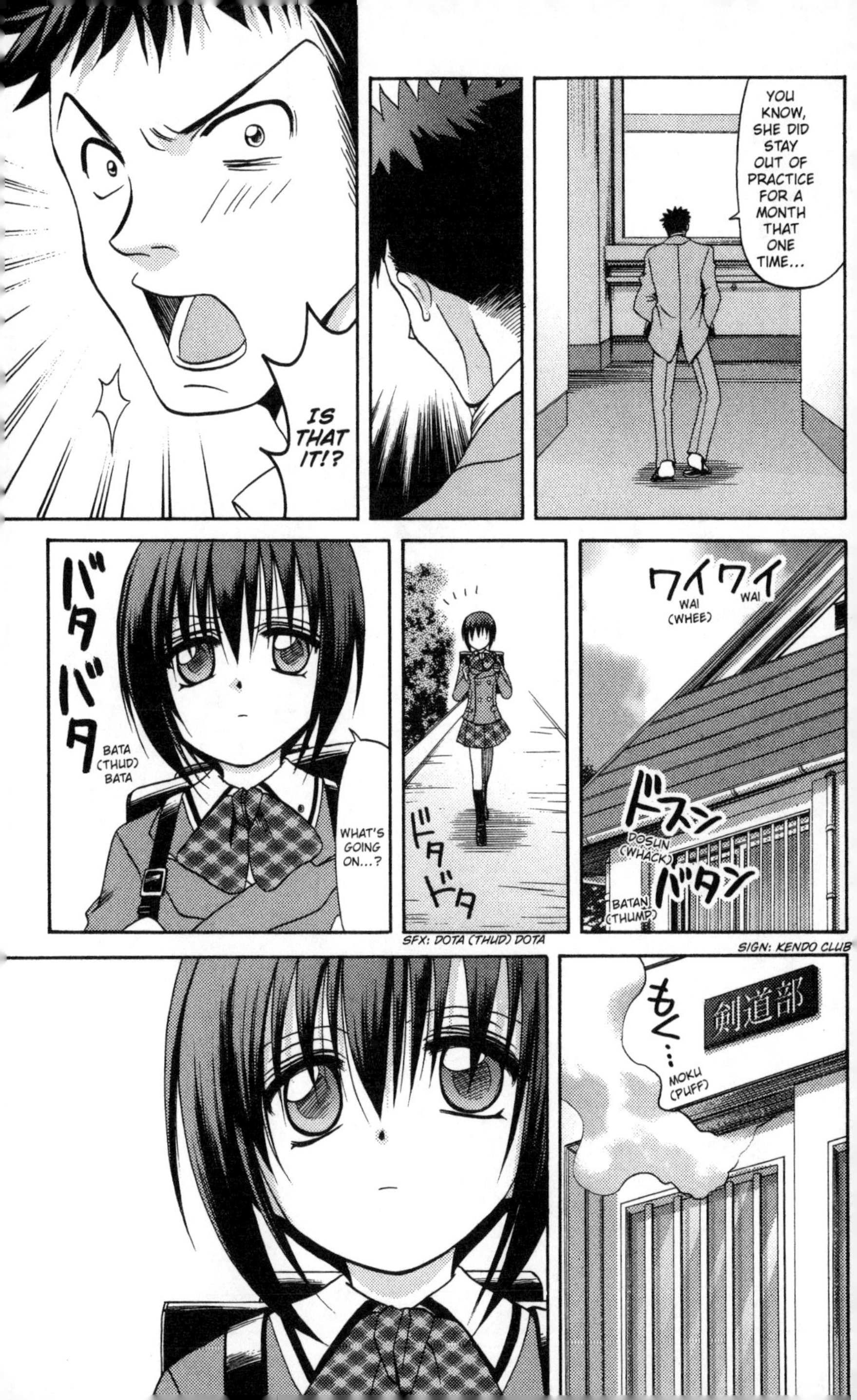
YOU KNOW, SHE DID STAY OUT OF PRACTICE FOR A MONTH THAT ONE TIME...
IS THAT IT!?
ワイワイ
WAI (WHEE) WAI
ドスン
DOSUN (WHACK)
バタン
BATAN (THUMP)
SIGN: KENDO CLUB
ドタドタ
SFX: DOTA (THUD) DOTA
バタバタ
BATA (THUD) BATA
WHAT'S GOING ON...?
剣道部
もく…
MOKU (PUFF)

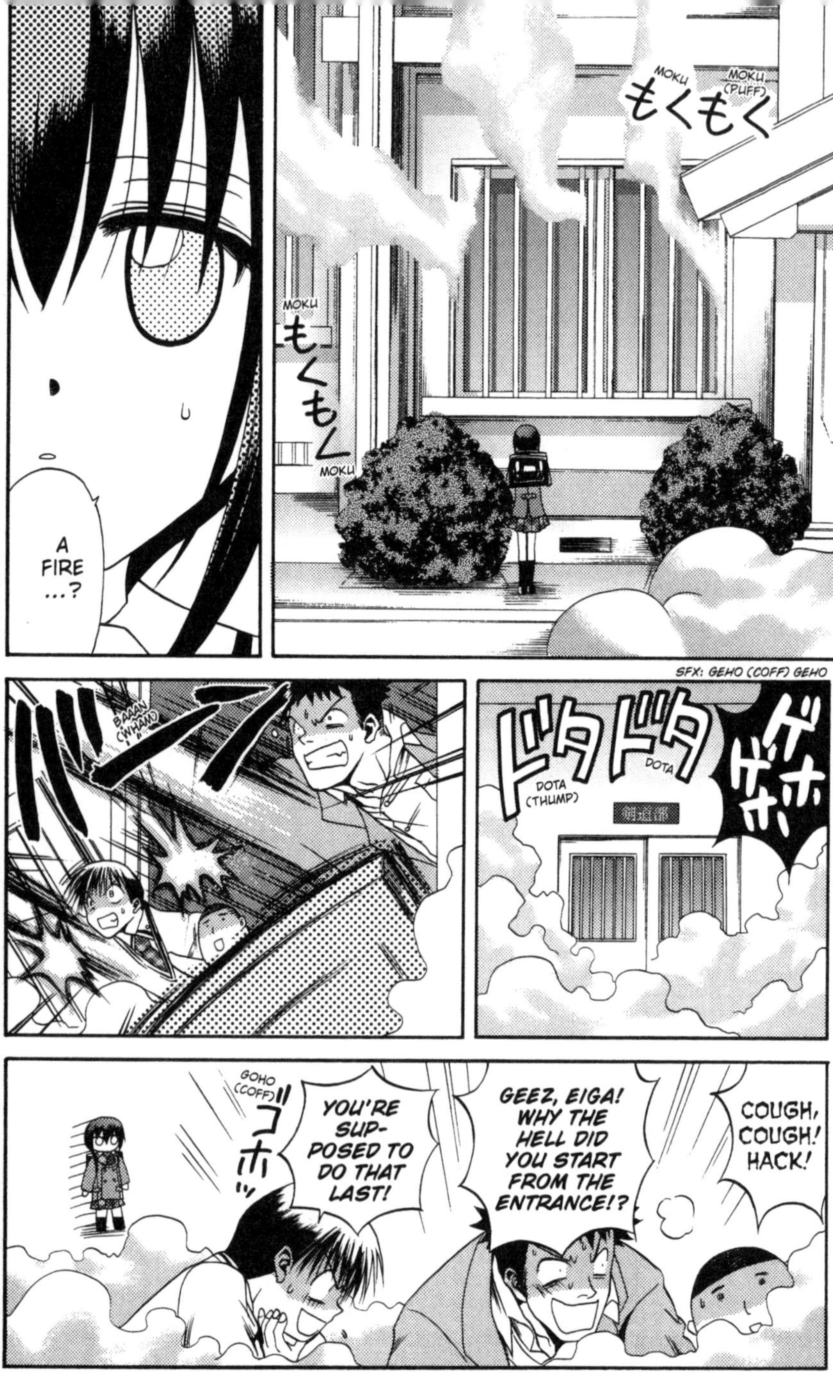
MOKU MOKU (PUFF)
もくもく
MOKU MOKU
もくもく
A FIRE ...?
SFX: GEHO (COFF) GEHO
DOTA (THUMP) DOTA
ドタドタ
ゲホゲホ
BAAAN (WHAM)
バーン
COUGH, COUGH! HACK!
GEEZ, EIGA! WHY THE HELL DID YOU START FROM THE ENTRANCE!?
YOU'RE SUP-POSED TO DO THAT LAST!
GOHO (COFF)
ゴホッ

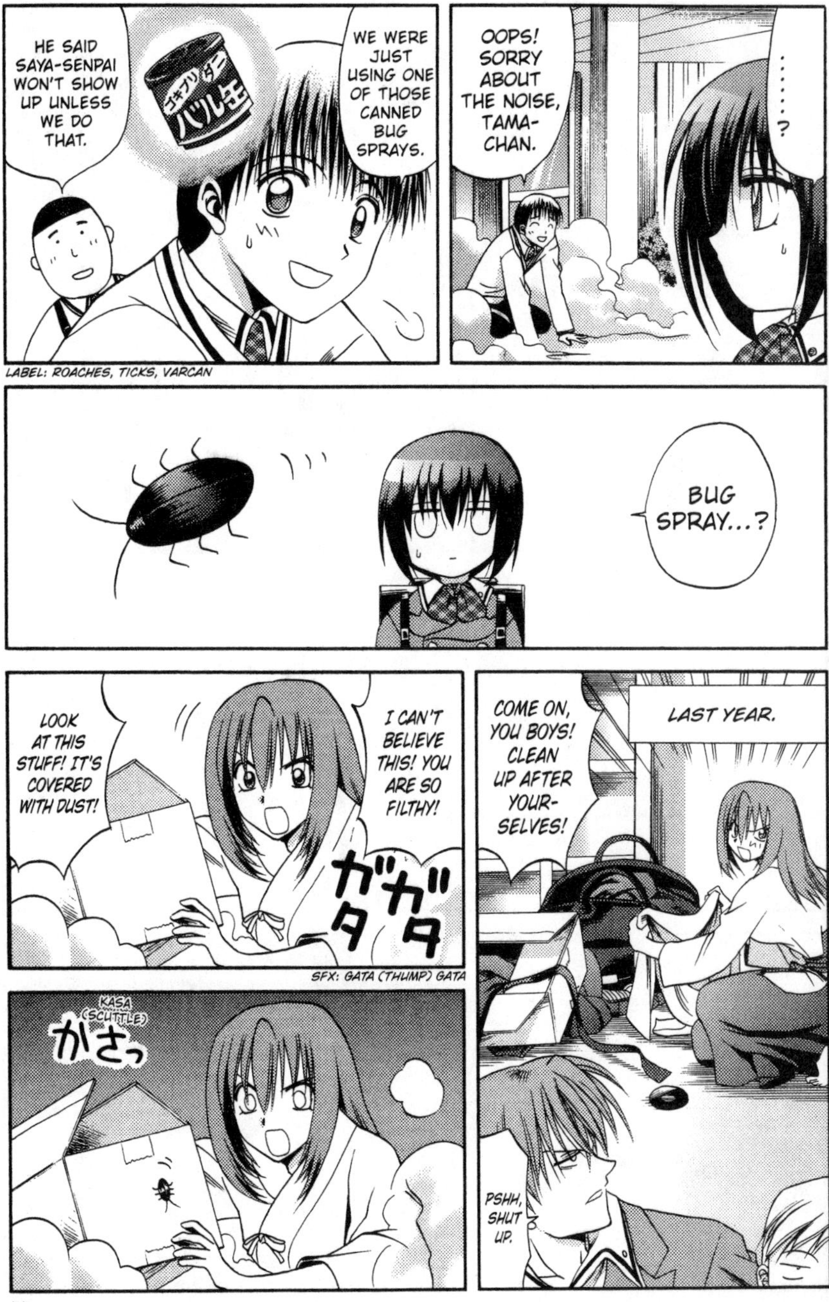
......?
OOPS! SORRY ABOUT THE NOISE, TAMA-CHAN.
WE WERE JUST USING ONE OF THOSE CANNED BUG SPRAYS.
HE SAID SAYA-SENPAI WON'T SHOW UP UNLESS WE DO THAT.
LABEL: ROACHES, TICKS, VARCAN
BUG SPRAY...?
LAST YEAR.
COME ON, YOU BOYS! CLEAN UP AFTER YOUR-SELVES!
PSHH, SHUT UP.
I CAN'T BELIEVE THIS! YOU ARE SO FILTHY!
LOOK AT THIS STUFF! IT'S COVERED WITH DUST!
ガタガタ
SFX: GATA (THUMP) GATA
かさっ
KASA (SCUTTLE)

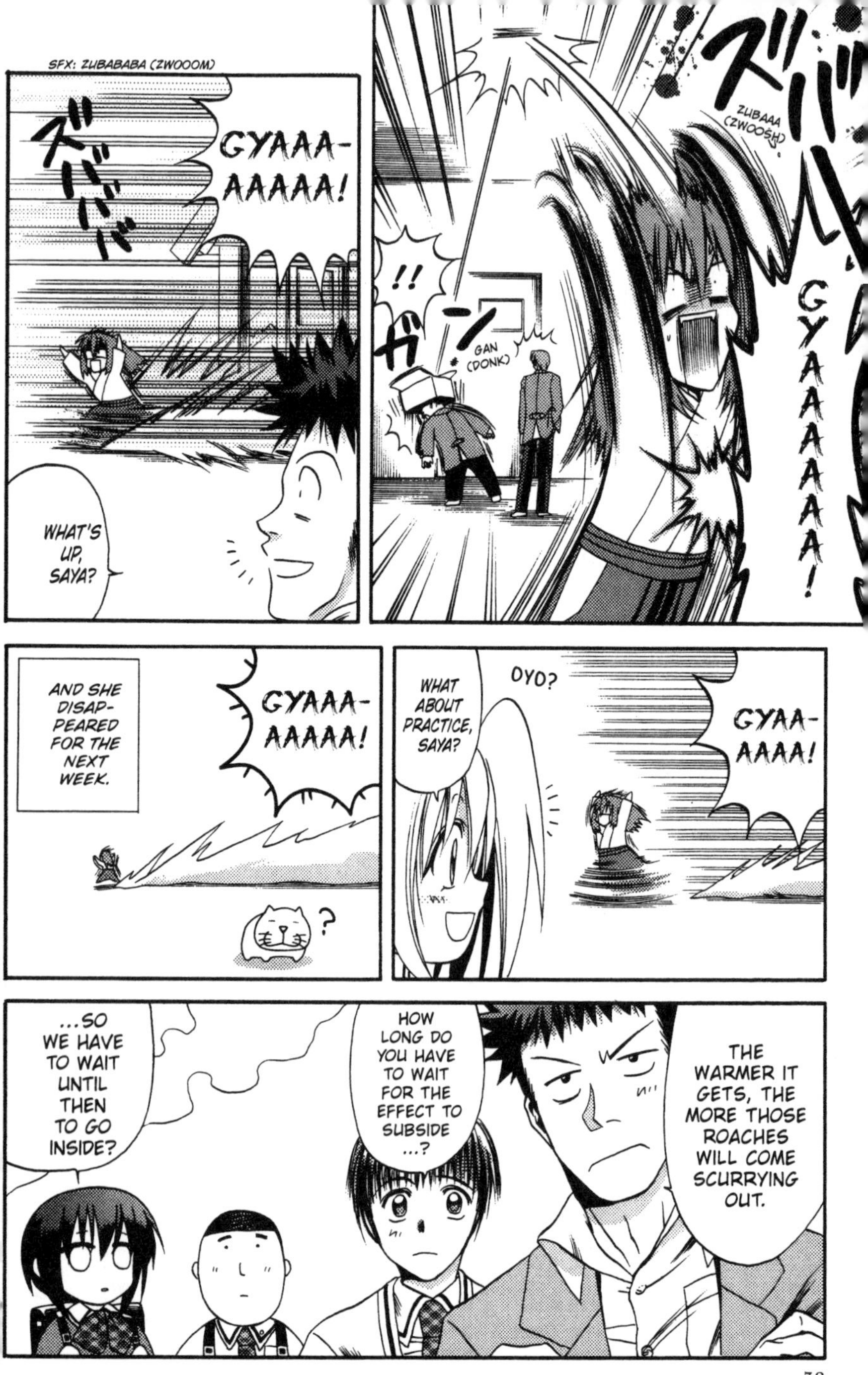

ZUBAAA (ZWOOSH)
GYAAAAAAAAA!
!!
GAN (DONK)
SFX: ZUBABABA (ZWOOOM)
GYAAA-AAAAA!
WHAT'S UP, SAYA?
GYAA-AAAA!
OYO?
WHAT ABOUT PRACTICE, SAYA?
GYAAA-AAAAA!
AND SHE DISAPPEARED FOR THE NEXT WEEK.
?
THE WARMER IT GETS, THE MORE THOSE ROACHES WILL COME SCURRYING OUT.
HOW LONG DO YOU HAVE TO WAIT FOR THE EFFECT TO SUBSIDE...?
...SO WE HAVE TO WAIT UNTIL THEN TO GO INSIDE?

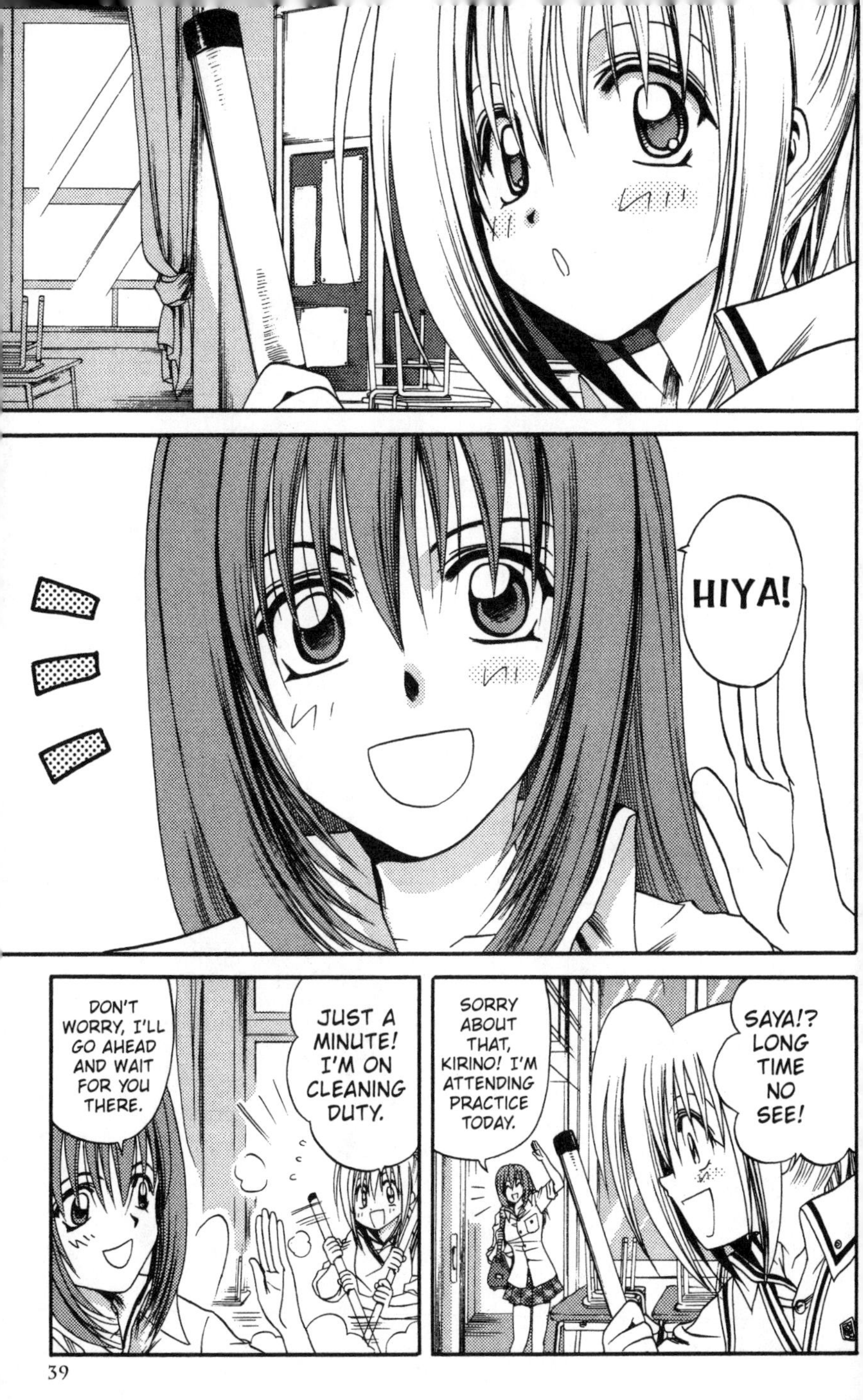
HIYA!
SAYA!? LONG TIME NO SEE!
SORRY ABOUT THAT, KIRINO! I'M ATTENDING PRACTICE TODAY.
JUST A MINUTE! I'M ON CLEANING DUTY.
DON'T WORRY, I'LL GO AHEAD AND WAIT FOR YOU THERE.

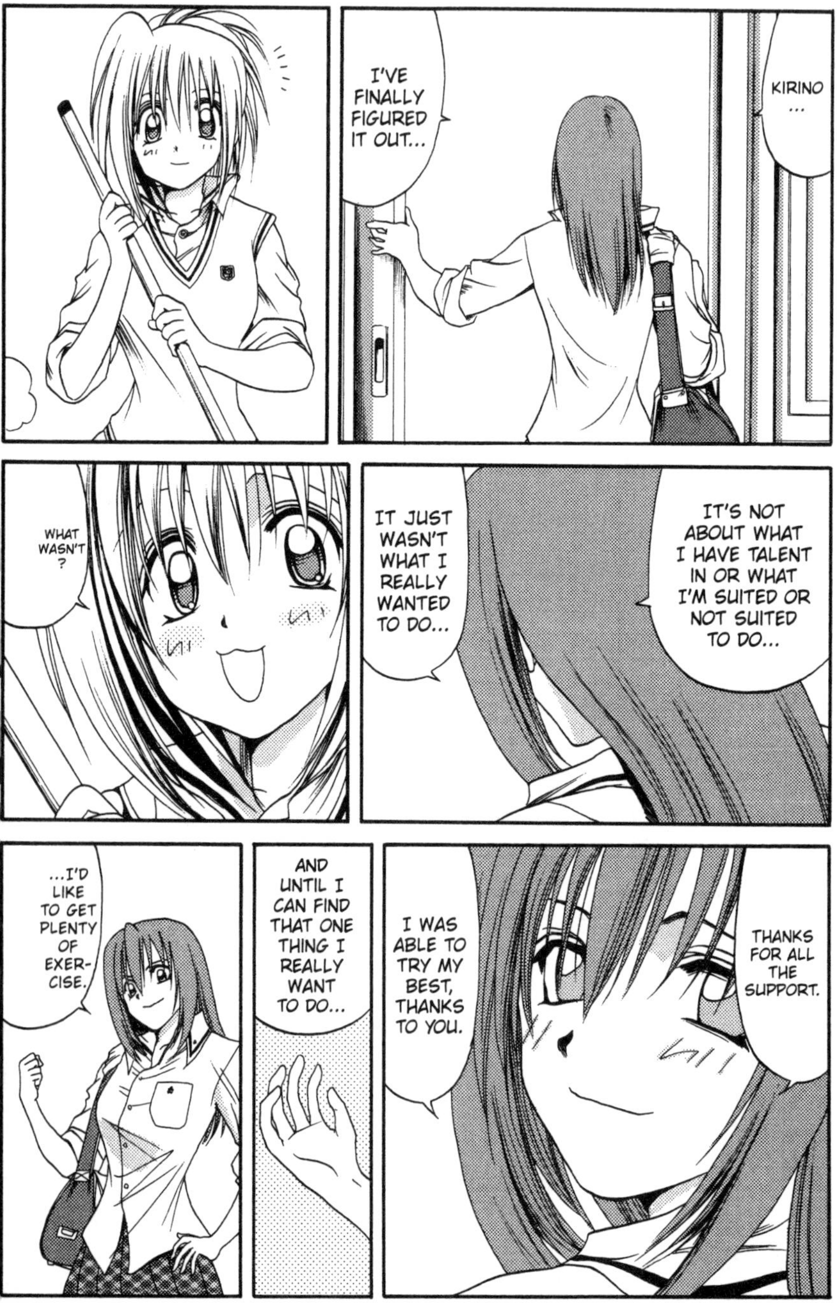
KIRINO ...
I'VE FINALLY FIGURED IT OUT...
IT'S NOT ABOUT WHAT I HAVE TALENT IN OR WHAT I'M SUITED OR NOT SUITED TO DO...
IT JUST WASN'T WHAT I REALLY WANTED TO DO...
WHAT WASN'T?
THANKS FOR ALL THE SUPPORT.
I WAS ABLE TO TRY MY BEST, THANKS TO YOU.
AND UNTIL I CAN FIND THAT ONE THING I REALLY WANT TO DO...
...I'D LIKE TO GET PLENTY OF EXERCISE.

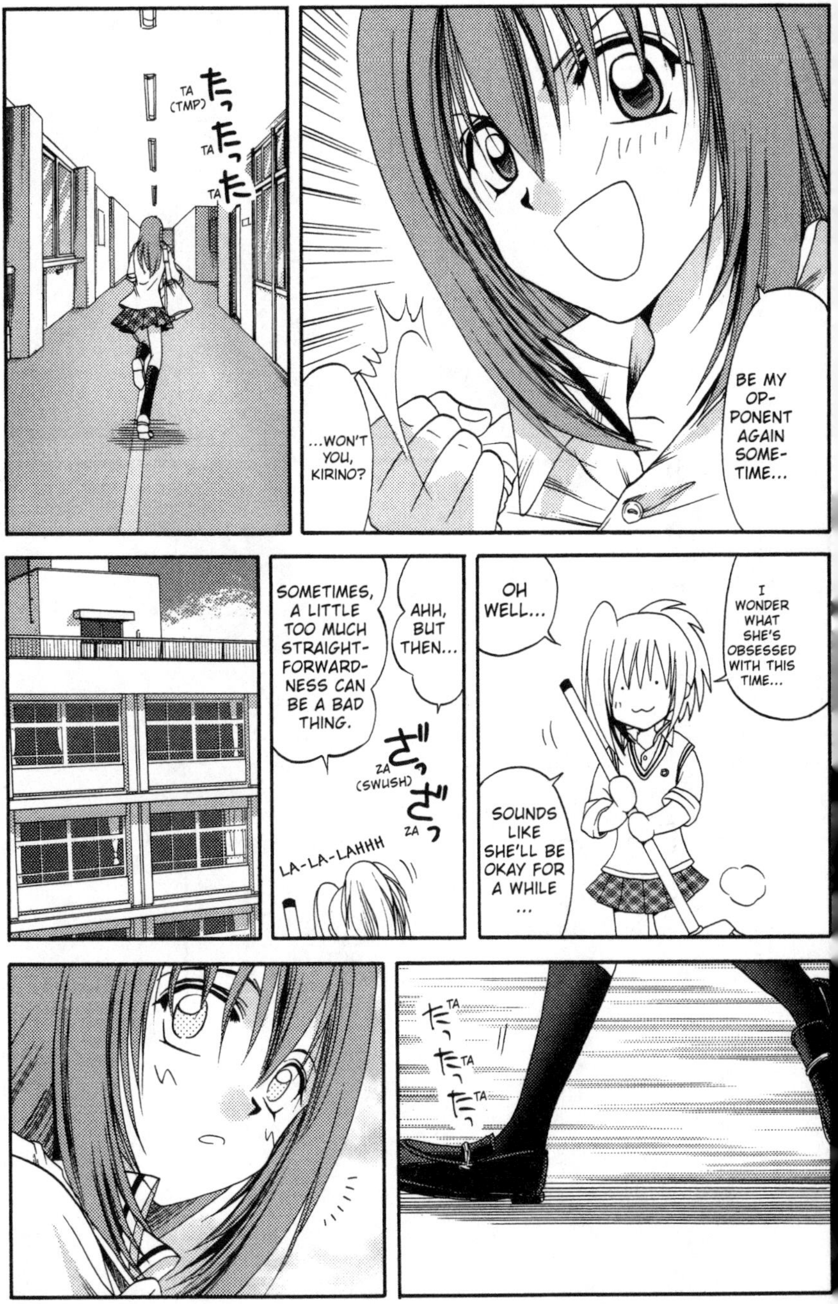
BE MY OPPONENT AGAIN SOMETIME...
...WON'T YOU, KIRINO?
TA (TMP) たっ
TA たっ
TA た
I WONDER WHAT SHE'S OBSESSED WITH THIS TIME...
OH WELL...
SOUNDS LIKE SHE'LL BE OKAY FOR A WHILE ...
AHH, BUT THEN...
SOMETIMES, A LITTLE TOO MUCH STRAIGHTFORWARDNESS CAN BE A BAD THING.
ZA (SWUSH) ざっ
ZA ざっ
LA-LA-LAHHH
TA たっ
TA たっ
TA たっ

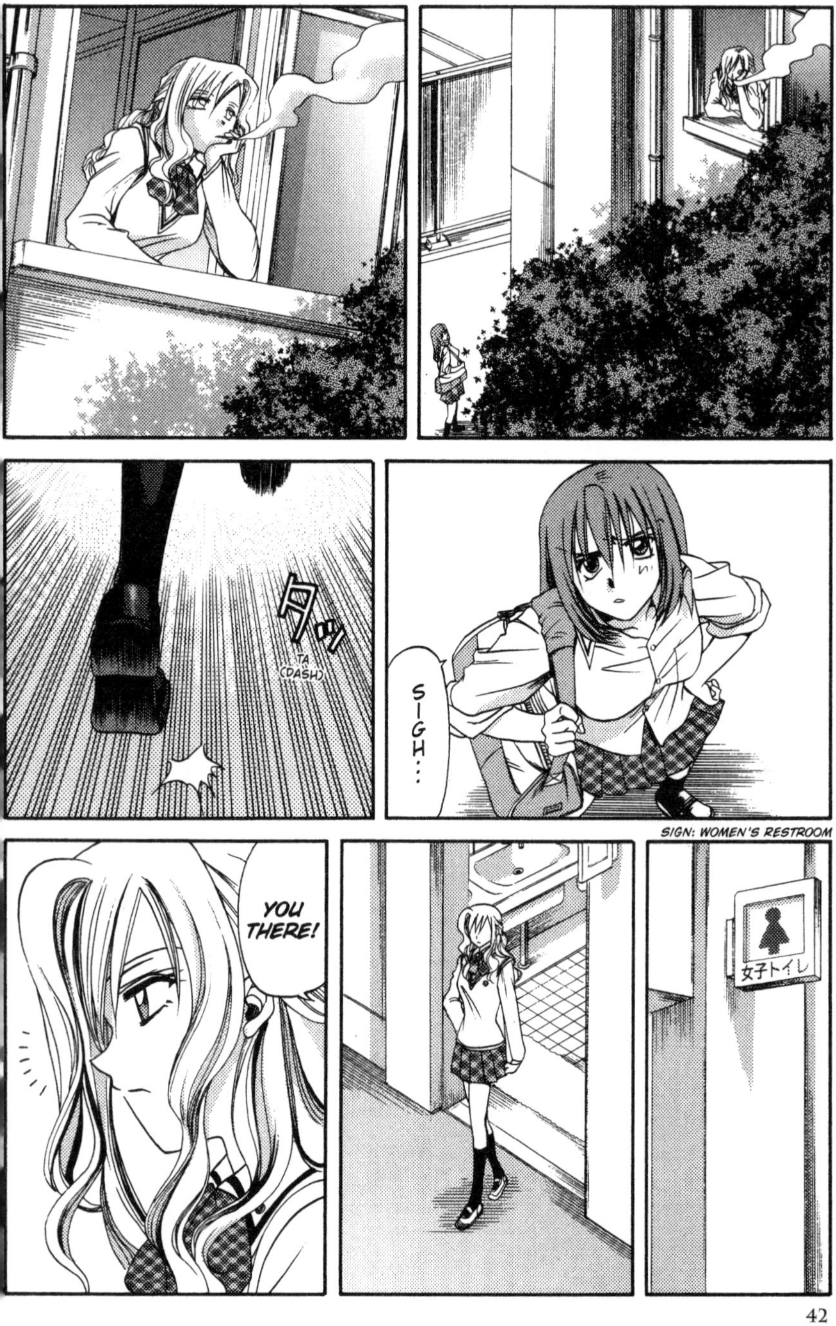
SIGH...
タッ
TA (DASH)
SIGN: WOMEN'S RESTROOM
女子トイレ
YOU THERE!

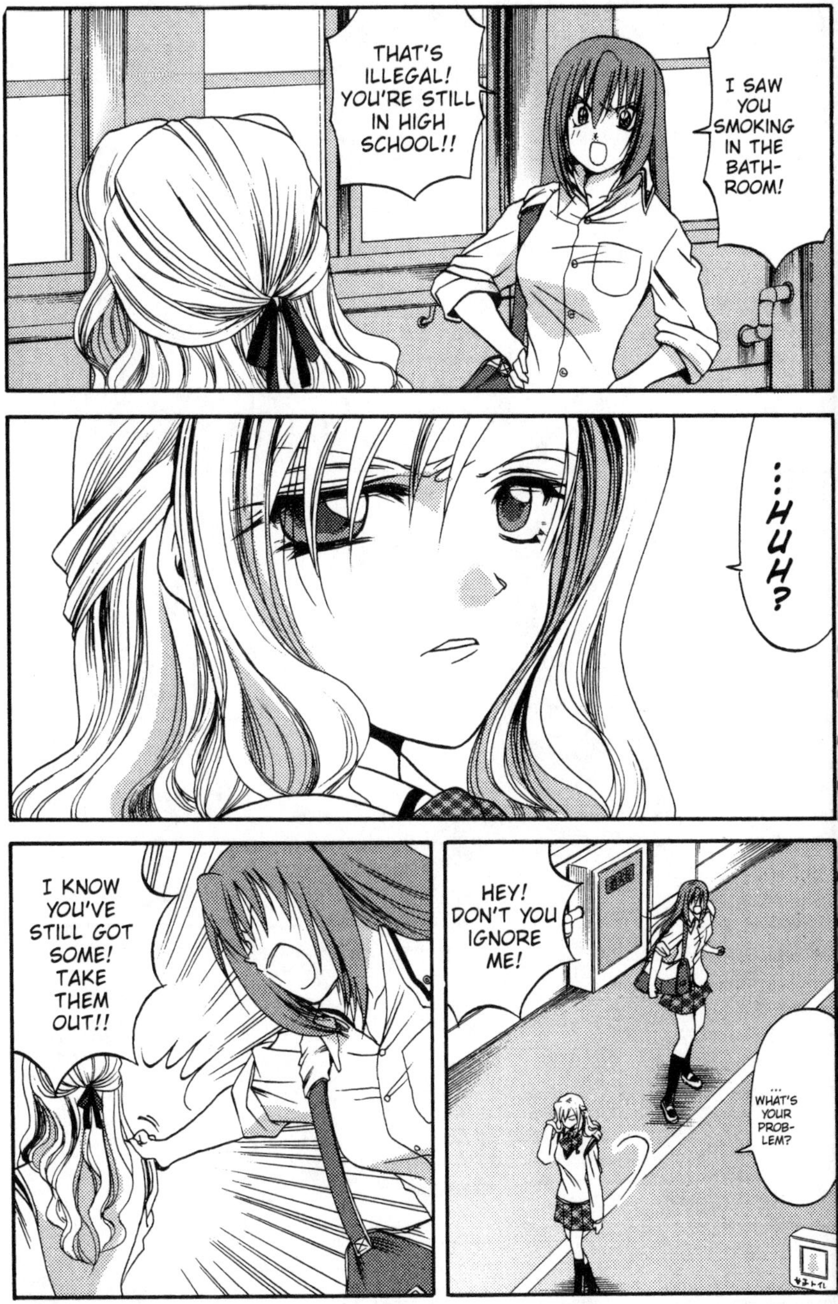
I SAW YOU SMOKING IN THE BATH-ROOM!
THAT'S ILLEGAL! YOU'RE STILL IN HIGH SCHOOL!!
...HUH?
HEY! DON'T YOU IGNORE ME!
...WHAT'S YOUR PROB-LEM?
I KNOW YOU'VE STILL GOT SOME! TAKE THEM OUT!!

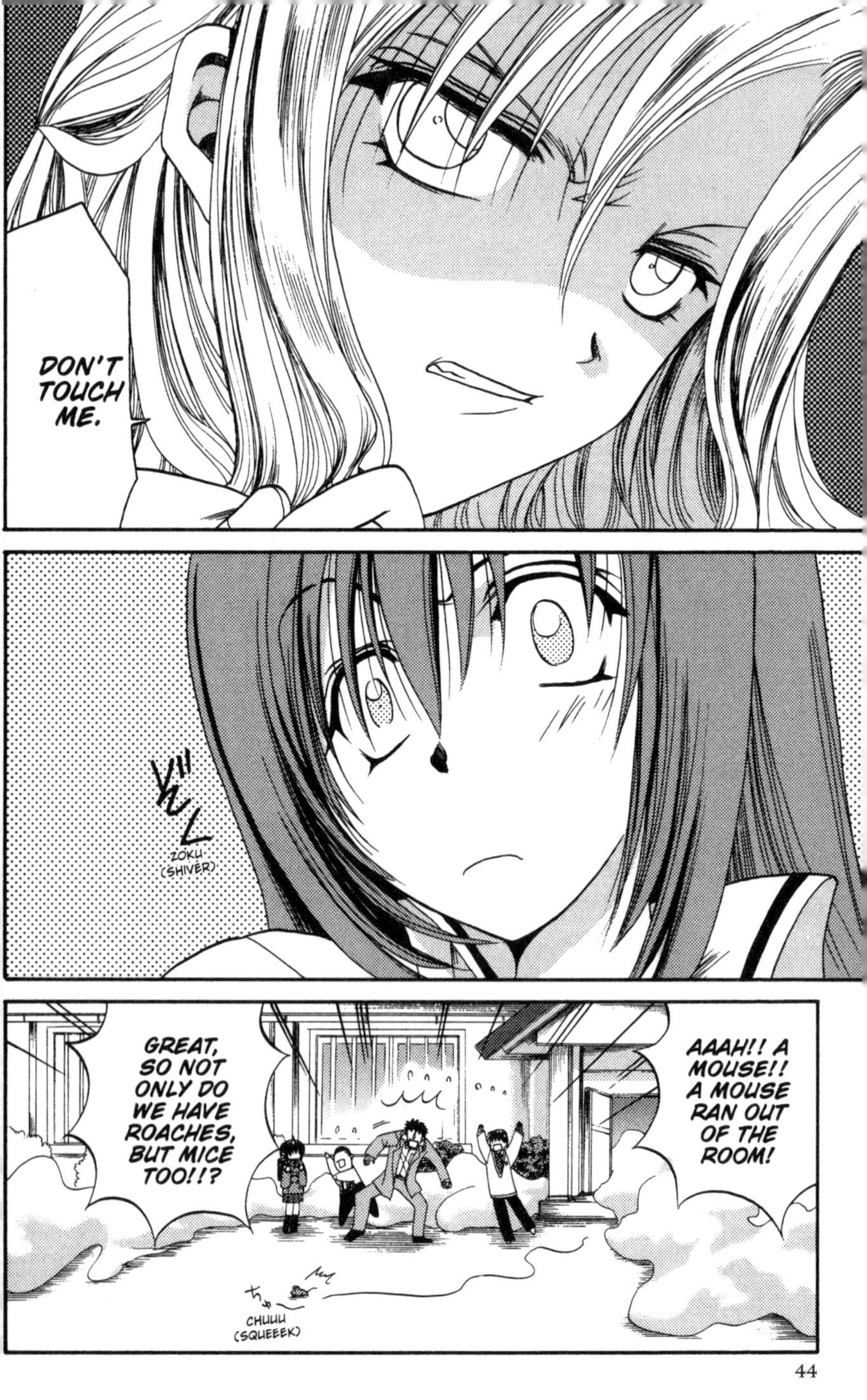
DON'T TOUCH ME.
ZOKU (SHIVER)
AAAH!! A MOUSE!! A MOUSE RAN OUT OF THE ROOM!
GREAT, SO NOT ONLY DO WE HAVE ROACHES, BUT MICE TOO!!?
CHUUU (SQUEEEK)

BAMBOO BLADE

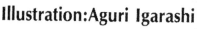
Illustration:Aguri Igarashi

Illustration:Masahiro Totsuka

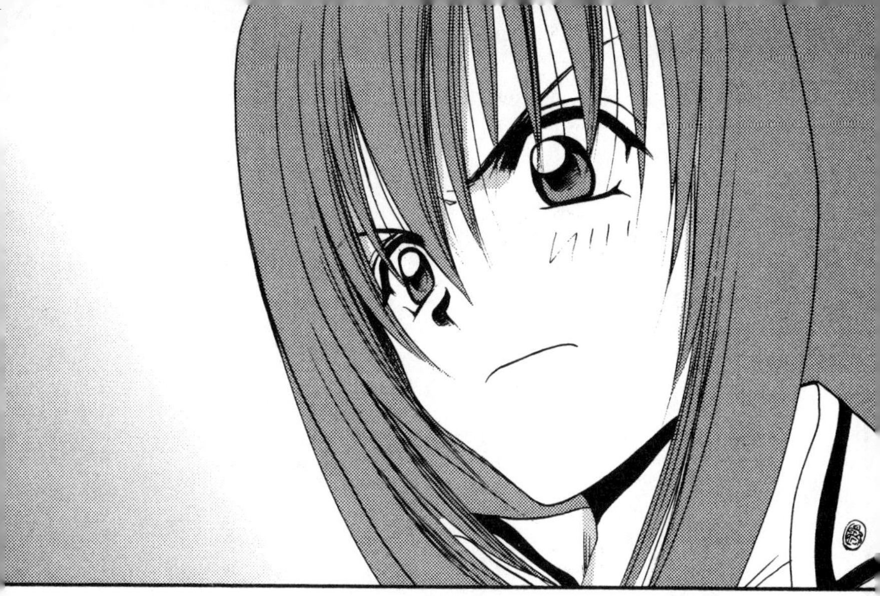

CHAPTER 13
MIYA-MIYA AND THE PANGOLIN

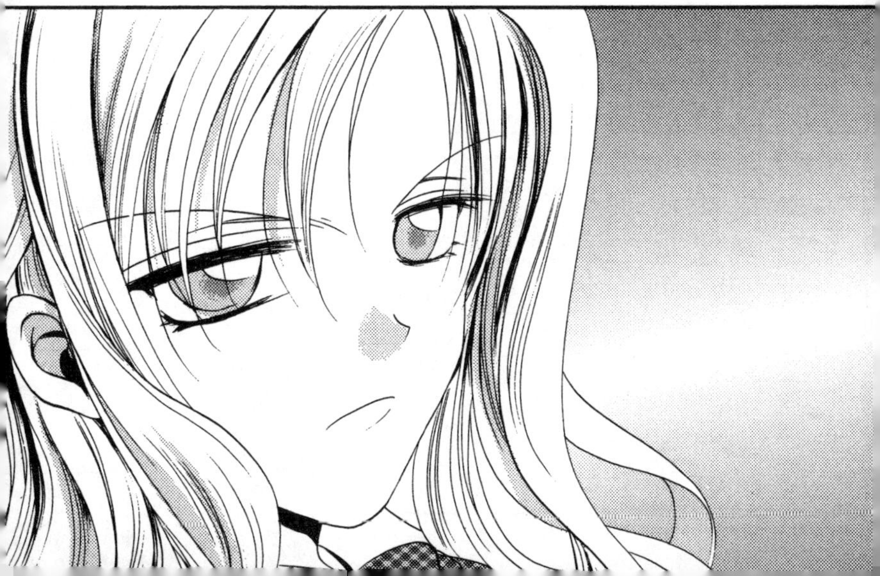

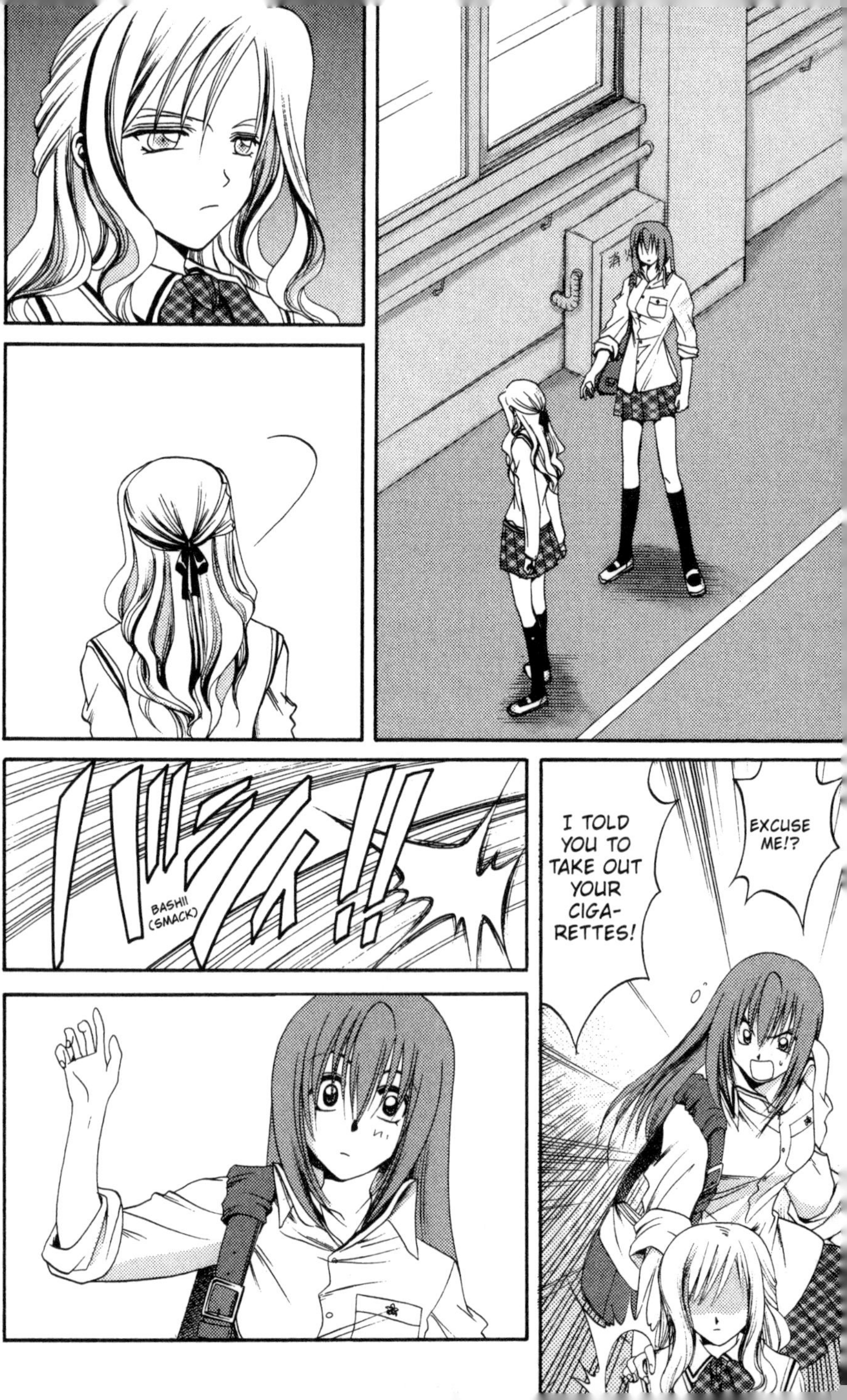
BASHII (SMACK)
EXCUSE ME!?
I TOLD YOU TO TAKE OUT YOUR CIGA-RETTES!

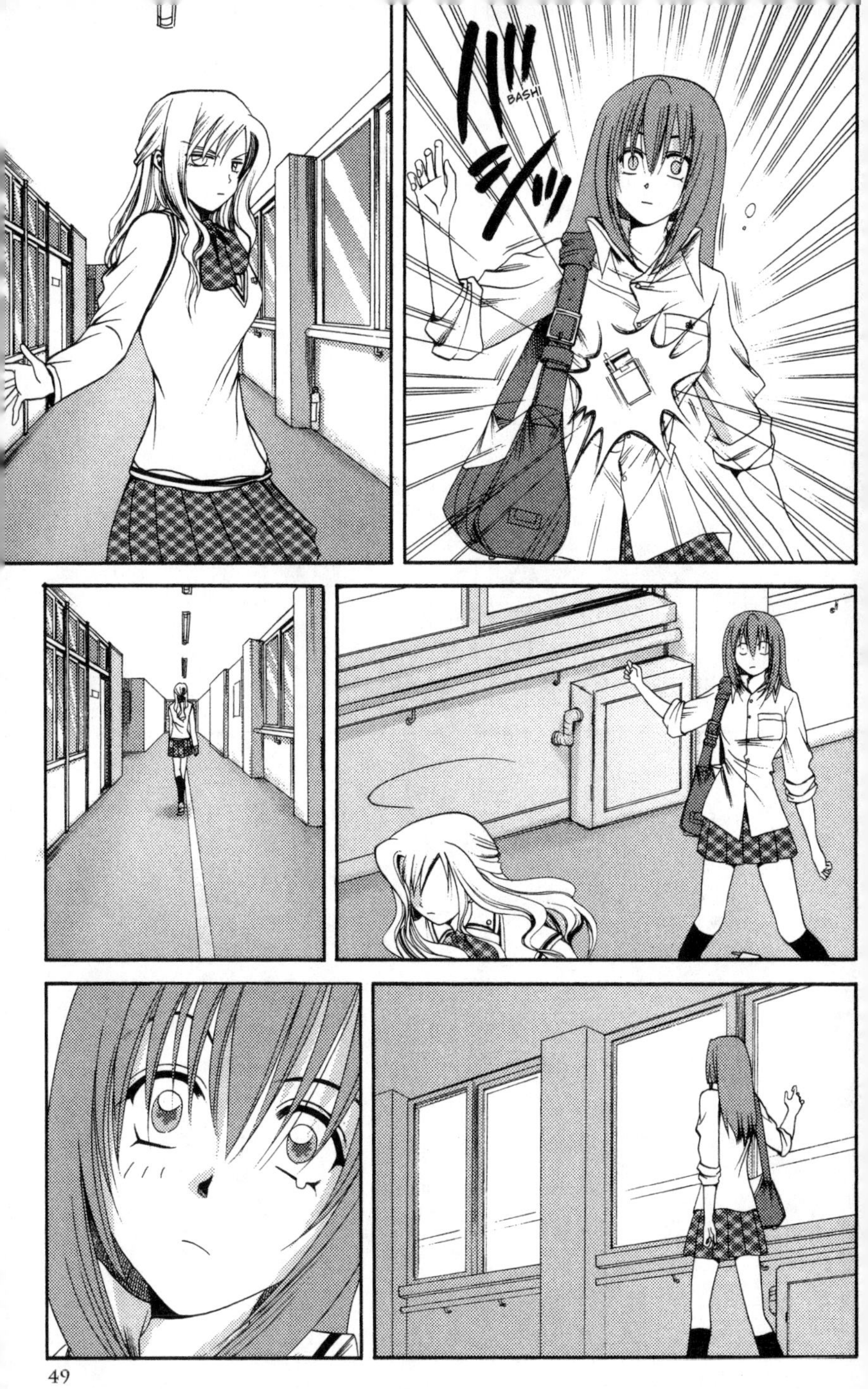
バシッ
BASHI

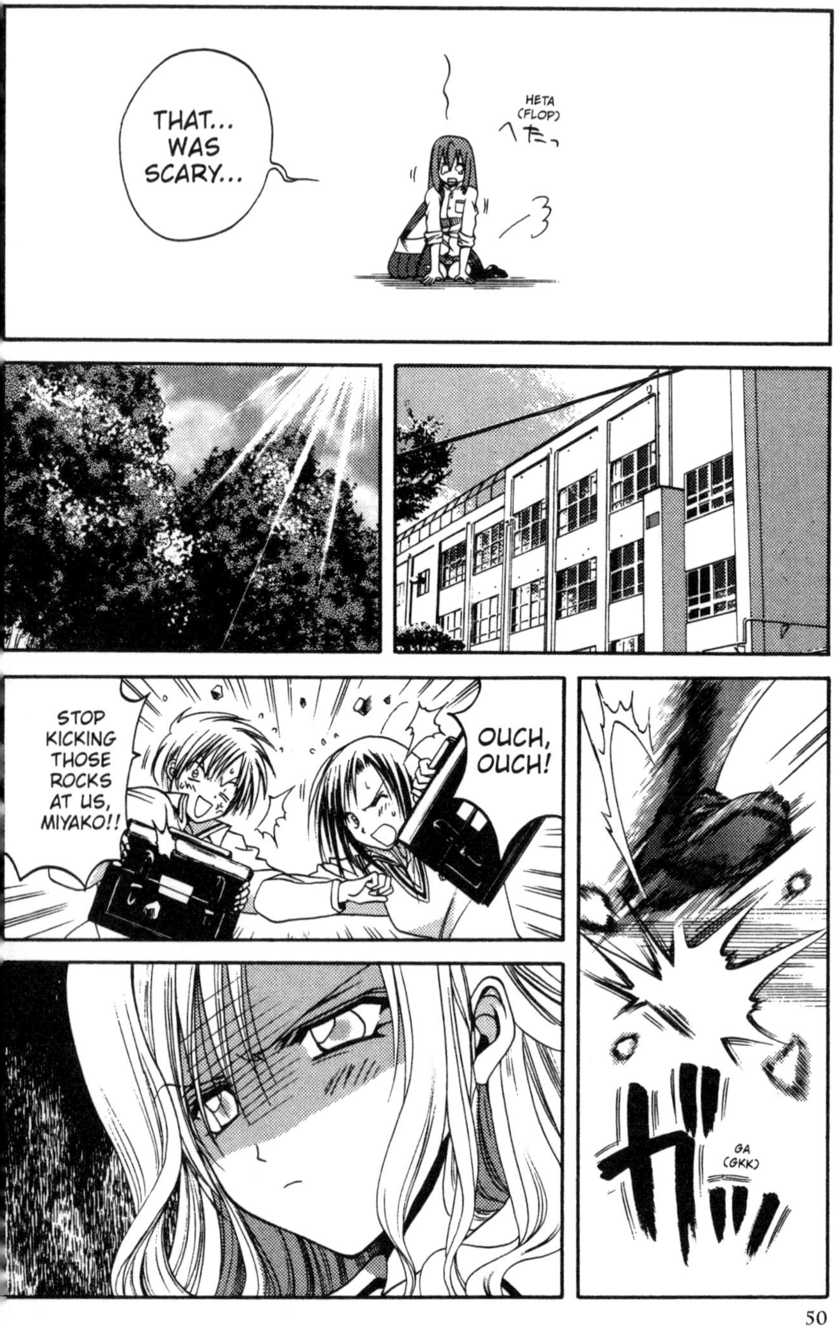
HETA (FLOP)
へたっ
THAT... WAS SCARY...
GA (GKK)
ガッ
OUCH, OUCH!
STOP KICKING THOSE ROCKS AT US, MIYAKO!!

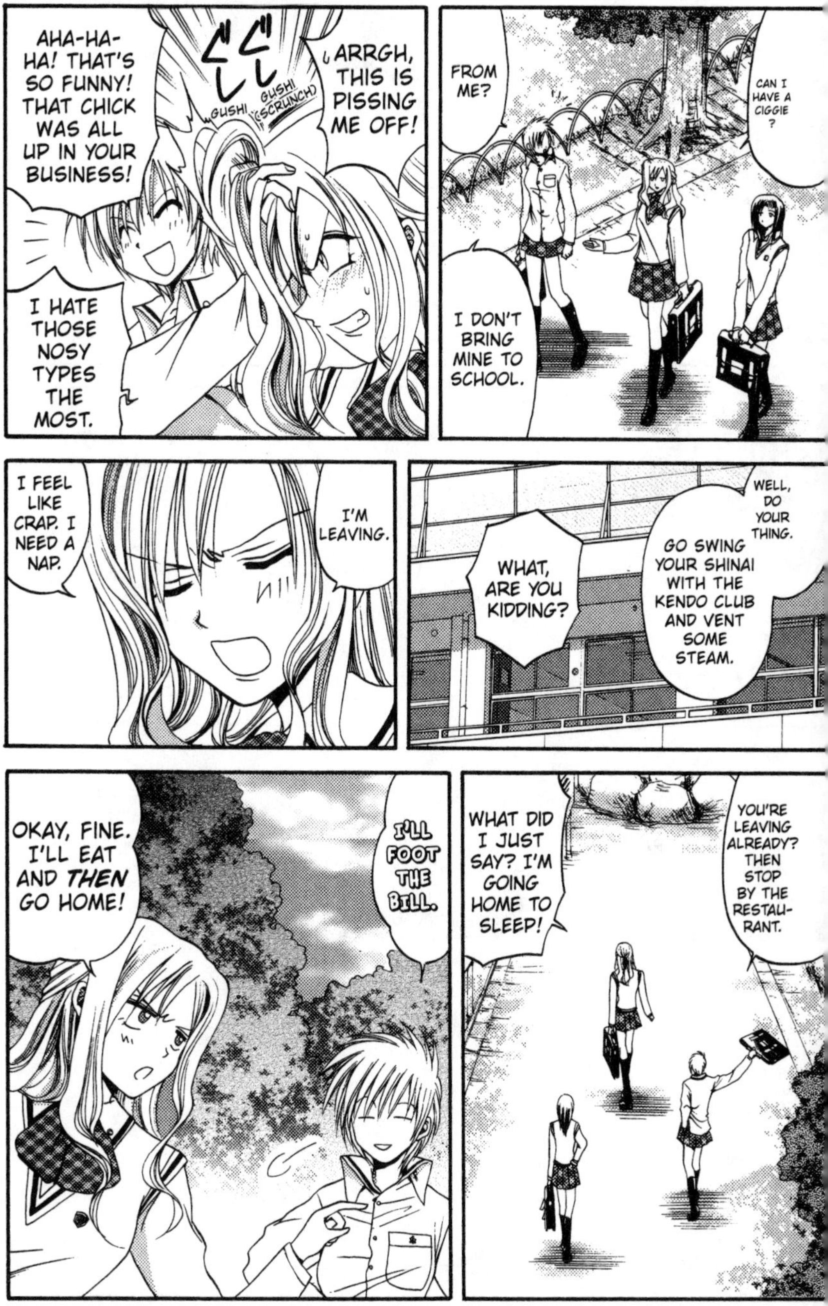
CAN I HAVE A CIGGIE?
FROM ME?
I DON'T BRING MINE TO SCHOOL.
ARRGH, THIS IS PISSING ME OFF!
ぐしぐし
GUSHI GUSHI (SCRUNCH)
AHA-HA-HA! THAT'S SO FUNNY! THAT CHICK WAS ALL UP IN YOUR BUSINESS!
I HATE THOSE NOSY TYPES THE MOST.
WELL, DO YOUR THING.
GO SWING YOUR SHINAI WITH THE KENDO CLUB AND VENT SOME STEAM.
WHAT, ARE YOU KIDDING?
I'M LEAVING.
I FEEL LIKE CRAP. I NEED A NAP.
YOU'RE LEAVING ALREADY? THEN STOP BY THE RESTAU-RANT.
WHAT DID I JUST SAY? I'M GOING HOME TO SLEEP!
I'LL FOOT THE BILL.
OKAY, FINE. I'LL EAT AND *THEN* GO HOME!

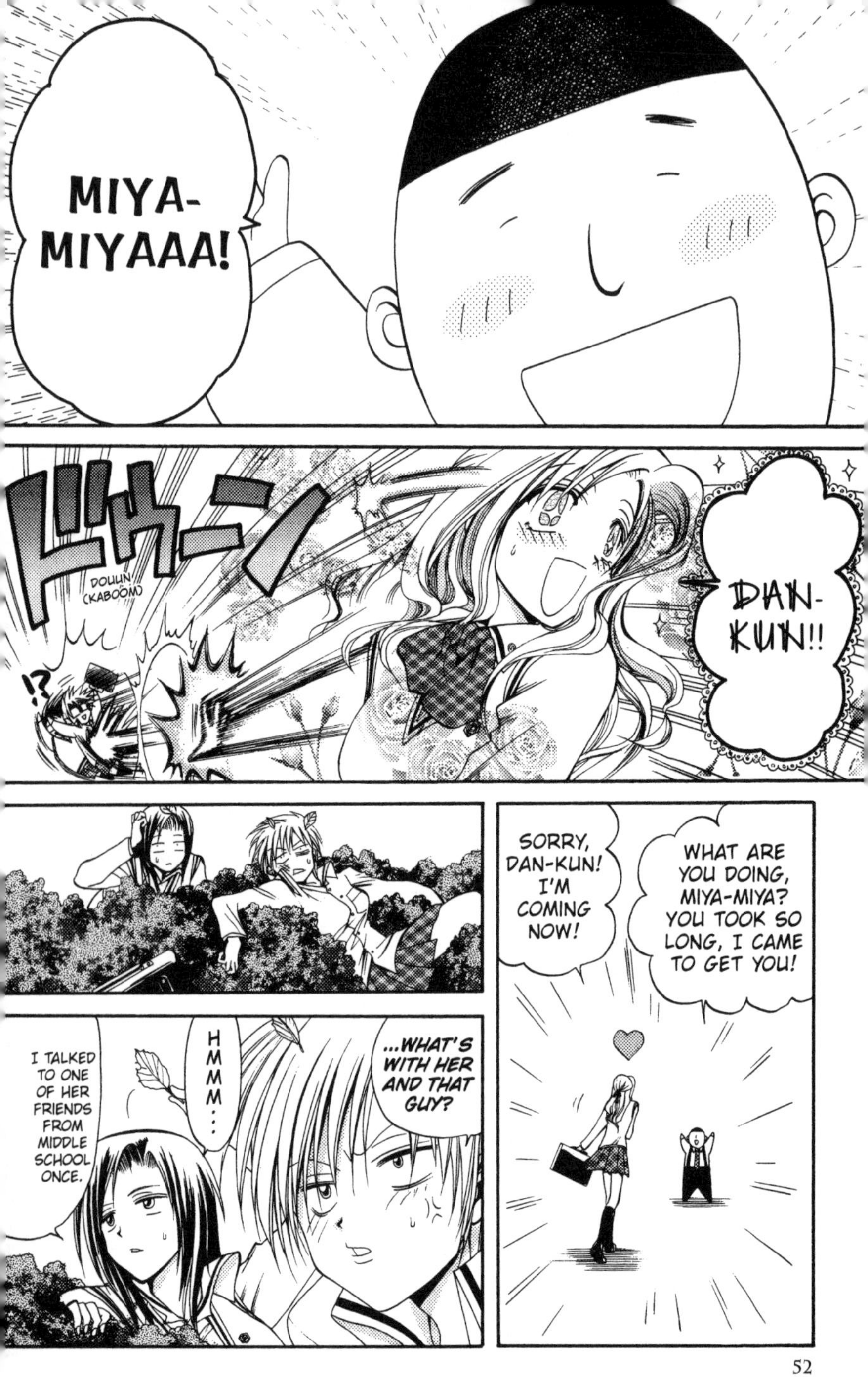
MIYA-MIYAAA!
DAN-KUN!!
ドゥーン
DOUUN (KABOOM)
WHAT ARE YOU DOING, MIYA-MIYA? YOU TOOK SO LONG, I CAME TO GET YOU!
SORRY, DAN-KUN! I'M COMING NOW!
...WHAT'S WITH HER AND THAT GUY?
HMMM...
I TALKED TO ONE OF HER FRIENDS FROM MIDDLE SCHOOL ONCE.

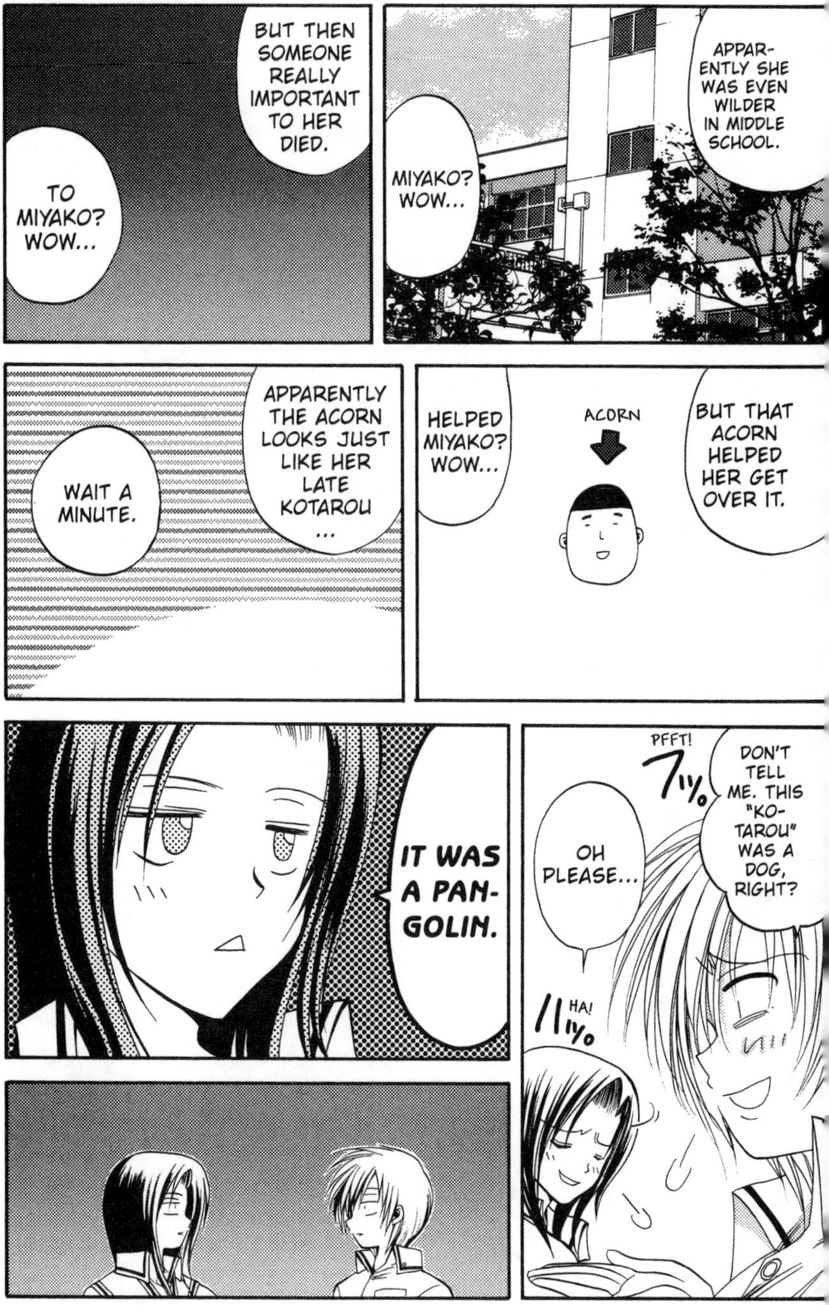
APPARENTLY SHE WAS EVEN WILDER IN MIDDLE SCHOOL.
MIYAKO? WOW...
BUT THEN SOMEONE REALLY IMPORTANT TO HER DIED.
TO MIYAKO? WOW...
BUT THAT ACORN HELPED HER GET OVER IT.
ACORN
HELPED MIYAKO? WOW...
APPARENTLY THE ACORN LOOKS JUST LIKE HER LATE KOTAROU ...
WAIT A MINUTE.
PFFT!
DON'T TELL ME. THIS "KOTAROU" WAS A DOG, RIGHT?
OH PLEASE...
HA!
IT WAS A PANGOLIN.

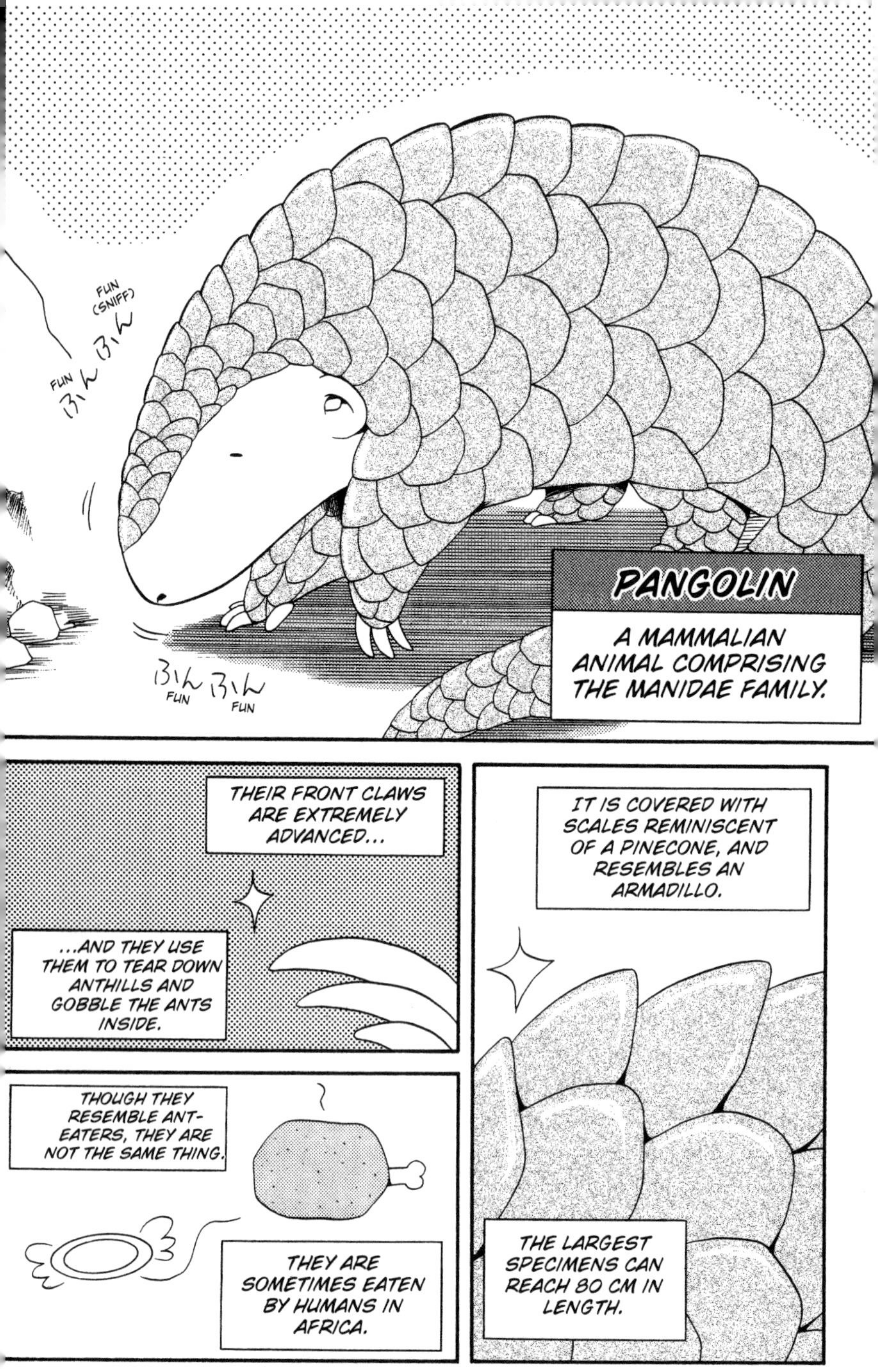
ふん ふん
FUN FUN (SNIFF)
PANGOLIN
A MAMMALIAN ANIMAL COMPRISING THE MANIDAE FAMILY.
ふん ふん
FUN FUN
IT IS COVERED WITH SCALES REMINISCENT OF A PINECONE, AND RESEMBLES AN ARMADILLO.
THE LARGEST SPECIMENS CAN REACH 80 CM IN LENGTH.
THEIR FRONT CLAWS ARE EXTREMELY ADVANCED...
...AND THEY USE THEM TO TEAR DOWN ANTHILLS AND GOBBLE THE ANTS INSIDE.
THOUGH THEY RESEMBLE ANT-EATERS, THEY ARE NOT THE SAME THING.
THEY ARE SOMETIMES EATEN BY HUMANS IN AFRICA.

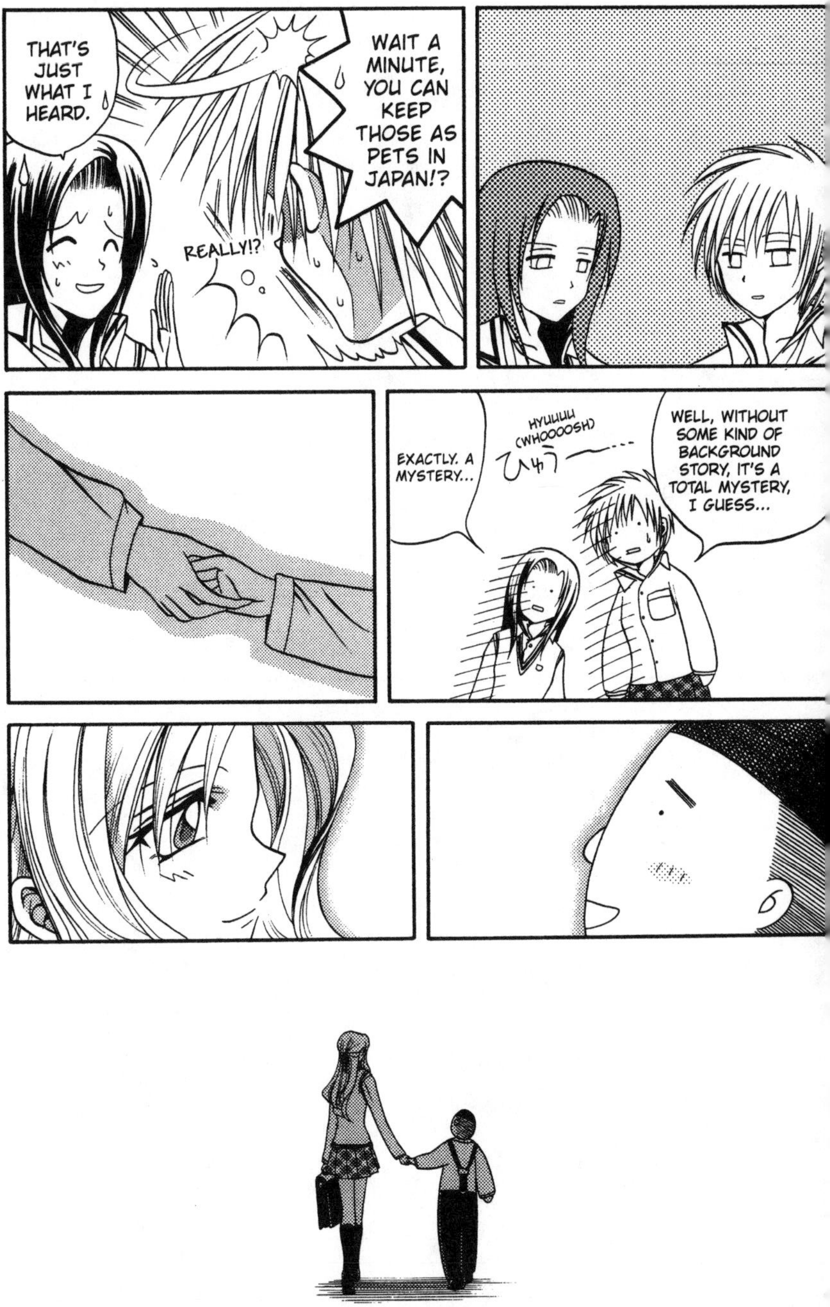
WAIT A MINUTE, YOU CAN KEEP THOSE AS PETS IN JAPAN!?
THAT'S JUST WHAT I HEARD.
REALLY!?
WELL, WITHOUT SOME KIND OF BACKGROUND STORY, IT'S A TOTAL MYSTERY, I GUESS...
HYUUUU (WHOOOOSH)
ひゅう
EXACTLY. A MYSTERY...

SIGN: MACHIDO PRIVATE SENIOR HIGH SCHOOL

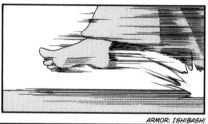

ARMOR: ISHIBASHI

OKAY.

BOYS, PRAC-TICE YOUR SWINGS.

PAAN (SWAACK)

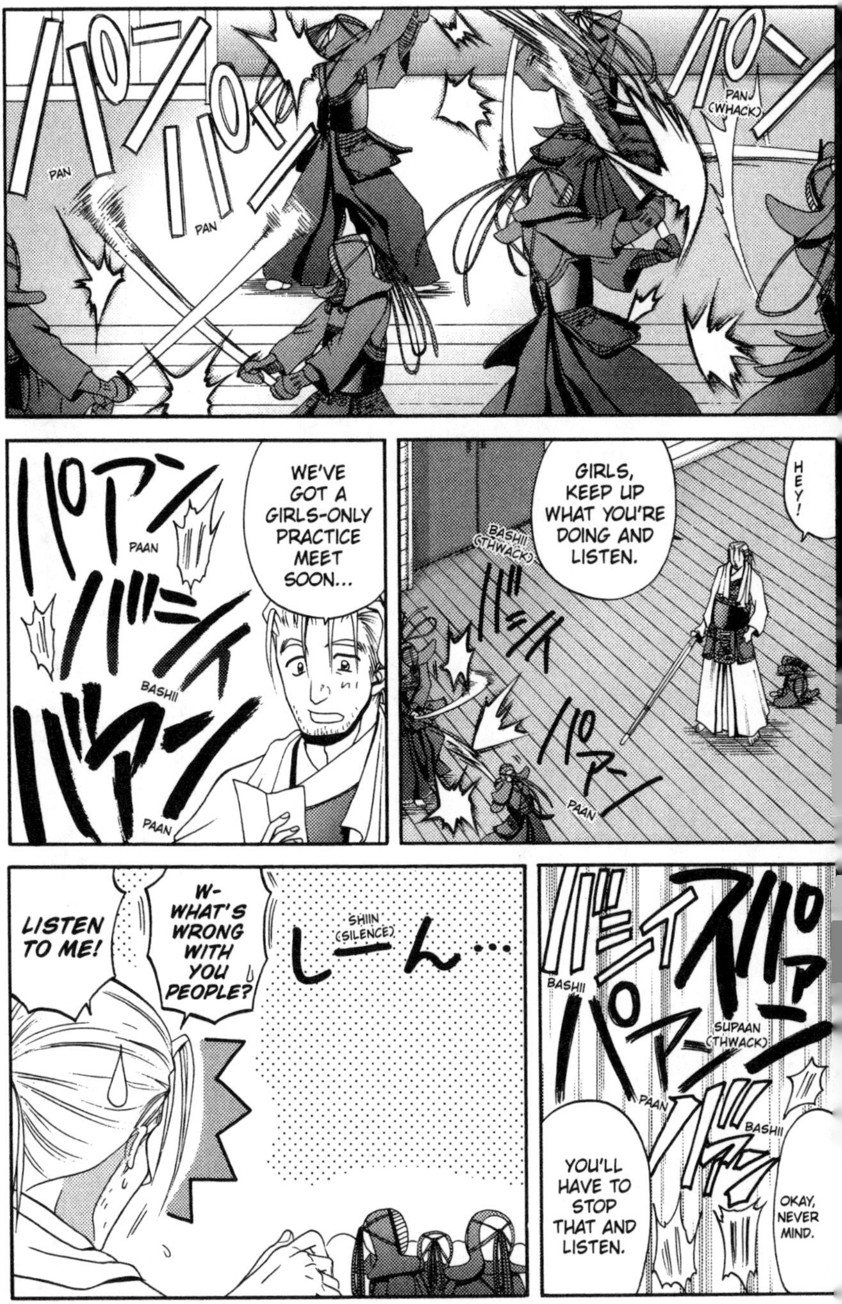
PAN (WHACK)
PAN
PAN
HEY!
GIRLS, KEEP UP WHAT YOU'RE DOING AND LISTEN.
BASHII (THWACK)
PAAN
WE'VE GOT A GIRLS-ONLY PRACTICE MEET SOON...
PAAN
BASHII
PAAN
BASHII
SUPAAN (THWACK)
PAAN
BASHII
YOU'LL HAVE TO STOP THAT AND LISTEN.
OKAY, NEVER MIND.
SHIIN (SILENCE)
W-WHAT'S WRONG WITH YOU PEOPLE?
LISTEN TO ME!

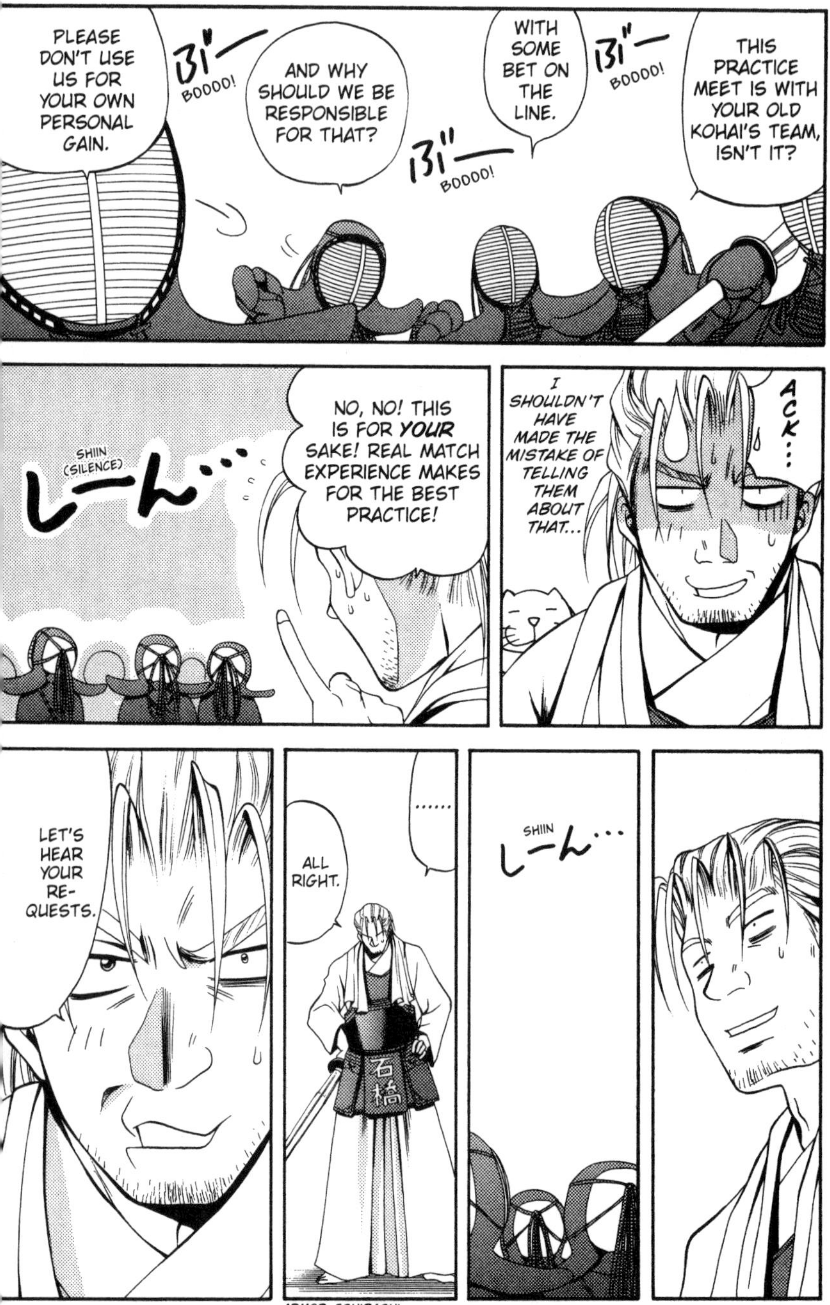
THIS PRACTICE MEET IS WITH YOUR OLD KOHAI'S TEAM, ISN'T IT?
ブー
BOOOO!
WITH SOME BET ON THE LINE.
ぶー
BOOOO!
ブー
BOOOO!
AND WHY SHOULD WE BE RESPONSIBLE FOR THAT?
PLEASE DON'T USE US FOR YOUR OWN PERSONAL GAIN.
ACK...
I SHOULDN'T HAVE MADE THE MISTAKE OF TELLING THEM ABOUT THAT...
NO, NO! THIS IS FOR *YOUR* SAKE! REAL MATCH EXPERIENCE MAKES FOR THE BEST PRACTICE!
しーん…
SHIIN (SILENCE)
しーん…
SHIIN
......
ALL RIGHT.
LET'S HEAR YOUR RE-QUESTS.
ARMOR: ISHIBASHI

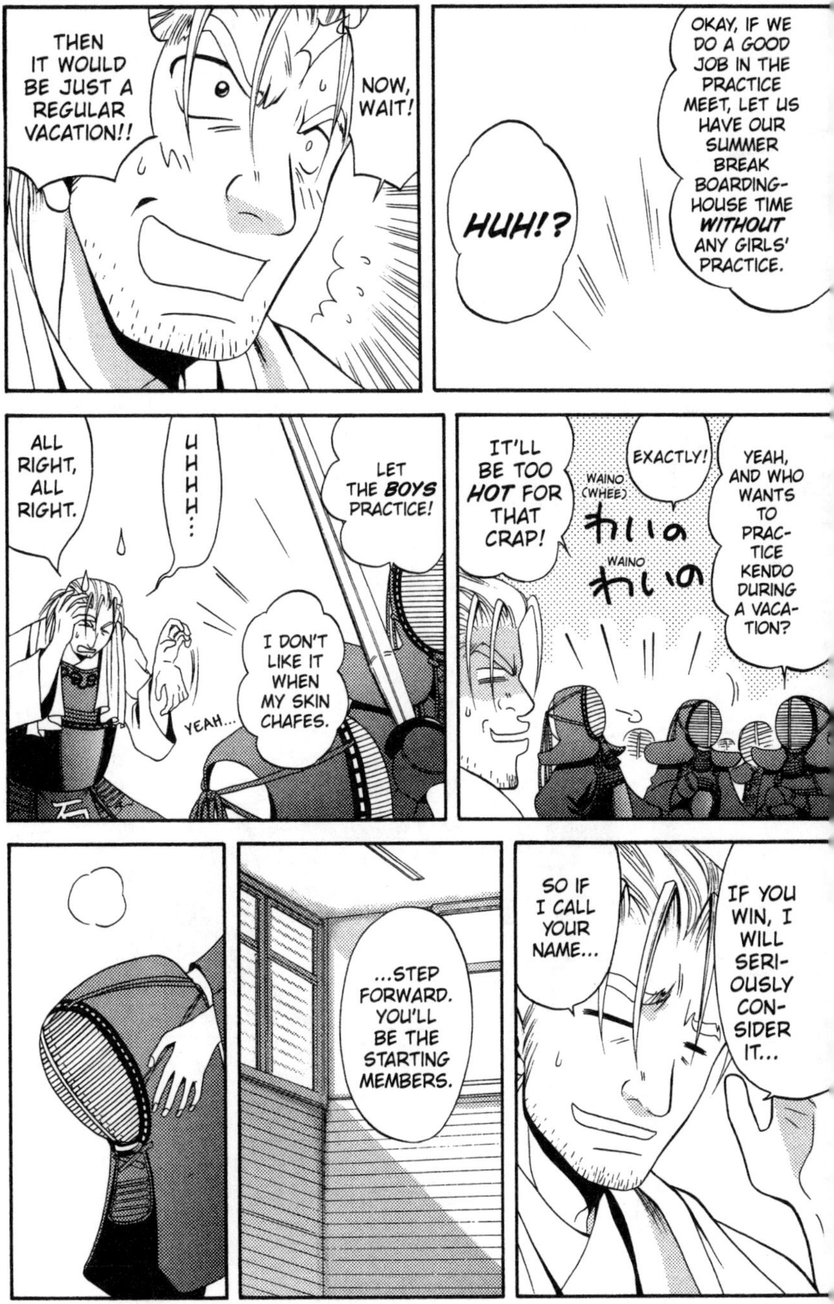
OKAY, IF WE DO A GOOD JOB IN THE PRACTICE MEET, LET US HAVE OUR SUMMER BREAK BOARDING-HOUSE TIME ***WITHOUT*** ANY GIRLS' PRACTICE.
HUH!?
NOW, WAIT!
THEN IT WOULD BE JUST A REGULAR VACATION!!
YEAH, AND WHO WANTS TO PRAC-TICE KENDO DURING A VACA-TION?
EXACTLY!
IT'LL BE TOO ***HOT*** FOR THAT CRAP!
WAINO (WHEE)
わいの
WAINO
わいの
LET THE ***BOYS*** PRACTICE!
I DON'T LIKE IT WHEN MY SKIN CHAFES.
UHHH...
YEAH...
ALL RIGHT, ALL RIGHT.
IF YOU WIN, I WILL SERI-OUSLY CON-SIDER IT...
SO IF I CALL YOUR NAME...
...STEP FORWARD. YOU'LL BE THE STARTING MEMBERS.

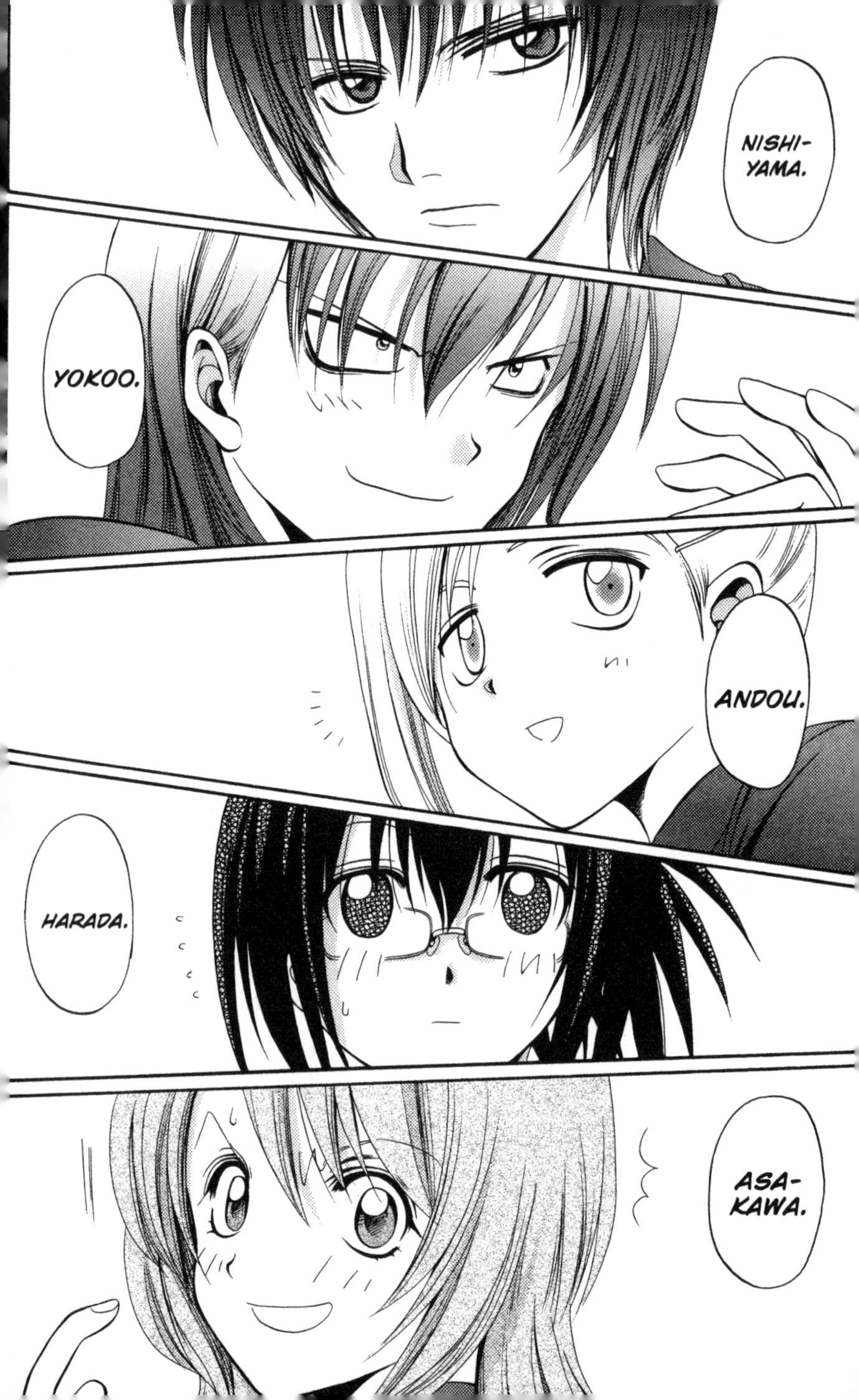
NISHI-YAMA.
YOKOO.
ANDOU.
HARADA.
ASA-KAWA.

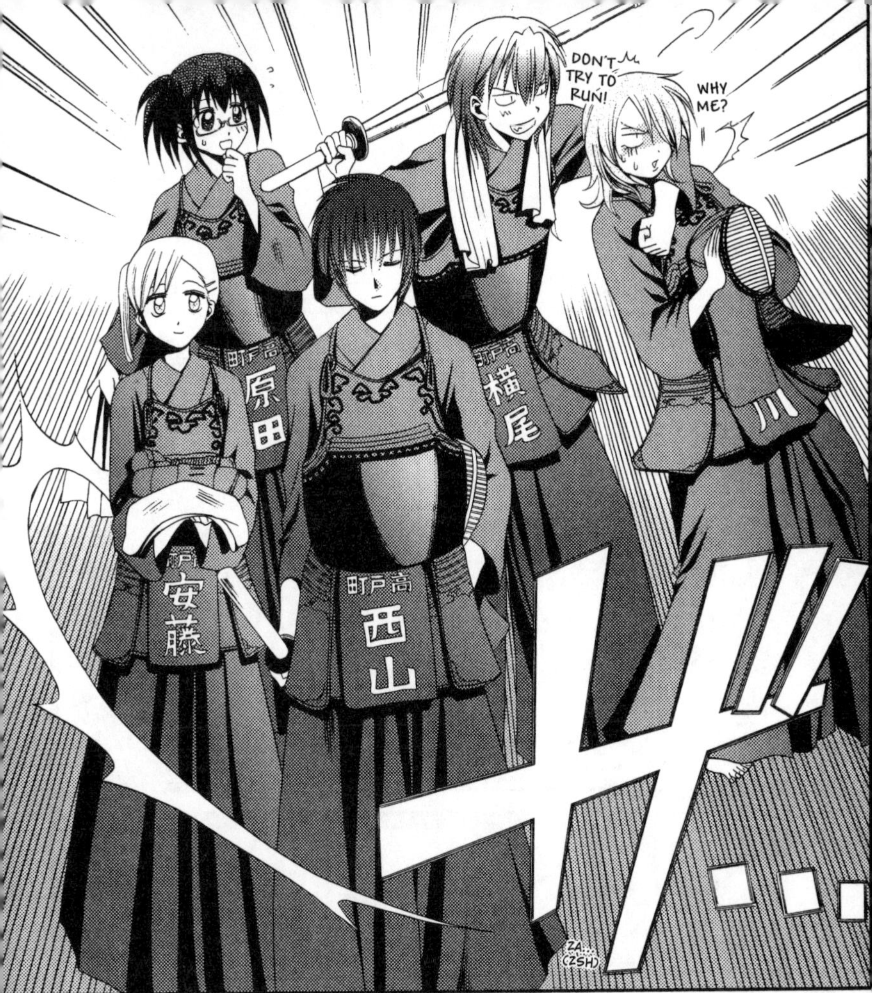
WHY ME?
DON'T TRY TO RUN!
町戸高 横尾
町戸高 原田
町戸高 西山
安藤
ザッ…
ZA... (ZSH)
ARMOR (L-R): MACHIDO HIGH-ANDOU / HARADA / NISHIYAMA / YOKOO / ASAKAWA

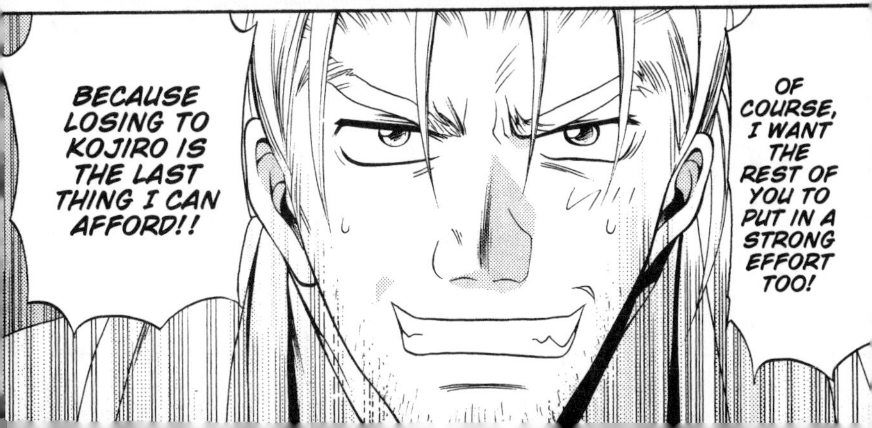
OF COURSE, I WANT THE REST OF YOU TO PUT IN A STRONG EFFORT TOO!
BECAUSE LOSING TO KOJIRO IS THE LAST THING I CAN AFFORD!!

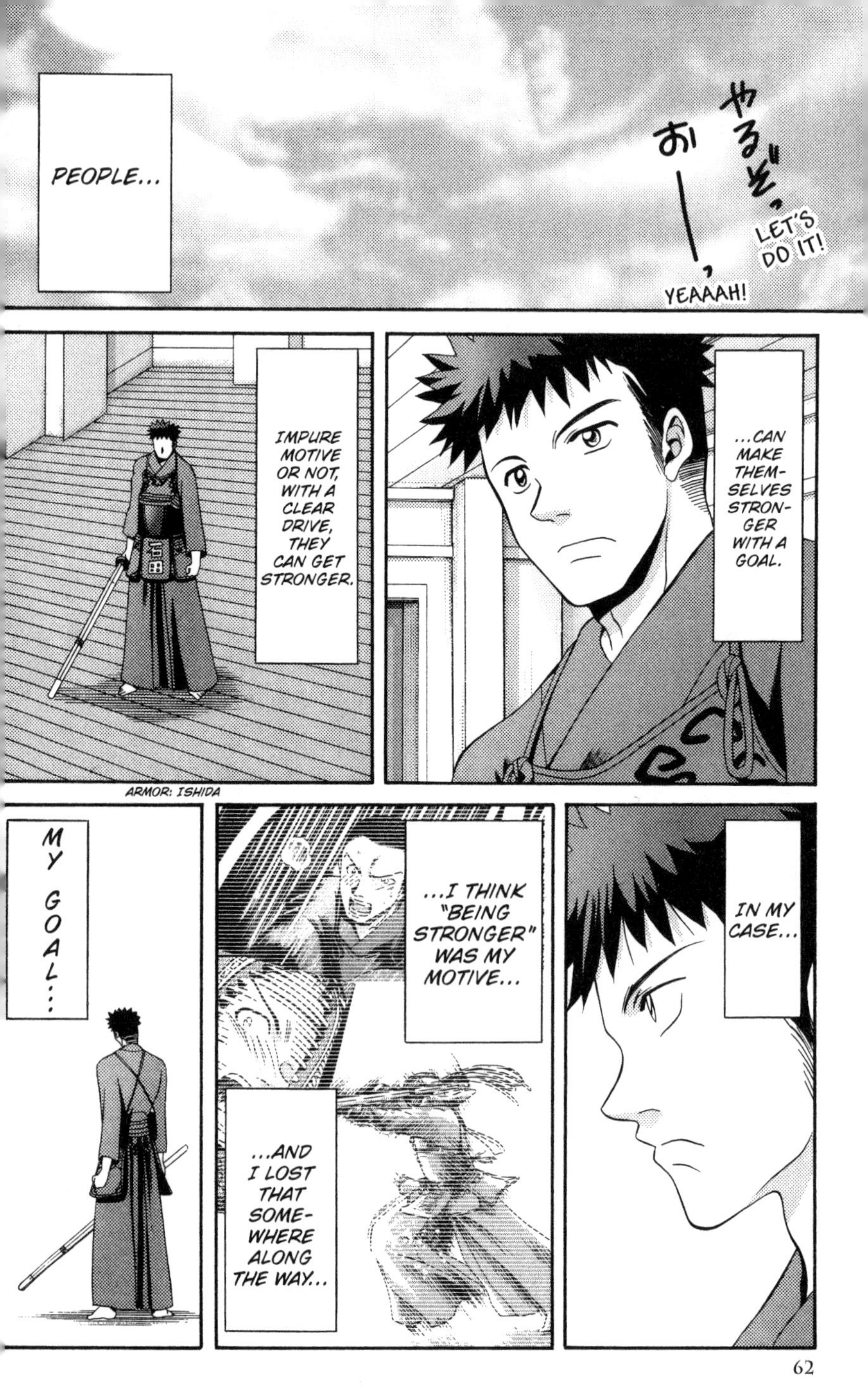
やるぞ、
LET'S DO IT!
おーー、
YEAAAH!
PEOPLE...
...CAN MAKE THEMSELVES STRONGER WITH A GOAL.
IMPURE MOTIVE OR NOT, WITH A CLEAR DRIVE, THEY CAN GET STRONGER.
ARMOR: ISHIDA
IN MY CASE...
...I THINK "BEING STRONGER" WAS MY MOTIVE...
...AND I LOST THAT SOMEWHERE ALONG THE WAY...
MY GOAL...

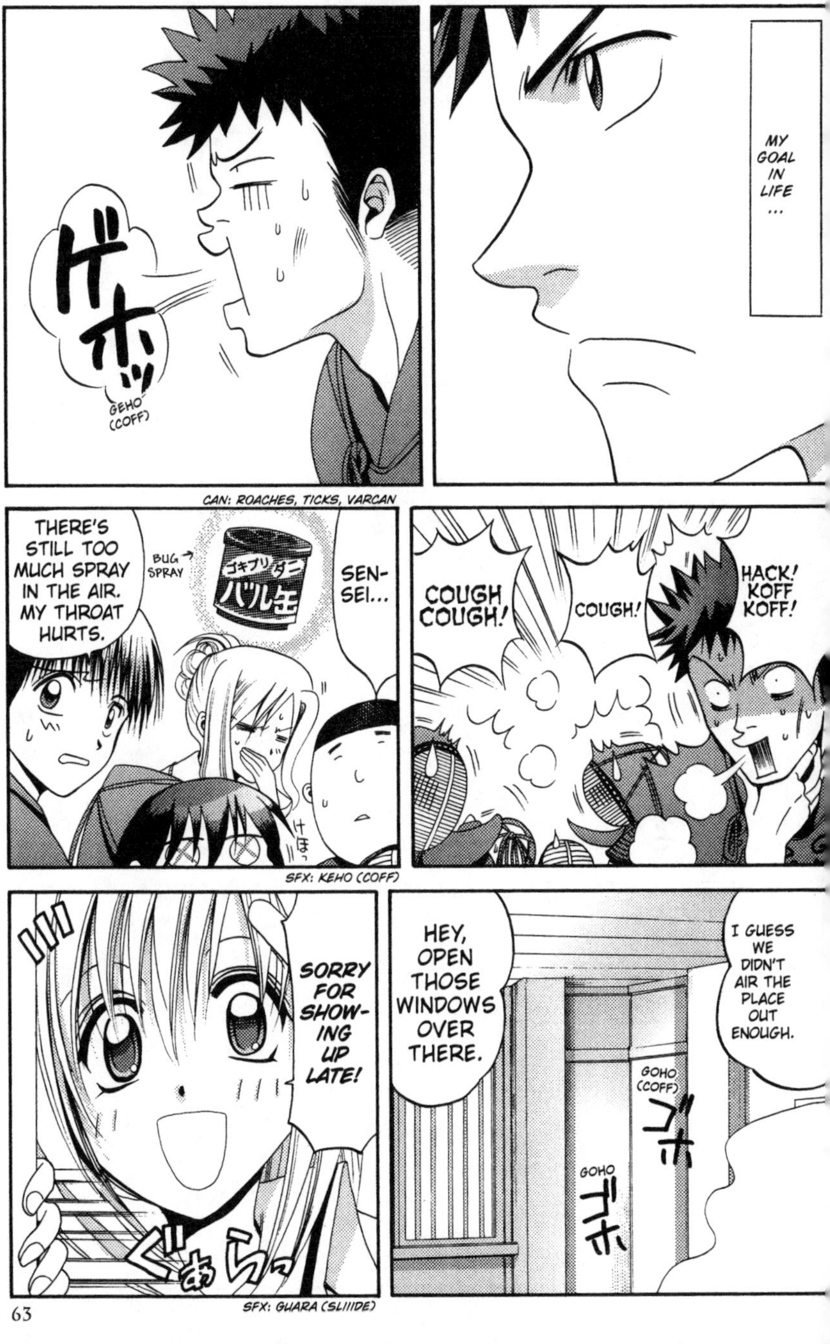
MY GOAL IN LIFE ...
ゲホッ
GEHO (COFF)
CAN: ROACHES, TICKS, VARCAN
HACK! KOFF KOFF!
COUGH!
COUGH COUGH!
SEN-SEI...
ゴキブリ ダニ バル缶
BUG SPRAY
THERE'S STILL TOO MUCH SPRAY IN THE AIR. MY THROAT HURTS.
けほっ
SFX: KEHO (COFF)
I GUESS WE DIDN'T AIR THE PLACE OUT ENOUGH.
GOHO (COFF)
ゴホ
GOHO
ゴホ
HEY, OPEN THOSE WINDOWS OVER THERE.
SORRY FOR SHOWING UP LATE!
ぐあらっ
SFX: GUARA (SLIIIDE)

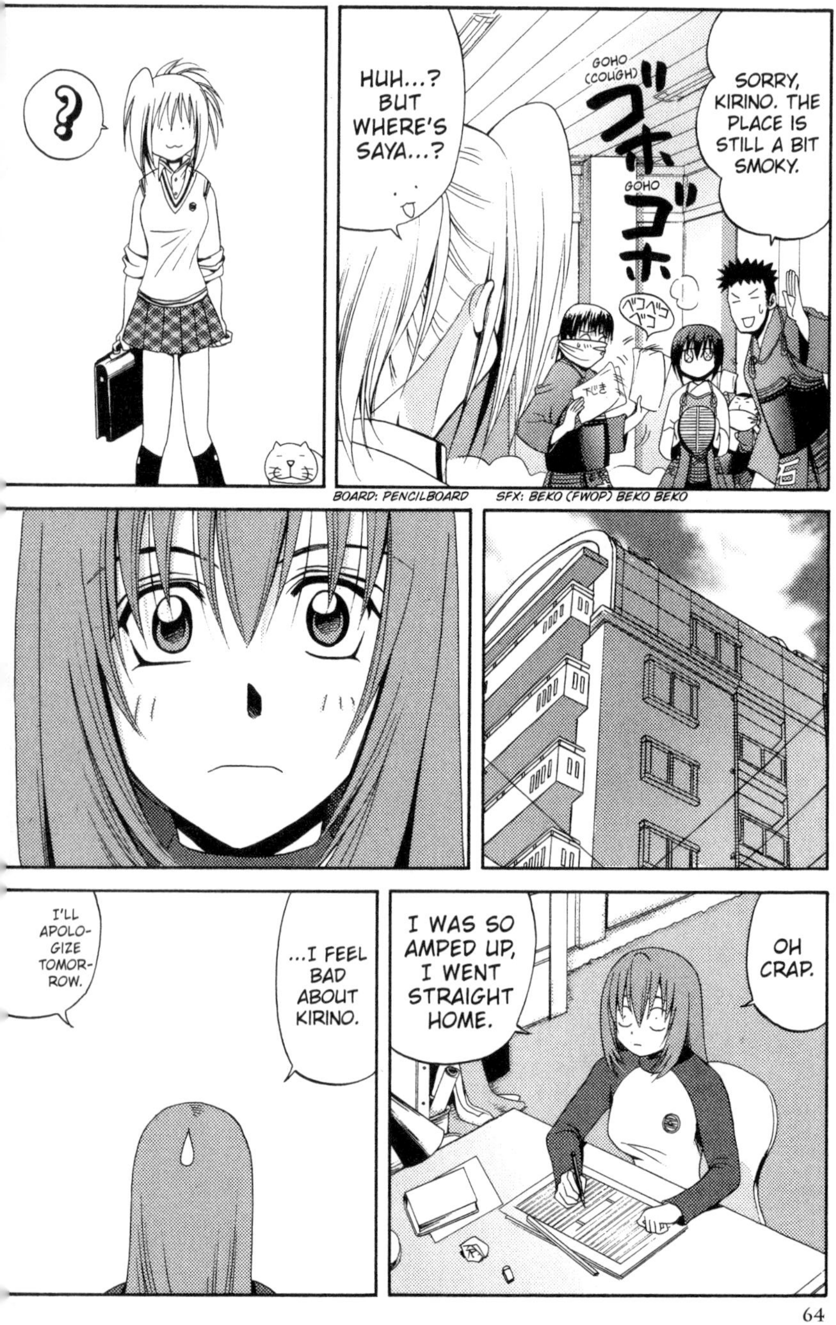
SORRY, KIRINO. THE PLACE IS STILL A BIT SMOKY.
GOHO (COUGH)
GOHO
HUH...? BUT WHERE'S SAYA...?
?
BOARD: PENCILBOARD
SFX: BEKO (FWOP) BEKO BEKO
OH CRAP.
I WAS SO AMPED UP, I WENT STRAIGHT HOME.
...I FEEL BAD ABOUT KIRINO.
I'LL APOLOGIZE TOMORROW.

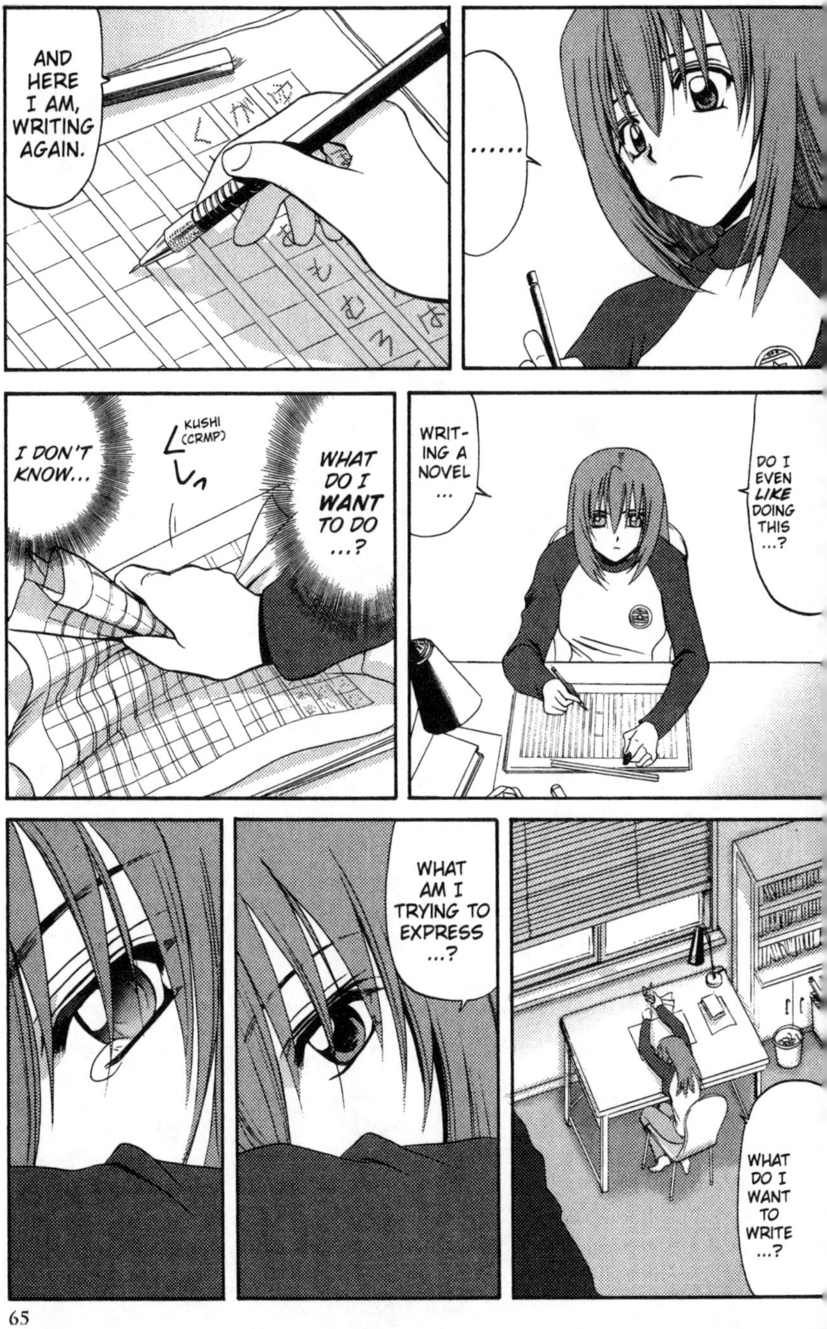
......
AND HERE I AM, WRITING AGAIN.
WRITING A NOVEL ...
DO I EVEN *LIKE* DOING THIS ...?
WHAT DO I WANT TO DO ...?
KUSHI (CRMP)
I DON'T KNOW...
WHAT DO I WANT TO WRITE ...?
WHAT AM I TRYING TO EXPRESS ...?

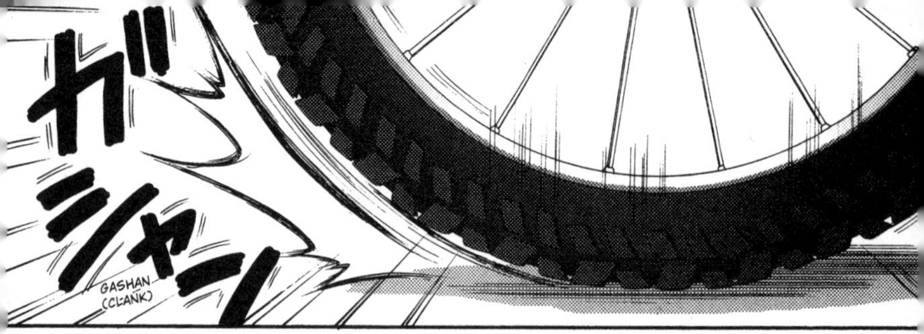
GASHAN
(CLANK)
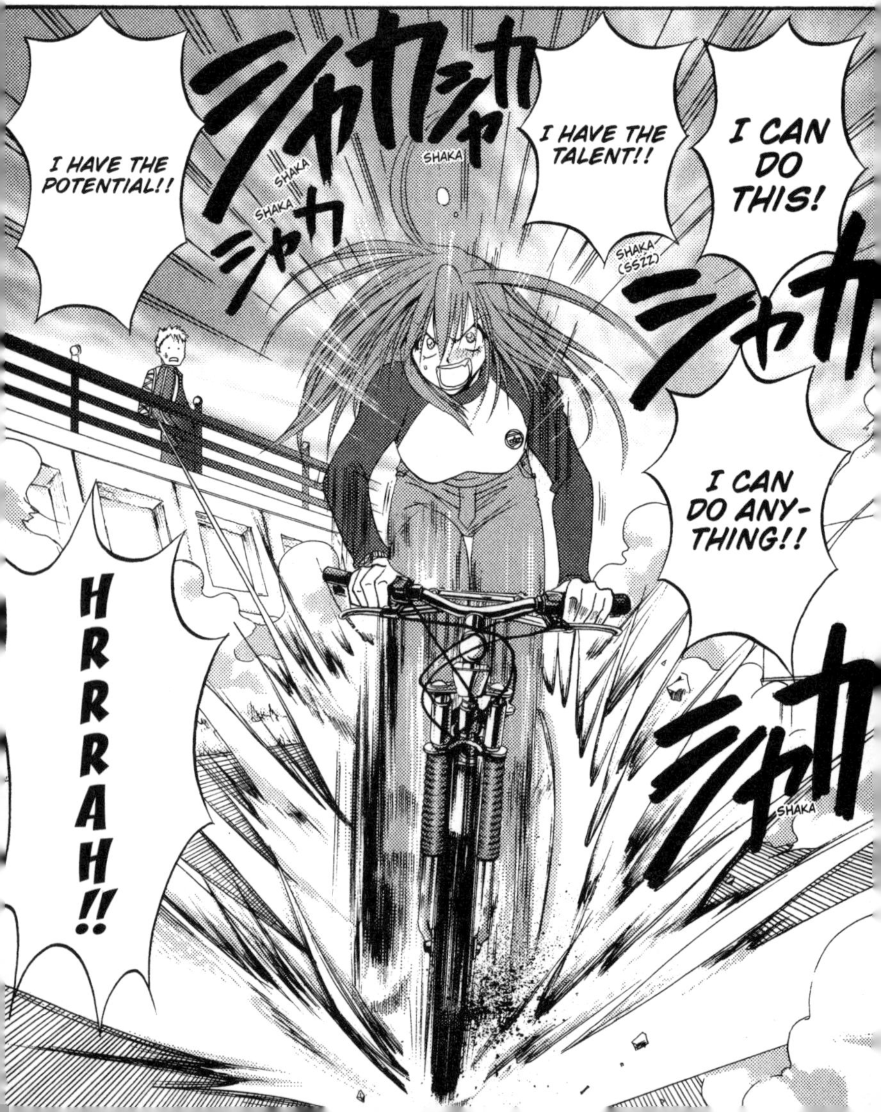
I CAN DO THIS!
I HAVE THE TALENT!!
SHAKA
SHAKA
SHAKA
I HAVE THE POTENTIAL!!
SHAKA (SSZZ)
I CAN DO ANY-THING!!
SHAKA
HRRRAH!!

BAMBOO BLADE

CHIBA-SAN AND NORMAL LIFE

SENSEI MADE ME DELIVER ALL THIS STUFF TO CAPTAIN KIRINO, JUST BECAUSE HE DIDN'T WANT TO...

HE'S SUCH A LAZY TEACHER.

SORRY YOU HAD TO COME TOO, TAMA-CHAN.

YEAH.

IT'S OKAY.

YOU KNOW, I WONDER WHAT CAPTAIN KIRINO DOES, NORMALLY.

I HATE TO SAY IT, BUT SHE'S A PRETTY WEIRD PERSON...

I WONDER IF SHE'S WEIRD ALL THE TIME.

ガラッ
GARA (THLUNK)

SFX: PINPON (PING PONG) PINPON PINPON

DAN-KUN!

♡

GO, KIRINO, GO!

THAT SEEMS NORMAL.

R-REALLY?

WHAT'S WITH THESE PEOPLE?

EVEN CONSIDERING TAMA-CHAN'S SENSE OF "NORMAL," THIS IS NOT IT.

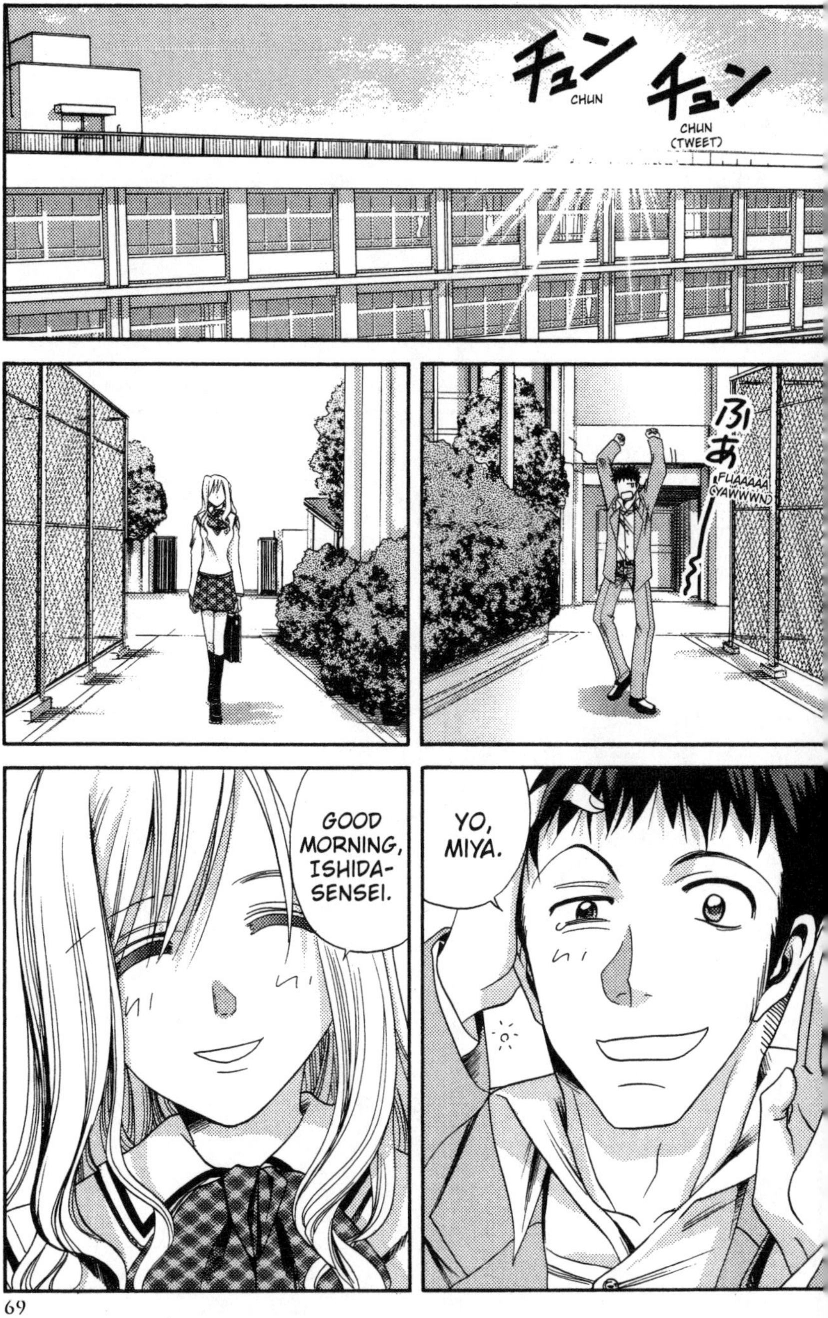
チュン
CHUN
チュン
CHUN (TWEET)
ふあ
FUAAAAA (YAWWWN)
YO, MIYA.
GOOD MORNING, ISHIDA-SENSEI.

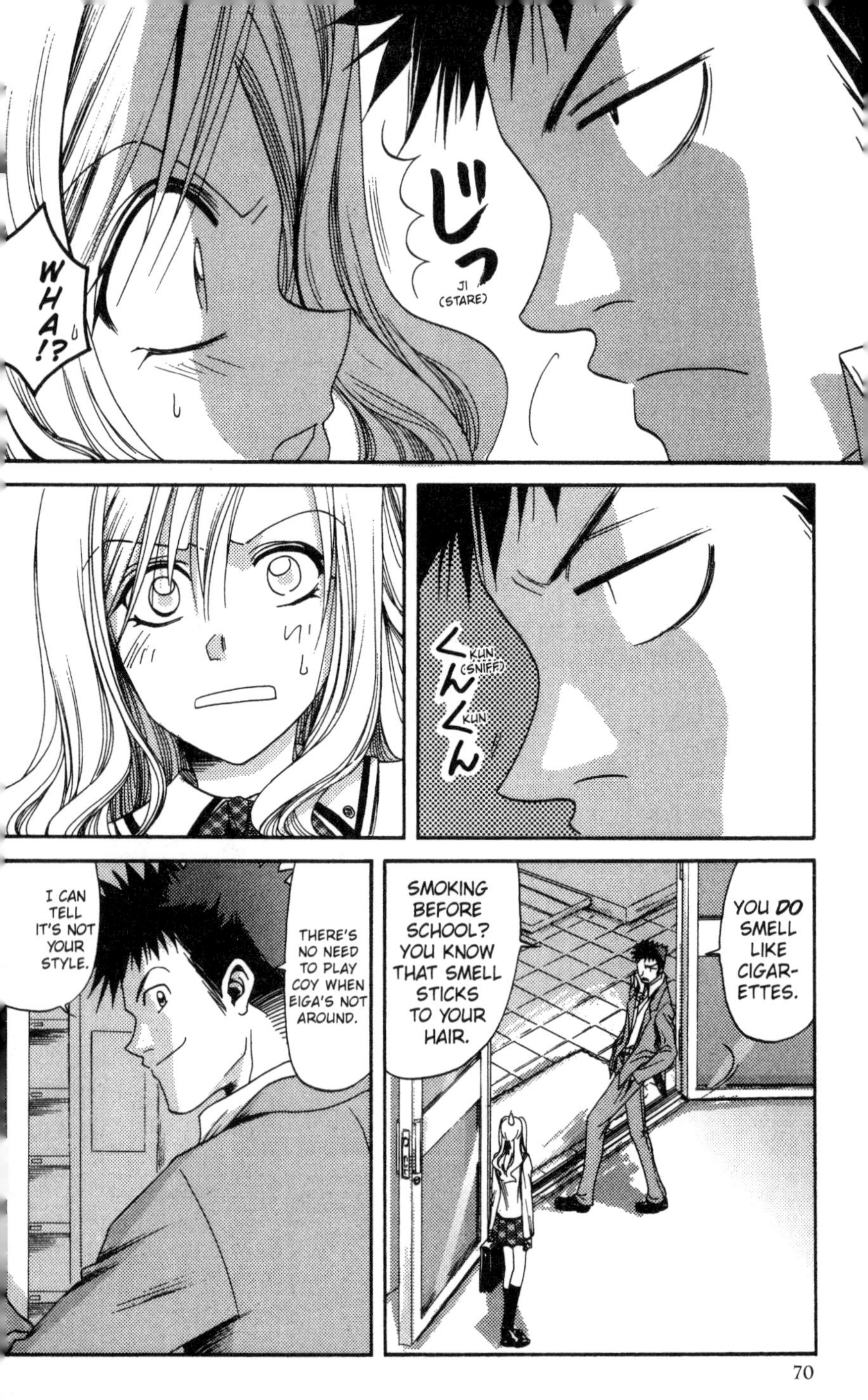
じっ
JI (STARE)
WHA!?
くんくん
KUN (SNIFF) KUN
YOU **DO** SMELL LIKE CIGARETTES.
SMOKING BEFORE SCHOOL? YOU KNOW THAT SMELL STICKS TO YOUR HAIR.
THERE'S NO NEED TO PLAY COY WHEN EIGA'S NOT AROUND.
I CAN TELL IT'S NOT YOUR STYLE.

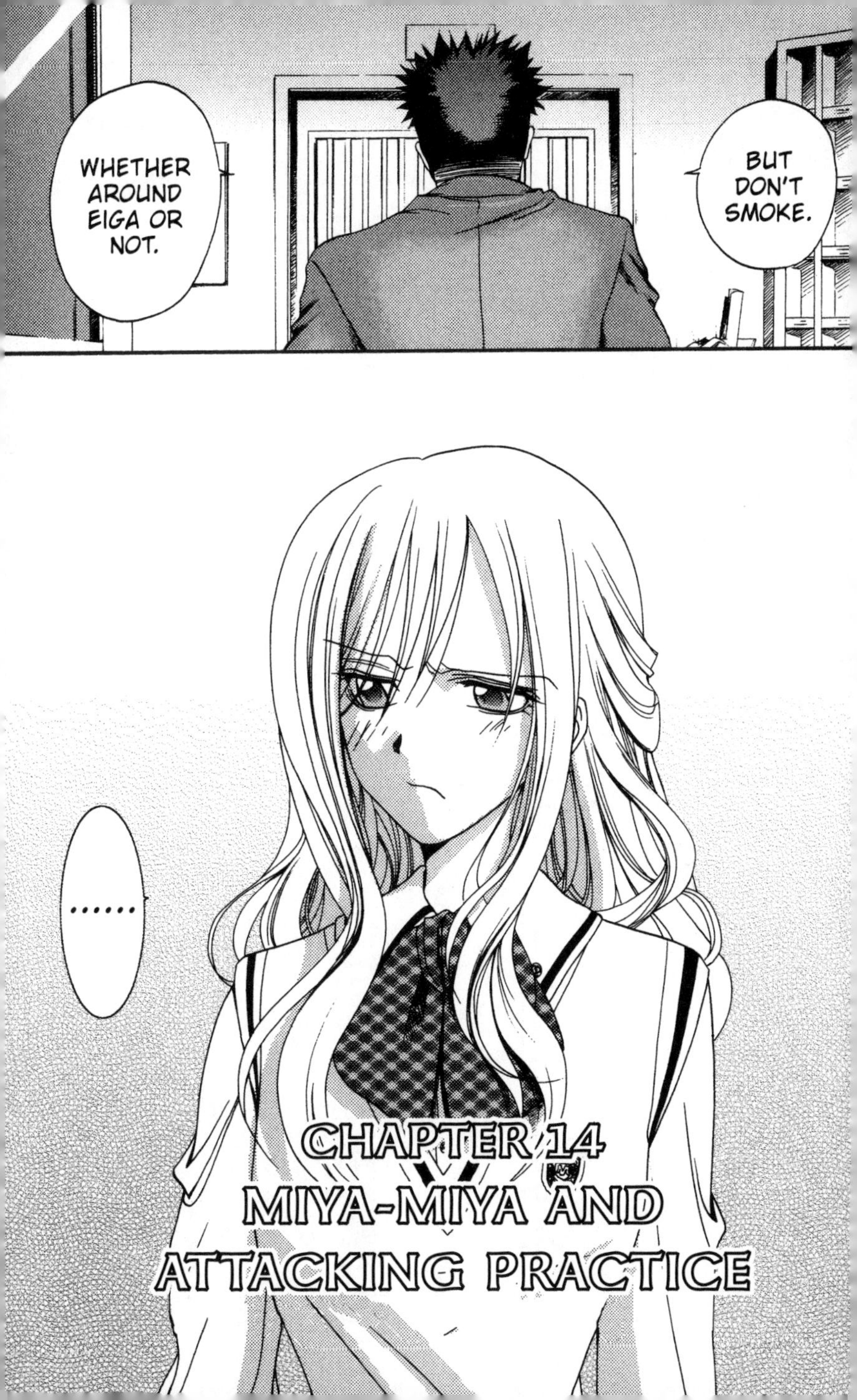
WHETHER AROUND EIGA OR NOT.
BUT DON'T SMOKE.
......
CHAPTER 14
MIYA-MIYA AND ATTACKING PRACTICE

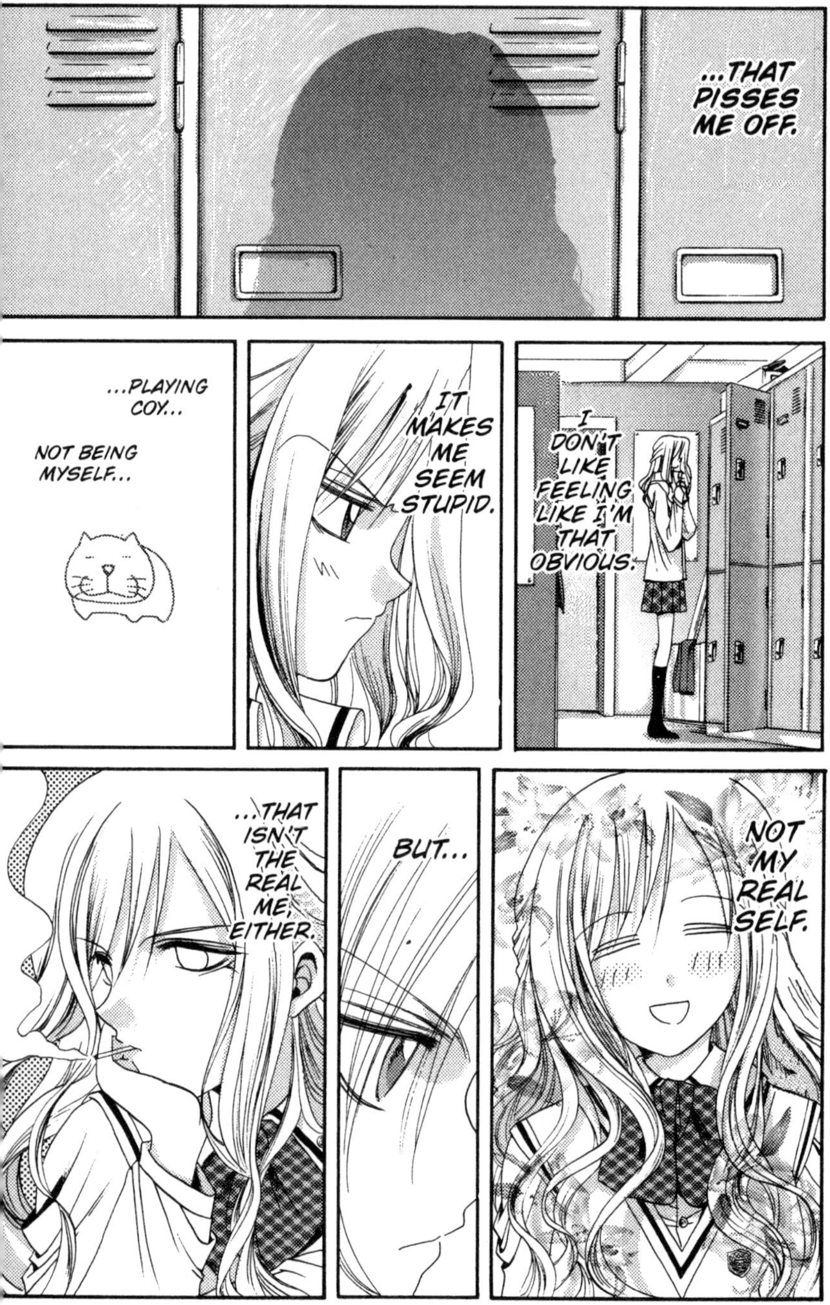
...THAT PISSES ME OFF.
I DON'T LIKE FEELING LIKE I'M THAT OBVIOUS.
IT MAKES ME SEEM STUPID.
...PLAYING COY...
NOT BEING MYSELF...
NOT MY REAL SELF.
BUT...
...THAT ISN'T THE REAL ME, EITHER.

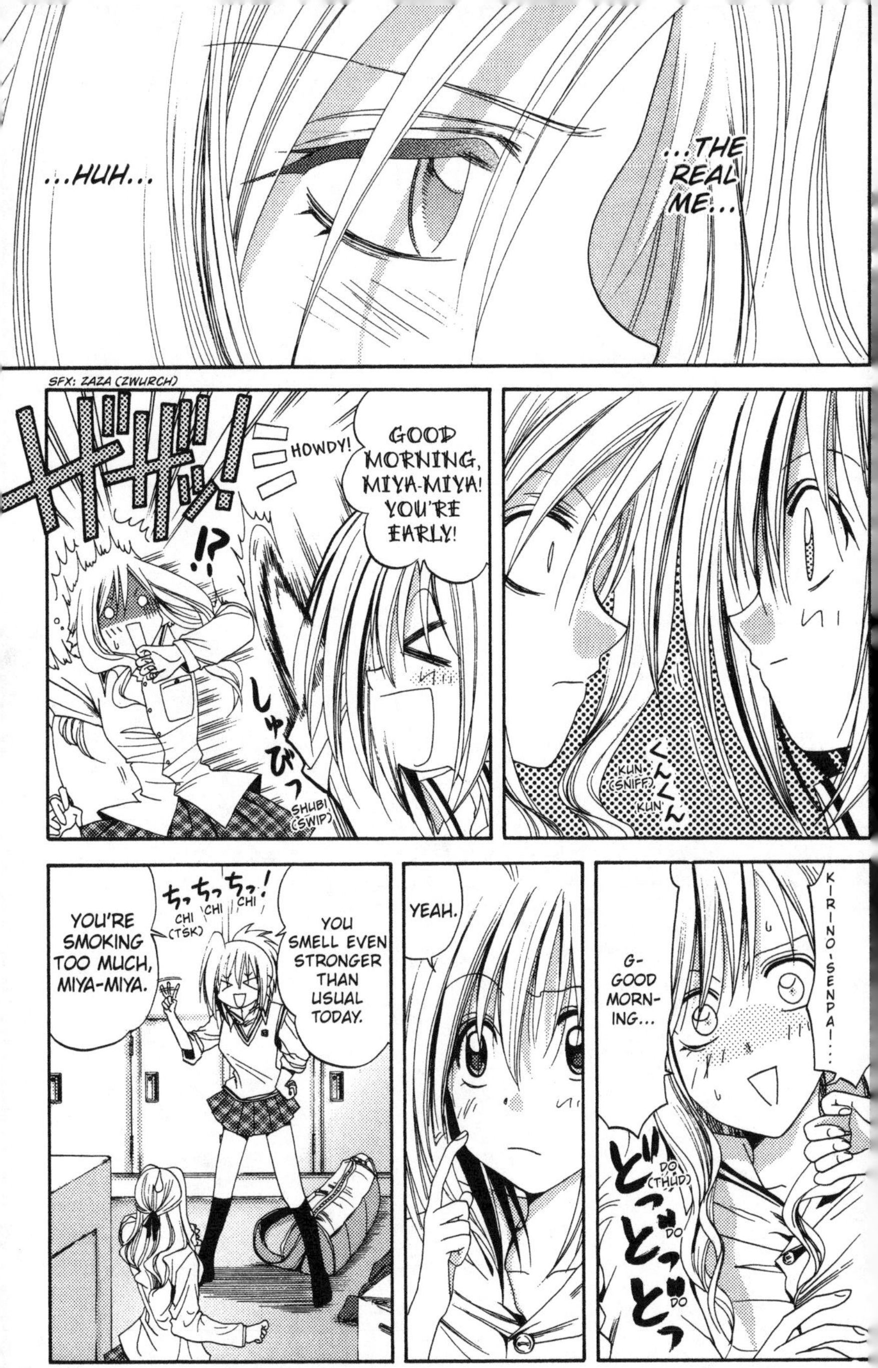
...THE REAL ME...
...HUH...
SFX: ZAZA (ZWURCH)
KUN (SNIFF) KUN
GOOD MORNING, MIYA-MIYA! YOU'RE EARLY!
HOWDY!
!?
SHUBI (SWIP)
KIRINO-SENPAI...
G-GOOD MORN-ING...
DO (THUD) DO DO
YEAH.
YOU SMELL EVEN STRONGER THAN USUAL TODAY.
CHI (TSK) CHI CHI
YOU'RE SMOKING TOO MUCH, MIYA-MIYA.

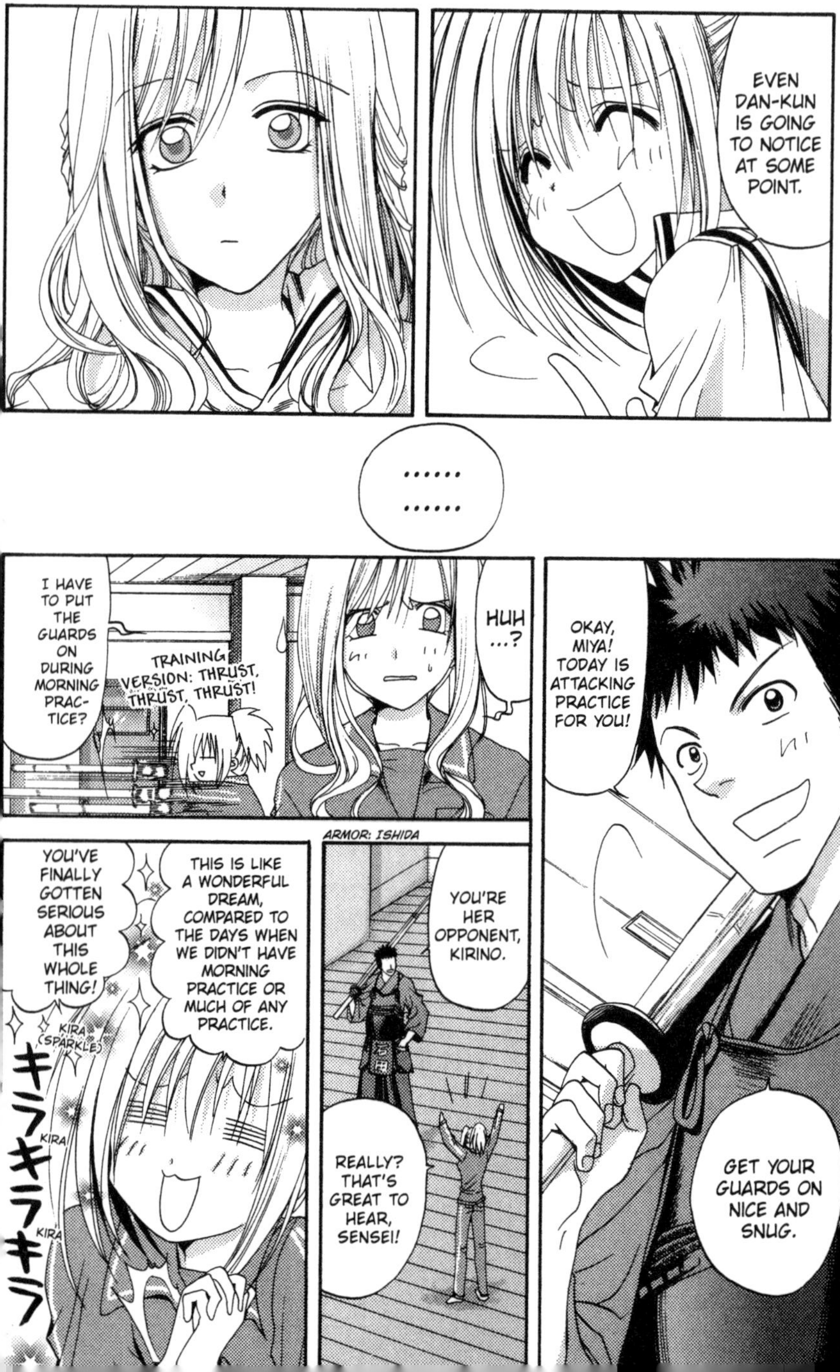
EVEN DAN-KUN IS GOING TO NOTICE AT SOME POINT.
…… ……
OKAY, MIYA! TODAY IS ATTACKING PRACTICE FOR YOU!
GET YOUR GUARDS ON NICE AND SNUG.
HUH ...?
TRAINING VERSION: THRUST, THRUST, THRUST!
I HAVE TO PUT THE GUARDS ON DURING MORNING PRACTICE?
ARMOR: ISHIDA
YOU'RE HER OPPONENT, KIRINO.
REALLY? THAT'S GREAT TO HEAR, SENSEI!
THIS IS LIKE A WONDERFUL DREAM, COMPARED TO THE DAYS WHEN WE DIDN'T HAVE MORNING PRACTICE OR MUCH OF ANY PRACTICE.
YOU'VE FINALLY GOTTEN SERIOUS ABOUT THIS WHOLE THING!
KIRA (SPARKLE)
キラキラキラ
KIRA
KIRA

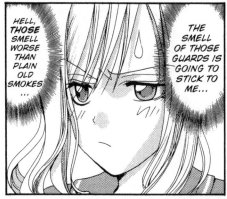

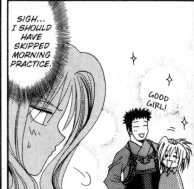

SIGH... I SHOULD HAVE SKIPPED MORNING PRACTICE.
GOOD GIRL!
THE SMELL OF THOSE GUARDS IS GOING TO STICK TO ME...
HELL, THOSE SMELL WORSE THAN PLAIN OLD SMOKES...
MAYBE I SHOULD JUST LEAVE.
BUT DAN-KUN WILL BE HERE SOON...
FURA (FLOP)
G...
GOOD... MORN... ING.
SAYAKO KUWAHARA...
...REPORTING FOR DUTY.

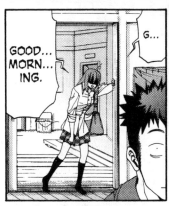

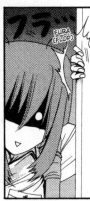

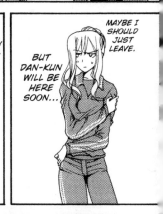

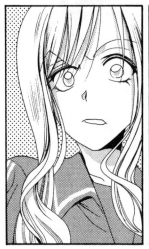

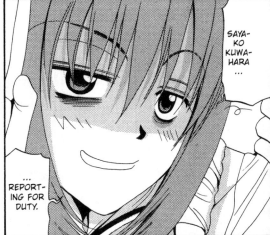

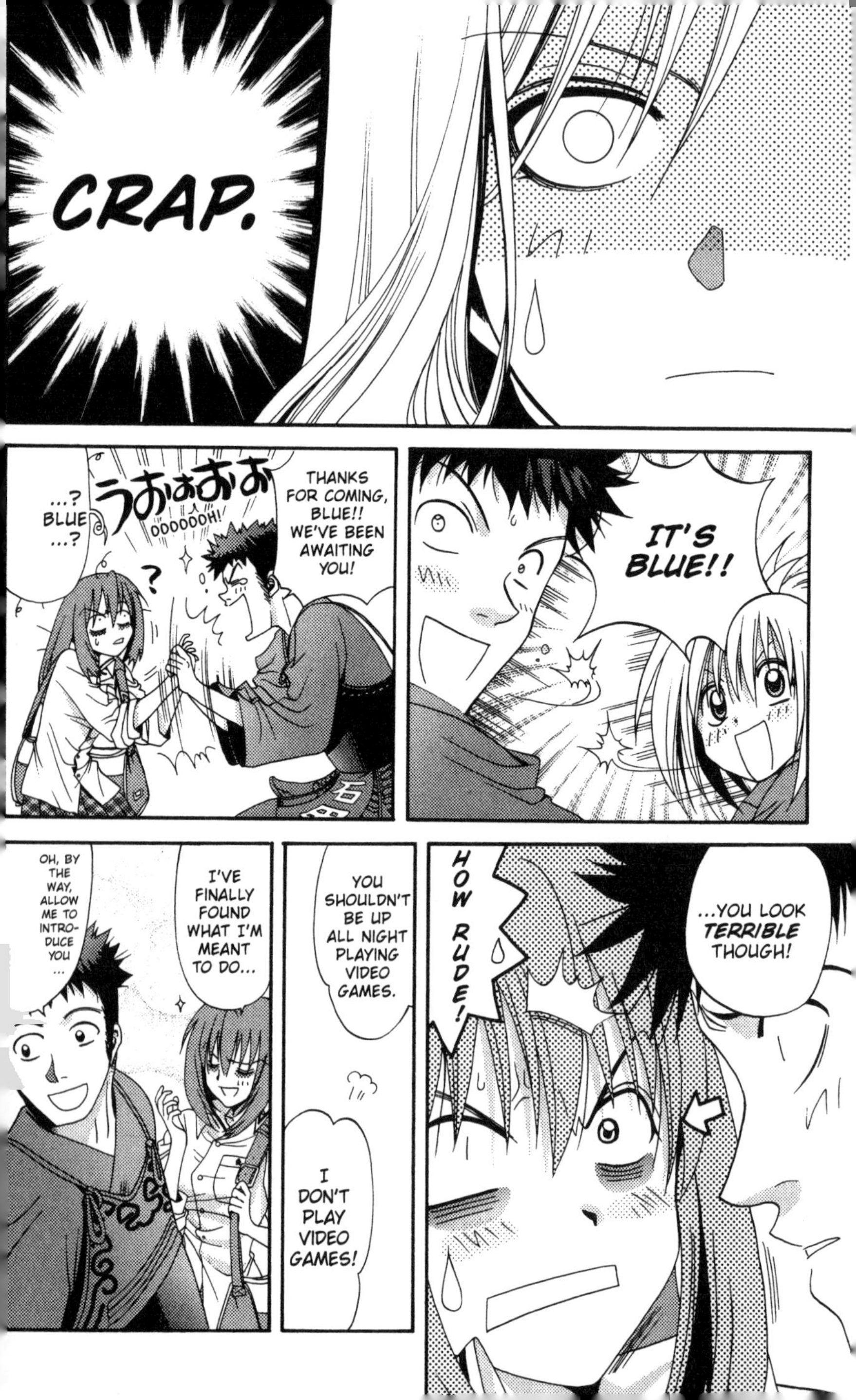
CRAP.
IT'S BLUE!!
THANKS FOR COMING, BLUE!! WE'VE BEEN AWAITING YOU!
うおぉおお
OOOOOOH!
...? BLUE ...?
?
...YOU LOOK TERRIBLE THOUGH!
HOW RUDE!
YOU SHOULDN'T BE UP ALL NIGHT PLAYING VIDEO GAMES.
I DON'T PLAY VIDEO GAMES!
I'VE FINALLY FOUND WHAT I'M MEANT TO DO...
OH, BY THE WAY, ALLOW ME TO INTRODUCE YOU ...

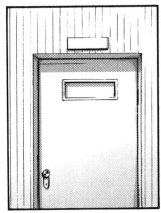

...HUH?

MIYA-
MIYA?

HMM
...

....

...IT'S
GUITAR.

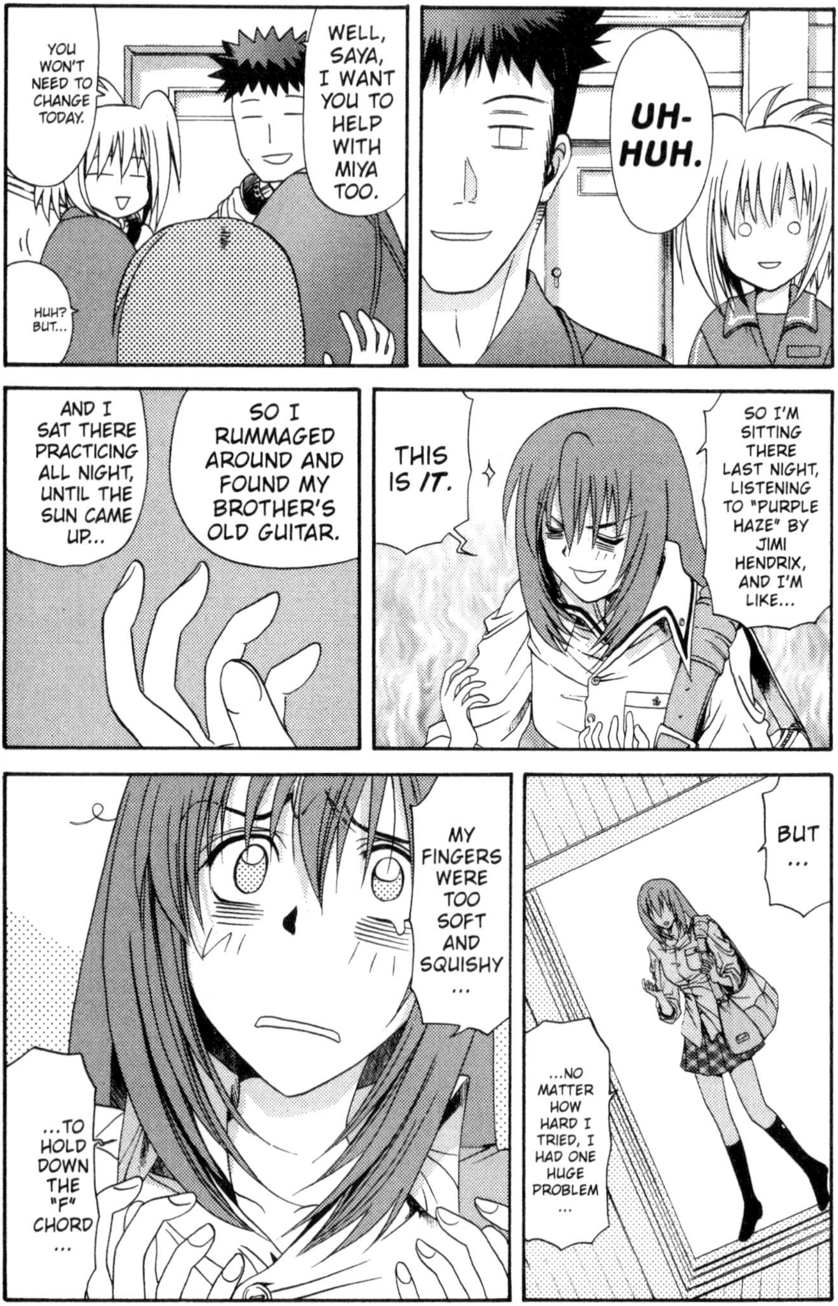
UH-HUH.
WELL, SAYA, I WANT YOU TO HELP WITH MIYA TOO.
YOU WON'T NEED TO CHANGE TODAY.
HUH? BUT...
SO I'M SITTING THERE LAST NIGHT, LISTENING TO "PURPLE HAZE" BY JIMI HENDRIX, AND I'M LIKE...
THIS IS *IT*.
SO I RUMMAGED AROUND AND FOUND MY BROTHER'S OLD GUITAR.
AND I SAT THERE PRACTICING ALL NIGHT, UNTIL THE SUN CAME UP...
BUT...
...NO MATTER HOW HARD I TRIED, I HAD ONE HUGE PROBLEM...
MY FINGERS WERE TOO SOFT AND SQUISHY...
...TO HOLD DOWN THE "F" CHORD...

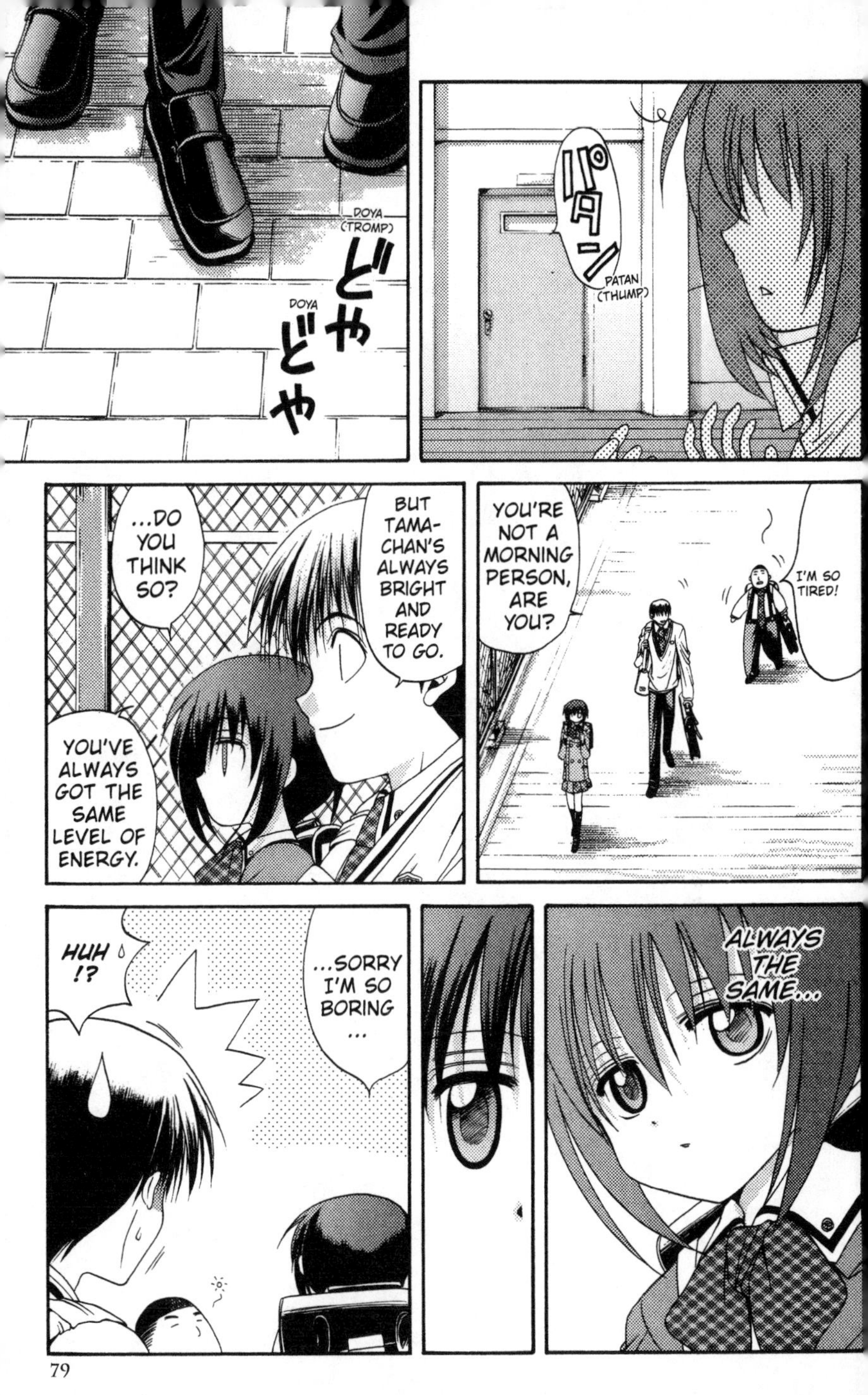
パタン
PATAN (THUMP)
どやどや
DOYA (TROMP) DOYA
I'M SO TIRED!
YOU'RE NOT A MORNING PERSON, ARE YOU?
BUT TAMA-CHAN'S ALWAYS BRIGHT AND READY TO GO.
...DO YOU THINK SO?
YOU'VE ALWAYS GOT THE SAME LEVEL OF ENERGY.
ALWAYS THE SAME...
...SORRY I'M SO BORING...
HUH!?

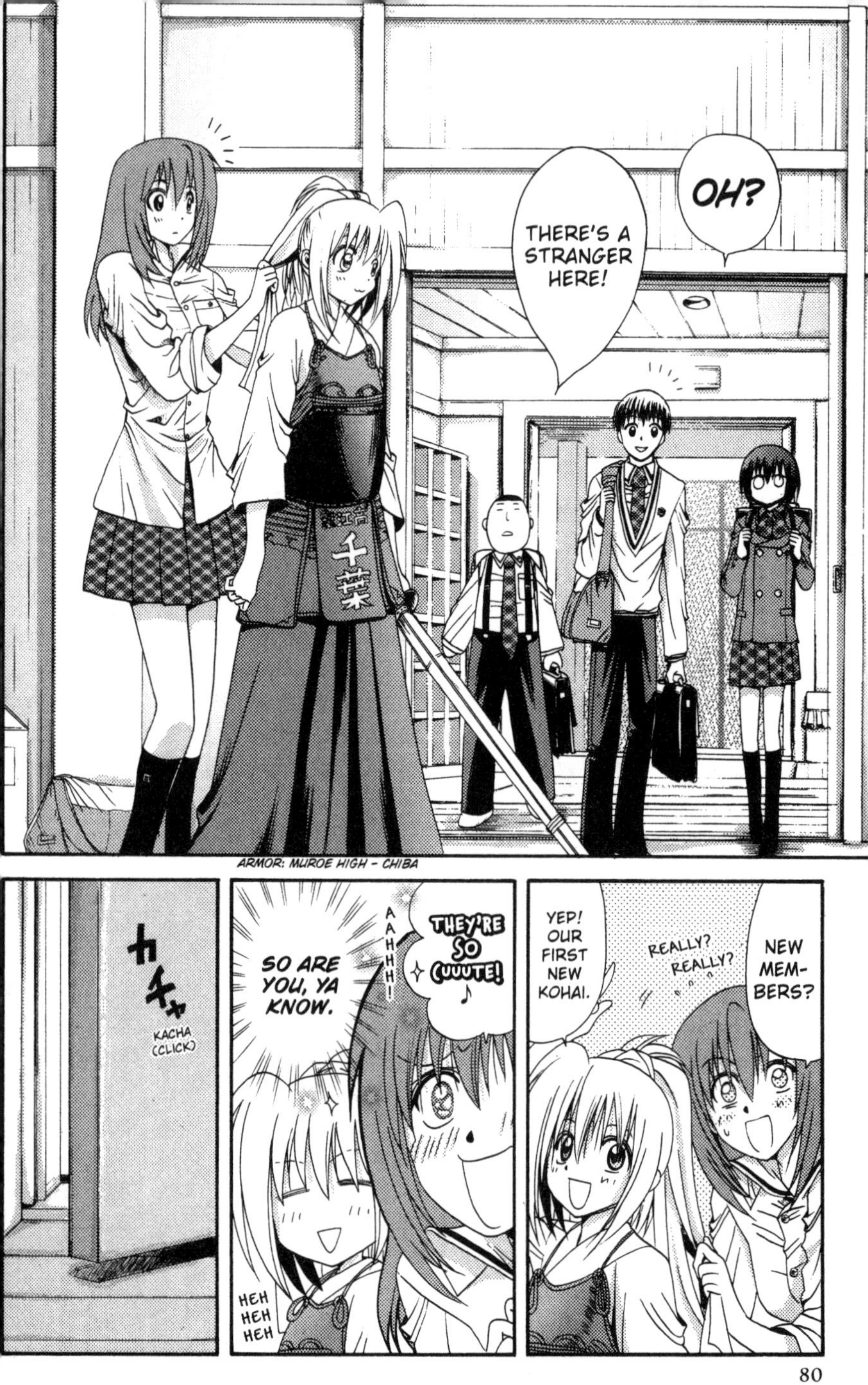
OH?
THERE'S A STRANGER HERE!
千葉
ARMOR: MUROE HIGH - CHIBA
NEW MEMBERS?
REALLY? REALLY?
YEP! OUR FIRST NEW KOHAI.
THEY'RE SO CUUUTE! ♪
AAHHH!
SO ARE YOU, YA KNOW.
HEH HEH HEH
カチャ
KACHA (CLICK)

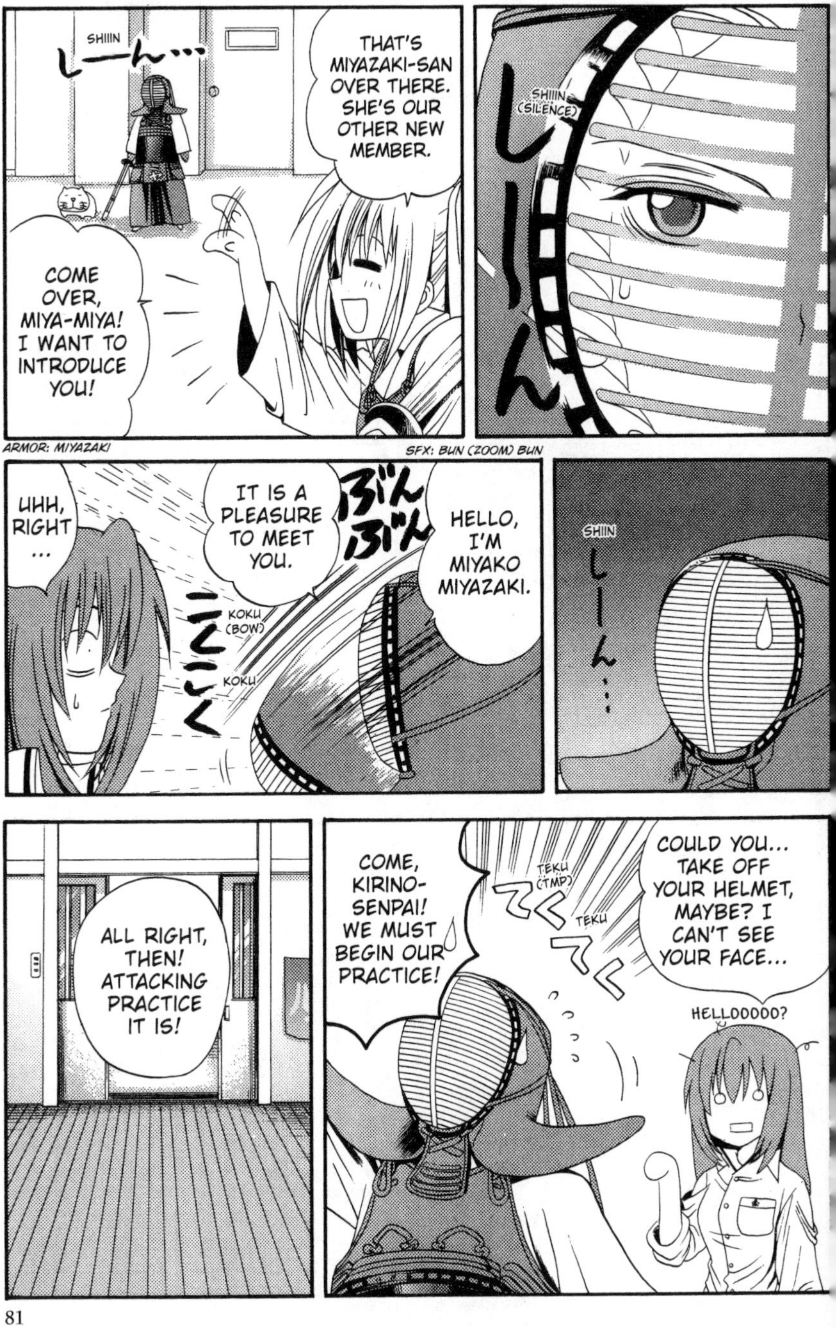
SHIIN (SILENCE)
しーん
SHIIN
しーん…
THAT'S MIYAZAKI-SAN OVER THERE. SHE'S OUR OTHER NEW MEMBER.
COME OVER, MIYA-MIYA! I WANT TO INTRODUCE YOU!
SFX: BUN (ZOOM) BUN
ARMOR: MIYAZAKI
SHIIN
しーん…
HELLO, I'M MIYAKO MIYAZAKI.
ぶんぶん
IT IS A PLEASURE TO MEET YOU.
KOKU (BOW)
こくこく
KOKU
UHH, RIGHT ...
COULD YOU... TAKE OFF YOUR HELMET, MAYBE? I CAN'T SEE YOUR FACE...
TEKU (TMP)
てく
TEKU
てく
COME, KIRINO-SENPAI! WE MUST BEGIN OUR PRACTICE!
HELLOOOOO?
ALL RIGHT, THEN! ATTACKING PRACTICE IT IS!

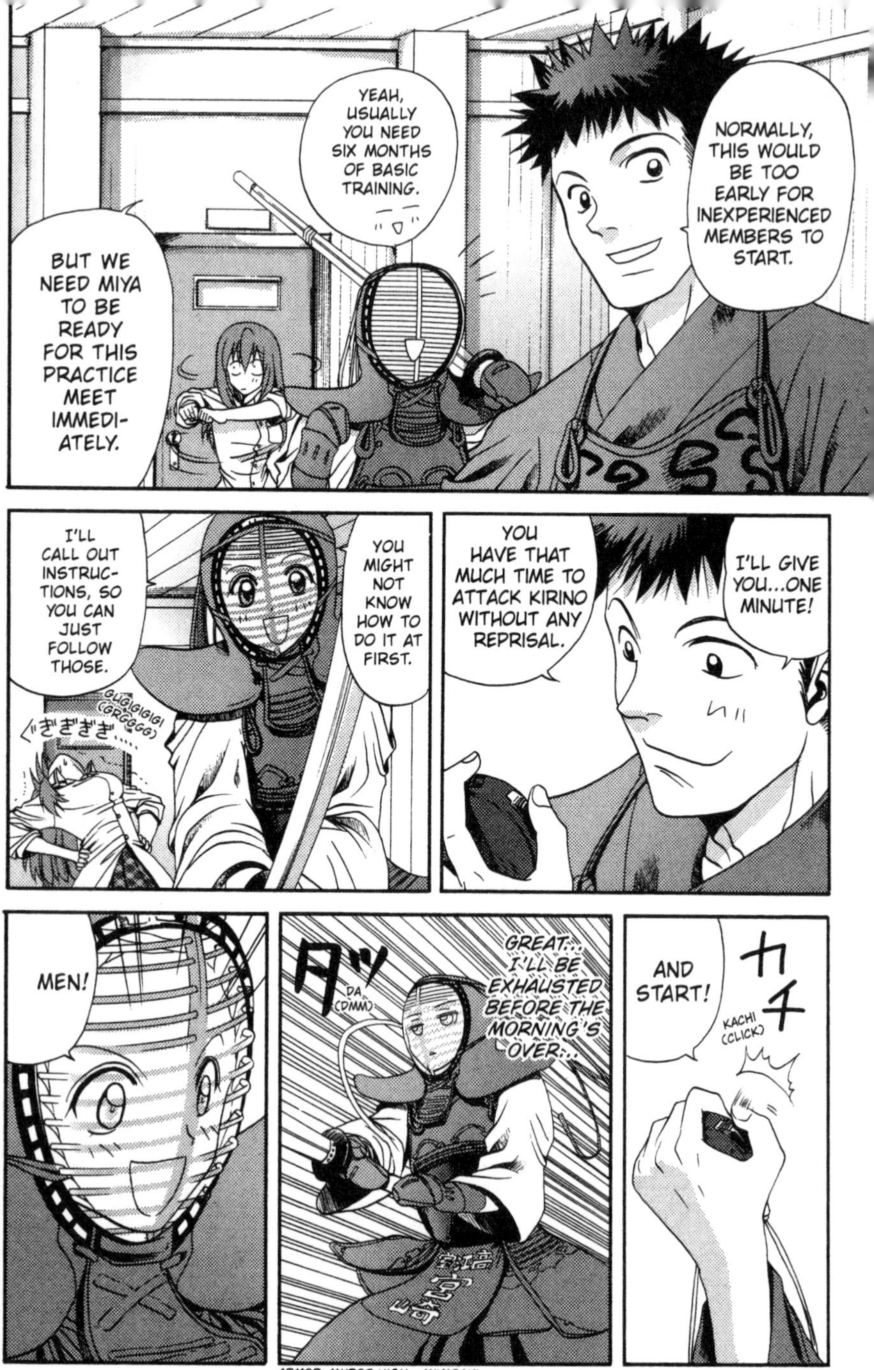
NORMALLY, THIS WOULD BE TOO EARLY FOR INEXPERIENCED MEMBERS TO START.
YEAH, USUALLY YOU NEED SIX MONTHS OF BASIC TRAINING.
BUT WE NEED MIYA TO BE READY FOR THIS PRACTICE MEET IMMEDI-ATELY.
I'LL GIVE YOU...ONE MINUTE!
YOU HAVE THAT MUCH TIME TO ATTACK KIRINO WITHOUT ANY REPRISAL.
YOU MIGHT NOT KNOW HOW TO DO IT AT FIRST.
I'LL CALL OUT INSTRUC-TIONS, SO YOU CAN JUST FOLLOW THOSE.
ぐぎぎぎぎ.....
GUGIGIGIGI (GRGGGG)
AND START!
カチ
KACHI (CLICK)
ダッ
DA (DMM)
GREAT... I'LL BE EXHAUSTED BEFORE THE MORNING'S OVER...
MEN!

ARMOR: MUROE HIGH - MIYAZAKI

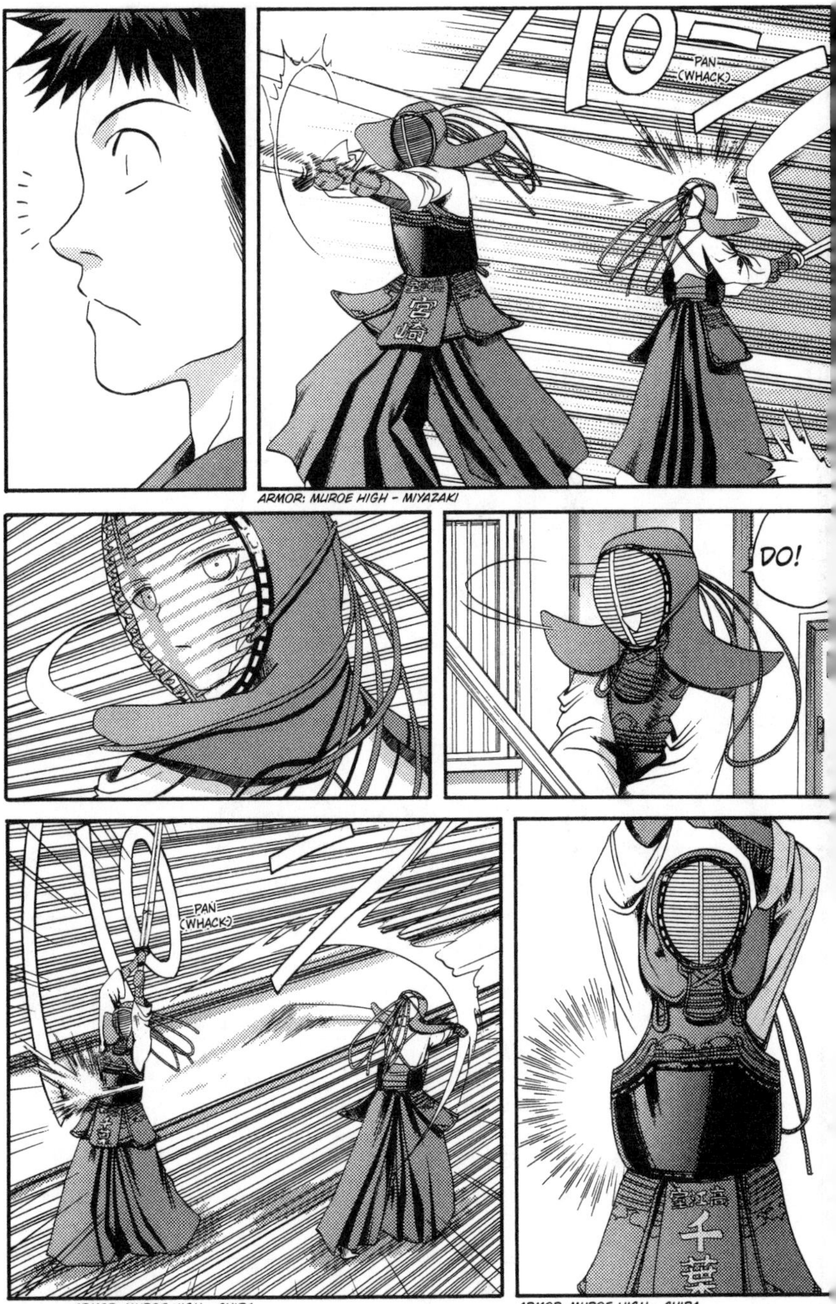
PAN
(WHACK)
DO!
PAN
(WHACK)
ARMOR: MUROE HIGH - MIYAZAKI

ARMOR: MUROE HIGH - CHIBA

ARMOR: MUROE HIGH - CHIBA

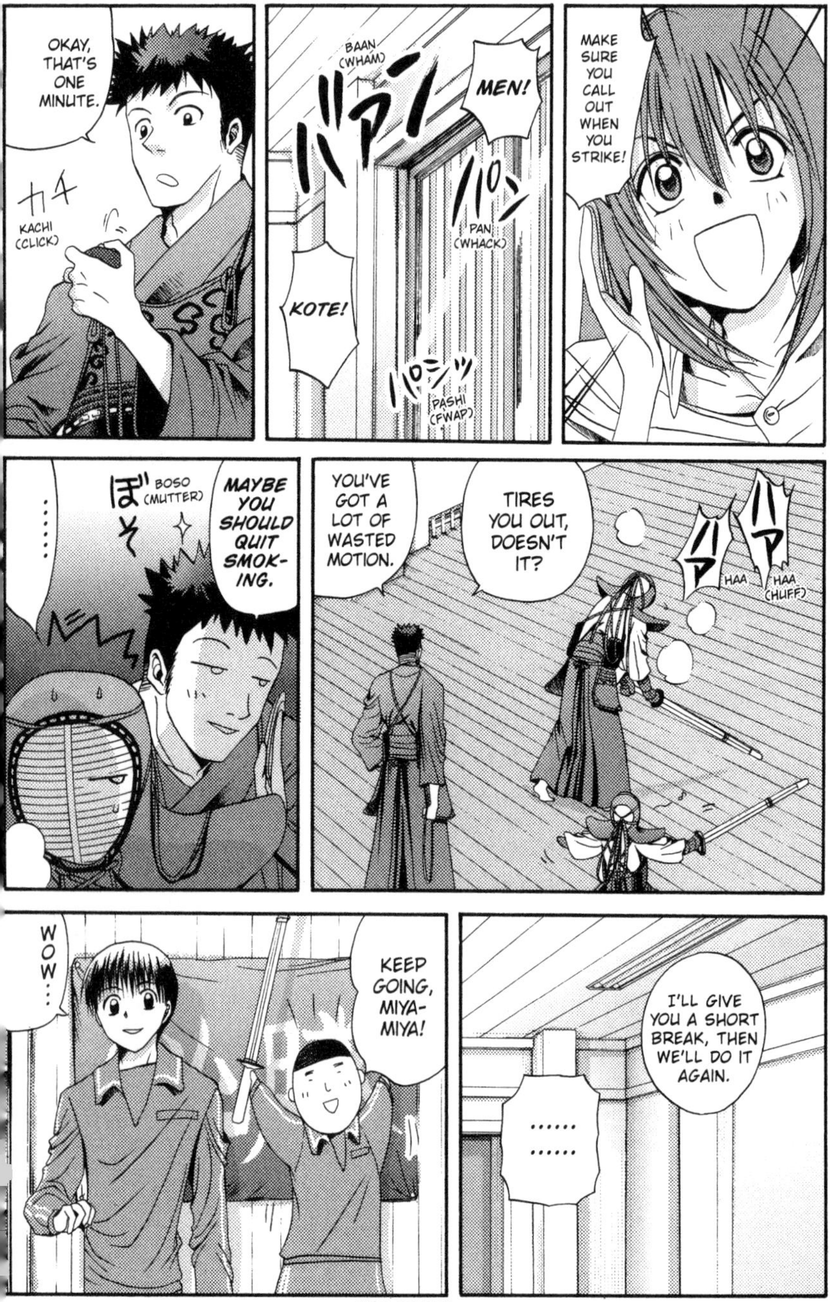
MAKE SURE YOU CALL OUT WHEN YOU STRIKE!
バアン
BAAN (WHAM)
MEN!
パン
PAN (WHACK)
KOTE!
パシッ
PASHI (FWAP)
OKAY, THAT'S ONE MINUTE.
カチ
KACHI (CLICK)
TIRES YOU OUT, DOESN'T IT?
YOU'VE GOT A LOT OF WASTED MOTION.
ハア ハア
HAA HAA (HUFF)
MAYBE YOU SHOULD QUIT SMOK-ING.
ぼそ
BOSO (MUTTER)
......
I'LL GIVE YOU A SHORT BREAK, THEN WE'LL DO IT AGAIN.
....
KEEP GOING, MIYA-MIYA!
WOW...

SIGN: VICTORY

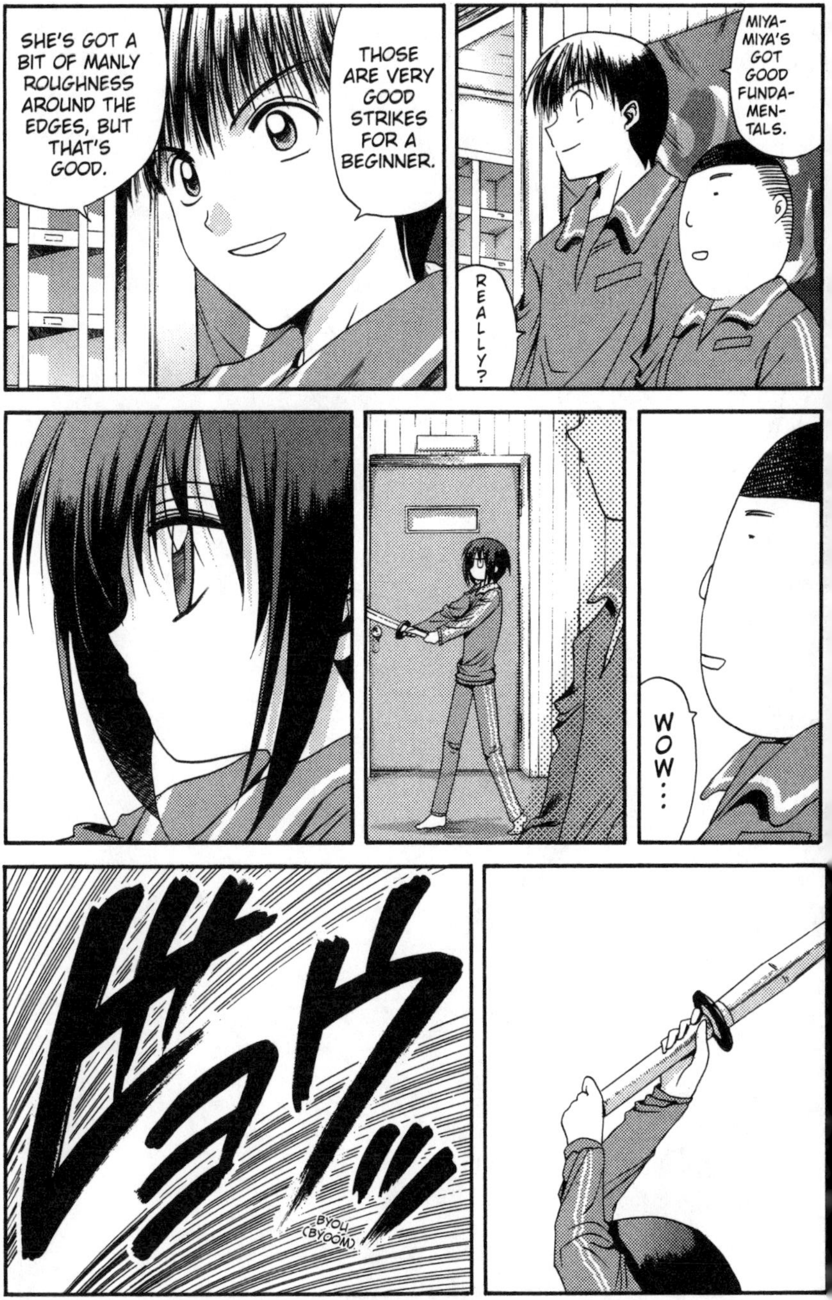
MIYA-MIYA'S GOT GOOD FUNDAMENTALS.
REALLY?
THOSE ARE VERY GOOD STRIKES FOR A BEGINNER.
SHE'S GOT A BIT OF MANLY ROUGHNESS AROUND THE EDGES, BUT THAT'S GOOD.
WOW...
BYOU (BYOOM)

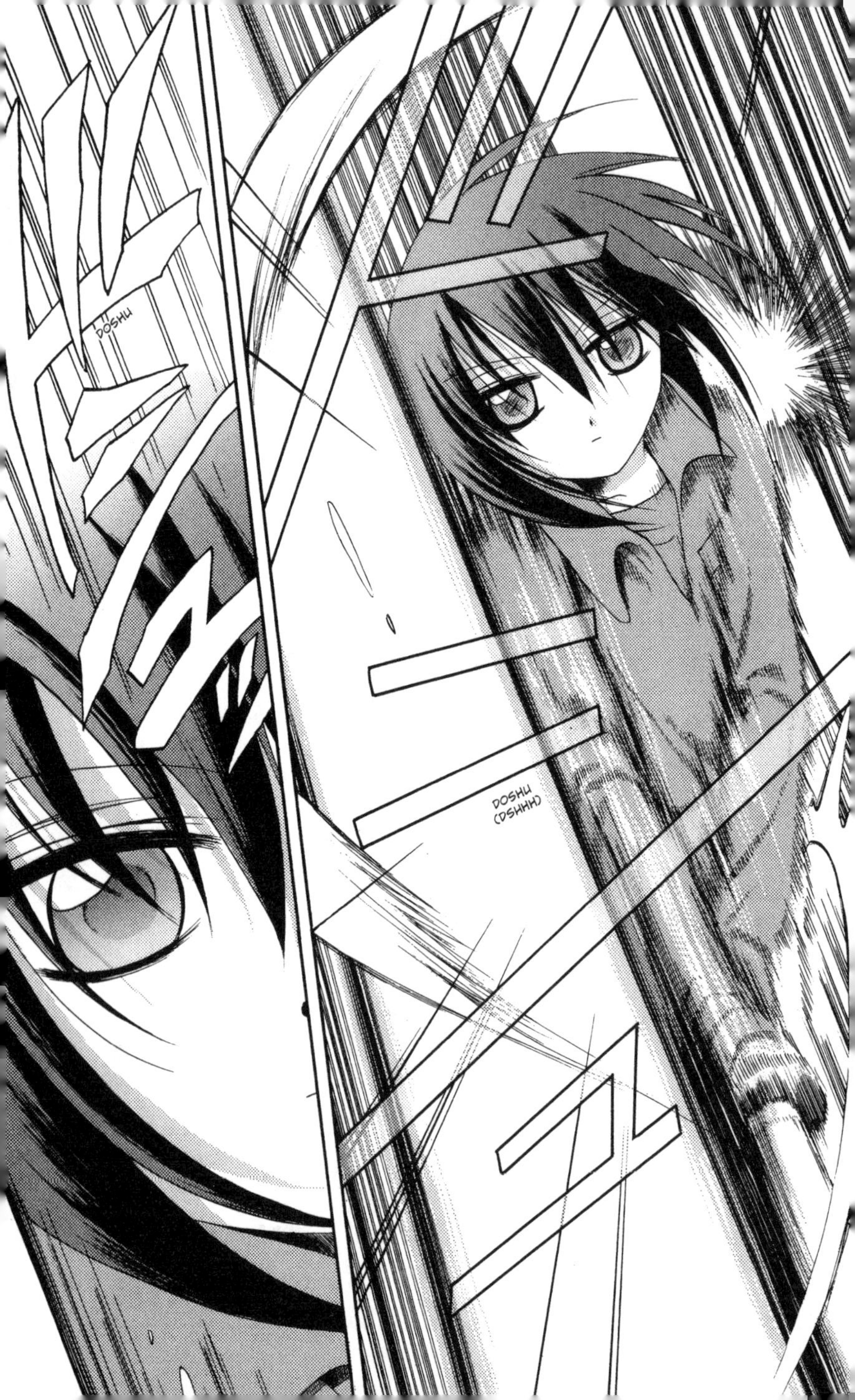
DOSHU
DOSHU
(DSHHH)

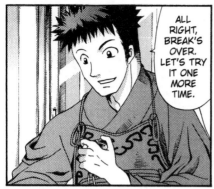

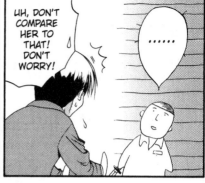

......
UH, DON'T COMPARE HER TO THAT! DON'T WORRY!
ALL RIGHT, BREAK'S OVER. LET'S TRY IT ONE MORE TIME.
ハア
HAA (HUFF)
ハア
HAA
WHAT A PAIN-IN-THE-ASS DAY...
PRACTICING AS SOON AS I GET TO SCHOOL.
BEING AROUND THAT PAIN-IN-THE-ASS GIRL.
あふぁ…
SFX: AFUA (YAWN)
BUT...

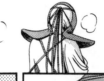

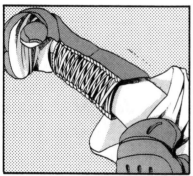

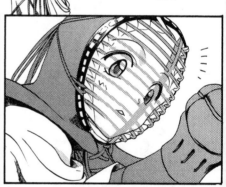

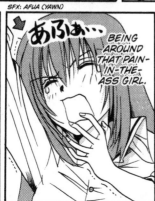

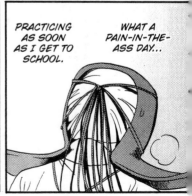

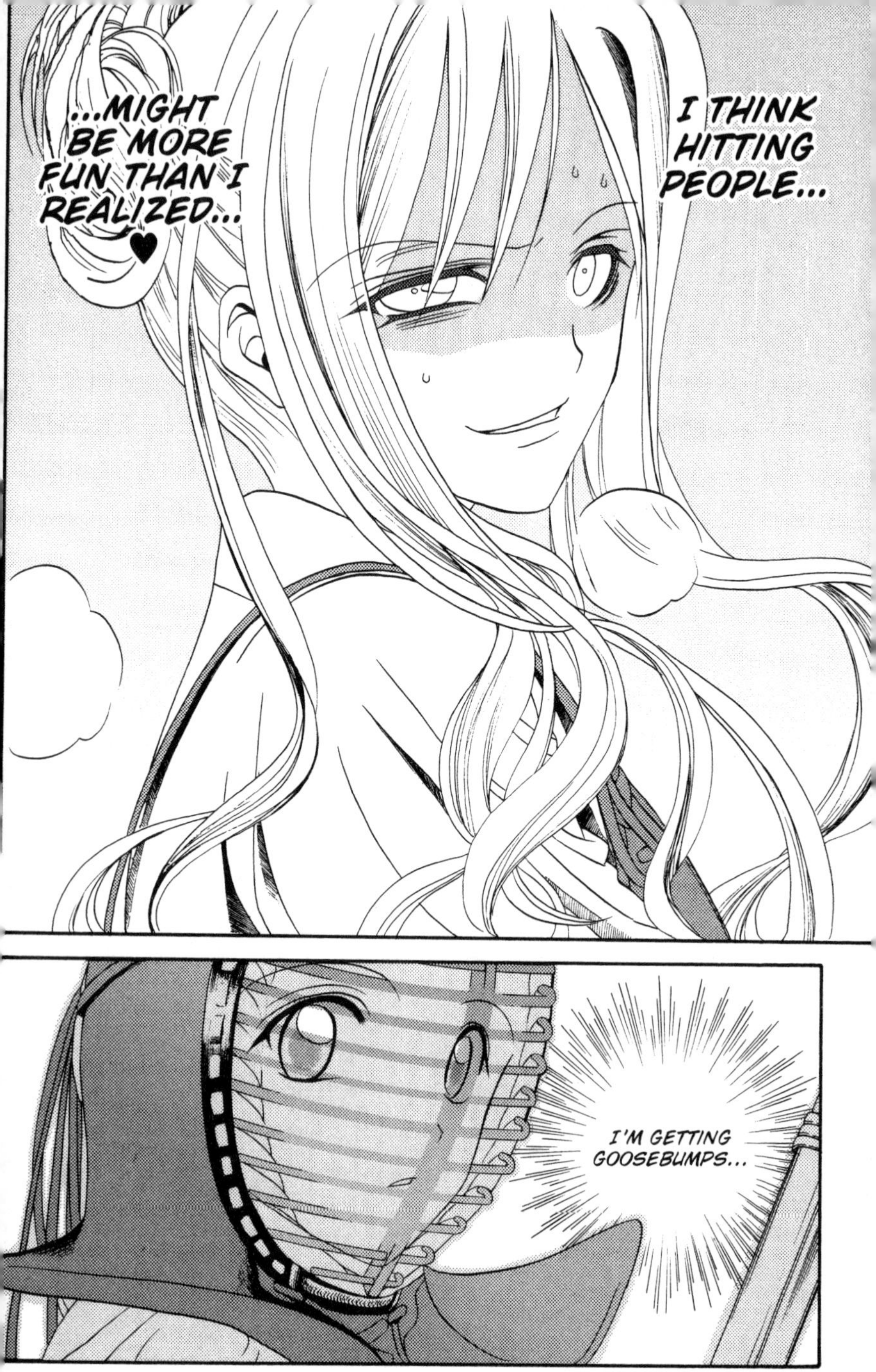
I THINK HITTING PEOPLE...
...MIGHT BE MORE FUN THAN I REALIZED... ♥
I'M GETTING GOOSEBUMPS...

BAMBOO BLADE

ISHIDA-SENSEI AND SELF-SUGGESTION

GOOOO (WHOOOSH)
I CAN DO IT! I CAN DO ANYTHING!! RAAAHHH!!
WHAT'S SAYA UP TO?
IT'S SELF-SUGGESTION! SHE'S TELLING HER BRAIN SHE CAN OVERCOME HER PROBLEMS.
OOOH.
ISN'T THAT CUTE? HO-HO-HO.
WHY DON'T YOU TRY IT, KOJIRO-SENSEI?
RIGHT!
RRAAAAAAAHHHH
I CAN DO IT! I CAN HANDLE THIS!
I KNOW I CAN DO IT!
OUT OF POVERTY.
SECOND DAY OF ATTEMPTED FASTING.
I CAN'T DO IT.
GUUUUUU (GRRRUMBLE)
LEND ME MONEY, NOBU-CHAN...
PHONE

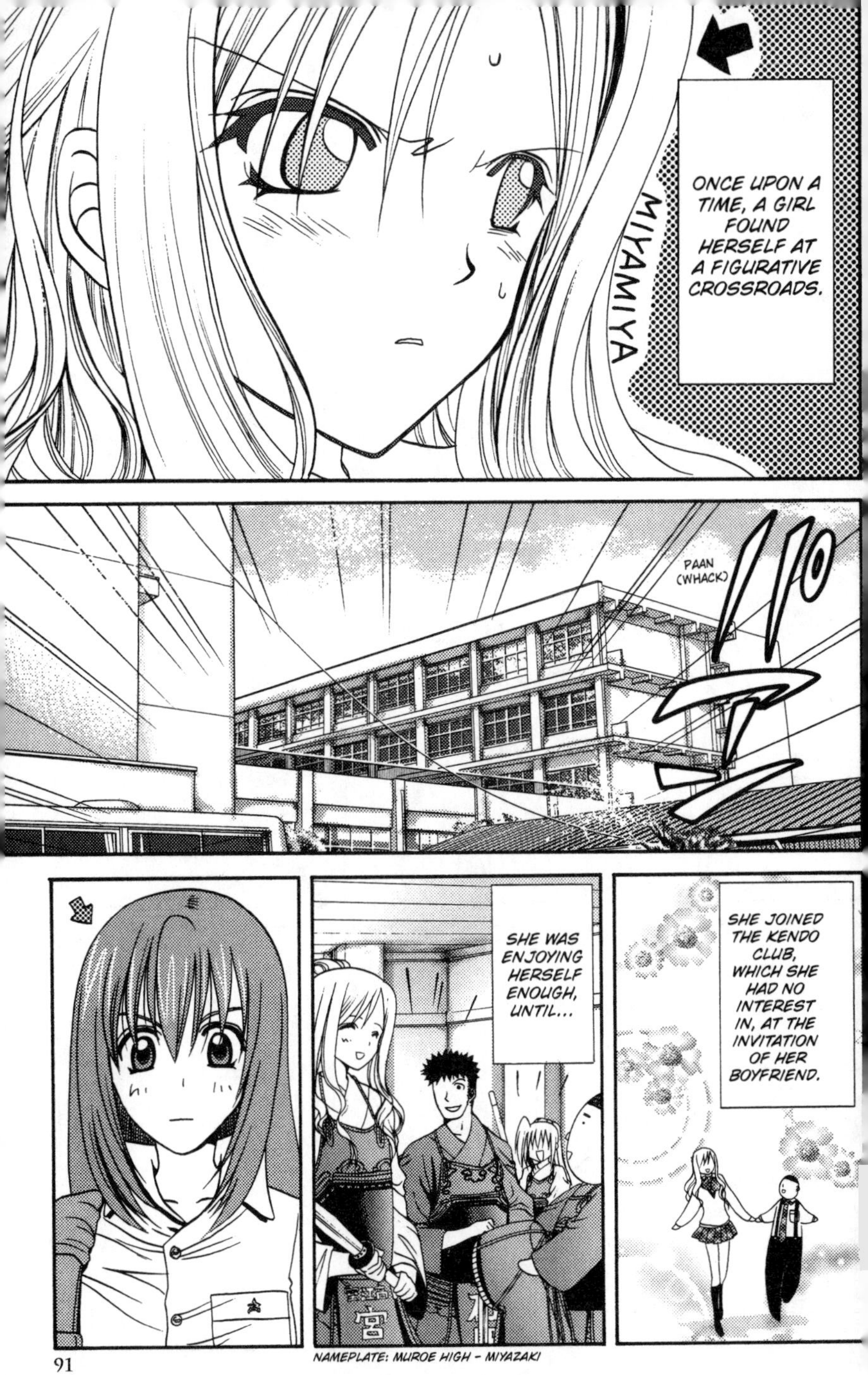
ONCE UPON A TIME, A GIRL FOUND HERSELF AT A FIGURATIVE CROSSROADS.
MIYAMIYA
PAAN (WHACK)
SHE JOINED THE KENDO CLUB, WHICH SHE HAD NO INTEREST IN, AT THE INVITATION OF HER BOYFRIEND.
SHE WAS ENJOYING HERSELF ENOUGH, UNTIL...

NAMEPLATE: MUROE HIGH - MIYAZAKI

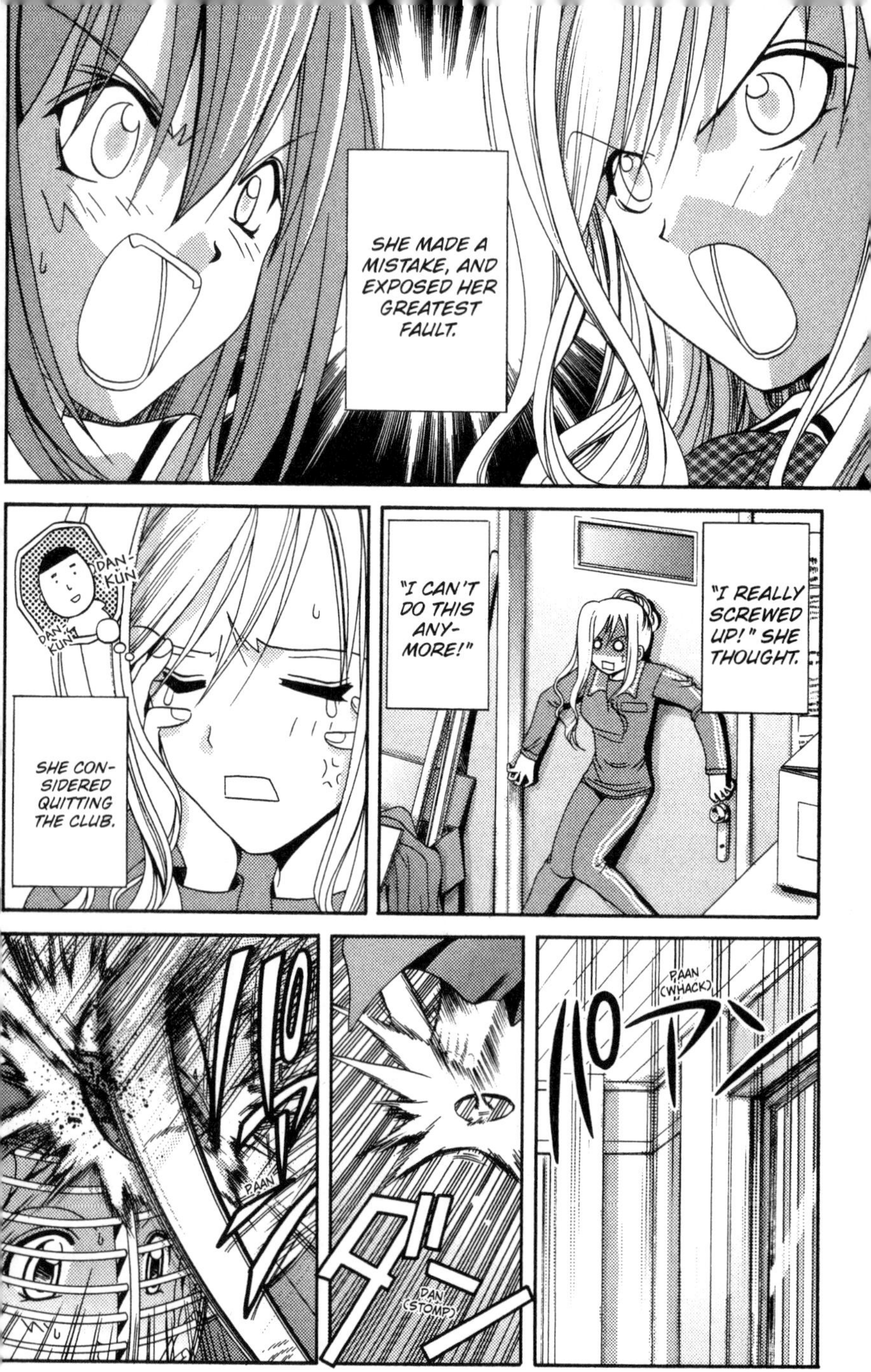
SHE MADE A MISTAKE, AND EXPOSED HER GREATEST FAULT.
"I REALLY SCREWED UP!" SHE THOUGHT.
"I CAN'T DO THIS ANYMORE!"
DAN-KUN
DAN-KUN
SHE CONSIDERED QUITTING THE CLUB.
PAAN (WHACK)
DAN (STOMP)
PAAN

BUT
...

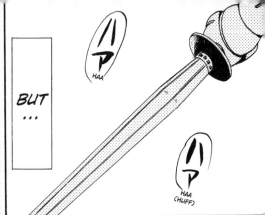

HAA

HAA
(CHUFF)

BAN!

KOTE
!!

BAN
(WHAM)

DO!!

...SHE HAD
AWAKENED TO THE
PLEASURES...

ZA
(ZSHH)

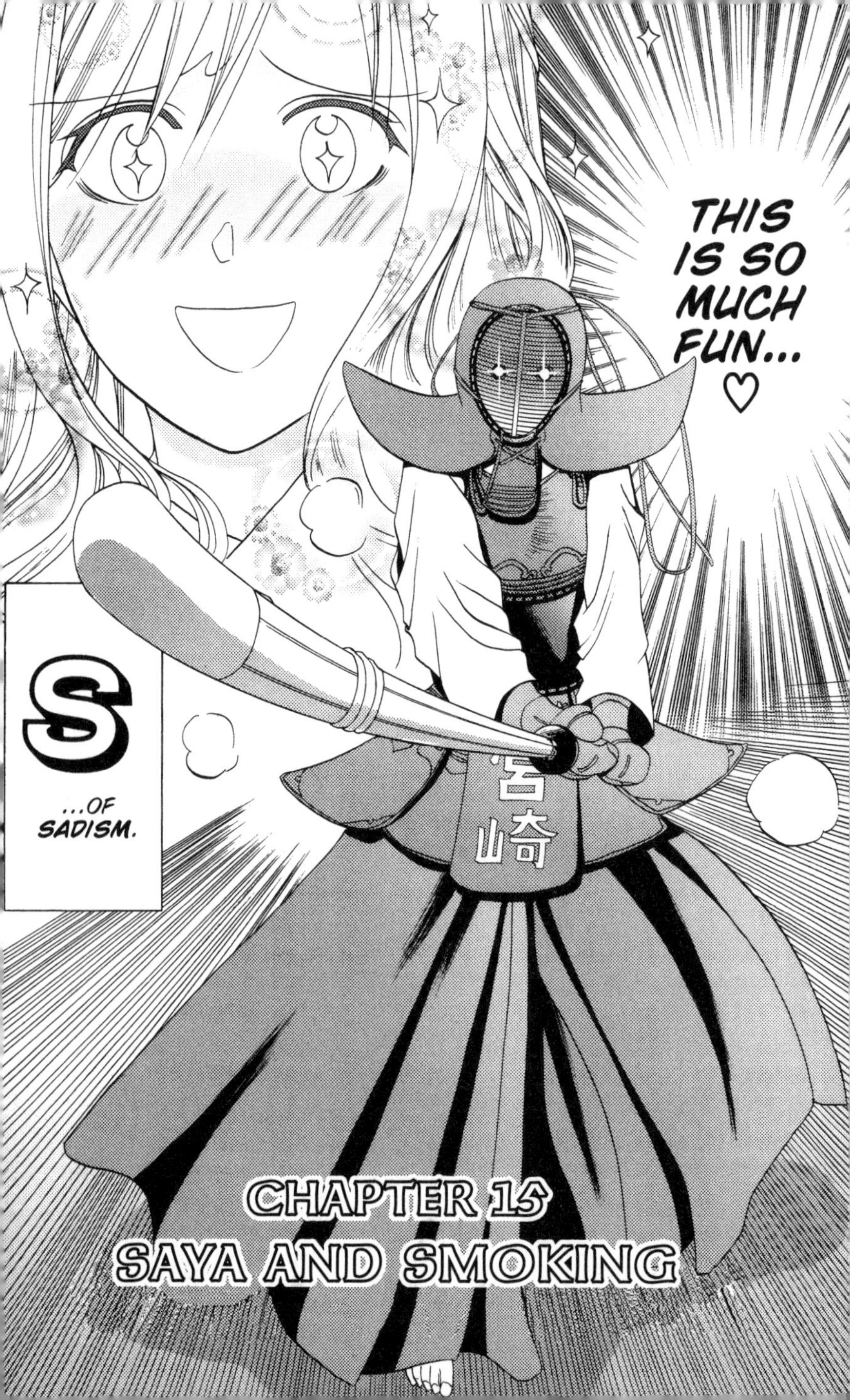
THIS IS SO MUCH FUN... ♡
S
...OF SADISM.
CHAPTER 15
SAYA AND SMOKING

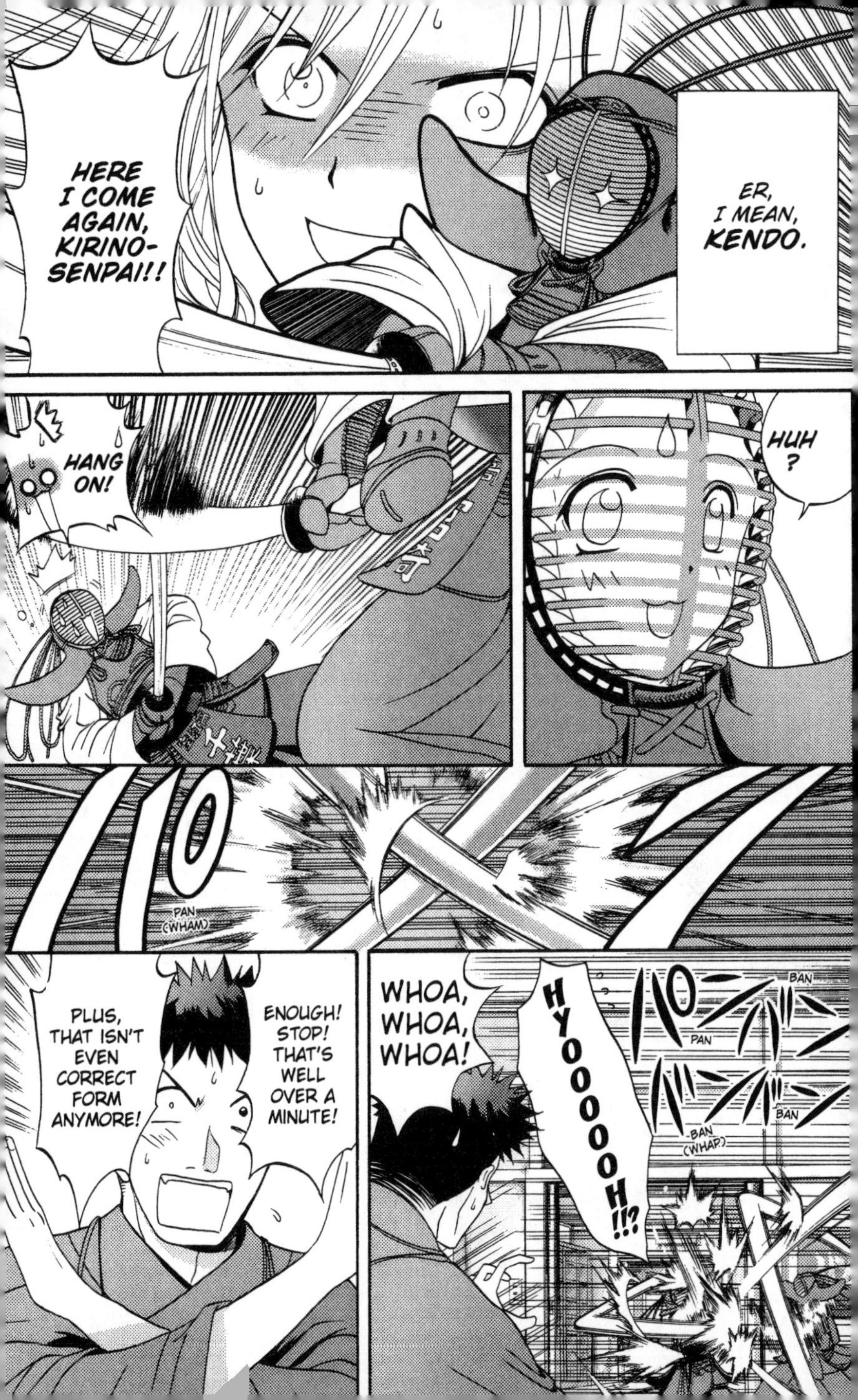
ER, I MEAN, KENDO.
HERE I COME AGAIN, KIRINO-SENPAI!!
HUH?
HANG ON!
PAN (WHAM)
BAN
PAN
BAN
BAN (WHAP)
HYOOOOOOH!!?
WHOA, WHOA, WHOA!
ENOUGH! STOP! THAT'S WELL OVER A MINUTE!
PLUS, THAT ISN'T EVEN CORRECT FORM ANYMORE!

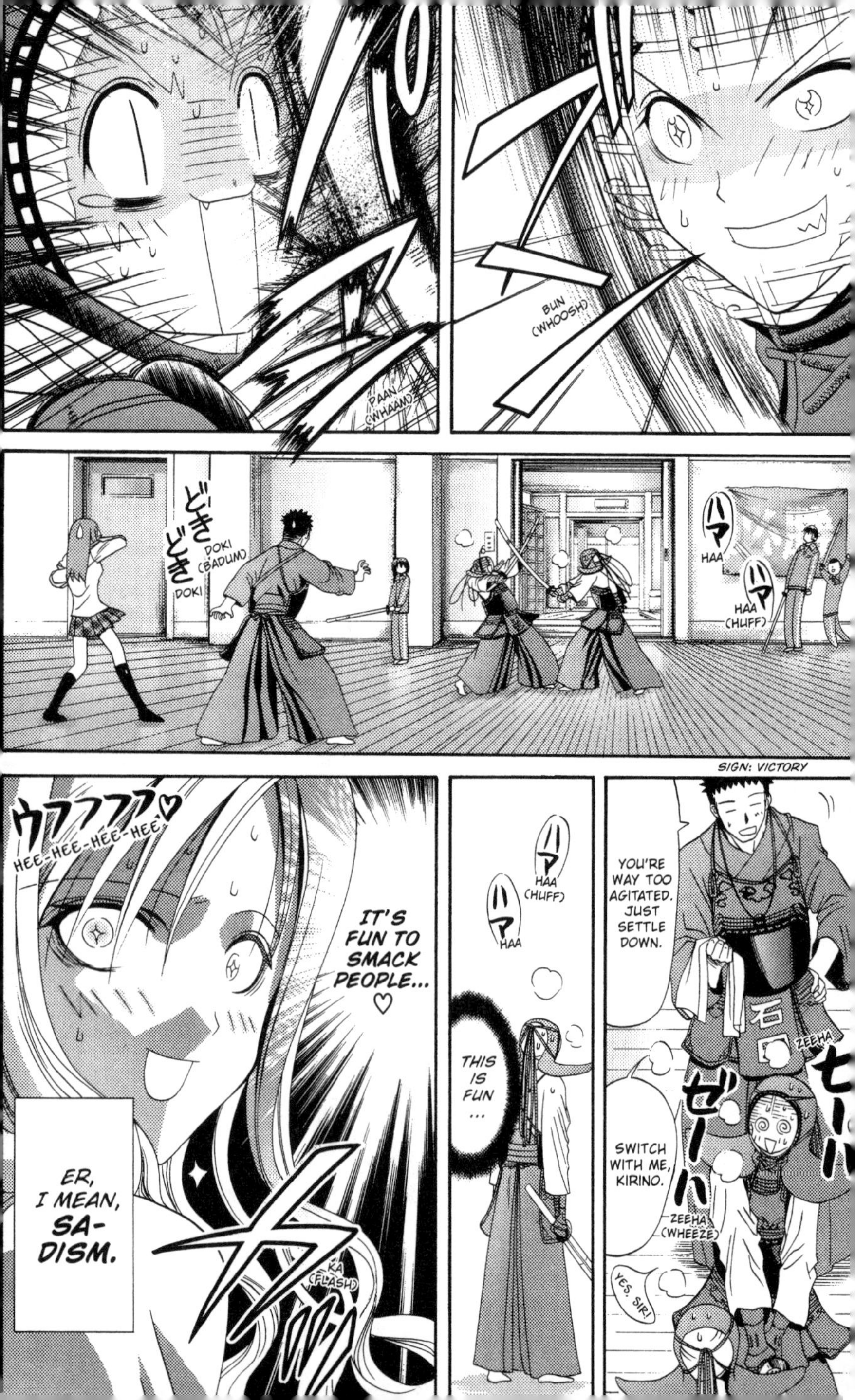
BUN (WHOOSH)
PAAN (WHAAM)
ハァ
HAA
ハァ
HAA (HUFF)
どきどき
DOKI (BADUM)
DOKI
SIGN: VICTORY
YOU'RE WAY TOO AGITATED. JUST SETTLE DOWN.
ZEEHA
SWITCH WITH ME, KIRINO.
ZEEHA (WHEEZE)
YES, SIR!
ハァ
HAA (HUFF)
ハァ
HAA
THIS IS FUN...
ウフフフフ♡
HEE-HEE-HEE-HEE
IT'S FUN TO SMACK PEOPLE...♡
ER, I MEAN, SA-DISM.
KA (FLASH)

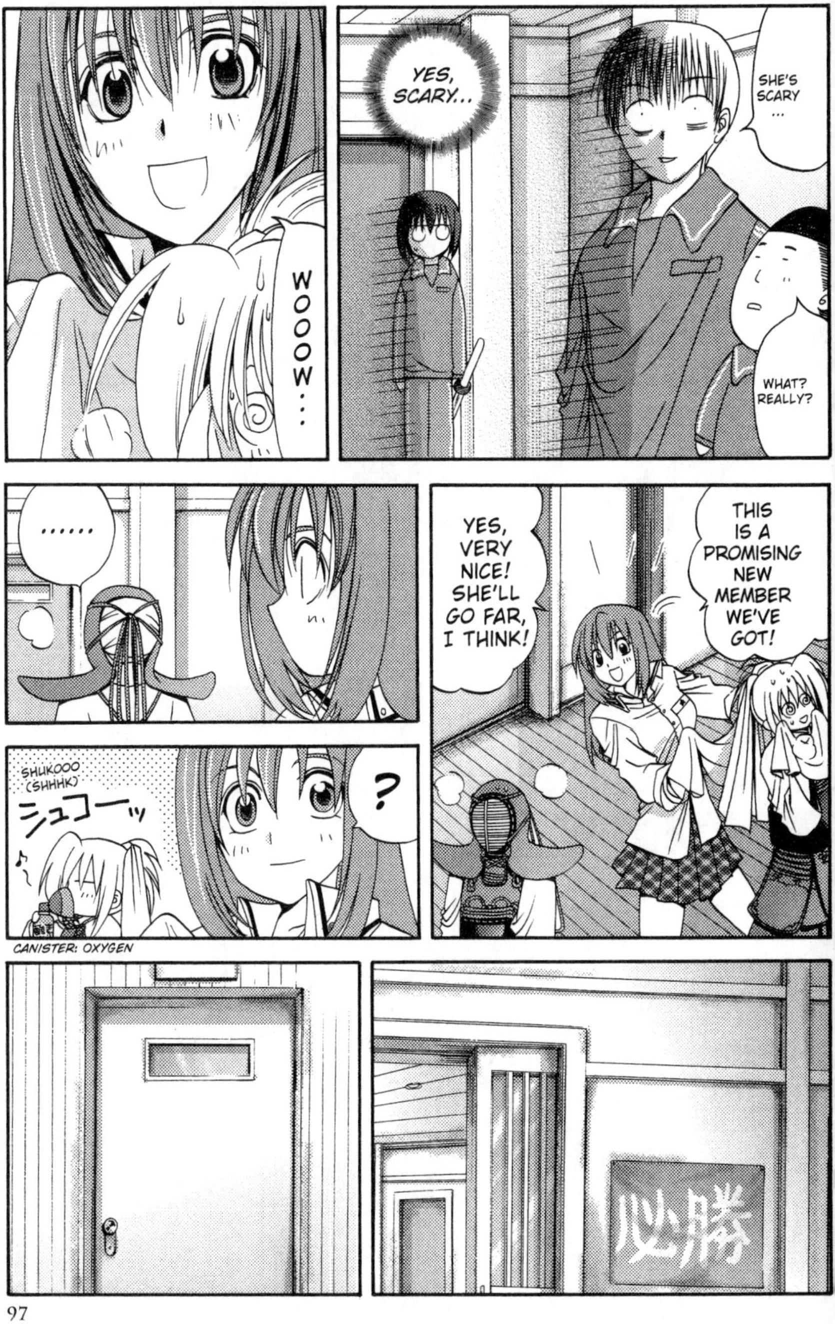
SHE'S SCARY ...
WHAT? REALLY?
YES, SCARY...
WOOOOW...
THIS IS A PROMISING NEW MEMBER WE'VE GOT!
YES, VERY NICE! SHE'LL GO FAR, I THINK!
......
?
SHUKOOO (SHHHK)
シュコーッ
CANISTER: OXYGEN
必勝

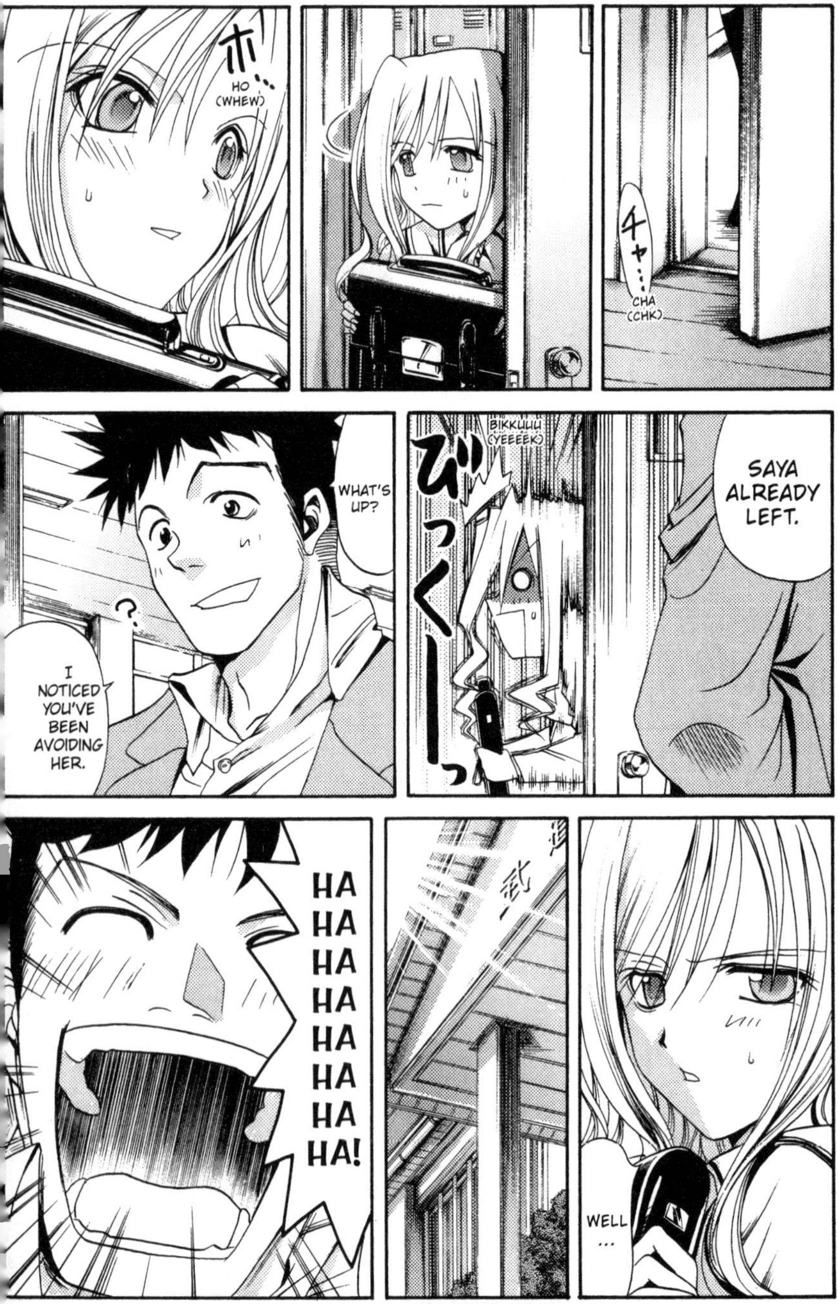
チャ…
CHA (CHK)
ホ…
HO (WHEW)
SAYA ALREADY LEFT.
びっくーっ
BIKKUUU (YEEEEK)
WHAT'S UP?
?
I NOTICED YOU'VE BEEN AVOIDING HER.
WELL ...
HA HA HA HA HA HA HA HA HA!

SIGN: MARTIAL ARTS HALL

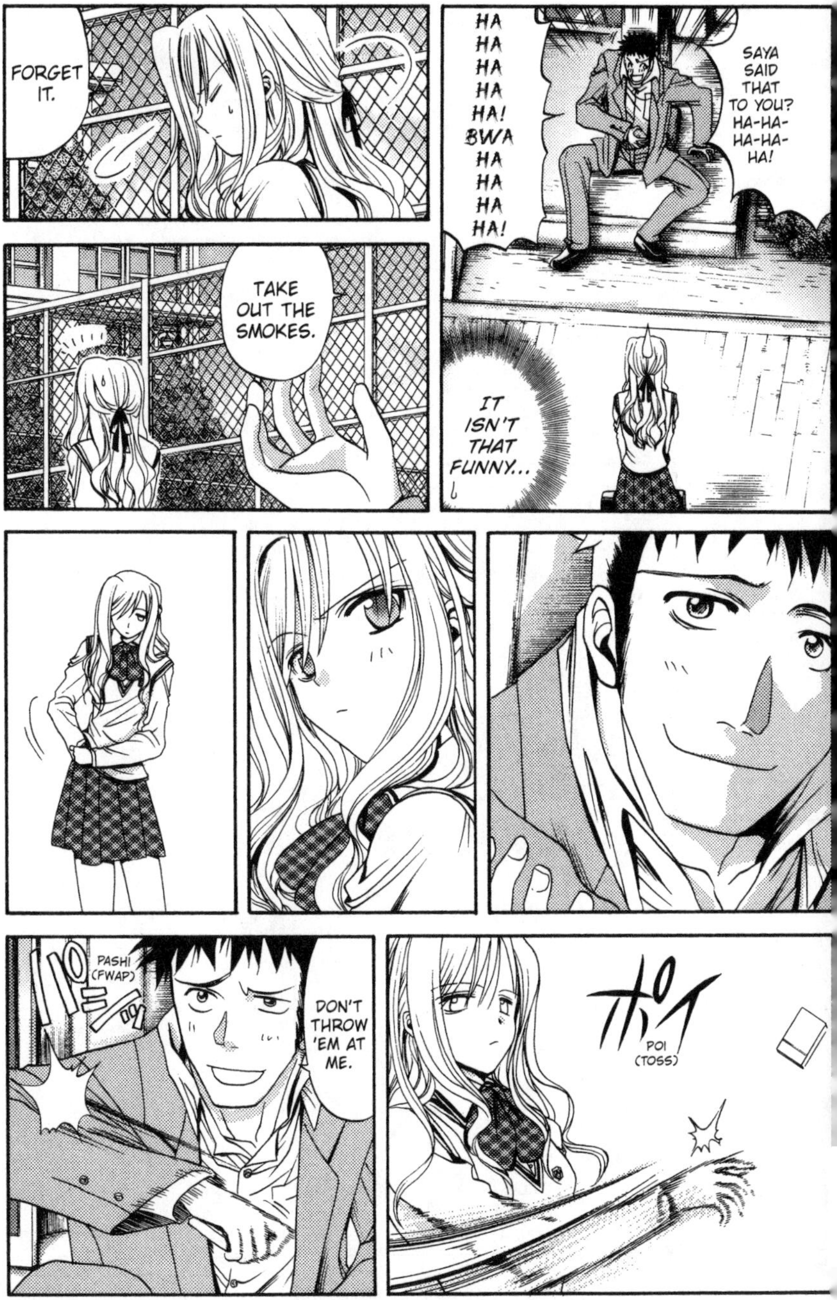
HA HA HA HA HA! BWA HA HA HA HA!
SAYA SAID THAT TO YOU? HA-HA-HA-HA-HA!
IT ISN'T THAT FUNNY...
FORGET IT.
TAKE OUT THE SMOKES.
POI (TOSS)
PASHI (FWAP)
DON'T THROW 'EM AT ME.

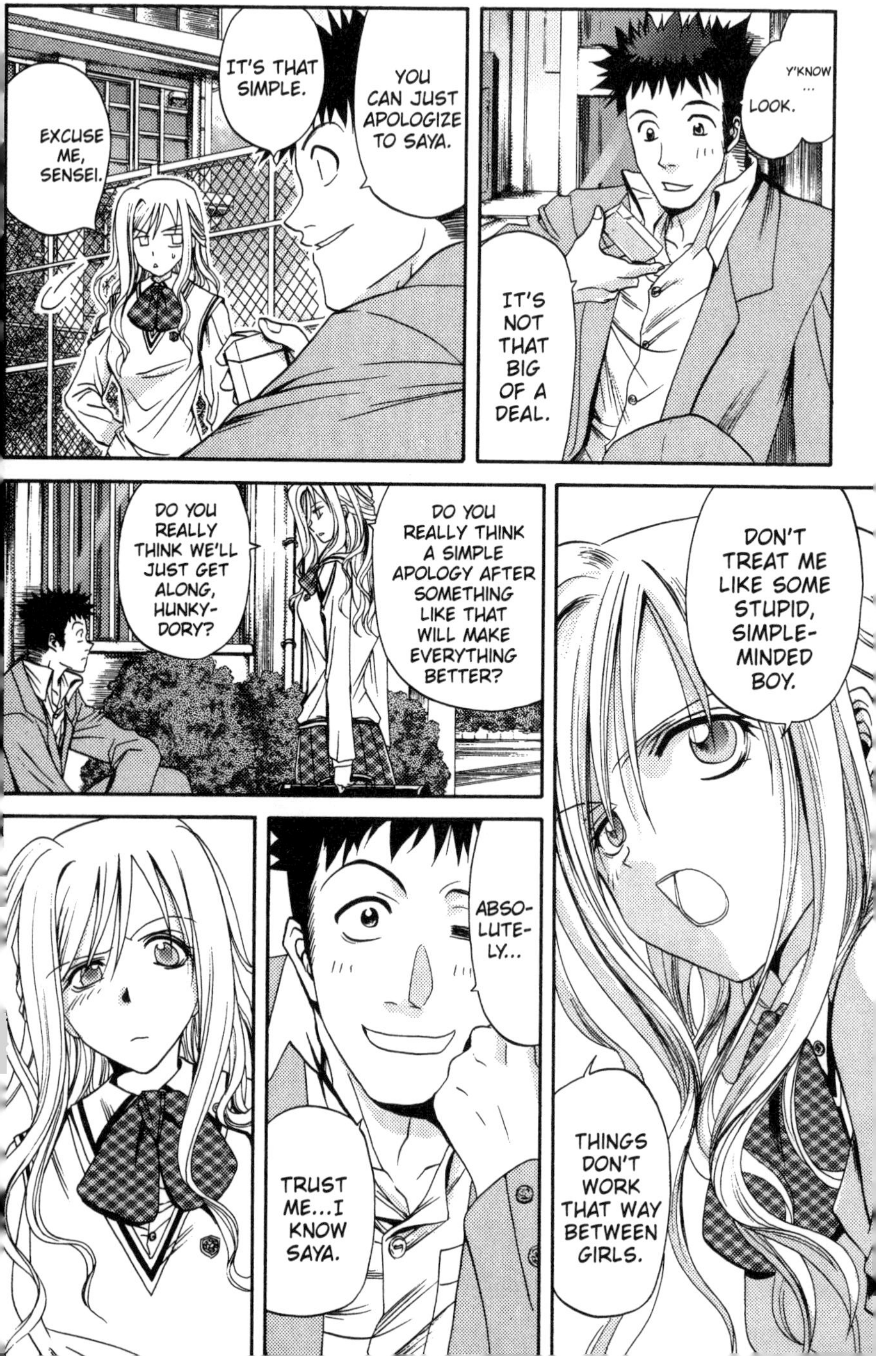
Y'KNOW... LOOK.
IT'S NOT THAT BIG OF A DEAL.
YOU CAN JUST APOLOGIZE TO SAYA.
IT'S THAT SIMPLE.
EXCUSE ME, SENSEI.
DON'T TREAT ME LIKE SOME STUPID, SIMPLE-MINDED BOY.
THINGS DON'T WORK THAT WAY BETWEEN GIRLS.
DO YOU REALLY THINK A SIMPLE APOLOGY AFTER SOMETHING LIKE THAT WILL MAKE EVERYTHING BETTER?
DO YOU REALLY THINK WE'LL JUST GET ALONG, HUNKY-DORY?
ABSO-LUTE-LY...
TRUST ME...I KNOW SAYA.

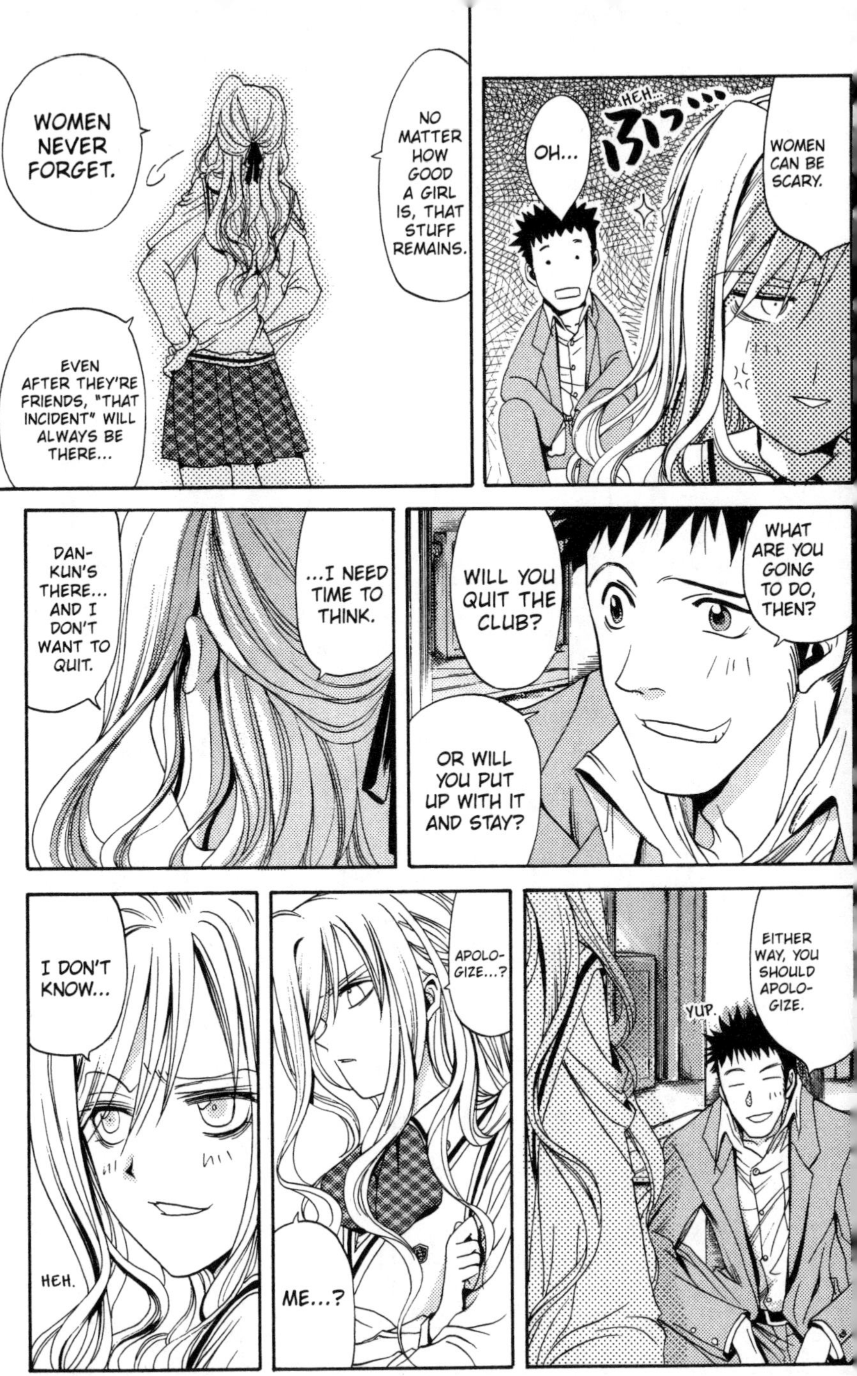
WOMEN CAN BE SCARY.
HEH...
ふっ…
OH...
NO MATTER HOW GOOD A GIRL IS, THAT STUFF REMAINS.
WOMEN NEVER FORGET.
EVEN AFTER THEY'RE FRIENDS, "THAT INCIDENT" WILL ALWAYS BE THERE...
WHAT ARE YOU GOING TO DO, THEN?
WILL YOU QUIT THE CLUB?
OR WILL YOU PUT UP WITH IT AND STAY?
...I NEED TIME TO THINK.
DAN-KUN'S THERE... AND I DON'T WANT TO QUIT.
EITHER WAY, YOU SHOULD APOLO-GIZE.
YUP.
APOLO-GIZE...?
ME...?
I DON'T KNOW...
HEH.

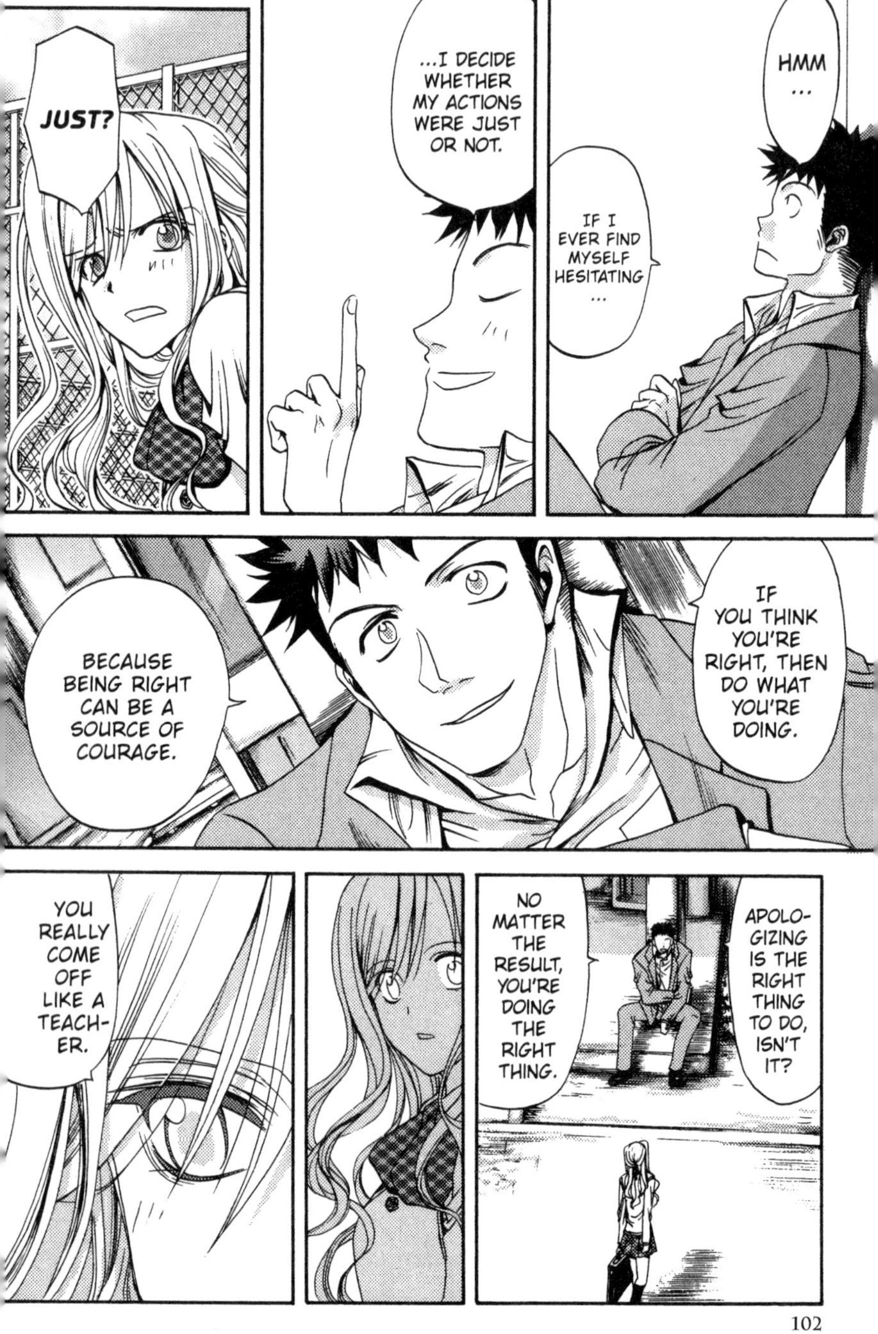
HMM...
IF I EVER FIND MYSELF HESITATING...
...I DECIDE WHETHER MY ACTIONS WERE JUST OR NOT.
JUST?
IF YOU THINK YOU'RE RIGHT, THEN DO WHAT YOU'RE DOING.
BECAUSE BEING RIGHT CAN BE A SOURCE OF COURAGE.
APOLOGIZING IS THE RIGHT THING TO DO, ISN'T IT?
NO MATTER THE RESULT, YOU'RE DOING THE RIGHT THING.
YOU REALLY COME OFF LIKE A TEACHER.

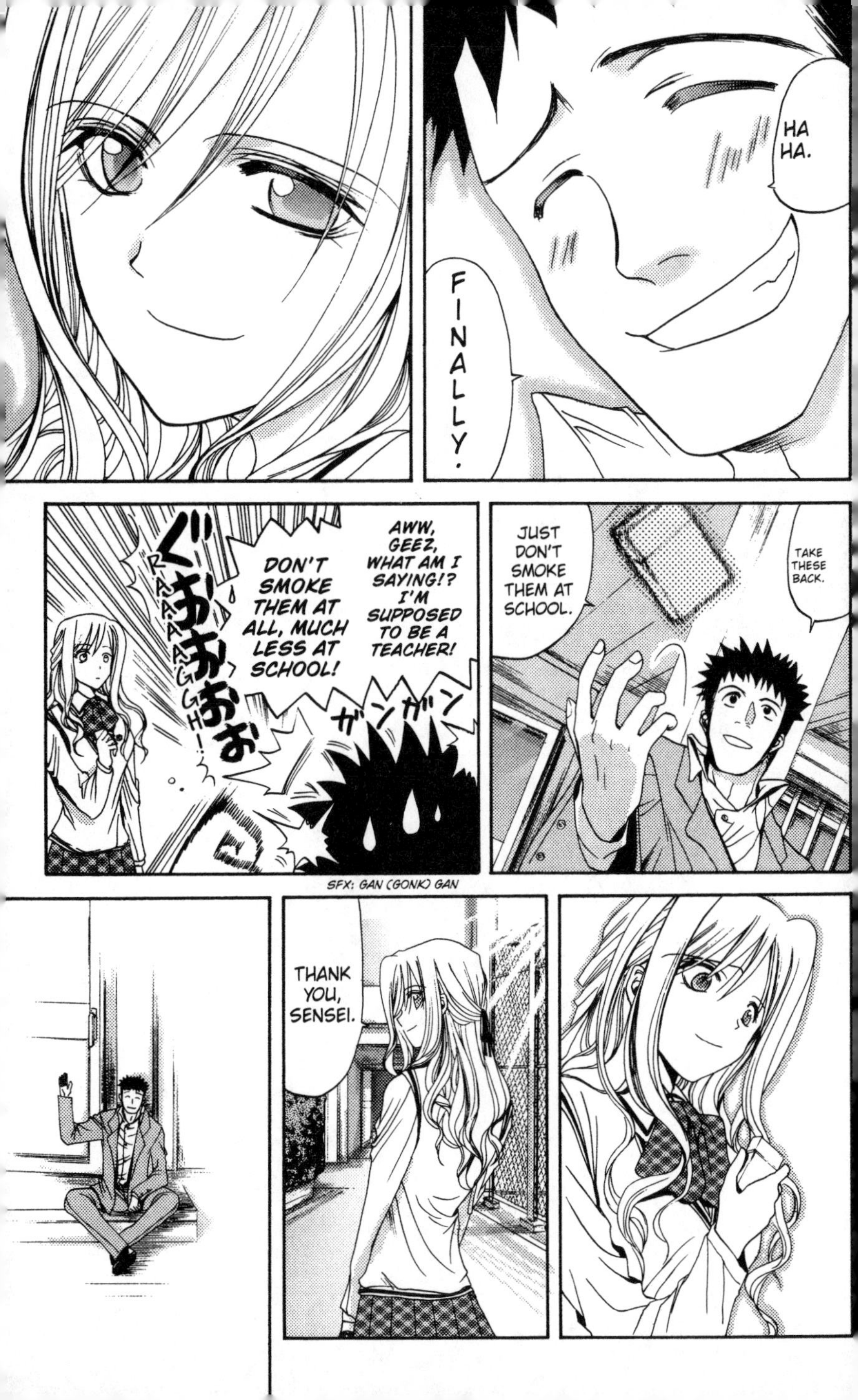
HA HA.
FINALLY.
TAKE THESE BACK.
JUST DON'T SMOKE THEM AT SCHOOL.
AWW, GEEZ, WHAT AM I SAYING!? I'M SUPPOSED TO BE A TEACHER!
DON'T SMOKE THEM AT ALL, MUCH LESS AT SCHOOL!
ぐおおおお
RAAAAGGH!!
ガンガン
SFX: GAN (GONK) GAN
THANK YOU, SENSEI.

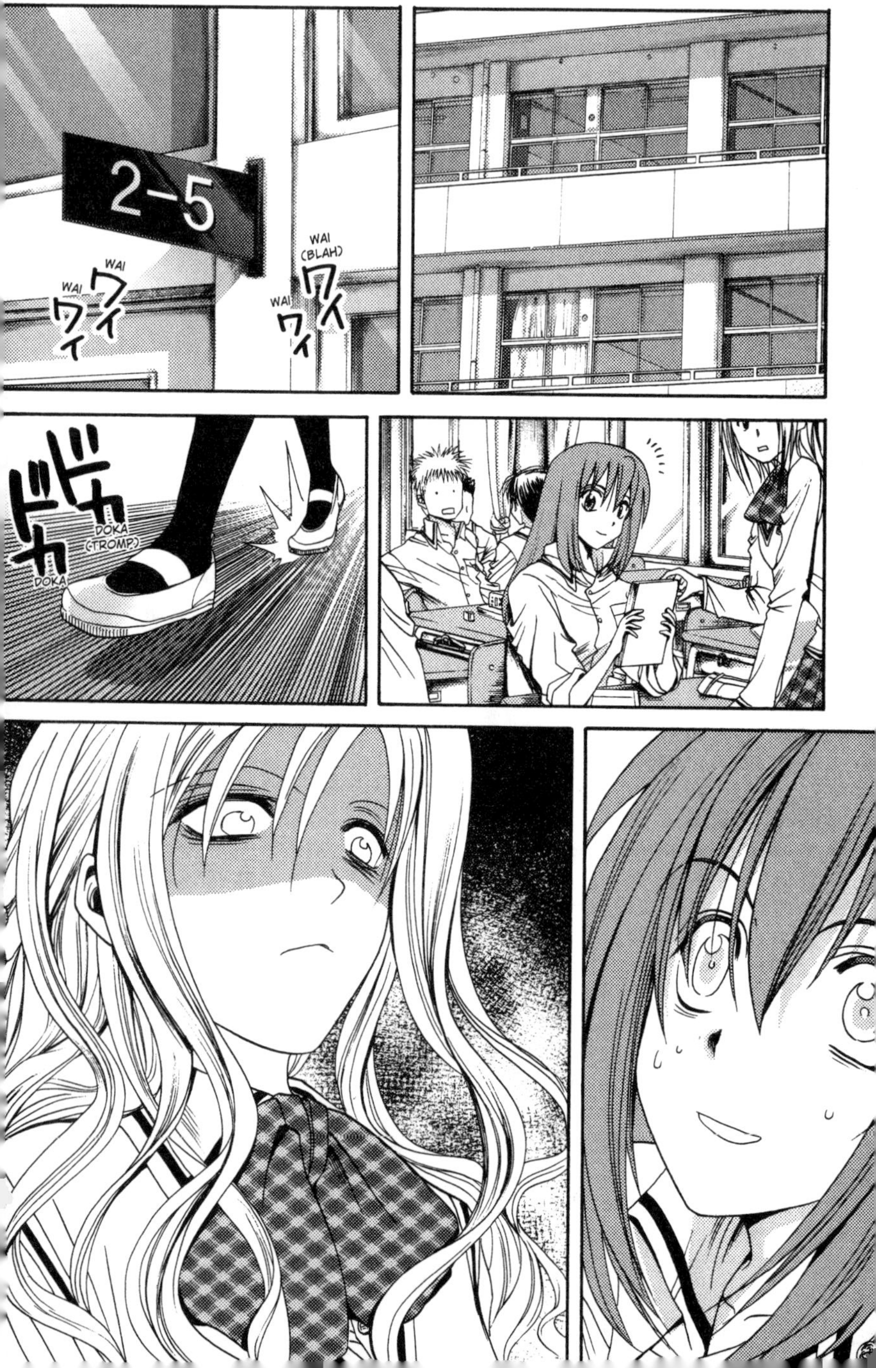
2-5
WAI (BLAH)
ワイ
WAI
ワイ
WAI
ワイ
WAI
ワイ
ドカ
DOKA (TROMP)
ドカ
DOKA

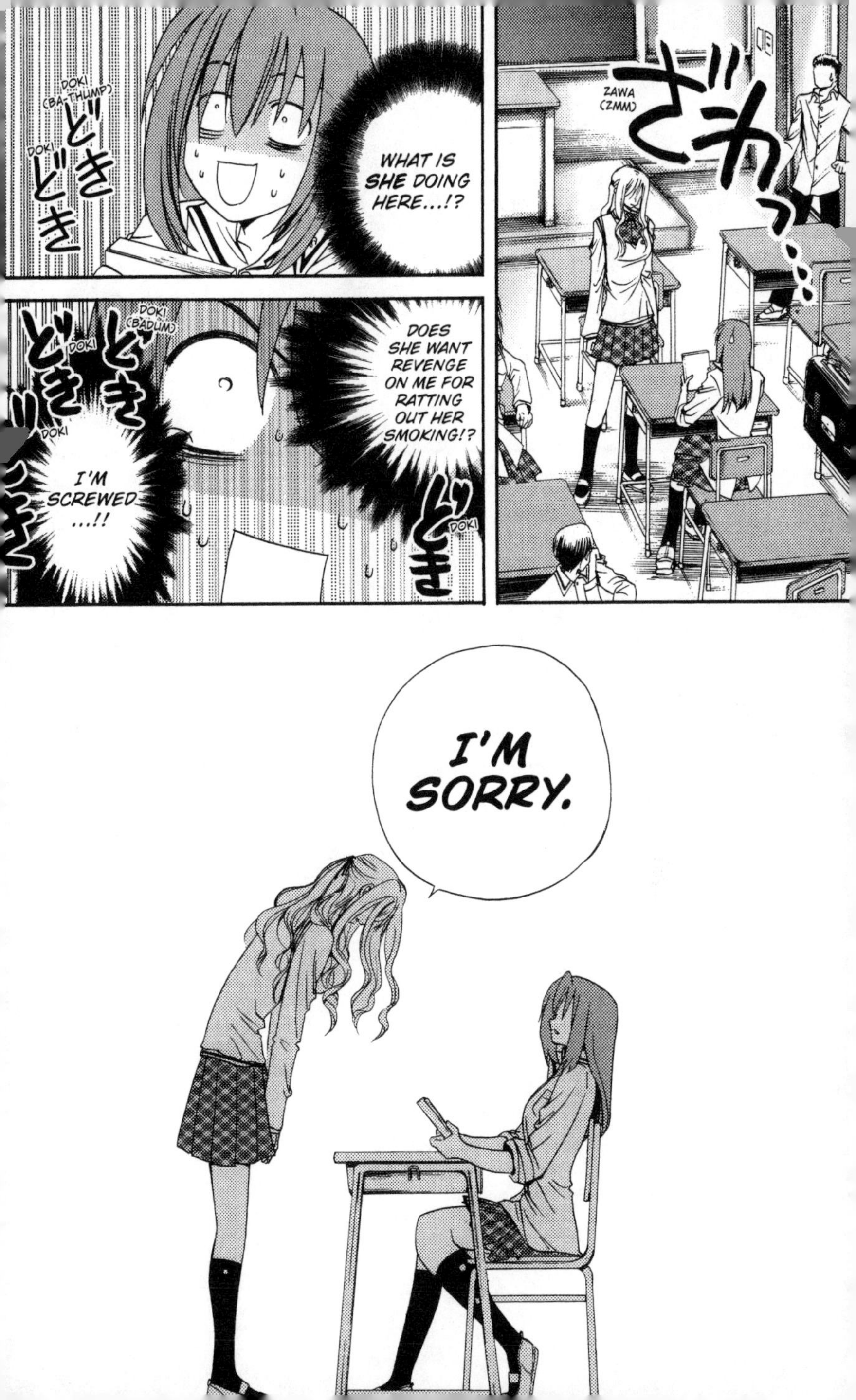
ざわっ…
ZAWA (ZMM)
どきどき
DOKI (BA-THUMP)
DOKI
WHAT IS SHE DOING HERE...!?
DOES SHE WANT REVENGE ON ME FOR RATTING OUT HER SMOKING!?
どき
DOKI! (BADUM)
どき
DOKI
どき
DOKI
I'M SCREWED...!!
どき
DOKI
I'M SORRY.

HANG ON TO THOSE.

I WON'T BE NEEDING THEM AT SCHOOL.

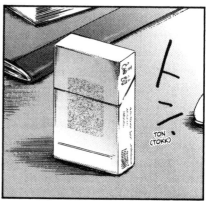

TON (TOKK)

?

?

?

...IT WOULD FINALLY...

AND SOON...

DAN-KUUUN! ♡

...BE TIME FOR THE MEET.

MIYA-MIYAAA!

BAMBOO BLADE

KAWAZOE-SAN AND SUMMER UNIFORMS

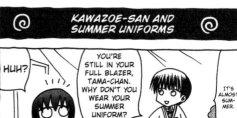

IT'S ALMOST SUMMER.
YOU'RE STILL IN YOUR FULL BLAZER, TAMA-CHAN. WHY DON'T YOU WEAR YOUR SUMMER UNIFORM?
HUH?
てくてく
TEKU TEKU (TMP)
SUMMER UNI
SUMMER UNI
SUMMER UNI
OH.
SUMMER HAIR
HOWA (FLUFF)
ほわ
HOWA
ほわ
......
CRAP! NOW SHE'S SHOCKED THAT EVEN THE CAT KNEW AND SHE DIDN'T!
DAMMIT, THAT STUPID CAT'S GONE ONE STEP TOO FAR TODAY!
HOWA HOWA
ほわほわ

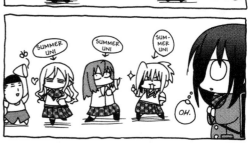

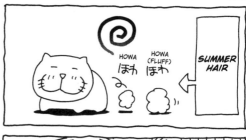

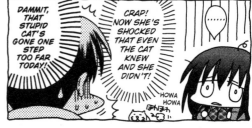

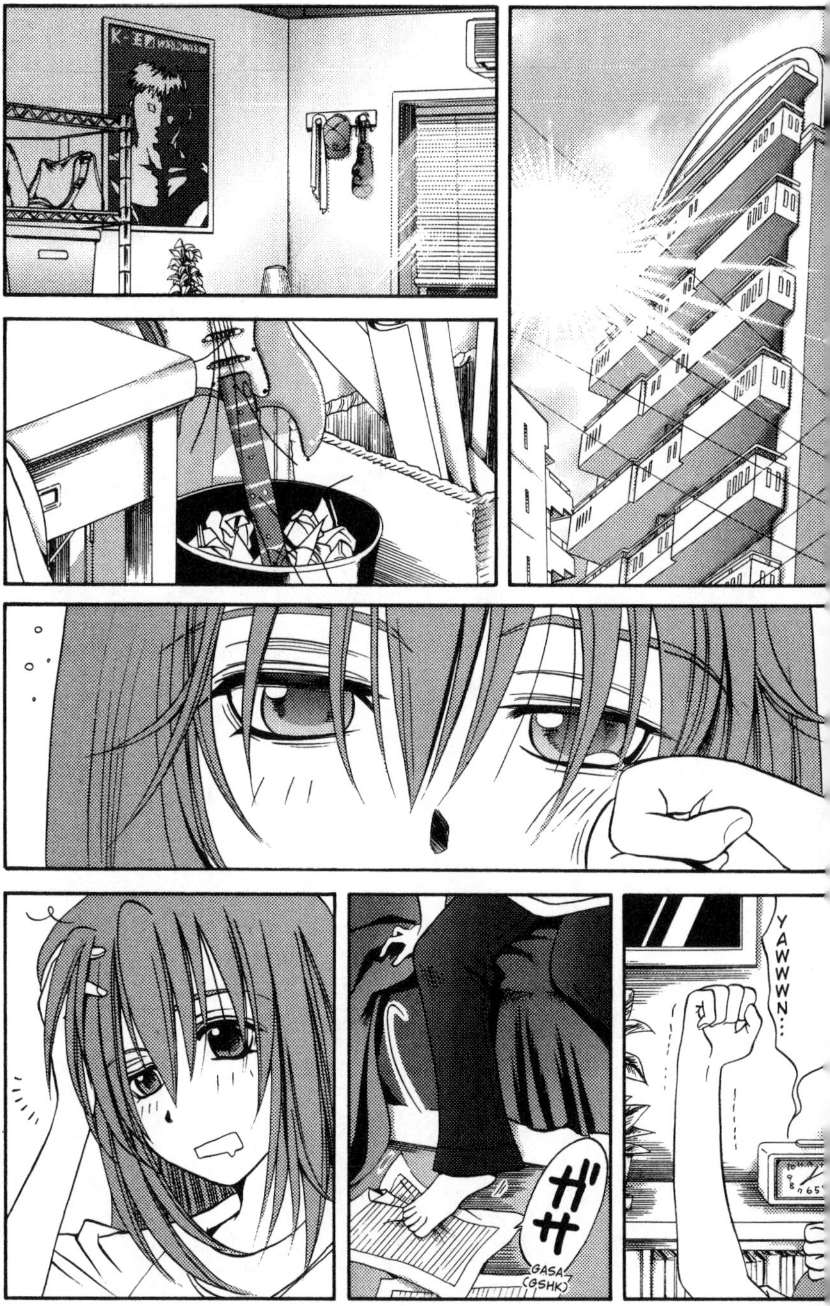
YAWWWN...
ガサ
GASA (GSHK)

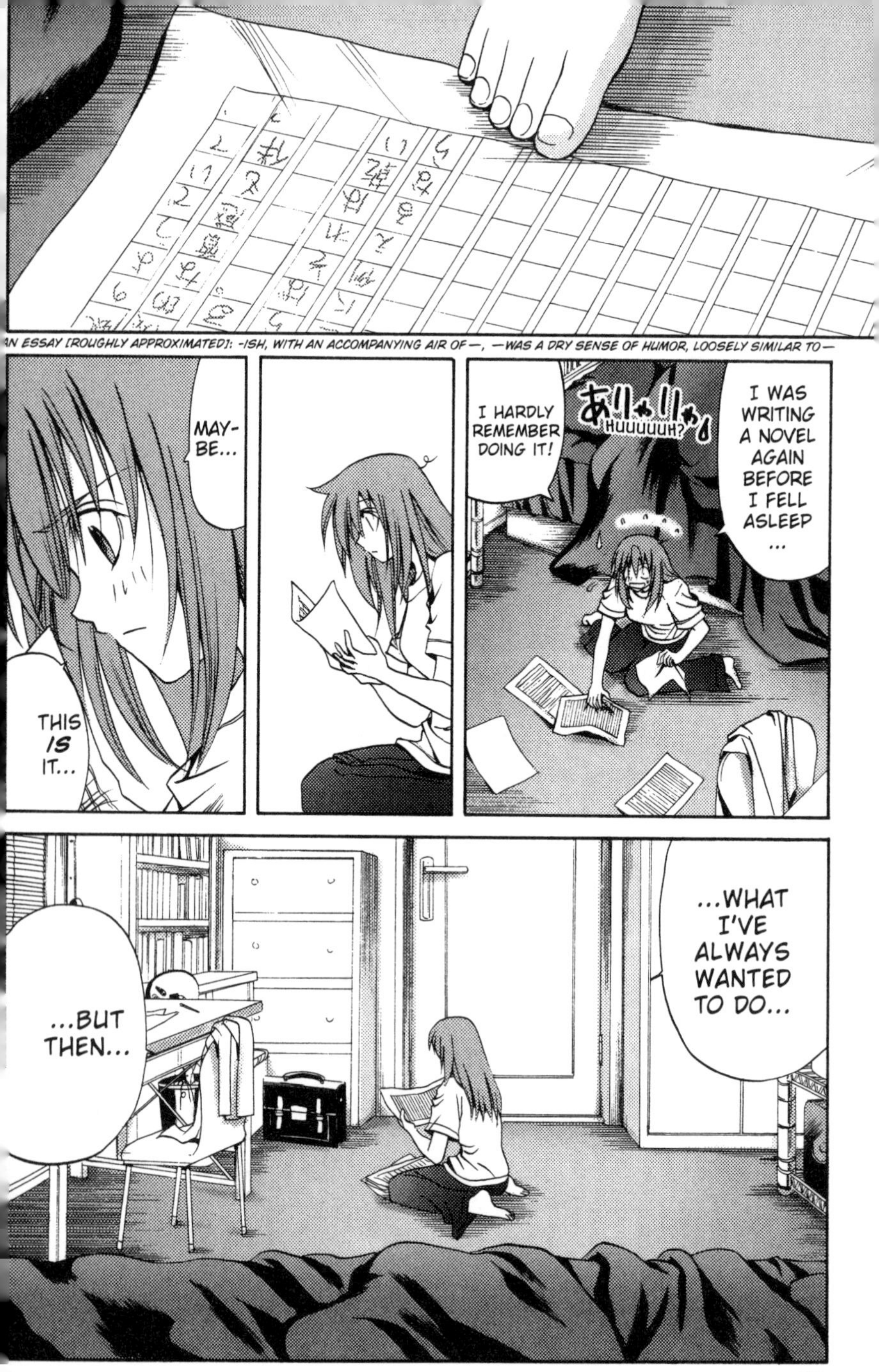
AN ESSAY [ROUGHLY APPROXIMATED]: -ISH, WITH AN ACCOMPANYING AIR OF—, —WAS A DRY SENSE OF HUMOR, LOOSELY SIMILAR TO—
I WAS WRITING A NOVEL AGAIN BEFORE I FELL ASLEEP ...
ありゃりゃ HUUUUUH?
I HARDLY REMEMBER DOING IT!
MAY-BE...
THIS *IS* IT...
...WHAT I'VE ALWAYS WANTED TO DO...
...BUT THEN...

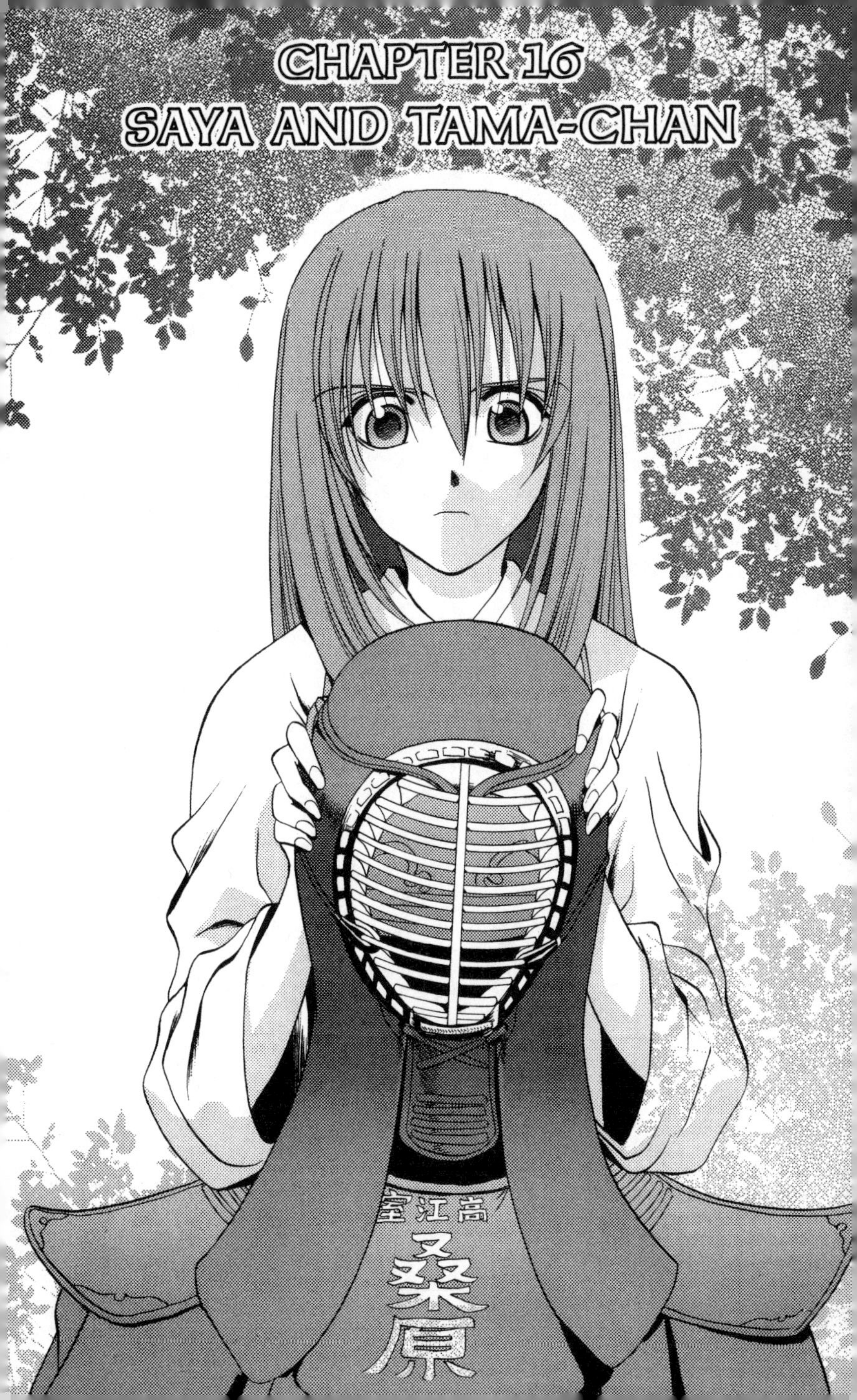
CHAPTER 16
SAYA AND TAMA-CHAN
室江高
桑原

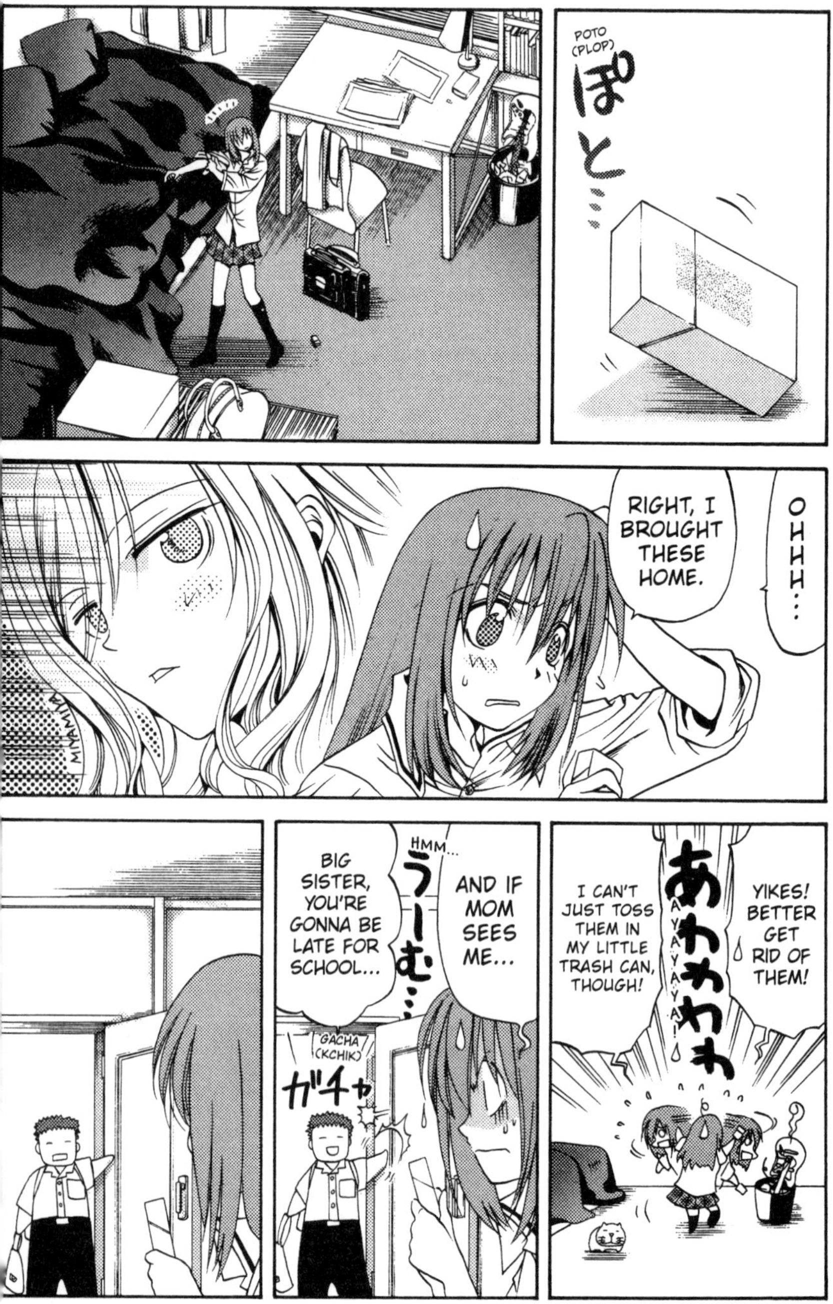
POTO (PLOP)
ぽと
OHHH...
RIGHT, I BROUGHT THESE HOME.
YIKES! BETTER GET RID OF THEM!
あわわわわ
AYAYAYAYA!
I CAN'T JUST TOSS THEM IN MY LITTLE TRASH CAN, THOUGH!
AND IF MOM SEES ME...
HMM...
うーむ
BIG SISTER, YOU'RE GONNA BE LATE FOR SCHOOL...
GACHA (KCHIK)
ガチャ

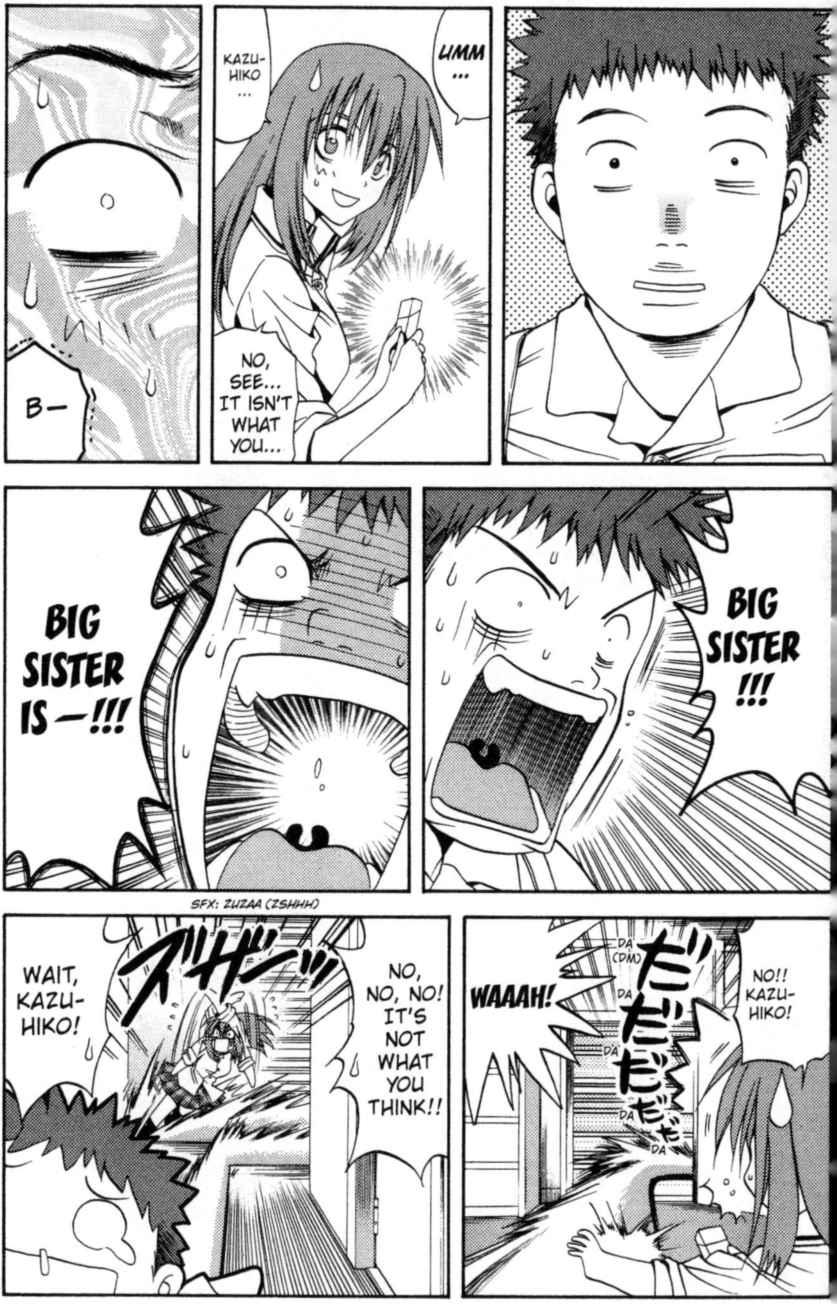
UMM...
KAZUHIKO...
NO, SEE... IT ISN'T WHAT YOU...
B—
BIG SISTER!!!
BIG SISTER IS—!!!
SFX: ZUZAA (ZSHHH)
NO!! KAZUHIKO!
DA (DM) DA DA DA DA
WAAAH!
NO, NO, NO! IT'S NOT WHAT YOU THINK!!
WAIT, KAZUHIKO!

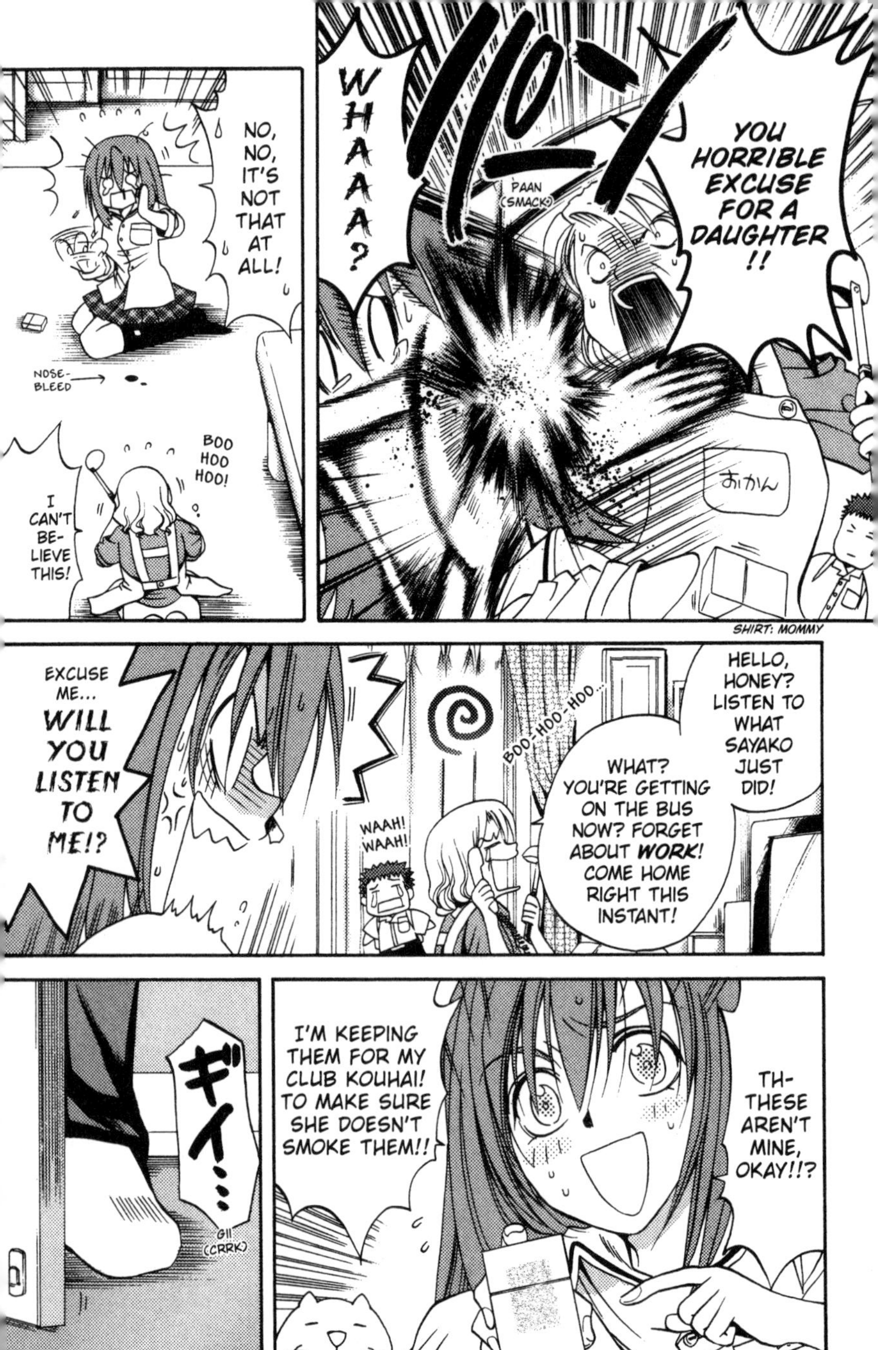
YOU HORRIBLE EXCUSE FOR A DAUGHTER!!
PAAN (SMACK)
WHAAAA?
おかん
SHIRT: MOMMY
NO, NO, IT'S NOT THAT AT ALL!
NOSE-BLEED
BOO HOO HOO!
I CAN'T BE-LIEVE THIS!
HELLO, HONEY? LISTEN TO WHAT SAYAKO JUST DID!
WHAT? YOU'RE GETTING ON THE BUS NOW? FORGET ABOUT WORK! COME HOME RIGHT THIS INSTANT!
BOO-HOO-HOO...
WAAH! WAAH!
EXCUSE ME... WILL YOU LISTEN TO ME!?
TH-THESE AREN'T MINE, OKAY!!?
I'M KEEPING THEM FOR MY CLUB KOUHAI! TO MAKE SURE SHE DOESN'T SMOKE THEM!!
ギイ…
GII (CRRK)

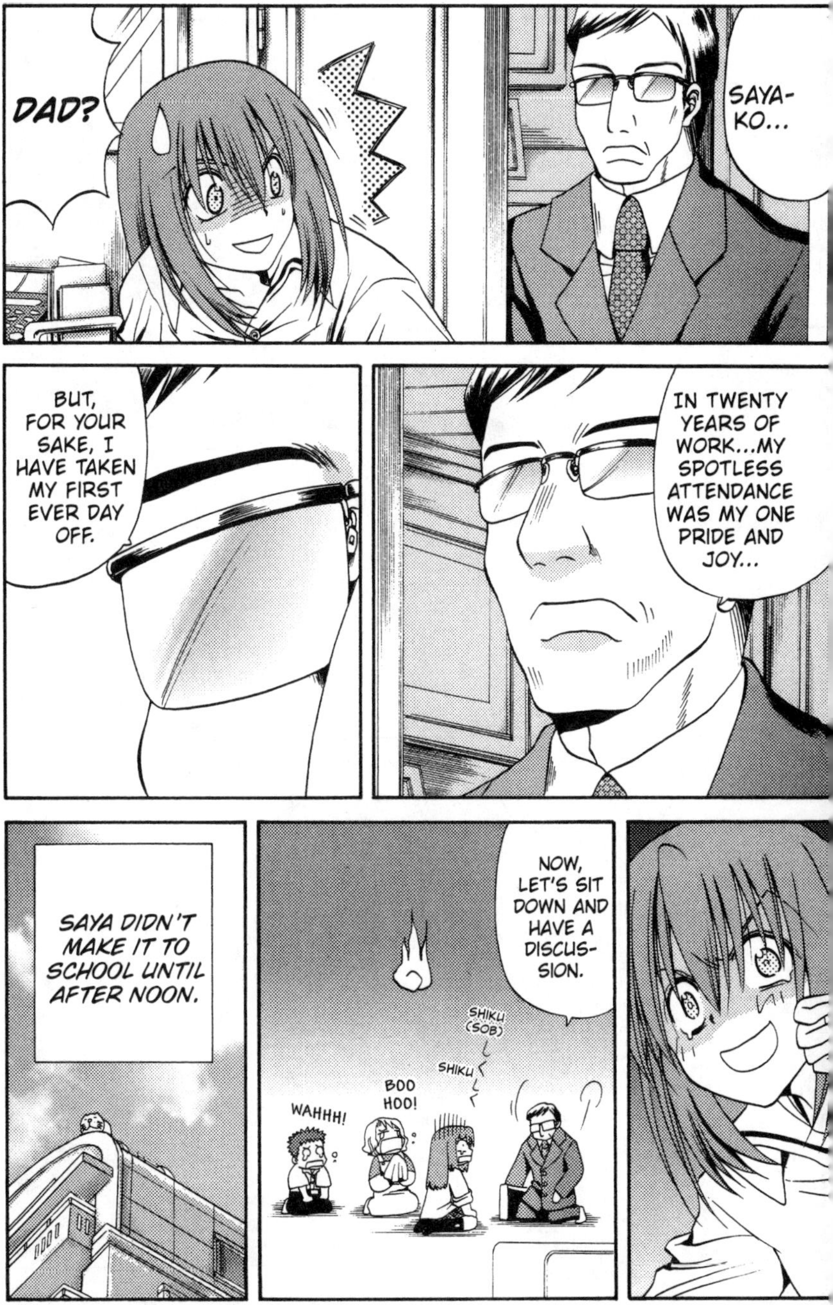
SAYA-KO...
DAD?
IN TWENTY YEARS OF WORK...MY SPOTLESS ATTENDANCE WAS MY ONE PRIDE AND JOY...
BUT, FOR YOUR SAKE, I HAVE TAKEN MY FIRST EVER DAY OFF.
NOW, LET'S SIT DOWN AND HAVE A DISCUS-SION.
SHIKU (SOB)
SHIKU
BOO HOO!
WAHHH!
SAYA DIDN'T MAKE IT TO SCHOOL UNTIL AFTER NOON.

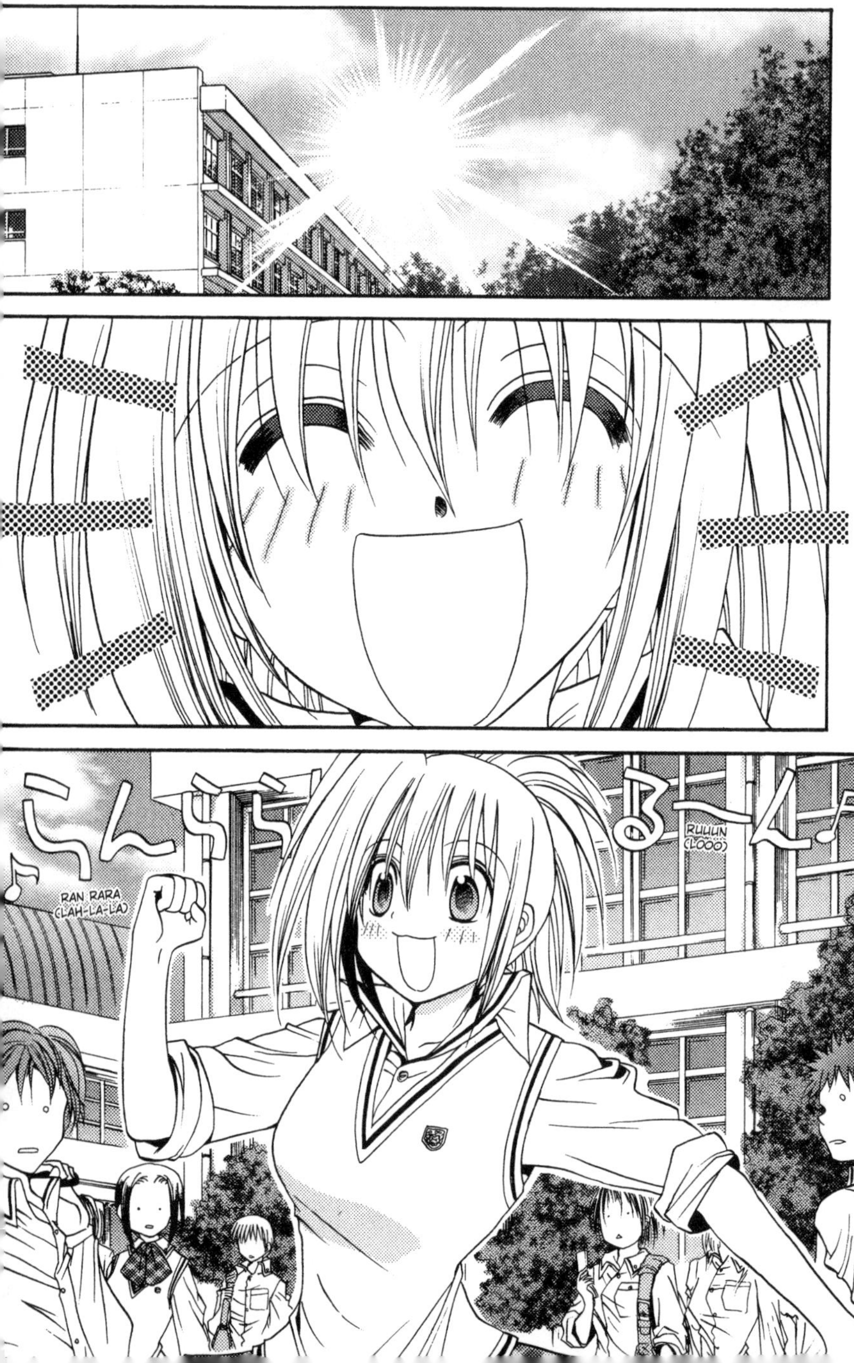

RAN RARA
(LAH-LA-LA)
RUUUN
(LOOO)

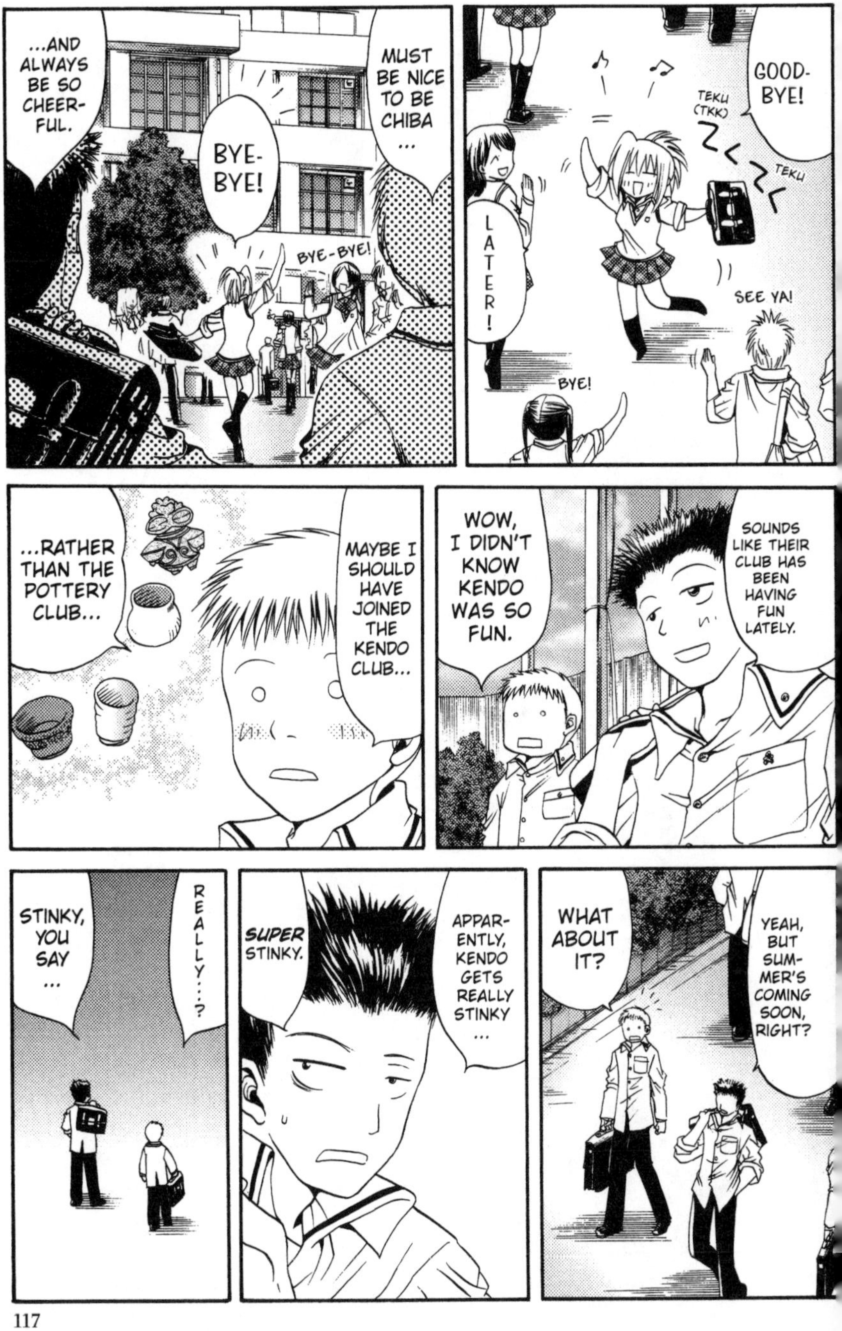
GOOD-BYE!
TEKU (TKK)
TEKU
LATER!
SEE YA!
BYE!
MUST BE NICE TO BE CHIBA...
BYE-BYE!
BYE-BYE!
...AND ALWAYS BE SO CHEERFUL.
SOUNDS LIKE THEIR CLUB HAS BEEN HAVING FUN LATELY.
WOW, I DIDN'T KNOW KENDO WAS SO FUN.
MAYBE I SHOULD HAVE JOINED THE KENDO CLUB...
...RATHER THAN THE POTTERY CLUB...
YEAH, BUT SUMMER'S COMING SOON, RIGHT?
WHAT ABOUT IT?
APPARENTLY, KENDO GETS REALLY STINKY...
SUPER STINKY.
REALLY...?
STINKY, YOU SAY...

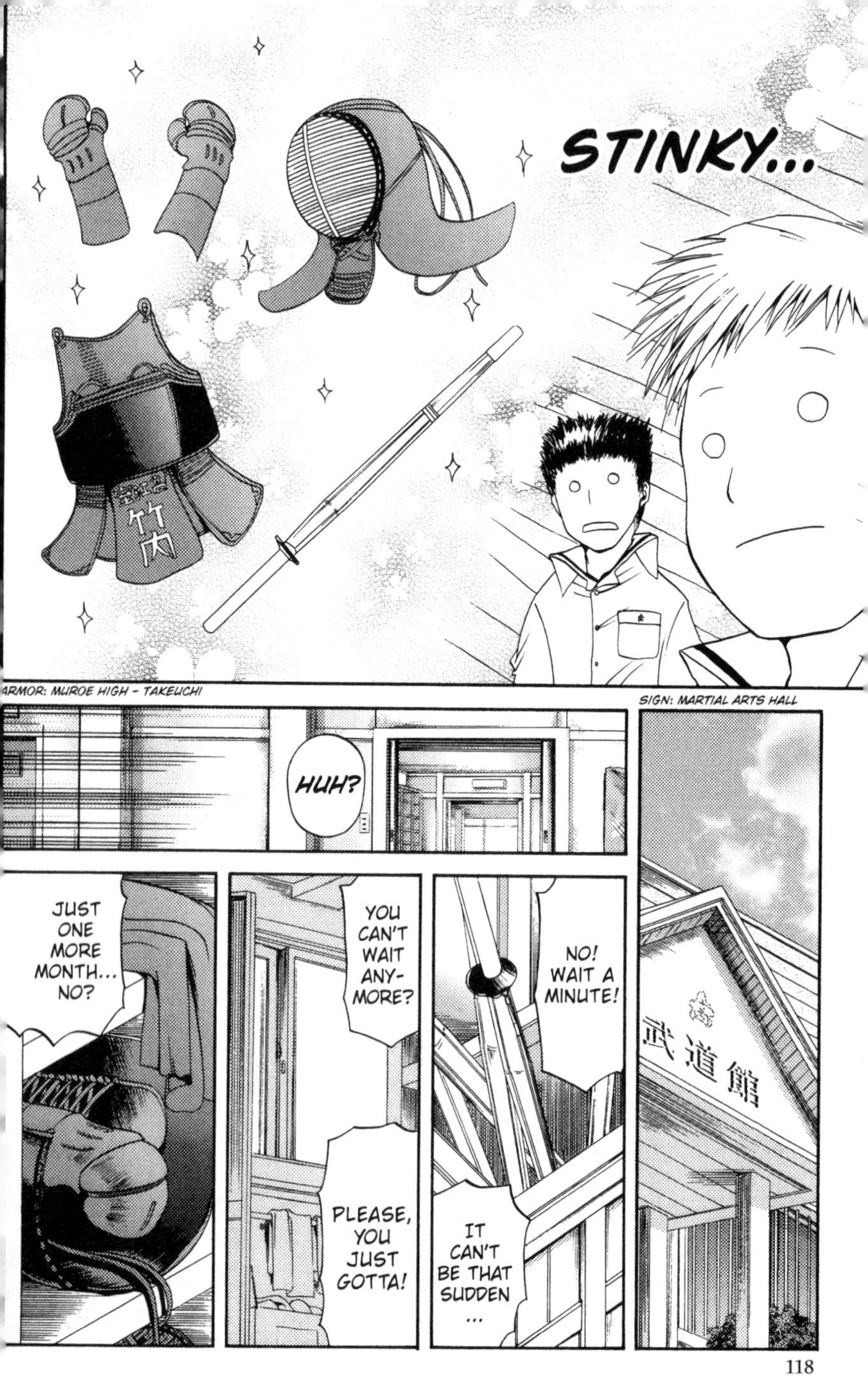
STINKY...
ARMOR: MUROE HIGH - TAKEUCHI
SIGN: MARTIAL ARTS HALL
武道館
HUH?
NO! WAIT A MINUTE!
IT CAN'T BE THAT SUDDEN ...
YOU CAN'T WAIT ANY-MORE?
PLEASE, YOU JUST GOTTA!
JUST ONE MORE MONTH... NO?

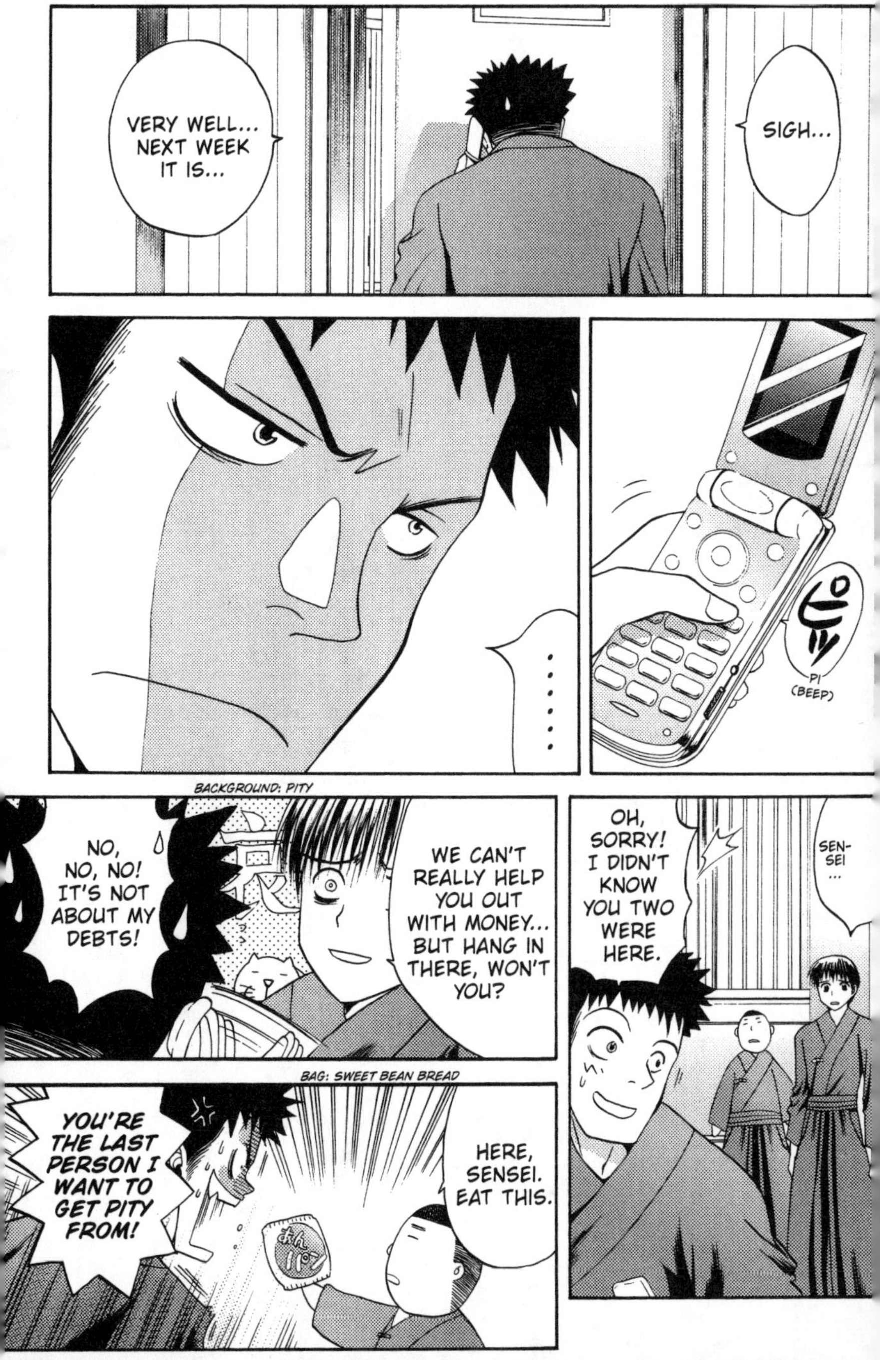
SIGH...
VERY WELL... NEXT WEEK IT IS...
ピッ
PI (BEEP)
......
SEN-SEI...
OH, SORRY! I DIDN'T KNOW YOU TWO WERE HERE.
BACKGROUND: PITY
WE CAN'T REALLY HELP YOU OUT WITH MONEY... BUT HANG IN THERE, WON'T YOU?
NO, NO, NO! IT'S NOT ABOUT MY DEBTS!
BAG: SWEET BEAN BREAD
HERE, SENSEI. EAT THIS.
YOU'RE THE LAST PERSON I WANT TO GET PITY FROM!

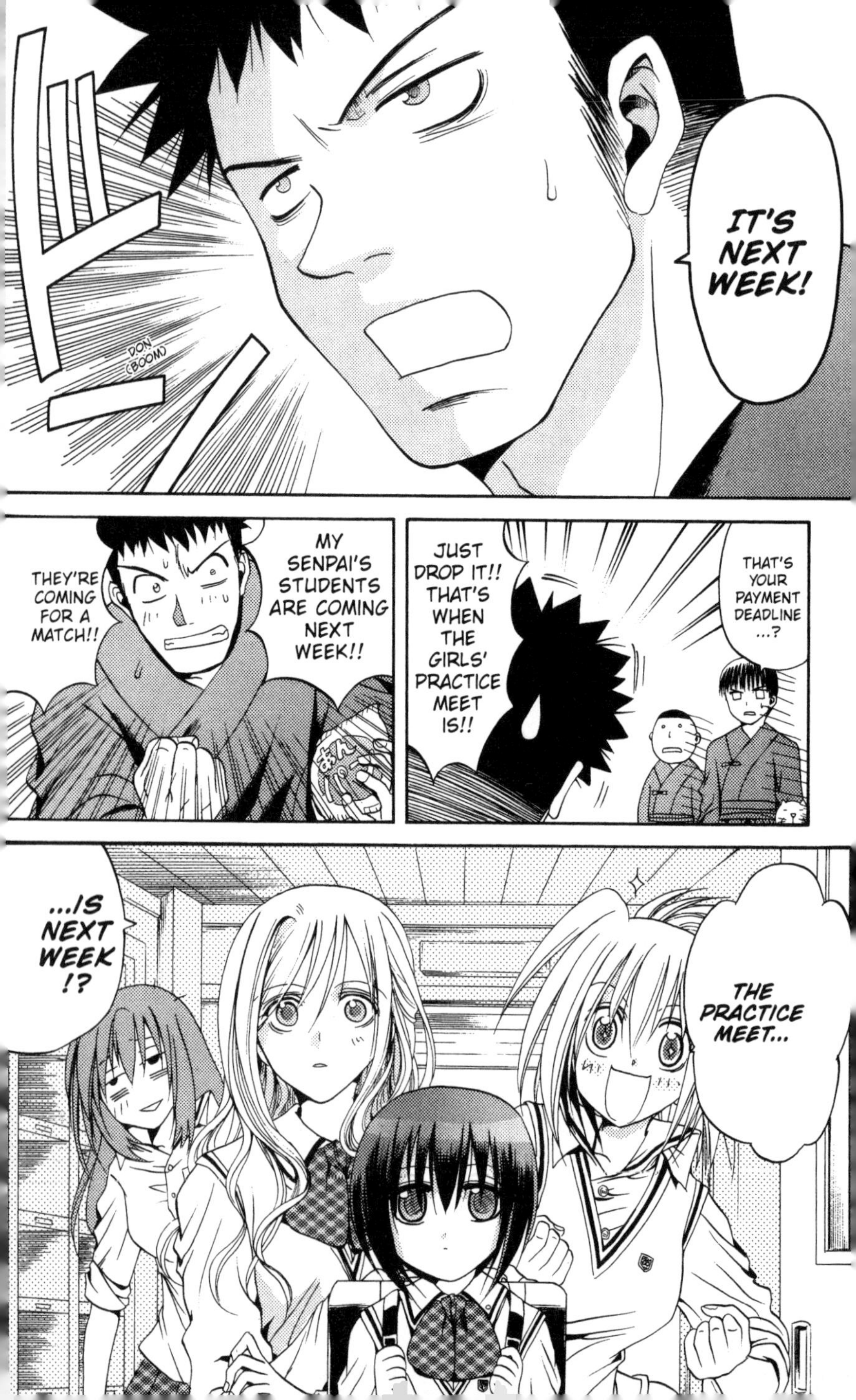
IT'S NEXT WEEK!
DON (BOOM)
THAT'S YOUR PAYMENT DEADLINE ...?
JUST DROP IT!! THAT'S WHEN THE GIRLS' PRACTICE MEET IS!!
MY SENPAI'S STUDENTS ARE COMING NEXT WEEK!!
THEY'RE COMING FOR A MATCH!!
THE PRACTICE MEET...
...IS NEXT WEEK !?

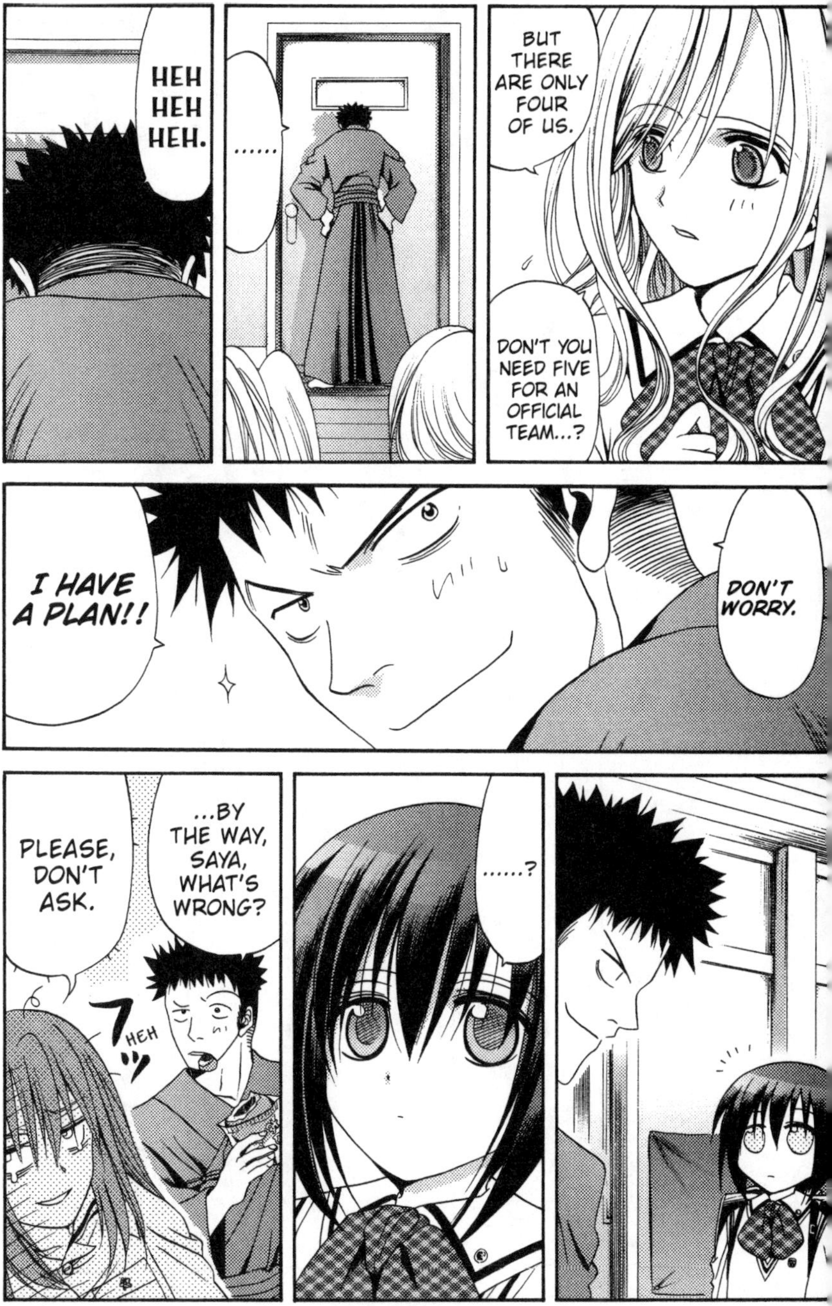
BUT THERE ARE ONLY FOUR OF US.
DON'T YOU NEED FIVE FOR AN OFFICIAL TEAM...?
......
HEH HEH HEH.
DON'T WORRY.
I HAVE A PLAN!!
......?
...BY THE WAY, SAYA, WHAT'S WRONG?
PLEASE, DON'T ASK.
HEH

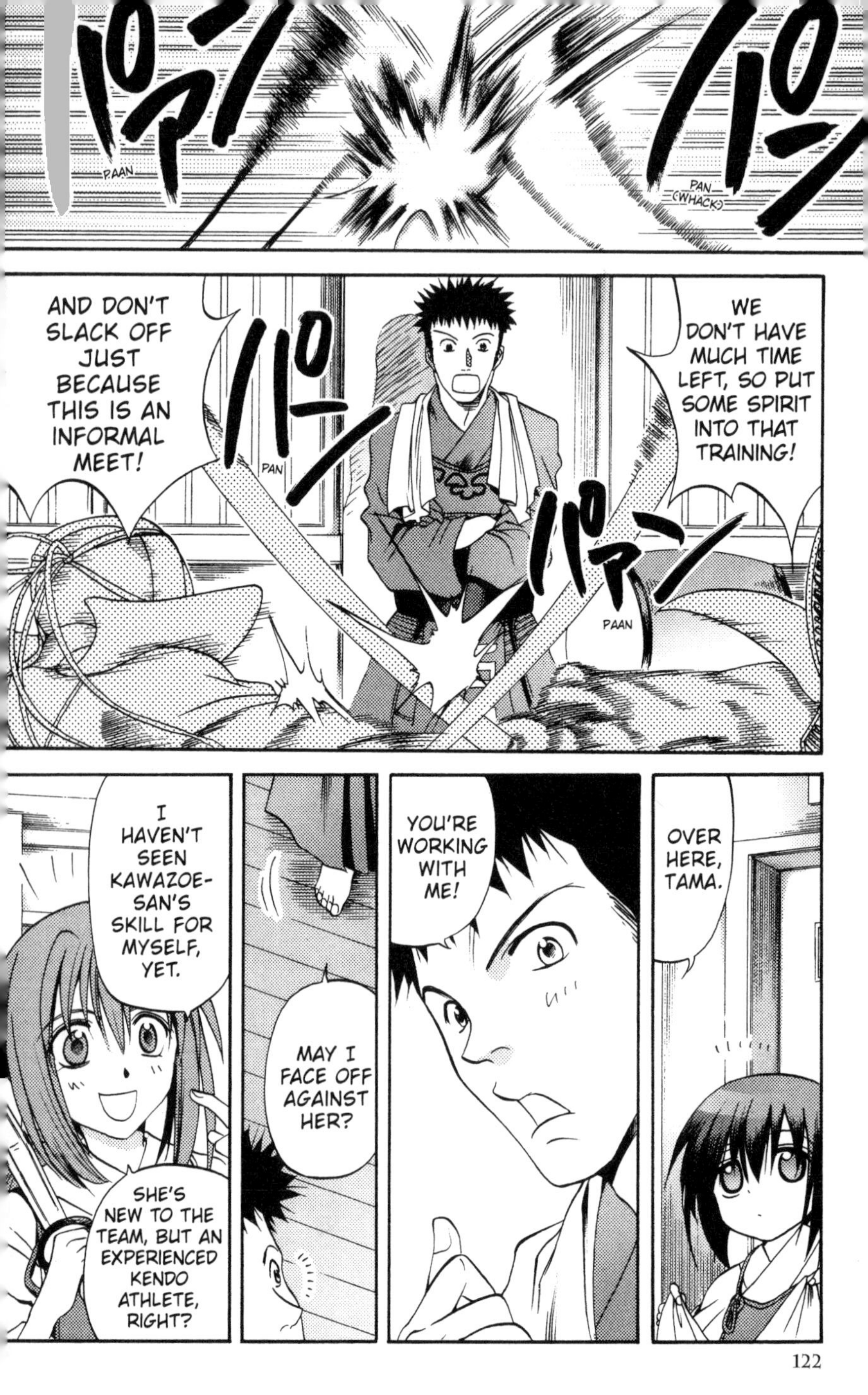
PAN
(WHACK)
PAAN
WE DON'T HAVE MUCH TIME LEFT, SO PUT SOME SPIRIT INTO THAT TRAINING!
PAAN
PAN
AND DON'T SLACK OFF JUST BECAUSE THIS IS AN INFORMAL MEET!
OVER HERE, TAMA.
YOU'RE WORKING WITH ME!
MAY I FACE OFF AGAINST HER?
I HAVEN'T SEEN KAWAZOE-SAN'S SKILL FOR MYSELF, YET.
SHE'S NEW TO THE TEAM, BUT AN EXPERIENCED KENDO ATHLETE, RIGHT?

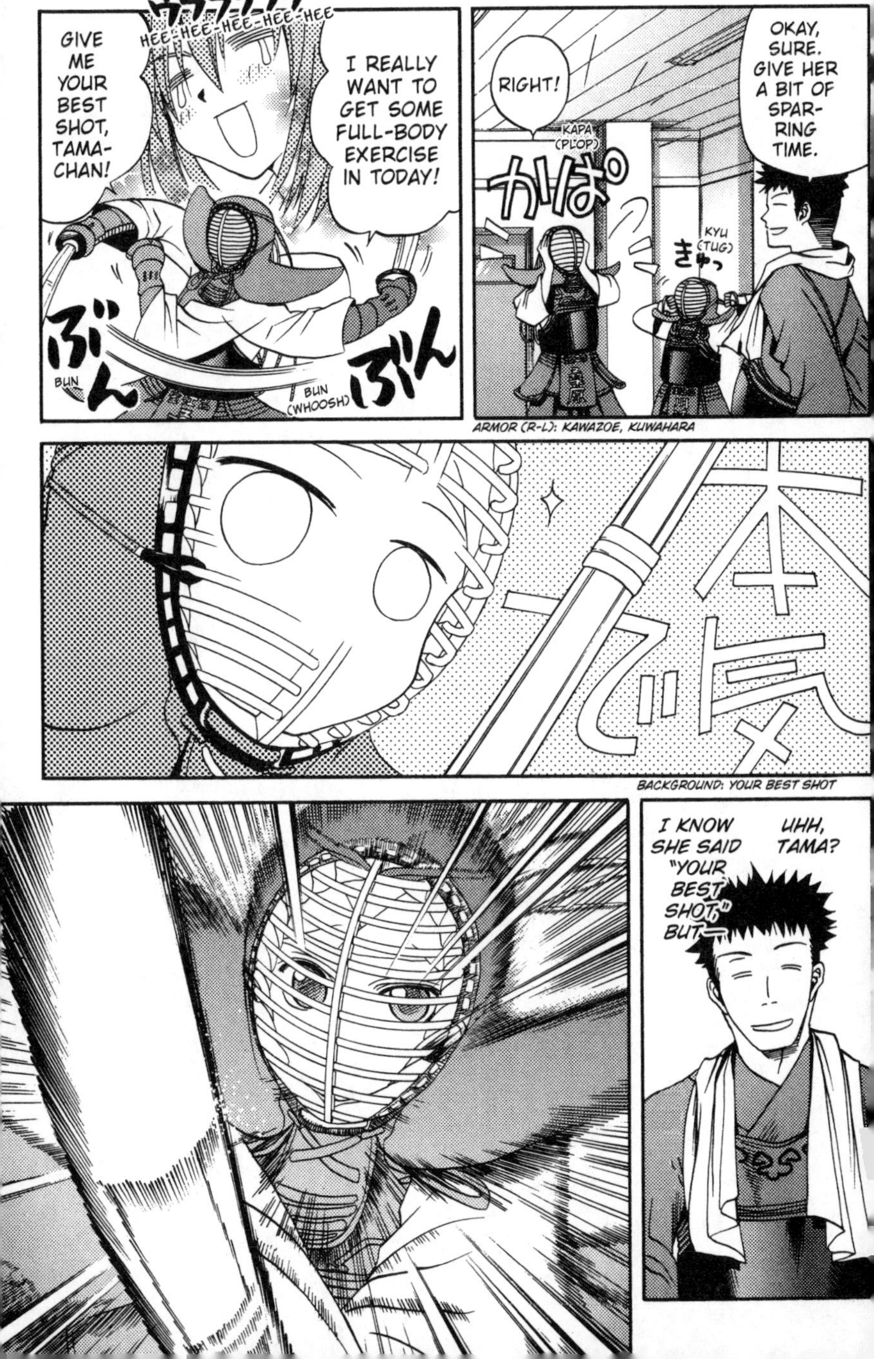
OKAY, SURE. GIVE HER A BIT OF SPAR-RING TIME.
KYU (TUG)
きゅっ
RIGHT!
KAPA (PLOP)
かぱ
HEE-HEE-HEE-HEE-HEE
I REALLY WANT TO GET SOME FULL-BODY EXERCISE IN TODAY!
GIVE ME YOUR BEST SHOT, TAMA-CHAN!
BUN (WHOOSH)
ぶん
BUN
ぶん
ARMOR (R-L): KAWAZOE, KUWAHARA
BACKGROUND: YOUR BEST SHOT
UHH, TAMA?
I KNOW SHE SAID "YOUR BEST SHOT," BUT—

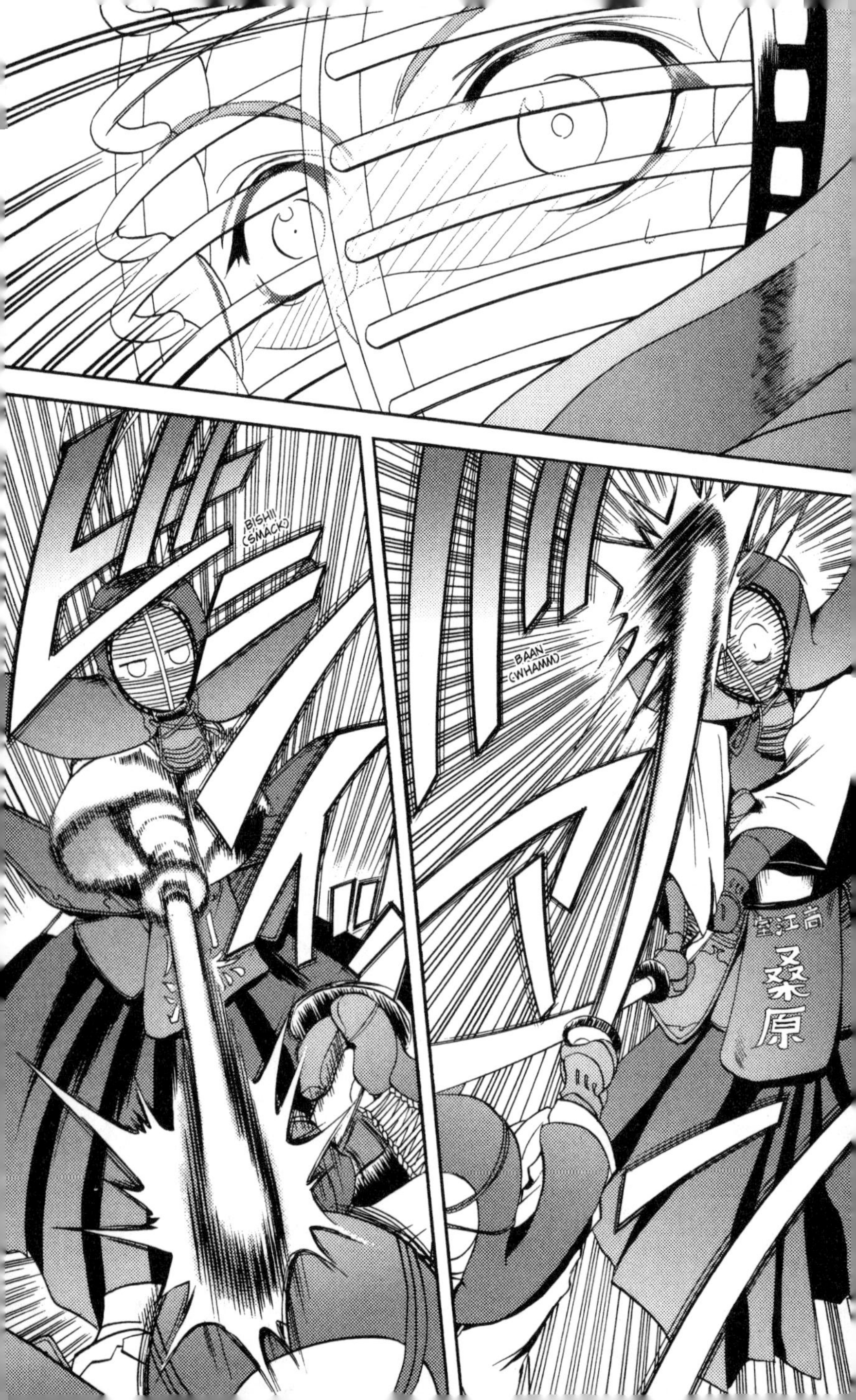
BAAN (WHAMM)
桑原
BISHII (SMACK)

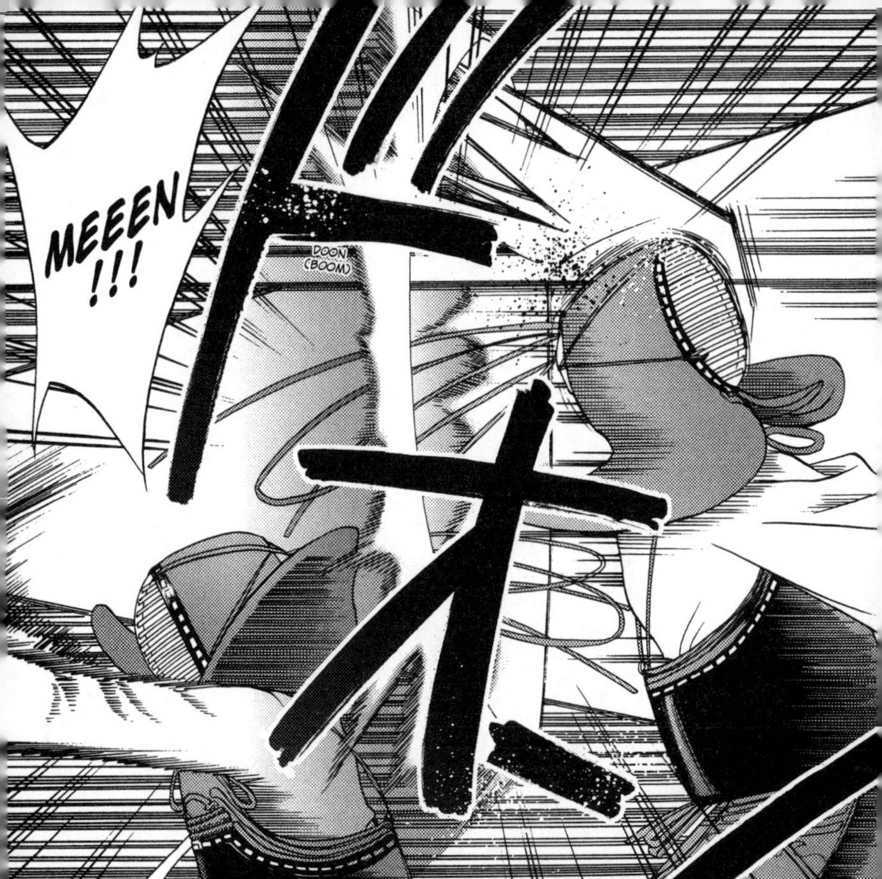
MEEEN!!!
DOON (BOOM)
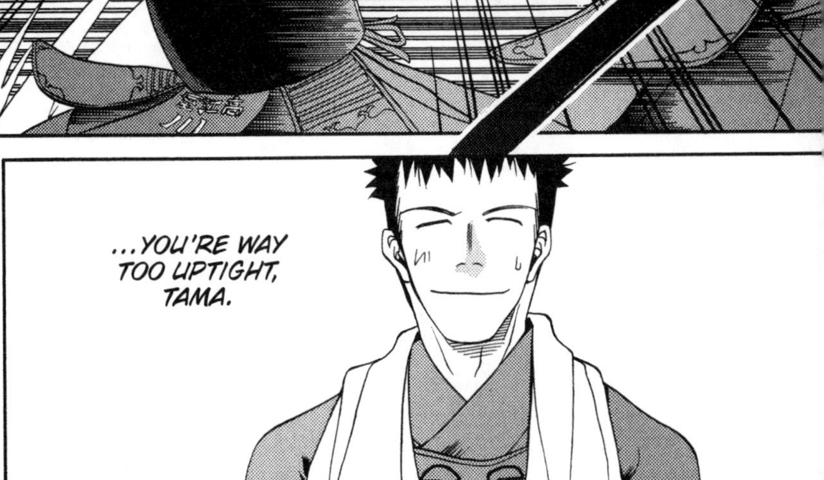
...YOU'RE WAY TOO UPTIGHT, TAMA.

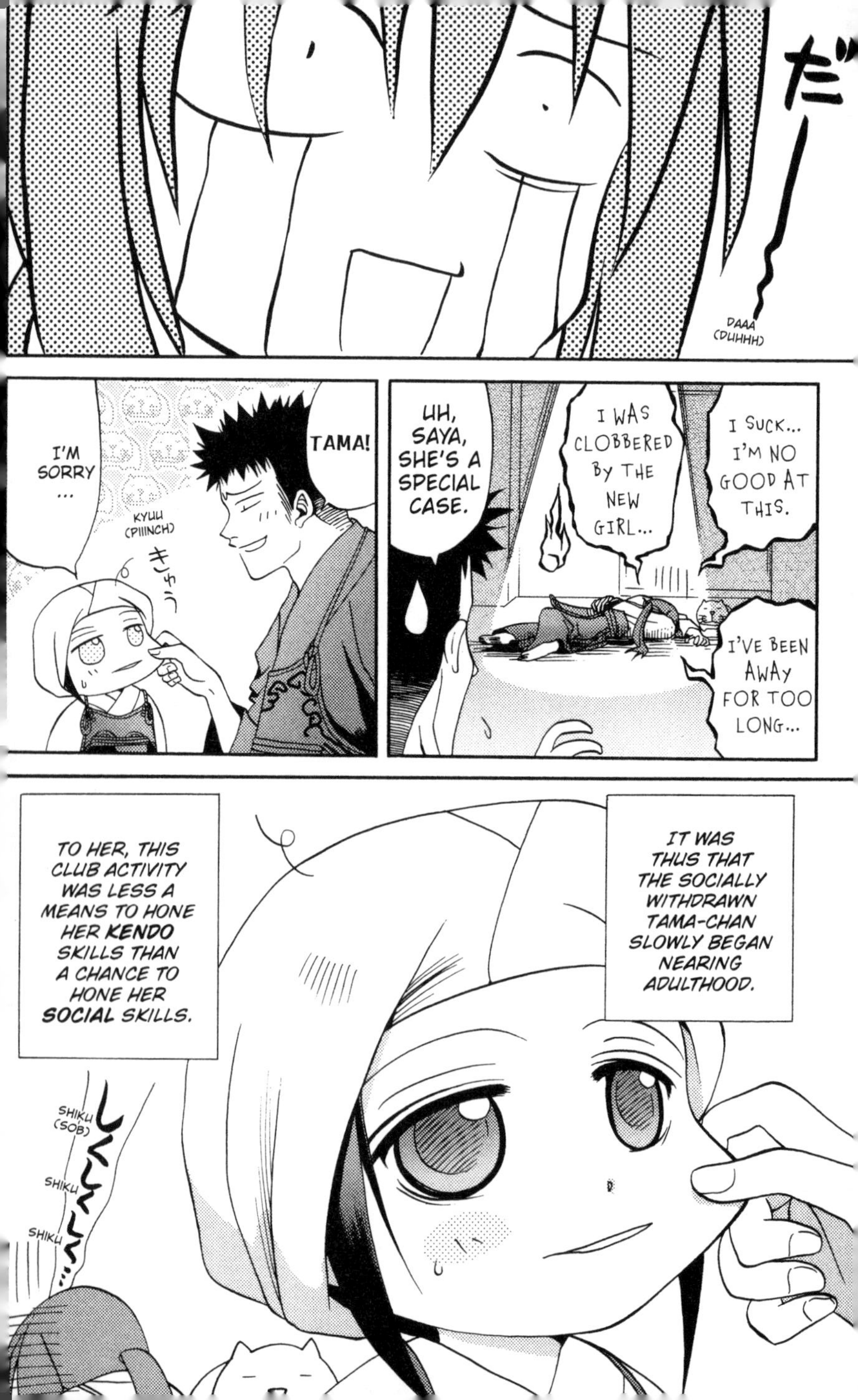
だーー
DAAA (DUHHH)
I SUCK... I'M NO GOOD AT THIS.
I WAS CLOBBERED BY THE NEW GIRL...
UH, SAYA, SHE'S A SPECIAL CASE.
I'VE BEEN AWAY FOR TOO LONG...
TAMA!
I'M SORRY...
キュう
KYUU (PIIINCH)
IT WAS THUS THAT THE SOCIALLY WITHDRAWN TAMA-CHAN SLOWLY BEGAN NEARING ADULTHOOD.
TO HER, THIS CLUB ACTIVITY WAS LESS A MEANS TO HONE HER **KENDO** SKILLS THAN A CHANCE TO HONE HER **SOCIAL** SKILLS.
しくしくしく…
SHIKU (SOB)
SHIKU
SHIKU

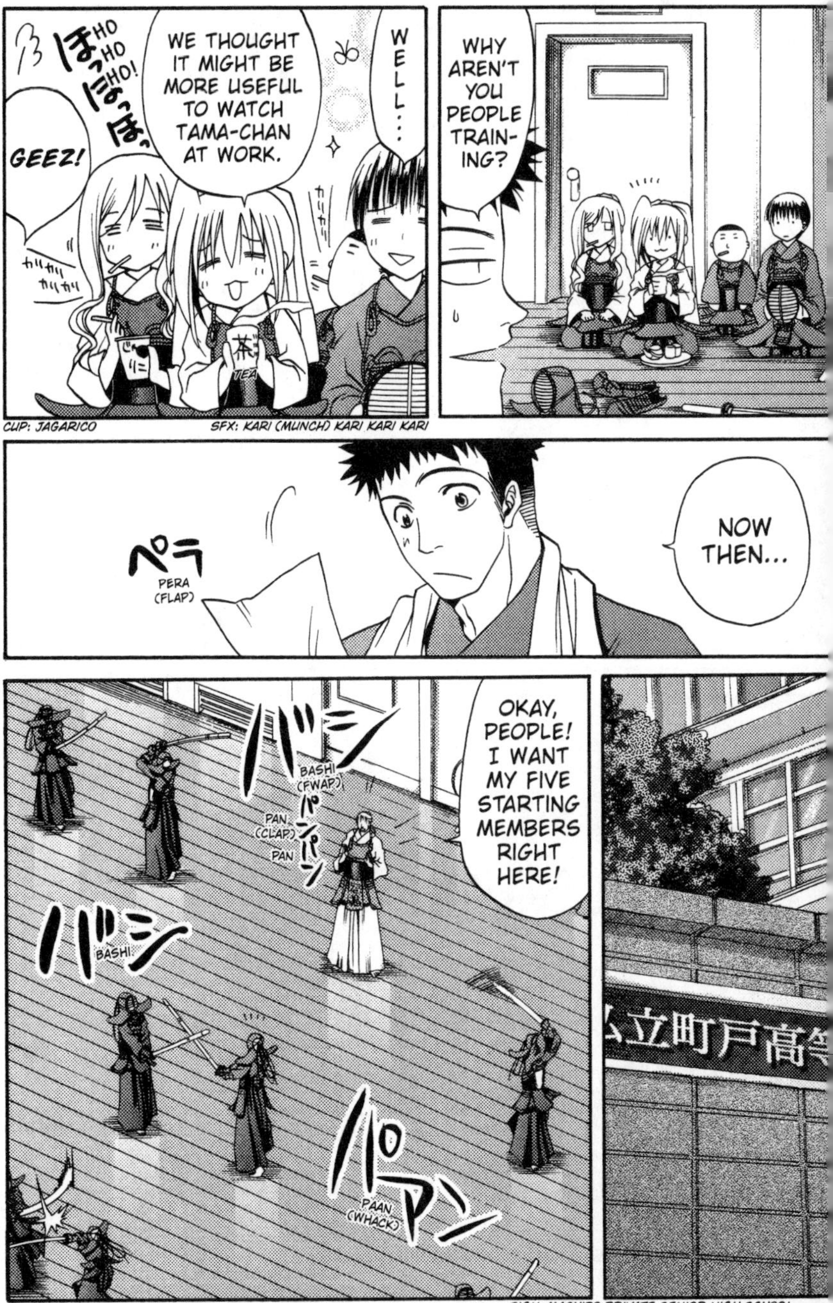
WHY AREN'T YOU PEOPLE TRAINING?
WELL...
WE THOUGHT IT MIGHT BE MORE USEFUL TO WATCH TAMA-CHAN AT WORK.
HO HO HO!
GEEZ!
TEA
NOW THEN...
PERA (FLAP)
OKAY, PEOPLE! I WANT MY FIVE STARTING MEMBERS RIGHT HERE!
BASHI (FWAP)
PAN (CLAP) PAN
BASHI
PAAN (WHACK)

CUP: JAGARICO

SFX: KARI (MUNCH) KARI KARI KARI

SIGN: MACHIDO PRIVATE SENIOR HIGH SCHOOL

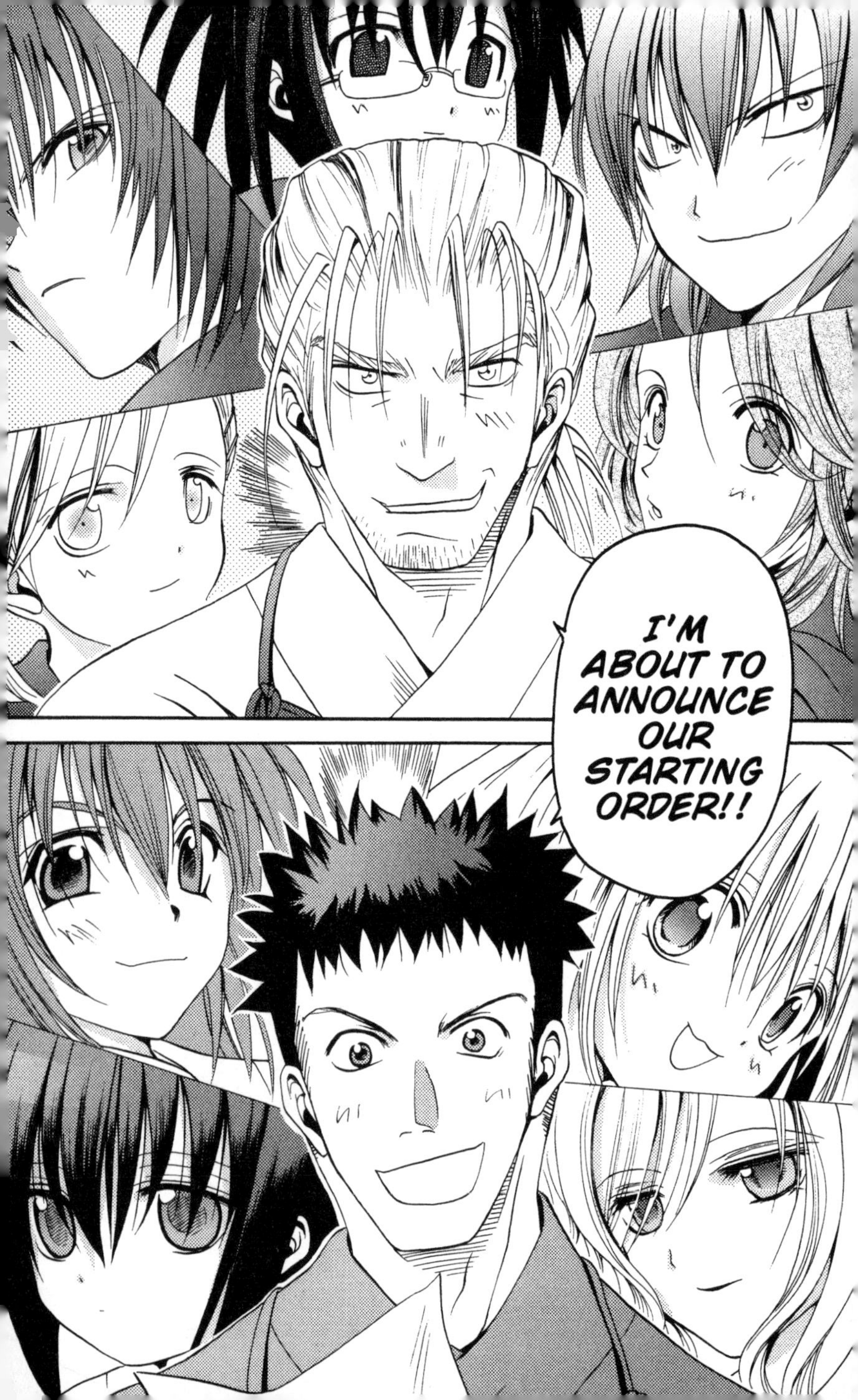
I'M ABOUT TO ANNOUNCE OUR STARTING ORDER!!

BAMBOO BLADE

ASAKAWA-SAN AND NAIL ART

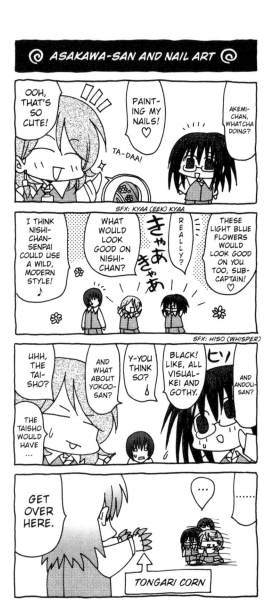

AKEMI-CHAN, WHATCHA DOING?
PAINT-ING MY NAILS! ♡
TA-DAA!
OOH, THAT'S SO CUTE!
SFX: KYAA (EEK) KYAA
THESE LIGHT BLUE FLOWERS WOULD LOOK GOOD ON YOU TOO, SUB-CAPTAIN! ♡
REALLY?
きゃあ きゃあ
WHAT WOULD LOOK GOOD ON NISHI-CHAN?
I THINK NISHI-CHAN-SENPAI COULD USE A WILD, MODERN STYLE! ♪
SFX: HISO (WHISPER)
AND ANDOU-SAN?
ヒソ
BLACK! LIKE, ALL VISUAL-KEI AND GOTHY.
Y-YOU THINK SO?
AND WHAT ABOUT YOKOO-SAN?
UHH, THE TAI-SHO?
THE TAISHO WOULD HAVE ...
......
...
GET OVER HERE.
TONGARI CORN

ALL RIGHT, FOLKS.

TIME TO ANNOUNCE OUR STARTING LINEUP!

| SENPO 先鋒 ADVANCE GUARD |
| JIHO 次鋒 SECOND GUARD |
| CHUKEN 中堅 CENTER OFFICER |
| FUKUSHO 副将 SECOND-IN-COMMAND |
| TAISHO 大将 GENERAL |

SAYAKO KUWAHARA, 2ND YEAR

KIRINO CHIBA, 2ND YEAR

MIYAKO MIYAZAKI, 1ST YEAR

TAMAKI KAWAZOE, 1ST YEAR

131

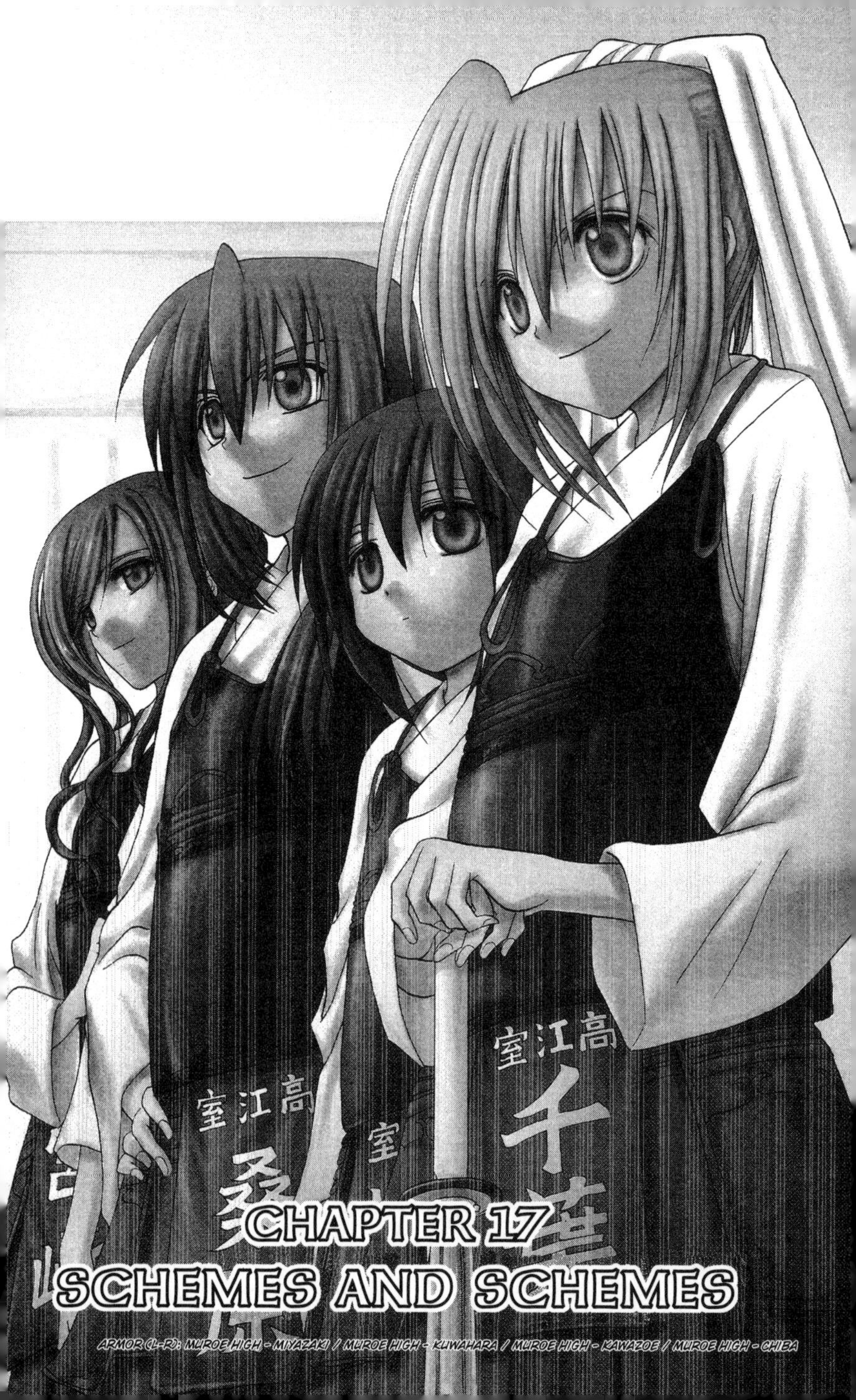
CHAPTER 17
SCHEMES AND SCHEMES
ARMOR (L-R): MUROE HIGH - MIYAZAKI / MUROE HIGH - KUWAHARA / MUROE HIGH - KAWAZOE / MUROE HIGH - CHIBA
室江高
室江高
室
千

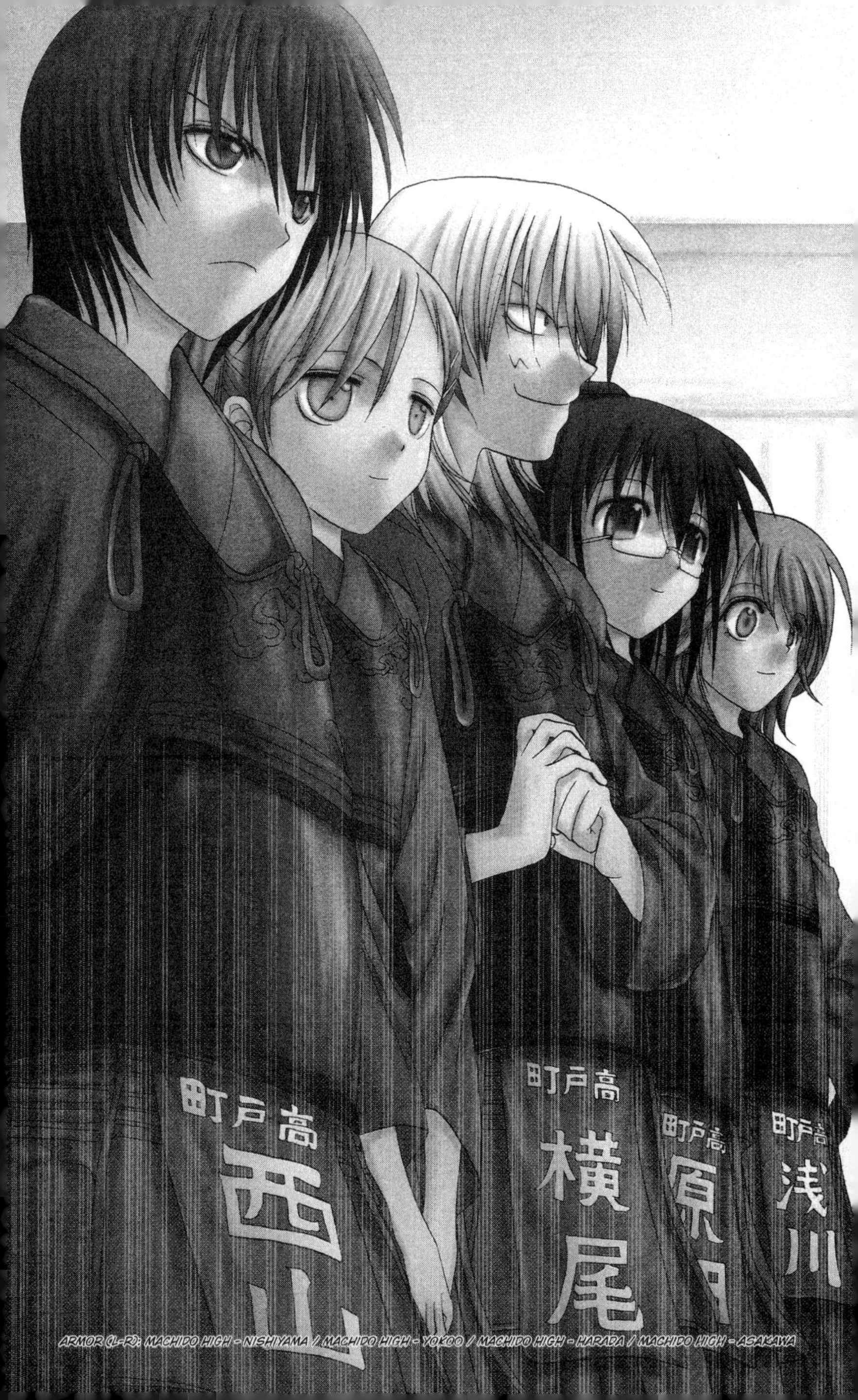
町戸高
西山
町戸高
横尾
町戸高
原
町戸高
浅川
ARMOR (L-R): MACHIDO HIGH - NISHIYAMA / MACHIDO HIGH - YOKOO / MACHIDO HIGH - HARADA / MACHIDO HIGH - ASAKAWA

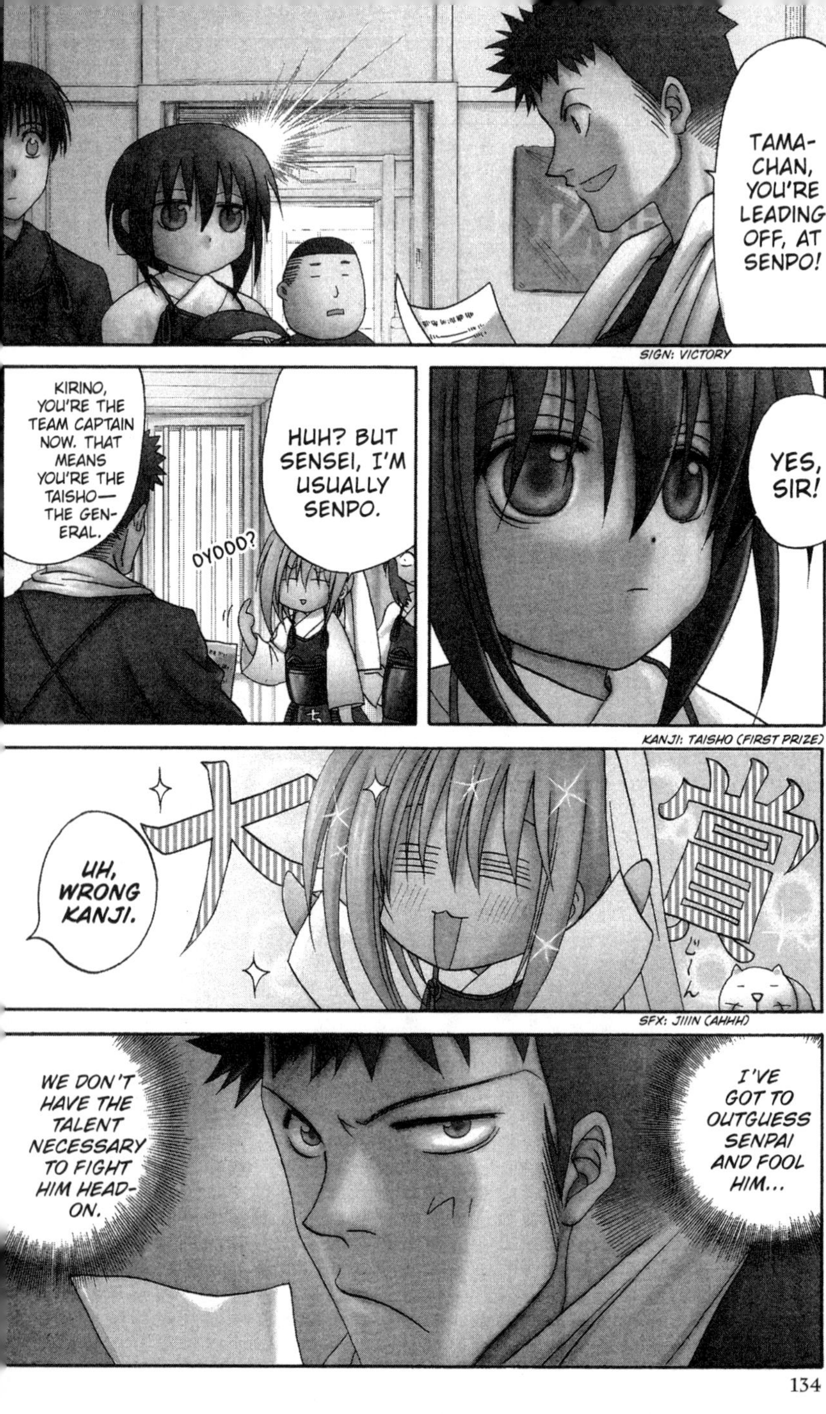
TAMA-CHAN, YOU'RE LEADING OFF, AT SENPO!
SIGN: VICTORY
YES, SIR!
HUH? BUT SENSEI, I'M USUALLY SENPO.
KIRINO, YOU'RE THE TEAM CAPTAIN NOW. THAT MEANS YOU'RE THE TAISHO— THE GENERAL.
OYOOO?
KANJI: TAISHO (FIRST PRIZE)
UH, WRONG KANJI.
SFX: JIIIN (AHHH)
I'VE GOT TO OUTGUESS SENPAI AND FOOL HIM...
WE DON'T HAVE THE TALENT NECESSARY TO FIGHT HIM HEAD-ON.

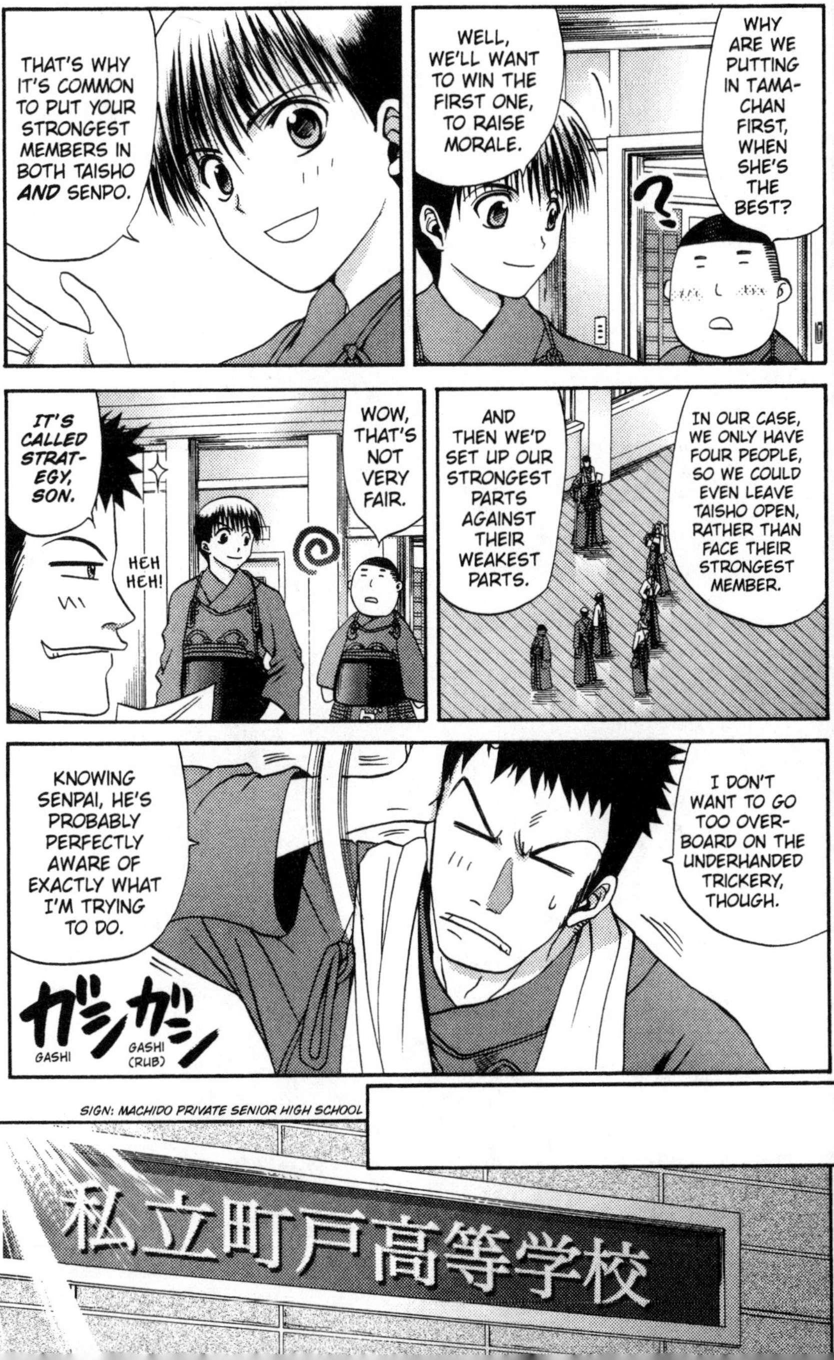
WHY ARE WE PUTTING IN TAMA-CHAN FIRST, WHEN SHE'S THE BEST?
?
WELL, WE'LL WANT TO WIN THE FIRST ONE, TO RAISE MORALE.
THAT'S WHY IT'S COMMON TO PUT YOUR STRONGEST MEMBERS IN BOTH TAISHO AND SENPO.
IN OUR CASE, WE ONLY HAVE FOUR PEOPLE, SO WE COULD EVEN LEAVE TAISHO OPEN, RATHER THAN FACE THEIR STRONGEST MEMBER.
AND THEN WE'D SET UP OUR STRONGEST PARTS AGAINST THEIR WEAKEST PARTS.
WOW, THAT'S NOT VERY FAIR.
HEH HEH!
IT'S CALLED STRAT-EGY, SON.
I DON'T WANT TO GO TOO OVER-BOARD ON THE UNDERHANDED TRICKERY, THOUGH.
KNOWING SENPAI, HE'S PROBABLY PERFECTLY AWARE OF EXACTLY WHAT I'M TRYING TO DO.
ガシガシ
GASHI GASHI (RUB)
SIGN: MACHIDO PRIVATE SENIOR HIGH SCHOOL
私立町戸高等学校

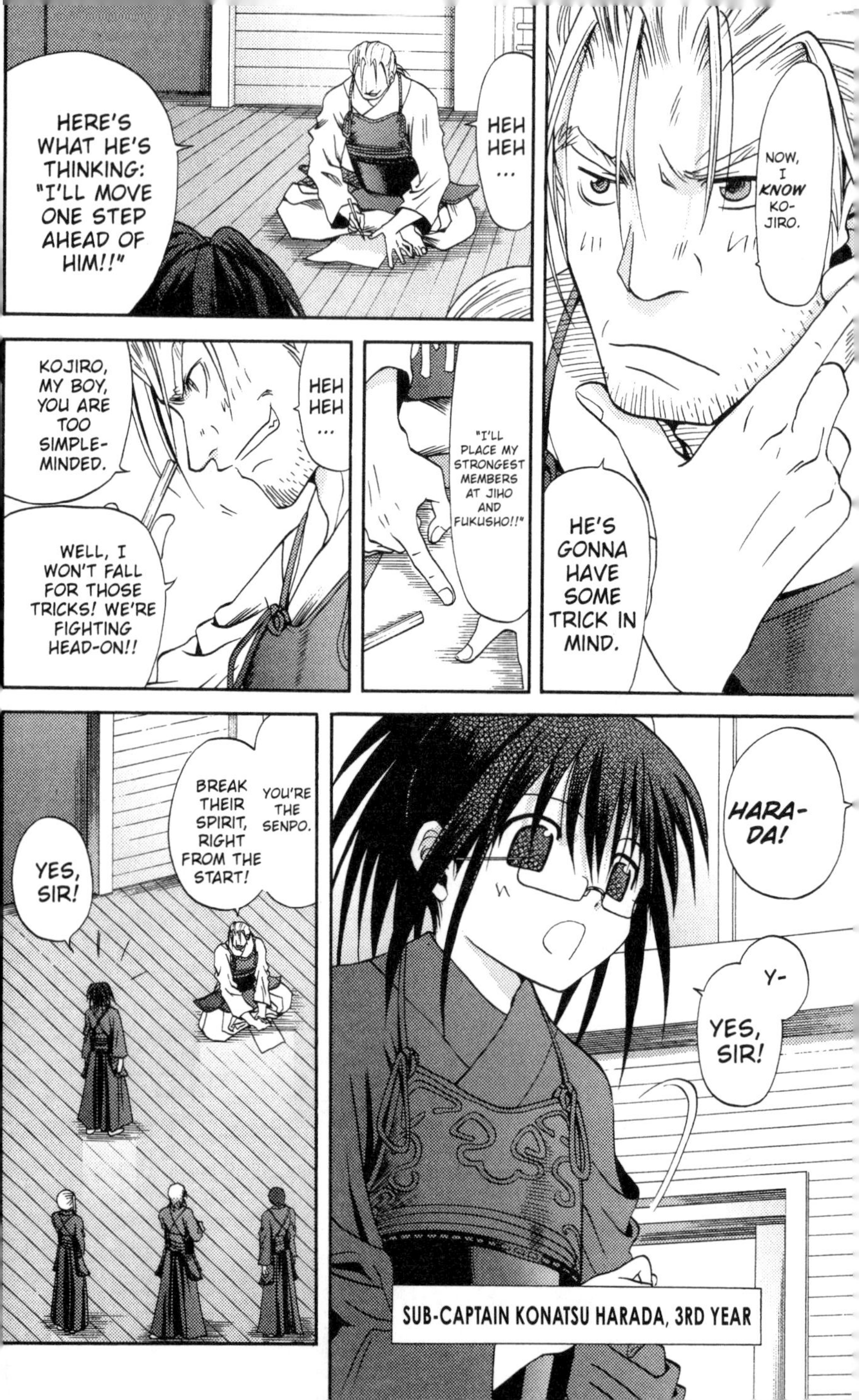
NOW, I KNOW KOJIRO.
HE'S GONNA HAVE SOME TRICK IN MIND.
HEH HEH ...
HERE'S WHAT HE'S THINKING: "I'LL MOVE ONE STEP AHEAD OF HIM!!"
"I'LL PLACE MY STRONGEST MEMBERS AT JIHO AND FUKUSHO!!"
HEH HEH ...
KOJIRO, MY BOY, YOU ARE TOO SIMPLE-MINDED.
WELL, I WON'T FALL FOR THOSE TRICKS! WE'RE FIGHTING HEAD-ON!!
HARADA!
Y- YES, SIR!
SUB-CAPTAIN KONATSU HARADA, 3RD YEAR
YOU'RE THE SENPO.
BREAK THEIR SPIRIT, RIGHT FROM THE START!
YES, SIR!

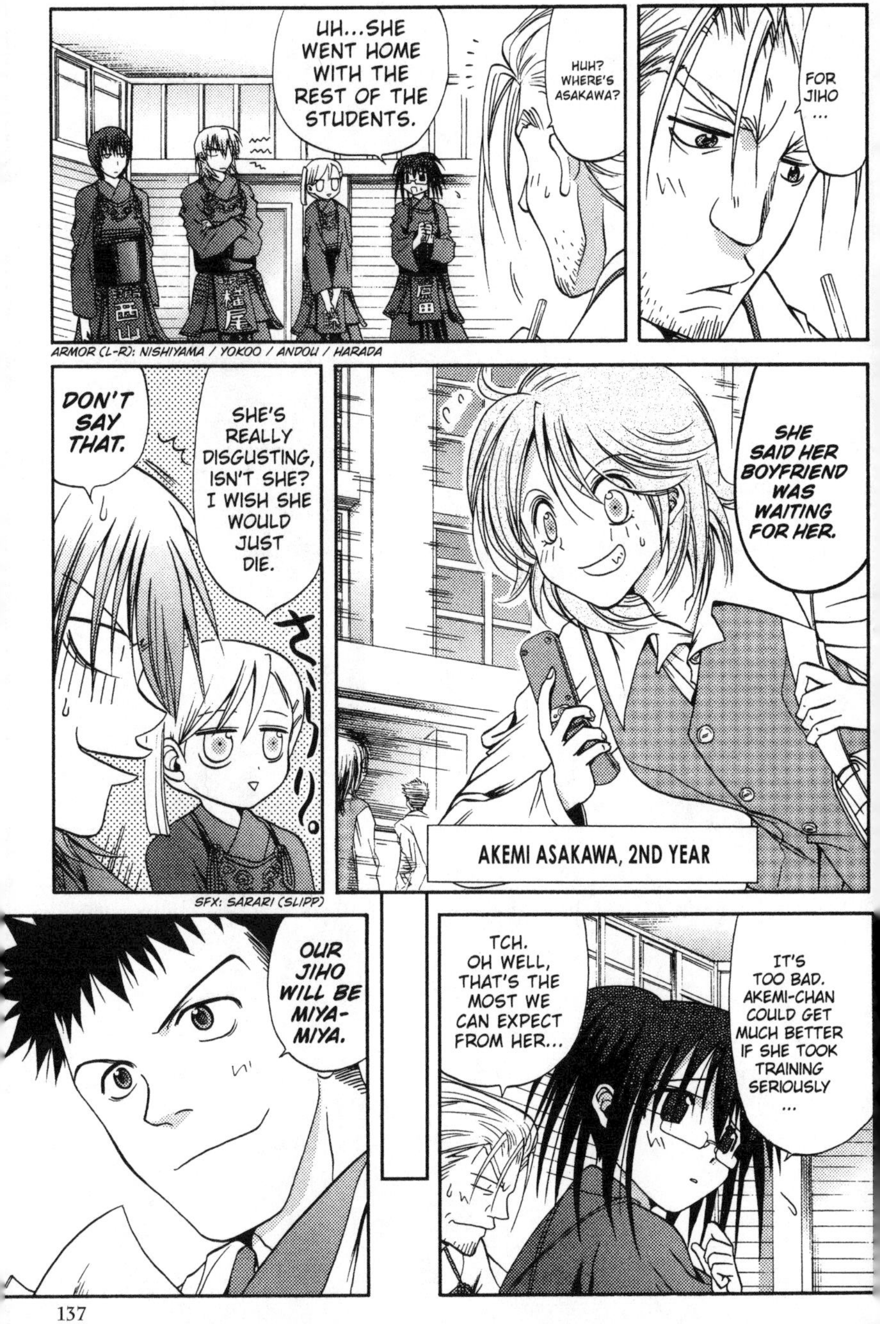
FOR JIHO ...
HUH? WHERE'S ASAKAWA?
UH...SHE WENT HOME WITH THE REST OF THE STUDENTS.
SHE SAID HER BOYFRIEND WAS WAITING FOR HER.
AKEMI ASAKAWA, 2ND YEAR
SHE'S REALLY DISGUSTING, ISN'T SHE? I WISH SHE WOULD JUST DIE.
DON'T SAY THAT.
IT'S TOO BAD. AKEMI-CHAN COULD GET MUCH BETTER IF SHE TOOK TRAINING SERIOUSLY ...
TCH. OH WELL, THAT'S THE MOST WE CAN EXPECT FROM HER...
OUR JIHO WILL BE MIYA-MIYA.
ARMOR (L-R): NISHIYAMA / YOKOO / ANDOU / HARADA

SFX: SARARI (SLIPP)

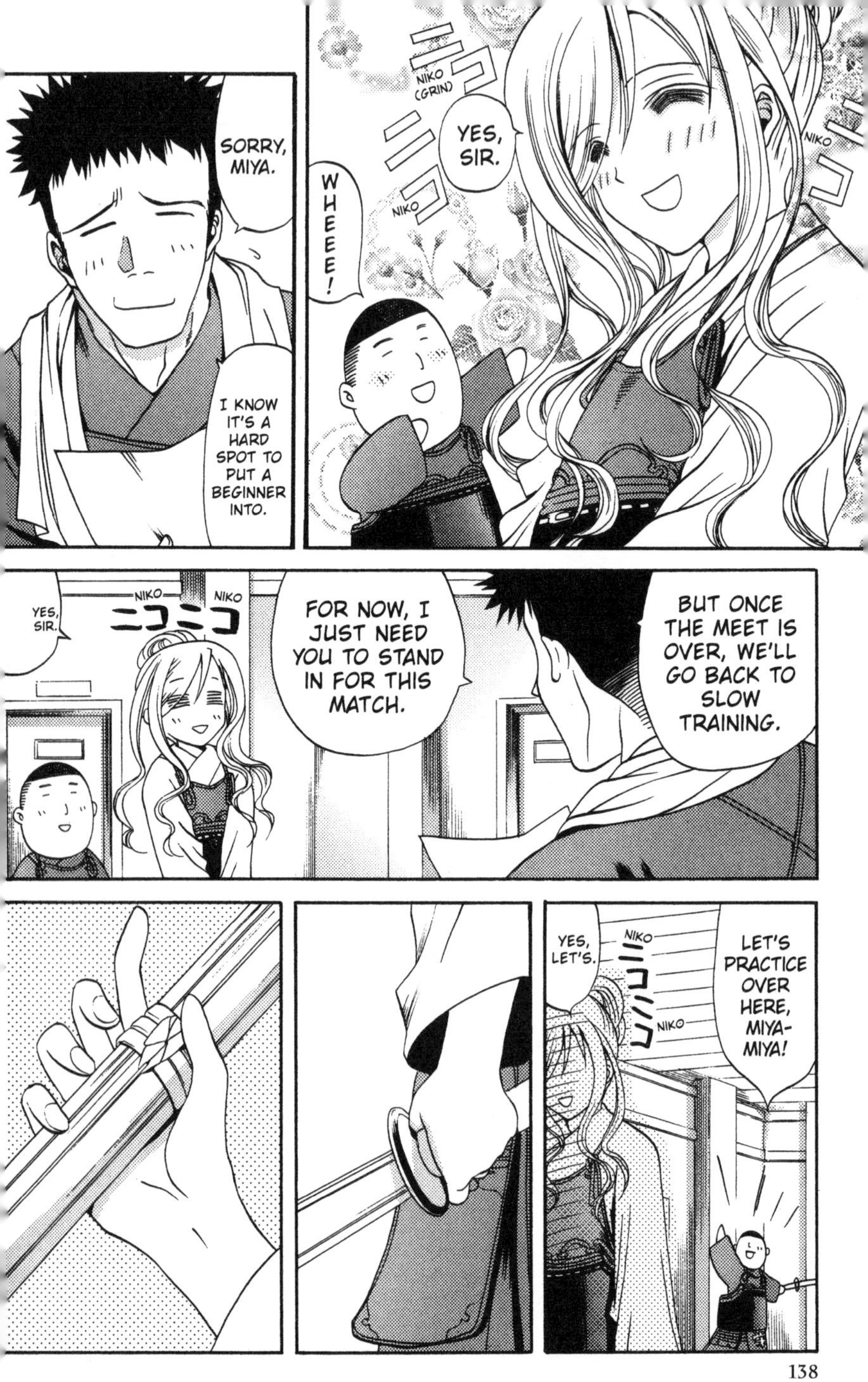
NIKO (GRIN)
YES, SIR.
NIKO
NIKO
WHEEEE!
SORRY, MIYA.
I KNOW IT'S A HARD SPOT TO PUT A BEGINNER INTO.
BUT ONCE THE MEET IS OVER, WE'LL GO BACK TO SLOW TRAINING.
FOR NOW, I JUST NEED YOU TO STAND IN FOR THIS MATCH.
NIKO NIKO
ニコニコ
YES, SIR.
LET'S PRACTICE OVER HERE, MIYA-MIYA!
NIKO
NIKO
YES, LET'S.

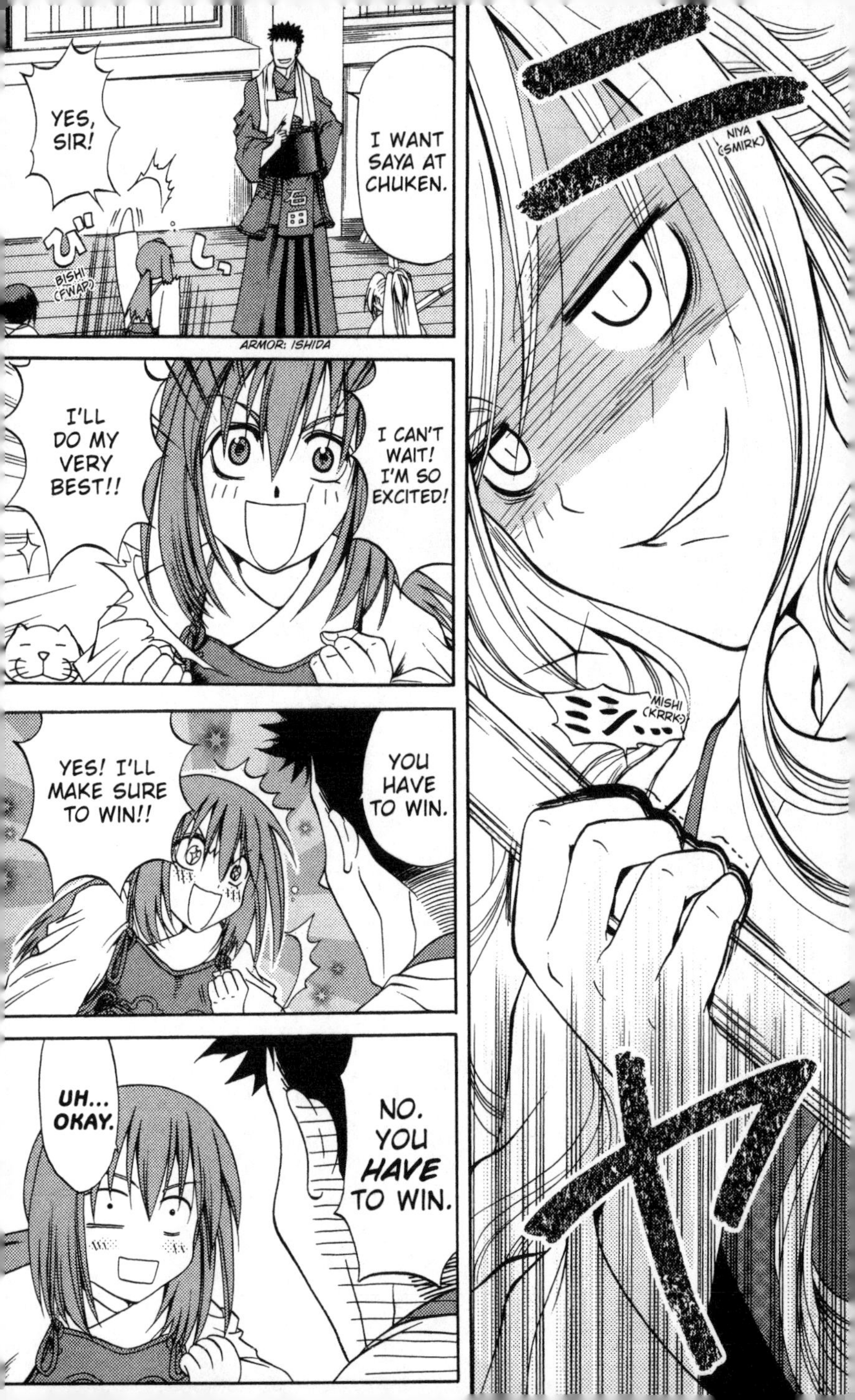
NIYA (SMIRK)
MISHI (KRRK)
I WANT SAYA AT CHUKEN.
YES, SIR!
BISHI (FWAP)
ARMOR: ISHIDA
I CAN'T WAIT! I'M SO EXCITED!
I'LL DO MY VERY BEST!!
YOU HAVE TO WIN.
YES! I'LL MAKE SURE TO WIN!!
NO. YOU *HAVE* TO WIN.
UH... OKAY.

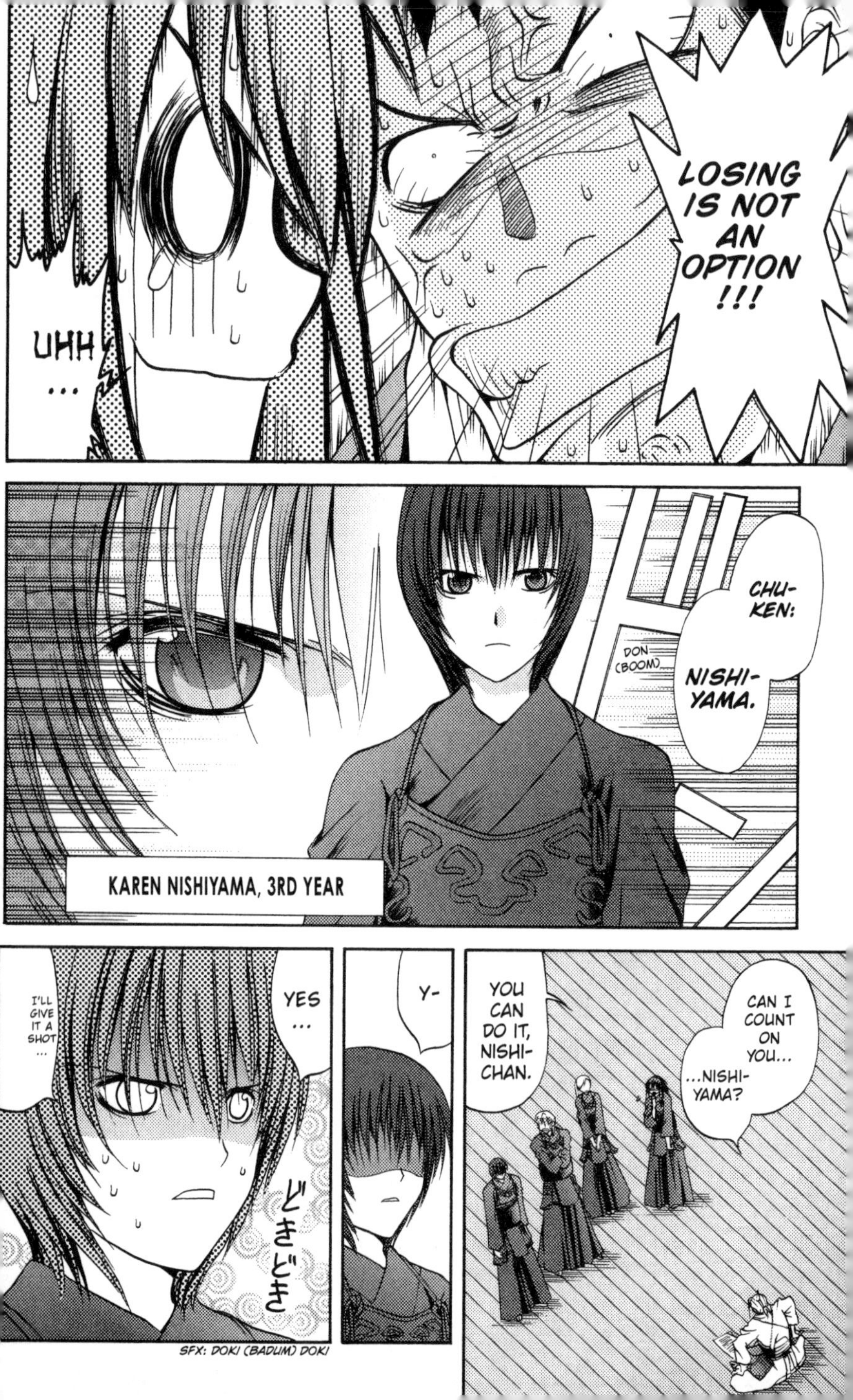
LOSING IS NOT AN OPTION!!!
UHH...
CHU-KEN:
NISHI-YAMA.
DON (BOOM)
KAREN NISHIYAMA, 3RD YEAR
CAN I COUNT ON YOU...
...NISHI-YAMA?
YOU CAN DO IT, NISHI-CHAN.
Y-
YES...
I'LL GIVE IT A SHOT...
どきどき
SFX: DOKI (BADUM) DOKI

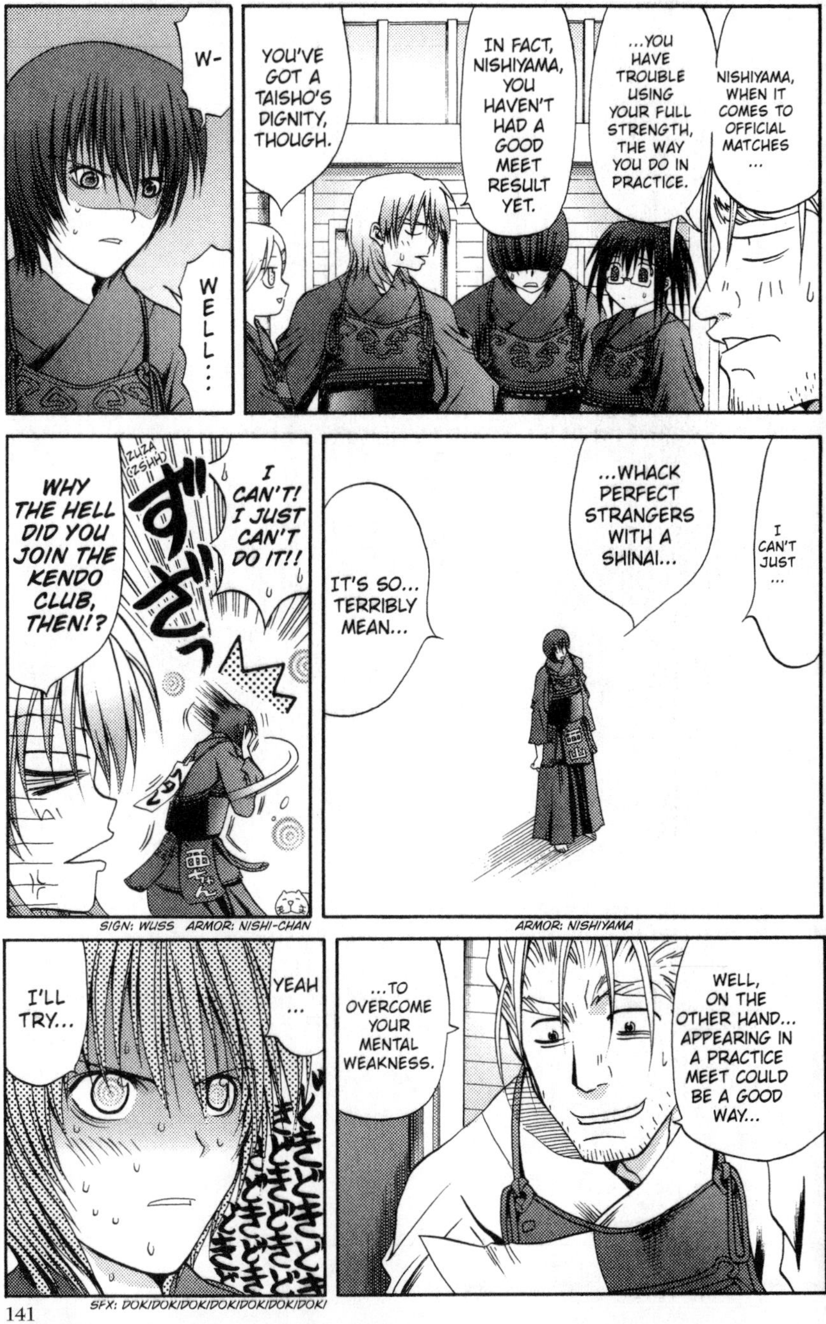
NISHIYAMA, WHEN IT COMES TO OFFICIAL MATCHES ...
...YOU HAVE TROUBLE USING YOUR FULL STRENGTH, THE WAY YOU DO IN PRACTICE.
IN FACT, NISHIYAMA, YOU HAVEN'T HAD A GOOD MEET RESULT YET.
YOU'VE GOT A TAISHO'S DIGNITY, THOUGH.
W-
WELL...
I CAN'T JUST ...
...WHACK PERFECT STRANGERS WITH A SHINAI...
IT'S SO... TERRIBLY MEAN...
ARMOR: NISHIYAMA
I CAN'T! I JUST CAN'T DO IT!!
ずざっ
ZUZA (ZSHHD)
WHY THE HELL DID YOU JOIN THE KENDO CLUB, THEN!?
SIGN: WUSS ARMOR: NISHI-CHAN
WELL, ON THE OTHER HAND... APPEARING IN A PRACTICE MEET COULD BE A GOOD WAY...
...TO OVERCOME YOUR MENTAL WEAKNESS.
YEAH ...
I'LL TRY...
SFX: DOKIDOKIDOKIDOKIDOKIDOKIDOKI

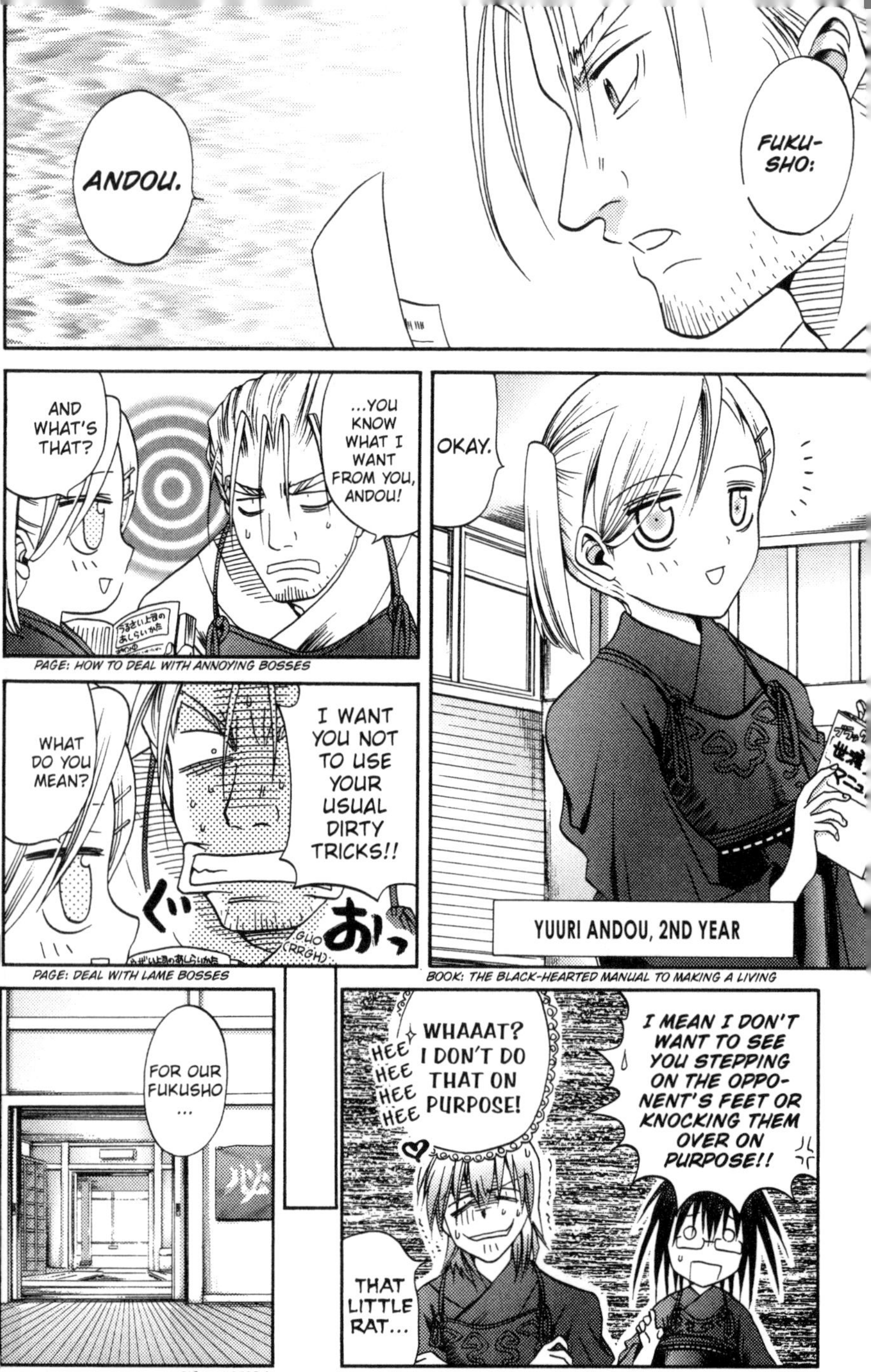
FUKU-SHO:
ANDOU.
OKAY.
YUURI ANDOU, 2ND YEAR
BOOK: THE BLACK-HEARTED MANUAL TO MAKING A LIVING
...YOU KNOW WHAT I WANT FROM YOU, ANDOU!
AND WHAT'S THAT?
PAGE: HOW TO DEAL WITH ANNOYING BOSSES
I WANT YOU NOT TO USE YOUR USUAL DIRTY TRICKS!!
WHAT DO YOU MEAN?
GUO (RRGH)
PAGE: DEAL WITH LAME BOSSES
I MEAN I DON'T WANT TO SEE YOU STEPPING ON THE OPPO-NENT'S FEET OR KNOCKING THEM OVER ON PURPOSE!!
WHAAAT? I DON'T DO THAT ON PURPOSE!
HEE HEE HEE HEE
THAT LITTLE RAT...
FOR OUR FUKUSHO ...
SIGN: VICTORY

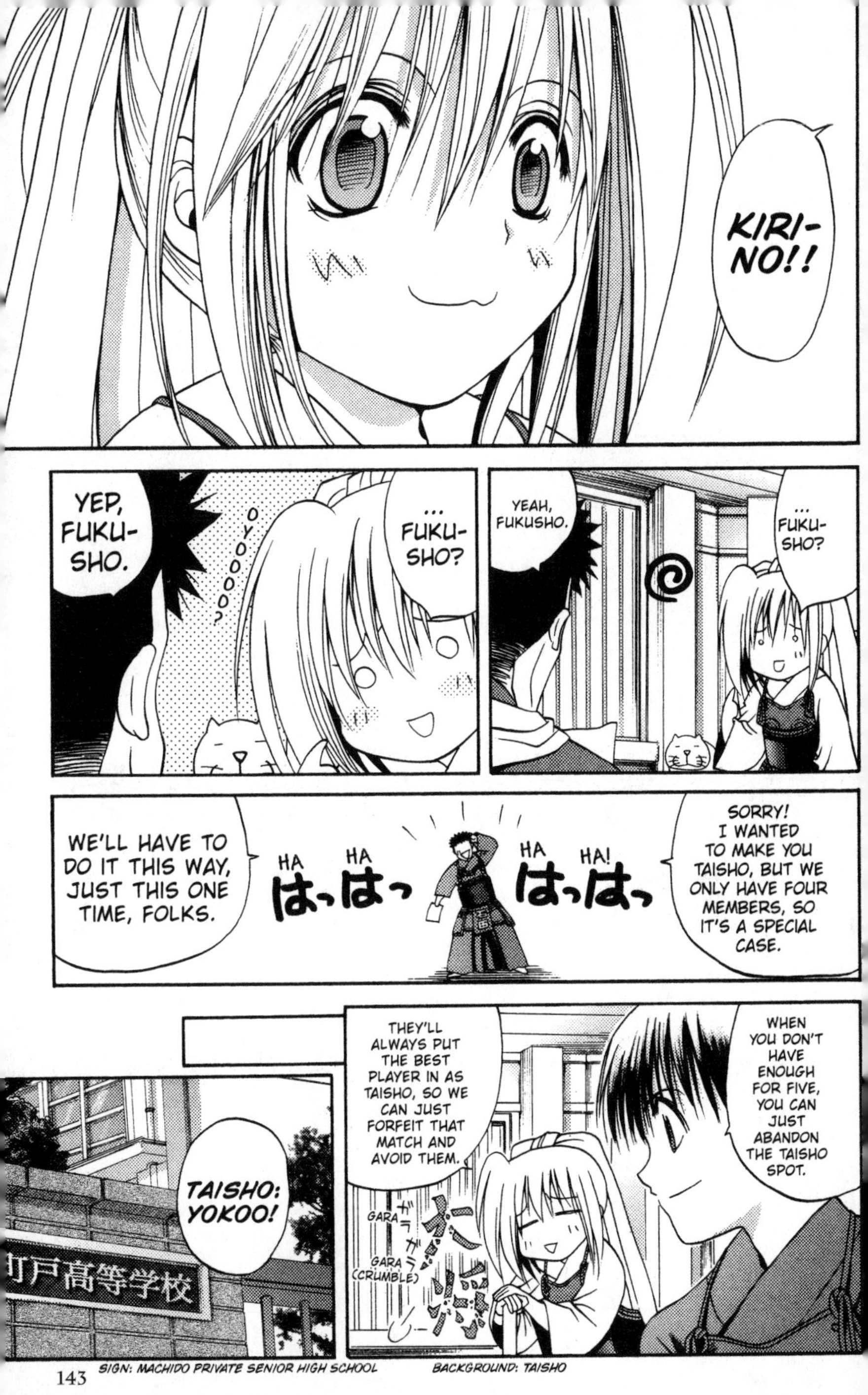
KIRI-NO!!
... FUKU-SHO?
YEAH, FUKUSHO.
... FUKU-SHO?
OYOOOOOO?
YEP, FUKU-SHO.
SORRY! I WANTED TO MAKE YOU TAISHO, BUT WE ONLY HAVE FOUR MEMBERS, SO IT'S A SPECIAL CASE.
HA HA!
はっはっ
HA HA
はっはっ
WE'LL HAVE TO DO IT THIS WAY, JUST THIS ONE TIME, FOLKS.
WHEN YOU DON'T HAVE ENOUGH FOR FIVE, YOU CAN JUST ABANDON THE TAISHO SPOT.
THEY'LL ALWAYS PUT THE BEST PLAYER IN AS TAISHO, SO WE CAN JUST FORFEIT THAT MATCH AND AVOID THEM.
GARA
GARA (CRUMBLE)
TAISHO: YOKOO!
戸高等学校

SIGN: MACHIDO PRIVATE SENIOR HIGH SCHOOL BACKGROUND: TAISHO

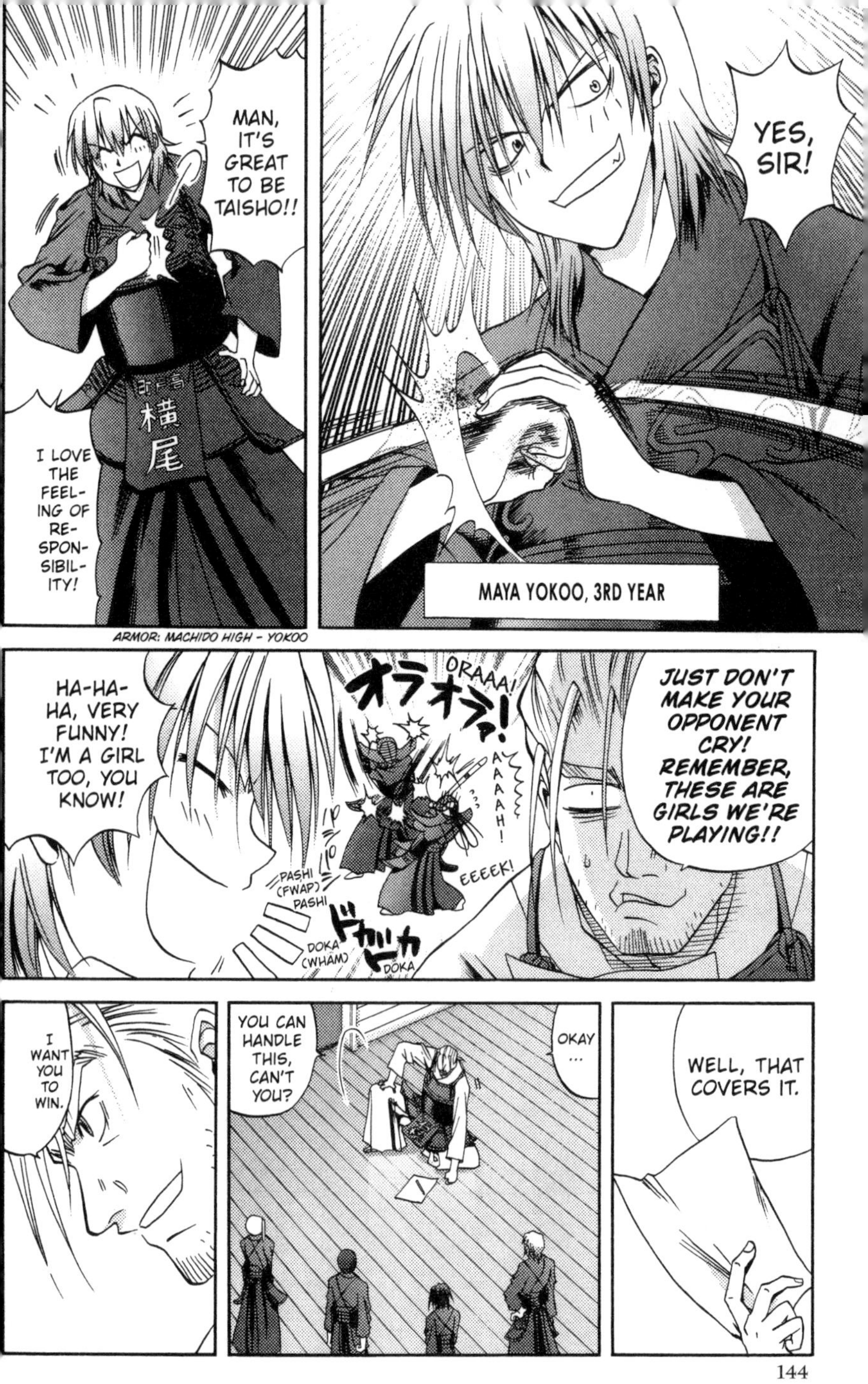
YES, SIR!
MAYA YOKOO, 3RD YEAR
MAN, IT'S GREAT TO BE TAISHO!!
I LOVE THE FEELING OF RESPONSIBILITY!
町戸高 横尾
ARMOR: MACHIDO HIGH - YOKOO
JUST DON'T MAKE YOUR OPPONENT CRY! REMEMBER, THESE ARE GIRLS WE'RE PLAYING!!
オラオラァ! ORAAA!
AAAAAH!
EEEEK!
HA-HA-HA, VERY FUNNY! I'M A GIRL TOO, YOU KNOW!
パシパシ PASHI (FWAP) PASHI
ドカドカ DOKA (WHAM) DOKA
WELL, THAT COVERS IT.
OKAY...
YOU CAN HANDLE THIS, CAN'T YOU?
I WANT YOU TO WIN.

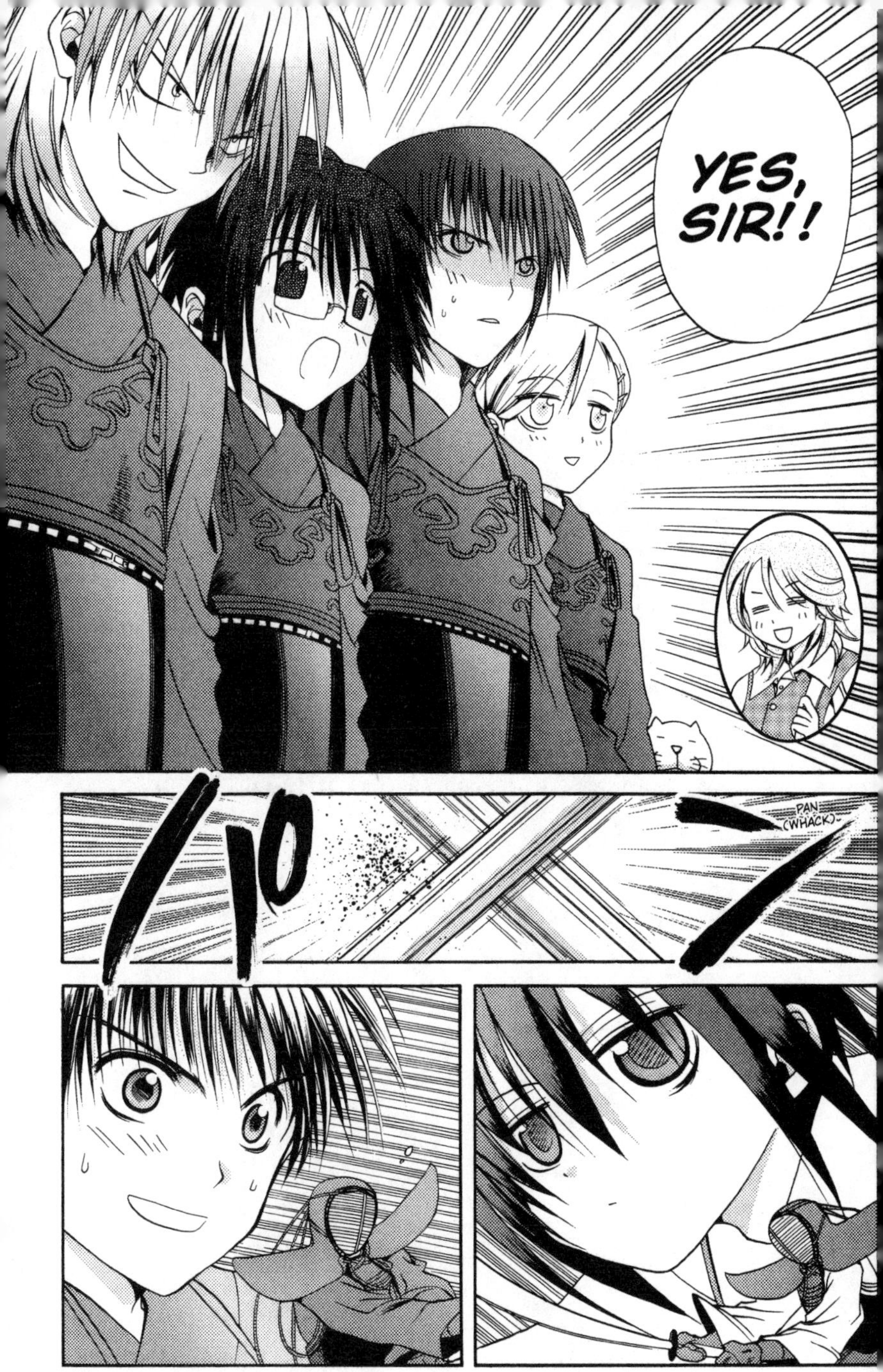
YES, SIR!!
PAN (WHACK)

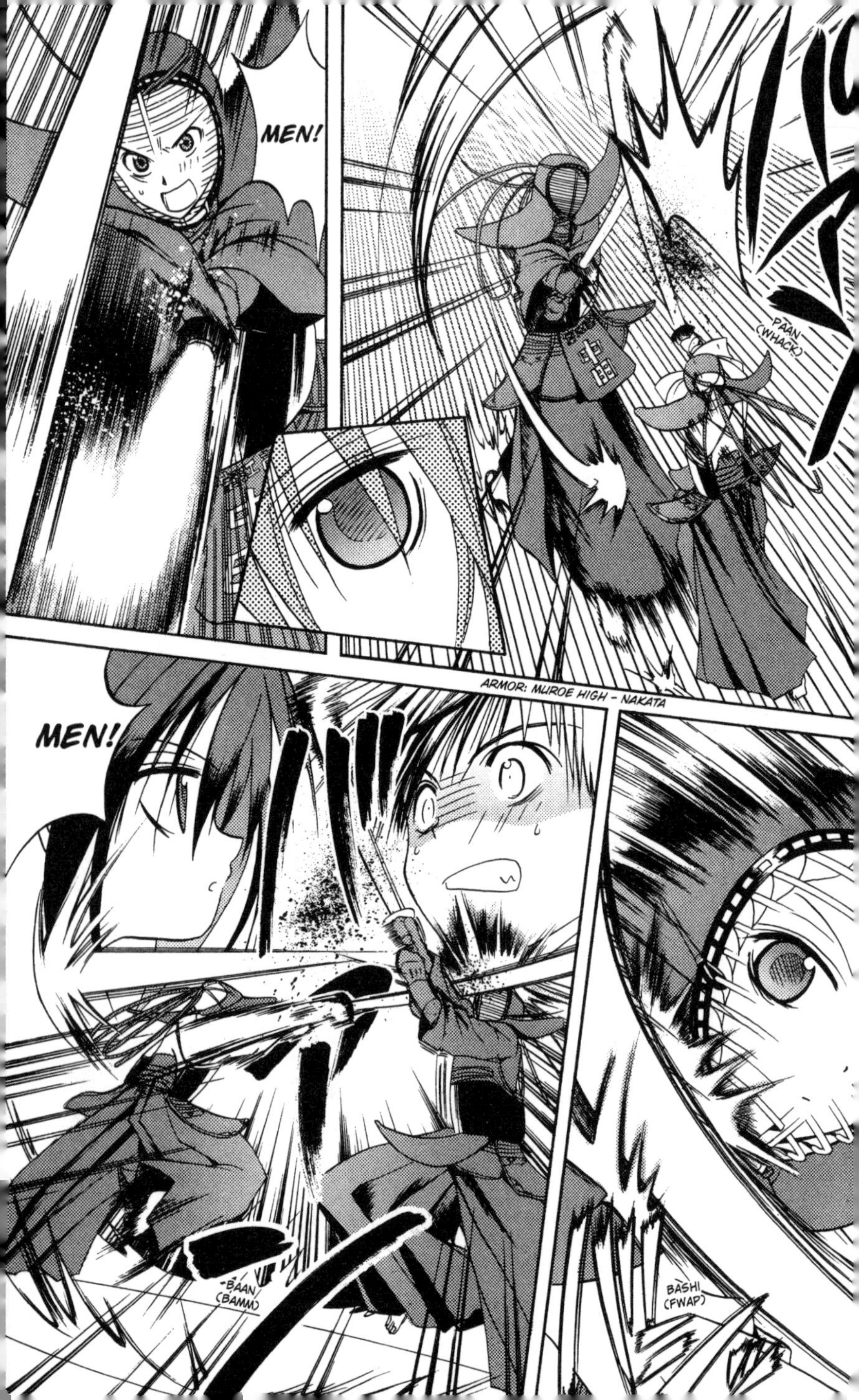
PAAN (WHACK)
ARMOR: MUROE HIGH - NAKATA
MEN!
BASHI (FWAP)
MEN!
BAAN (BAMM)

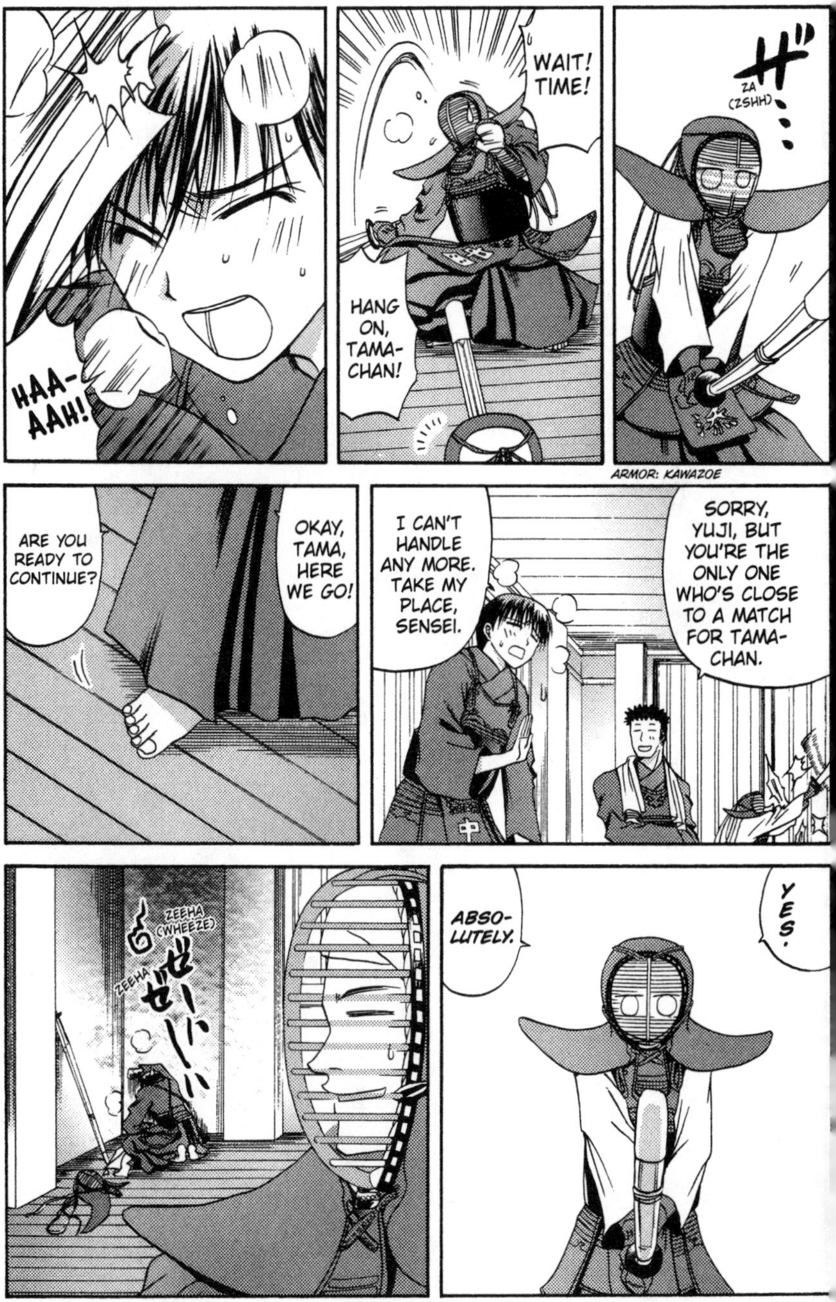
ZA (ZSHH)
ARMOR: KAWAZOE
WAIT! TIME!
HANG ON, TAMA-CHAN!
HAA-AAH!
SORRY, YUJI, BUT YOU'RE THE ONLY ONE WHO'S CLOSE TO A MATCH FOR TAMA-CHAN.
I CAN'T HANDLE ANY MORE. TAKE MY PLACE, SENSEI.
OKAY, TAMA, HERE WE GO!
ARE YOU READY TO CONTINUE?
YES.
ABSO-LUTELY.
ZEEHA (WHEEZE)
ZEEHA

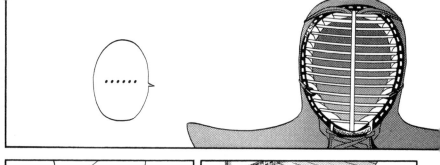

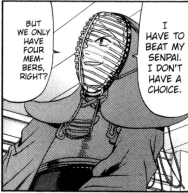

......
SAY, TAMA.
I HAVE TO BEAT MY SENPAI. I DON'T HAVE A CHOICE.
BUT WE ONLY HAVE FOUR MEM-BERS, RIGHT?
THAT'S A DIS-ADVAN-TAGE.
WE'RE IN BIG TROUBLE.
......
RIGHT...
...BUT, YOU SEE...
...WE'RE ACTUALLY NOT.
THIS TEAM...
...HAS ONE MORE MEM-BER...

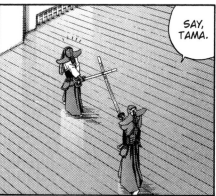

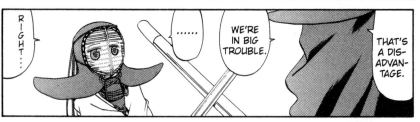

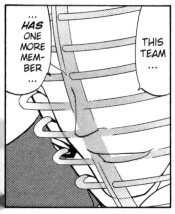

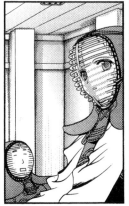

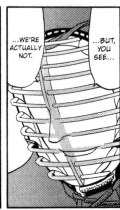

...A FIFTH MEMBER...

WE DO HAVE...

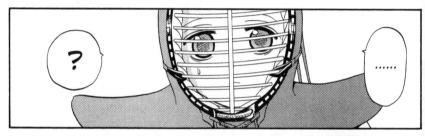

?

......

SHE'LL COME TO SAVE US, WHEN WE'RE IN TROUBLE...

BLADE BRAVER.

SHE'S AN AGENT OF GOOD, WHO FIGHTS TO SAVE OTHERS.

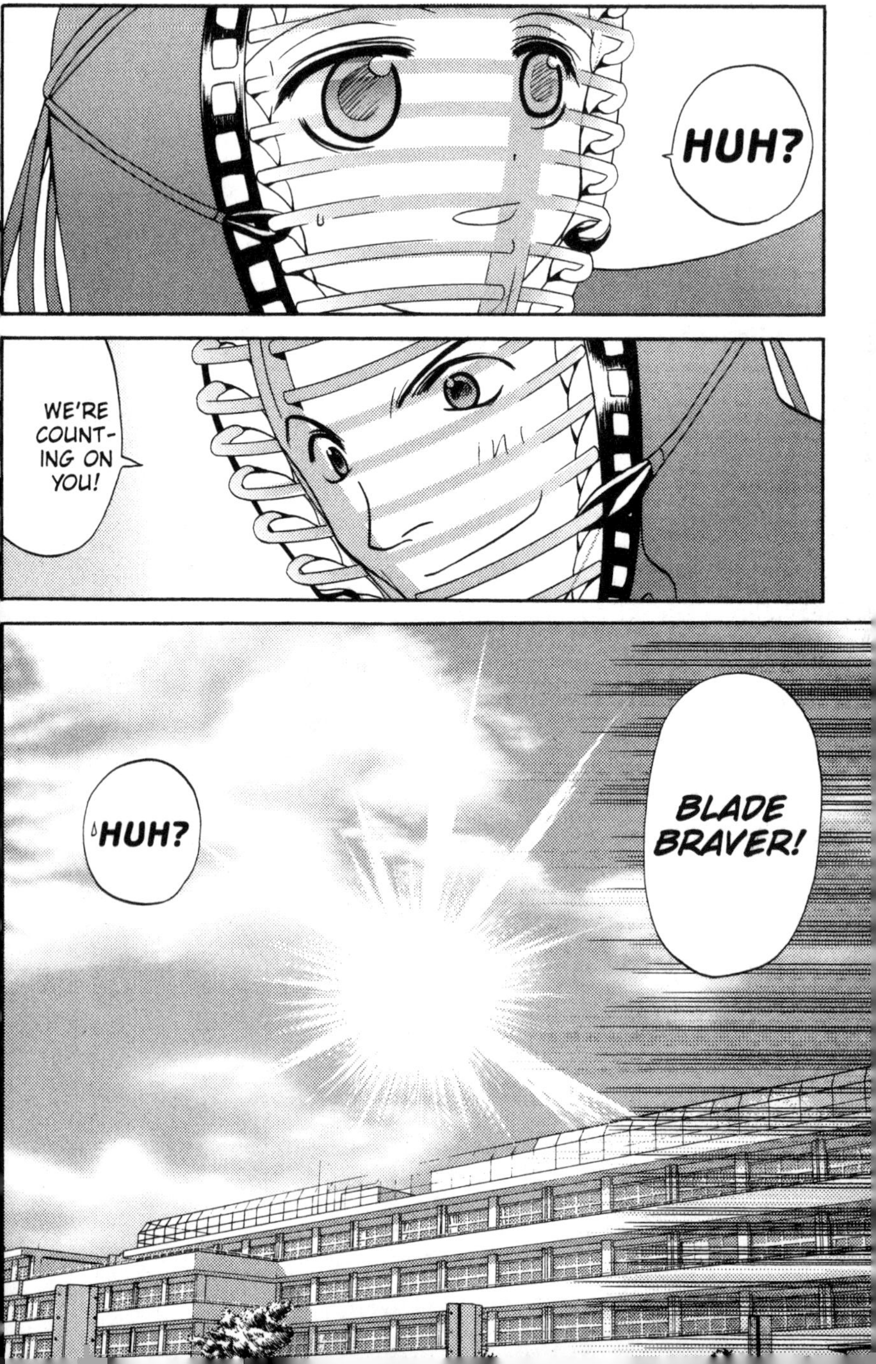
HUH?
WE'RE COUNTING ON YOU!
BLADE BRAVER!
HUH?

BAMBOO BLADE

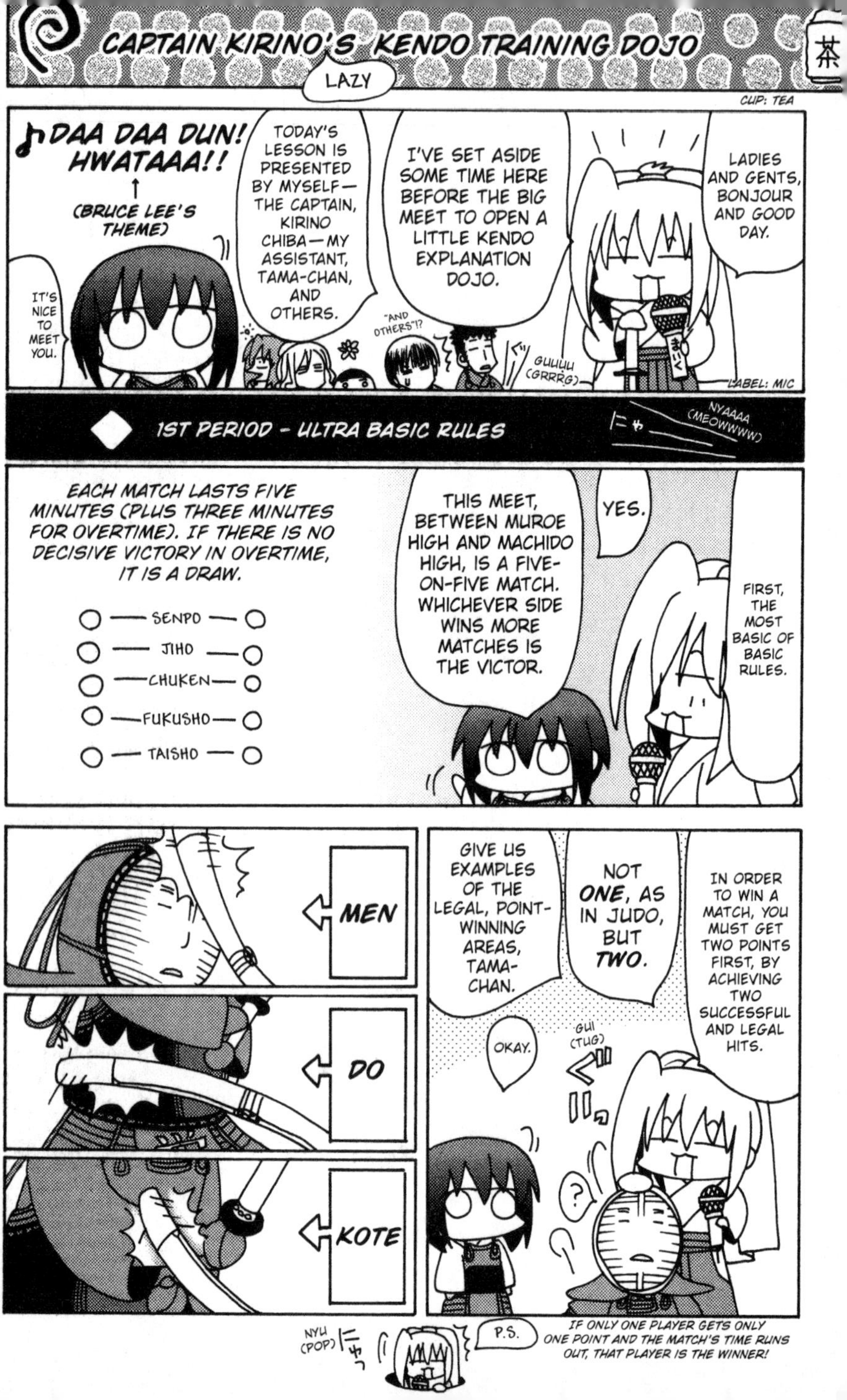
CAPTAIN KIRINO'S KENDO TRAINING DOJO
LAZY
CUP: TEA
LADIES AND GENTS, BONJOUR AND GOOD DAY.
I'VE SET ASIDE SOME TIME HERE BEFORE THE BIG MEET TO OPEN A LITTLE KENDO EXPLANATION DOJO.
TODAY'S LESSON IS PRESENTED BY MYSELF—THE CAPTAIN, KIRINO CHIBA—MY ASSISTANT, TAMA-CHAN, AND OTHERS.
♪DAA DAA DUN! HWATAAA!!
(BRUCE LEE'S THEME)
LABEL: MIC
GUUUU (GRRRG)
"AND OTHERS"!?
IT'S NICE TO MEET YOU.
1ST PERIOD - ULTRA BASIC RULES
NYAAAA (MEOWWWW)
FIRST, THE MOST BASIC OF BASIC RULES.
YES.
THIS MEET, BETWEEN MUROE HIGH AND MACHIDO HIGH, IS A FIVE-ON-FIVE MATCH. WHICHEVER SIDE WINS MORE MATCHES IS THE VICTOR.
EACH MATCH LASTS FIVE MINUTES (PLUS THREE MINUTES FOR OVERTIME). IF THERE IS NO DECISIVE VICTORY IN OVERTIME, IT IS A DRAW.
SENPO
JIHO
CHUKEN
FUKUSHO
TAISHO
IN ORDER TO WIN A MATCH, YOU MUST GET TWO POINTS FIRST, BY ACHIEVING TWO SUCCESSFUL AND LEGAL HITS.
NOT ONE, AS IN JUDO, BUT TWO.
GIVE US EXAMPLES OF THE LEGAL, POINT-WINNING AREAS, TAMA-CHAN.
GUI (TUG)
OKAY.
MEN
DO
KOTE
P.S.
IF ONLY ONE PLAYER GETS ONLY ONE POINT AND THE MATCH'S TIME RUNS OUT, THAT PLAYER IS THE WINNER!
NYU (POP)

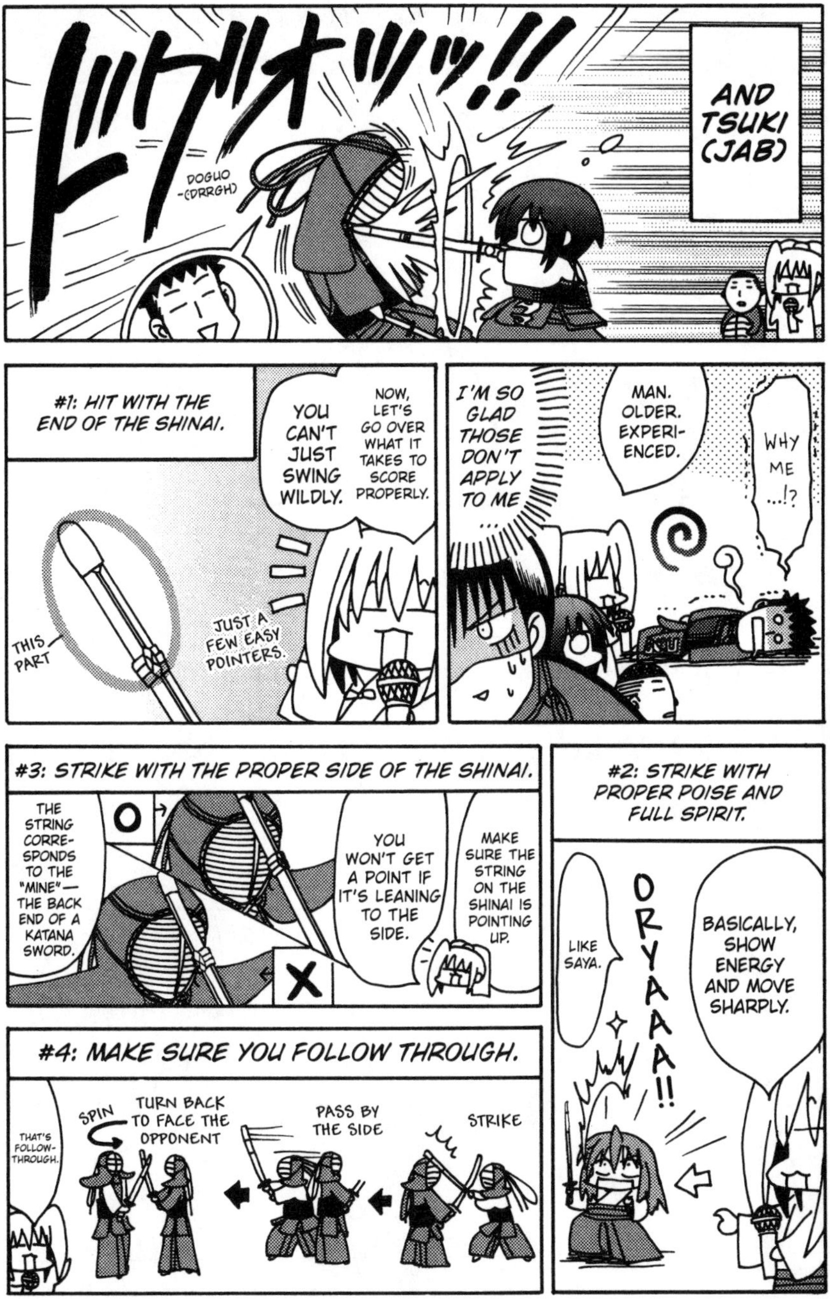
AND TSUKI (JAB)
ドゥゴオッッッ!!
DOGUO -(DRRGH)
WHY ME ...!?
MAN. OLDER. EXPERI-ENCED.
I'M SO GLAD THOSE DON'T APPLY TO ME ...
NOW, LET'S GO OVER WHAT IT TAKES TO SCORE PROPERLY.
YOU CAN'T JUST SWING WILDLY.
#1: HIT WITH THE END OF THE SHINAI.
JUST A FEW EASY POINTERS.
THIS PART
#2: STRIKE WITH PROPER POISE AND FULL SPIRIT.
BASICALLY, SHOW ENERGY AND MOVE SHARPLY.
ORYAAA!!
LIKE SAYA.
#3: STRIKE WITH THE PROPER SIDE OF THE SHINAI.
MAKE SURE THE STRING ON THE SHINAI IS POINTING UP.
YOU WON'T GET A POINT IF IT'S LEANING TO THE SIDE.
O
X
THE STRING CORRE-SPONDS TO THE "MINE"—THE BACK END OF A KATANA SWORD.
#4: MAKE SURE YOU FOLLOW THROUGH.
STRIKE
PASS BY THE SIDE
TURN BACK TO FACE THE OPPONENT
SPIN
THAT'S FOLLOW-THROUGH.

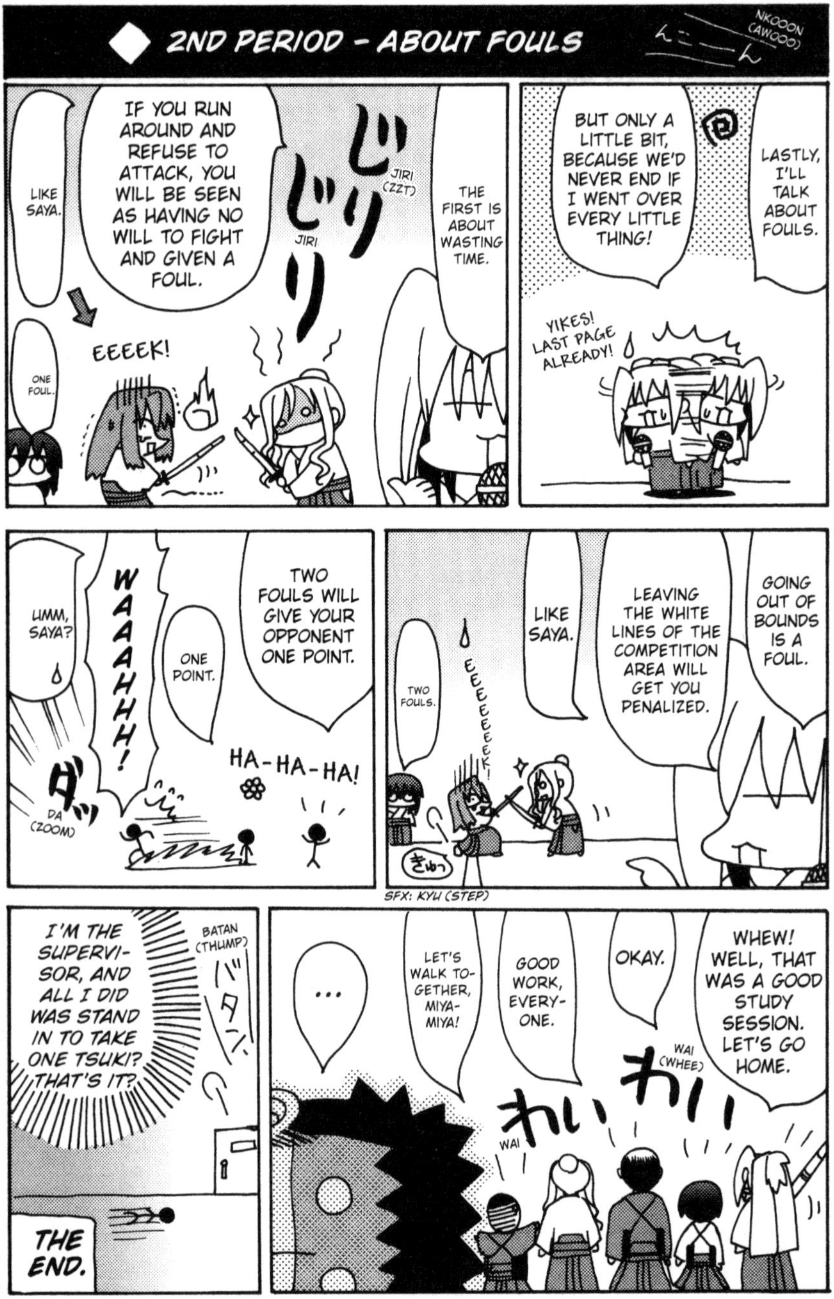
2ND PERIOD - ABOUT FOULS
NKOOON (AWOOO)
LASTLY, I'LL TALK ABOUT FOULS.
BUT ONLY A LITTLE BIT, BECAUSE WE'D NEVER END IF I WENT OVER EVERY LITTLE THING!
YIKES! LAST PAGE ALREADY!
THE FIRST IS ABOUT WASTING TIME.
JIRI (ZZT)
JIRI
IF YOU RUN AROUND AND REFUSE TO ATTACK, YOU WILL BE SEEN AS HAVING NO WILL TO FIGHT AND GIVEN A FOUL.
LIKE SAYA.
EEEEK!
ONE FOUL.
GOING OUT OF BOUNDS IS A FOUL.
LEAVING THE WHITE LINES OF THE COMPETITION AREA WILL GET YOU PENALIZED.
LIKE SAYA.
EEEEEEEEK!
TWO FOULS.
SFX: KYU (STEP)
TWO FOULS WILL GIVE YOUR OPPONENT ONE POINT.
ONE POINT.
HA-HA-HA!
WAAAAHHH!
UMM, SAYA?
DA (ZOOM)
WHEW! WELL, THAT WAS A GOOD STUDY SESSION. LET'S GO HOME.
OKAY.
GOOD WORK, EVERY-ONE.
LET'S WALK TO-GETHER, MIYA-MIYA!
...
WAI (WHEE)
WAI
I'M THE SUPERVI-SOR, AND ALL I DID WAS STAND IN TO TAKE ONE TSUKI? THAT'S IT?
BATAN (THUMP)
THE END.

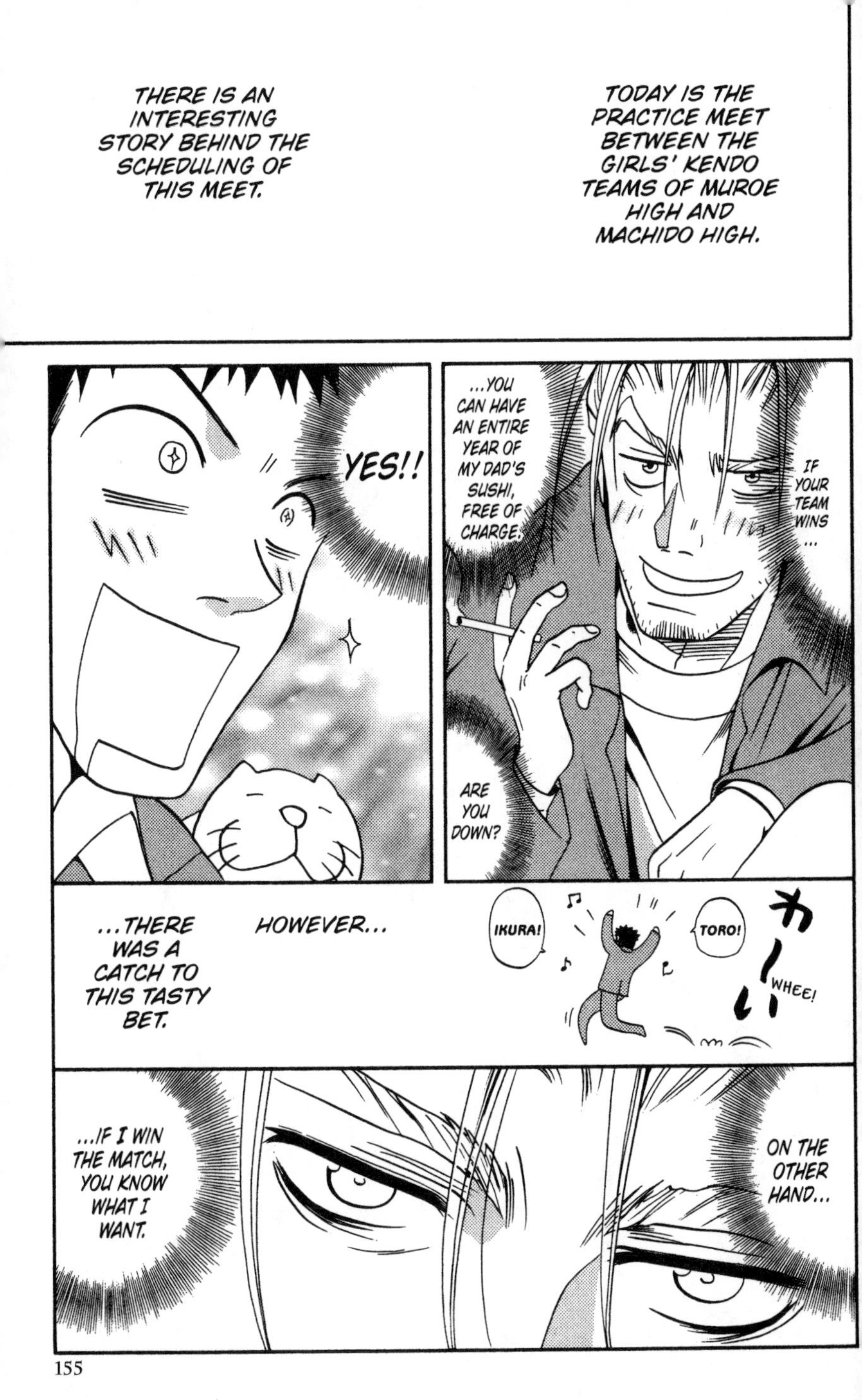
TODAY IS THE PRACTICE MEET BETWEEN THE GIRLS' KENDO TEAMS OF MUROE HIGH AND MACHIDO HIGH.
THERE IS AN INTERESTING STORY BEHIND THE SCHEDULING OF THIS MEET.
IF YOUR TEAM WINS...
...YOU CAN HAVE AN ENTIRE YEAR OF MY DAD'S SUSHI, FREE OF CHARGE.
ARE YOU DOWN?
YES!!
わーい
WHEE!
TORO!
IKURA!
HOWEVER...
...THERE WAS A CATCH TO THIS TASTY BET.
ON THE OTHER HAND...
...IF I WIN THE MATCH, YOU KNOW WHAT I WANT.

CHAPTER 18
MUROE HIGH AND MACHIDO HIGH

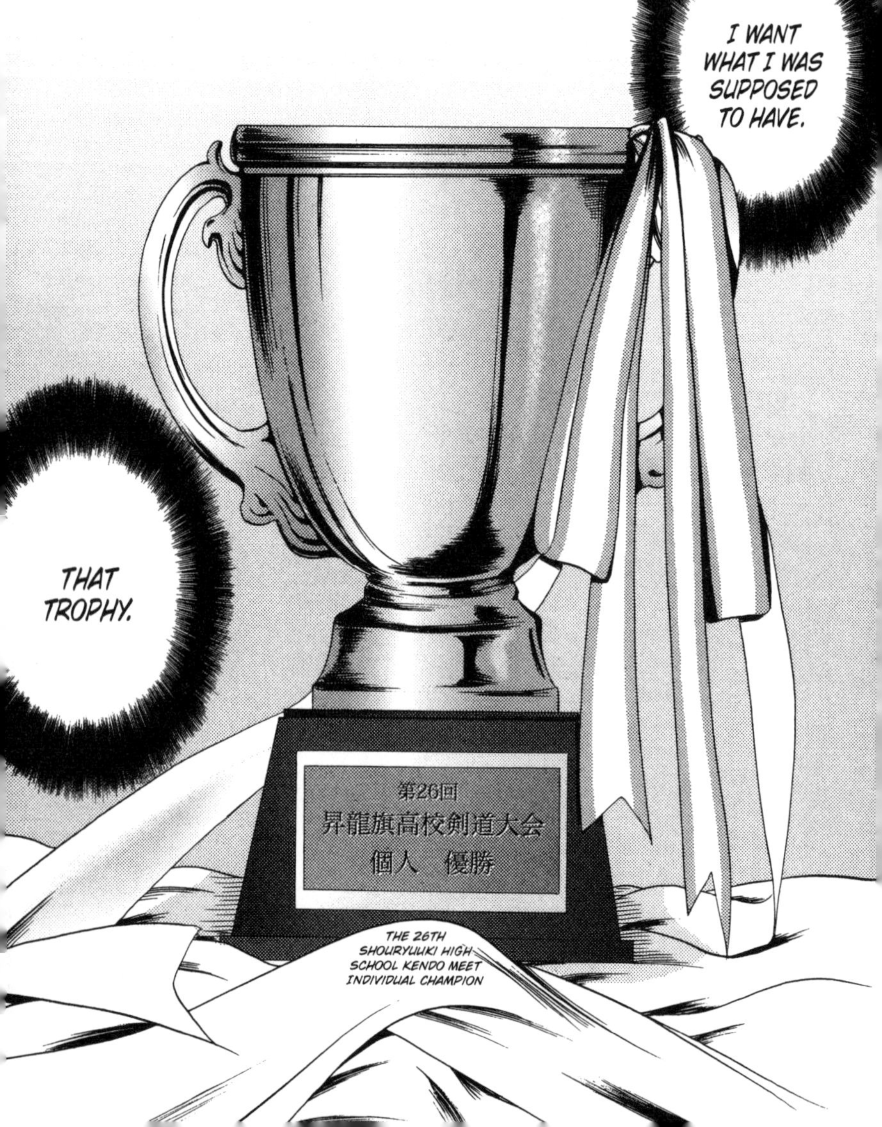
I WANT WHAT I WAS SUPPOSED TO HAVE.
THAT TROPHY.
第26回
昇龍旗高校剣道大会
個人　優勝
THE 26TH SHOURYUUKI HIGH SCHOOL KENDO MEET INDIVIDUAL CHAMPION

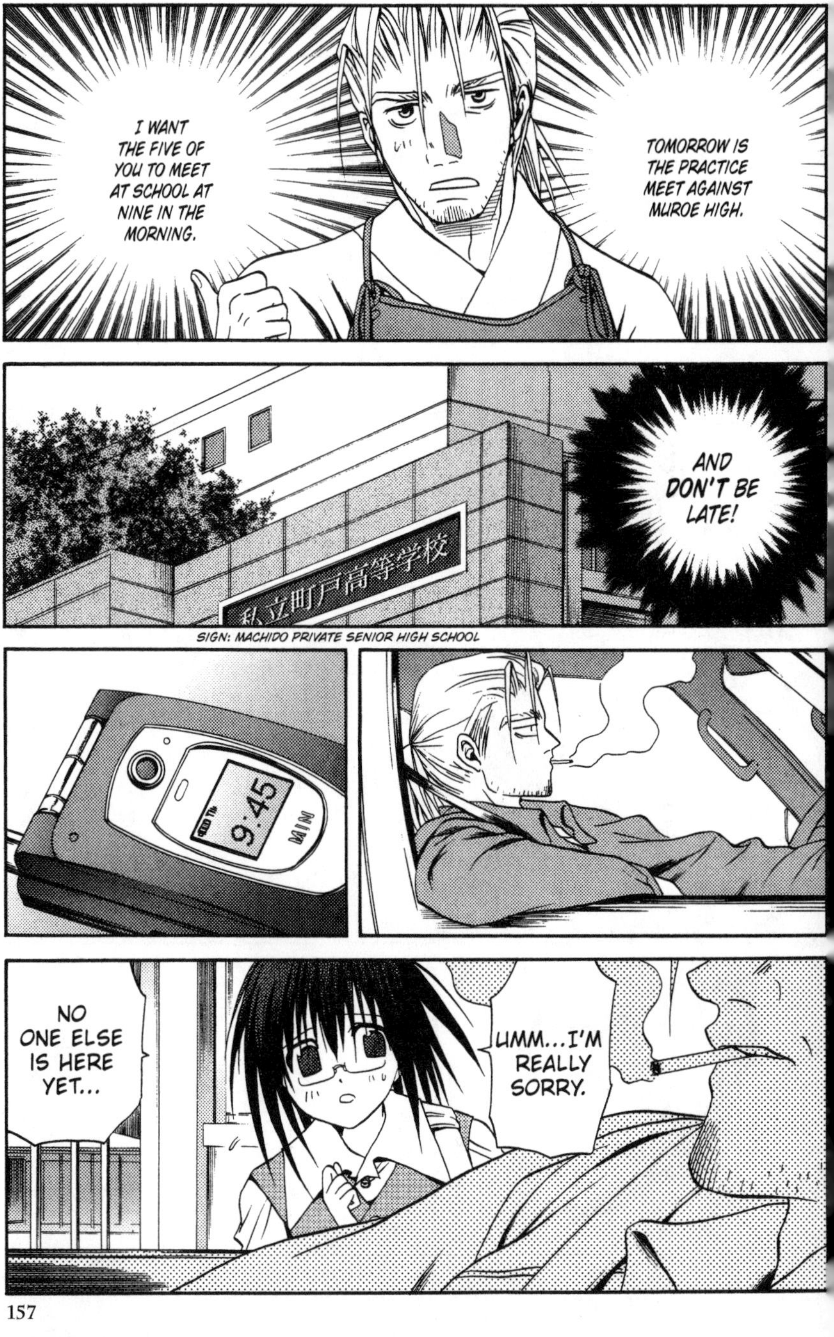
TOMORROW IS THE PRACTICE MEET AGAINST MUROE HIGH.
I WANT THE FIVE OF YOU TO MEET AT SCHOOL AT NINE IN THE MORNING.
AND DON'T BE LATE!
私立町戸高等学校
SIGN: MACHIDO PRIVATE SENIOR HIGH SCHOOL
9:45
MIN
UMM...I'M REALLY SORRY.
NO ONE ELSE IS HERE YET...

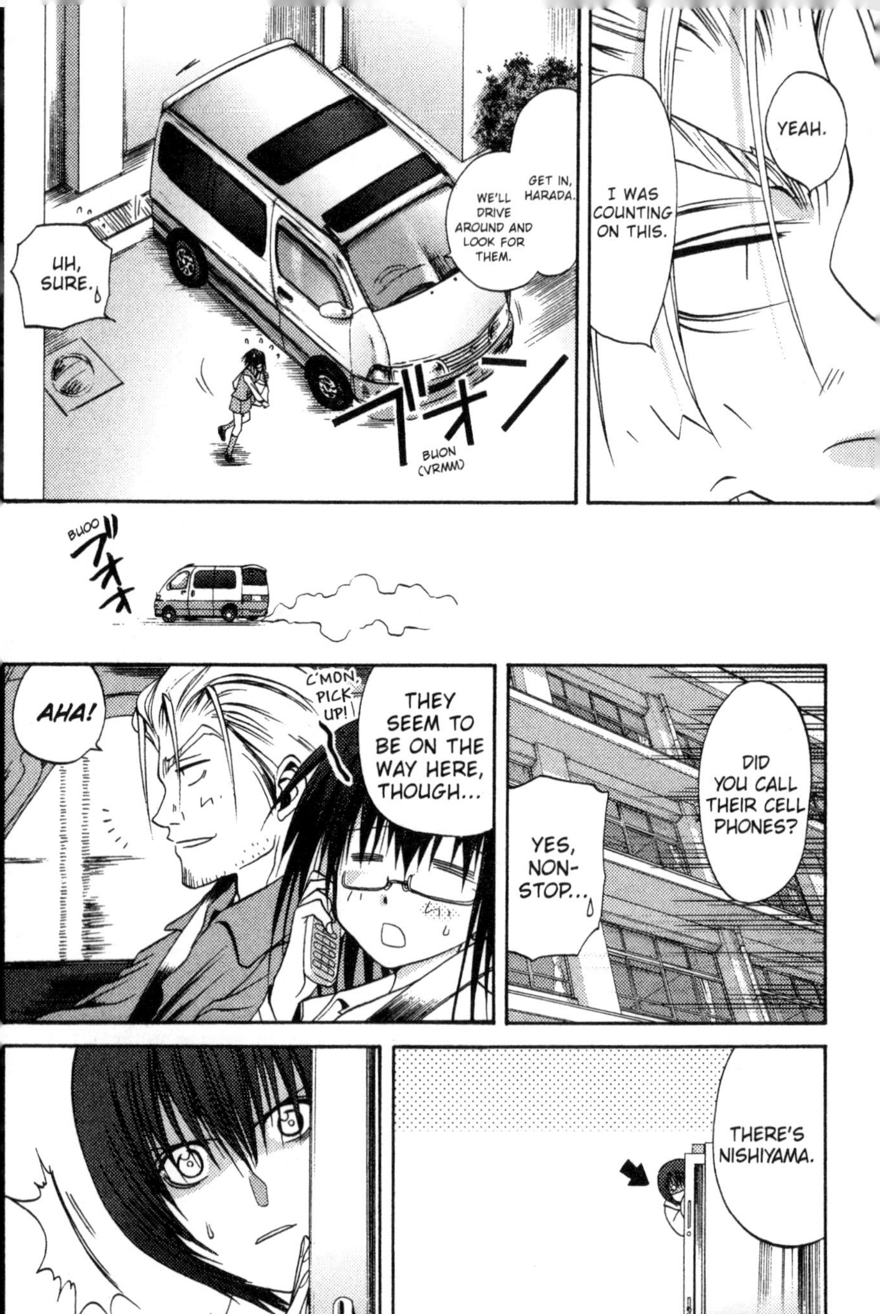
YEAH.
I WAS COUNTING ON THIS.
GET IN, HARADA.
WE'LL DRIVE AROUND AND LOOK FOR THEM.
UH, SURE.
BUON (VRMM)
BUOO
DID YOU CALL THEIR CELL PHONES?
YES, NON-STOP...
THEY SEEM TO BE ON THE WAY HERE, THOUGH...
C'MON, PICK UP!
AHA!
THERE'S NISHIYAMA.

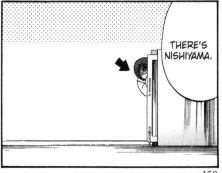

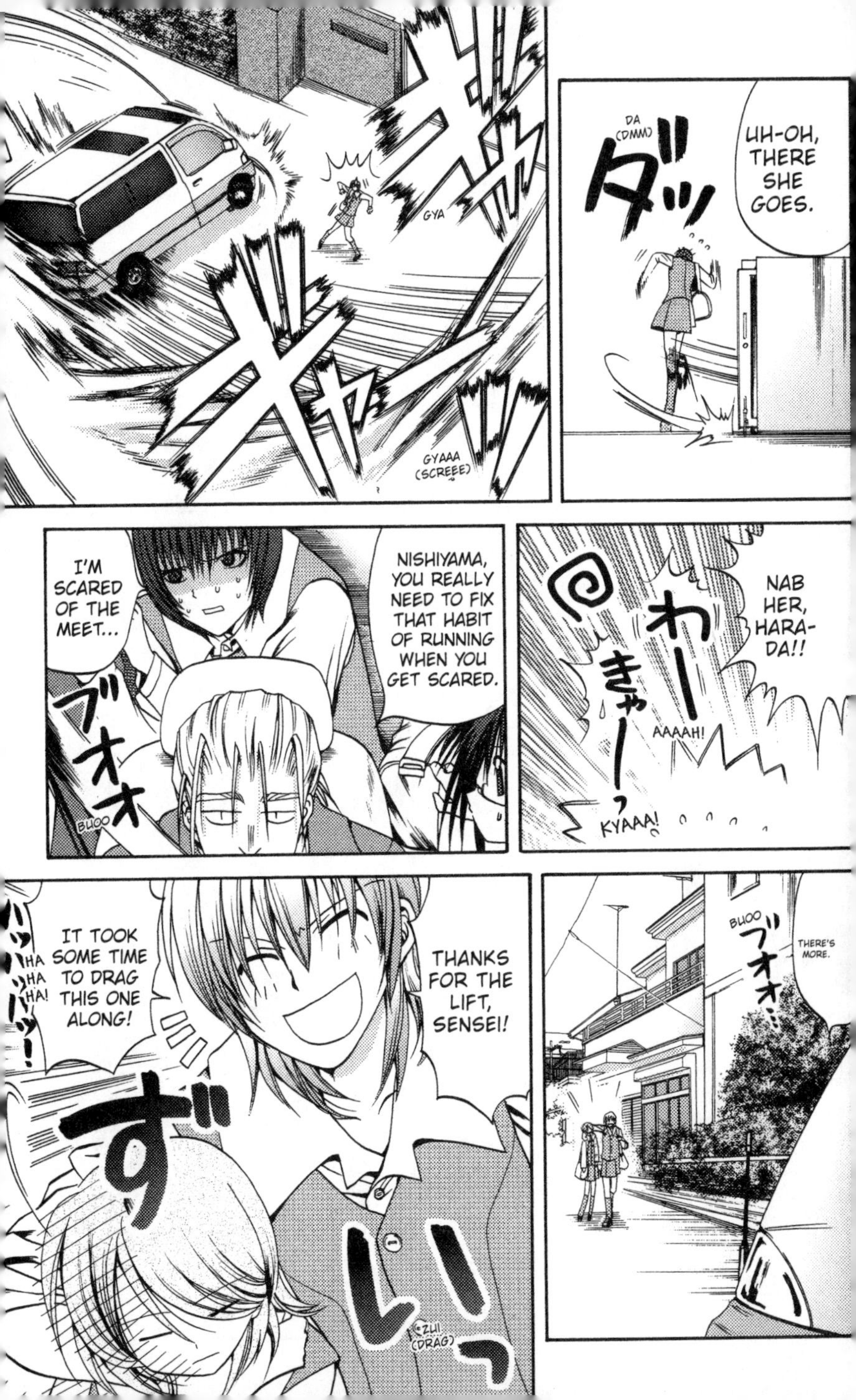
UH-OH, THERE SHE GOES.
DA (DMM)
GYA
GYAAA (SCREEE)
NAB HER, HARADA!!
AAAAH!
KYAAA!
NISHIYAMA, YOU REALLY NEED TO FIX THAT HABIT OF RUNNING WHEN YOU GET SCARED.
I'M SCARED OF THE MEET...
BUOO
THERE'S MORE.
BUOO
THANKS FOR THE LIFT, SENSEI!
IT TOOK SOME TIME TO DRAG THIS ONE ALONG!
HA HA HA!
ZUI (DRAG)

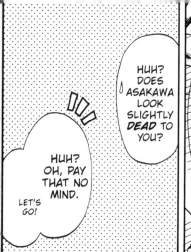

HUH? DOES ASAKAWA LOOK SLIGHTLY DEAD TO YOU?
HUH? OH, PAY THAT NO MIND.
LET'S GO!
BUOOOO (VRMMM)
ブオォォォ
ANDOU'S THE ONLY ONE LEFT NOW.
ANDOU-SAN'S THE ONLY PERSON I COULDN'T REACH.
I GUESS WE'LL HAVE TO STOP AT HER HOUSE, THEN.
DOES ANYONE KNOW THE WAY?
安藤

SIGN: ANDOU

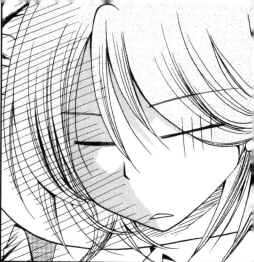

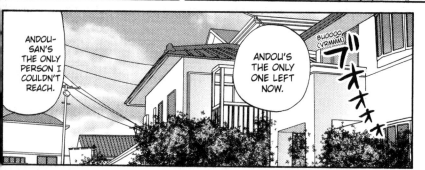

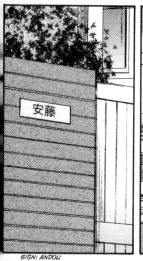

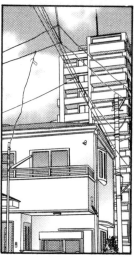

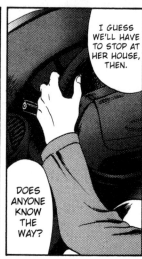

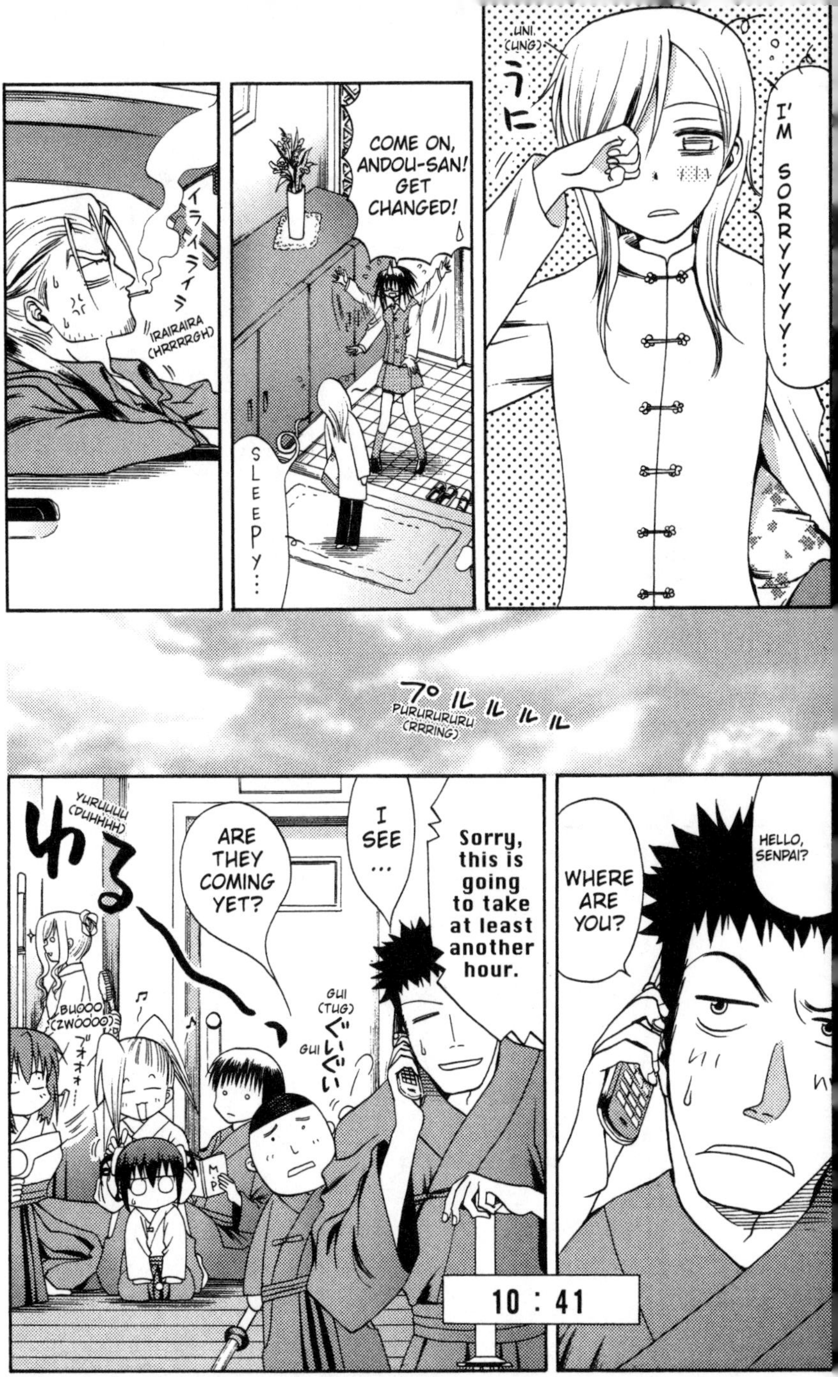
UNI (UNG)
うに
I'M SORRYYYYYY...
COME ON, ANDOU-SAN! GET CHANGED!
SLEEPY...
イライライラ
IRAIRAIRA (HRRRRGH)
プルルルルル
PURURURURU (RRRING)
HELLO, SENPAI?
WHERE ARE YOU?
Sorry, this is going to take at least another hour.
I SEE ...
ARE THEY COMING YET?
ゆる～～～
YURUUUU (DUHHHH)
ぐいぐい
GUI (TUG)
GUI
ブオオォ…
BUOOO (ZWOOOO)
10 : 41

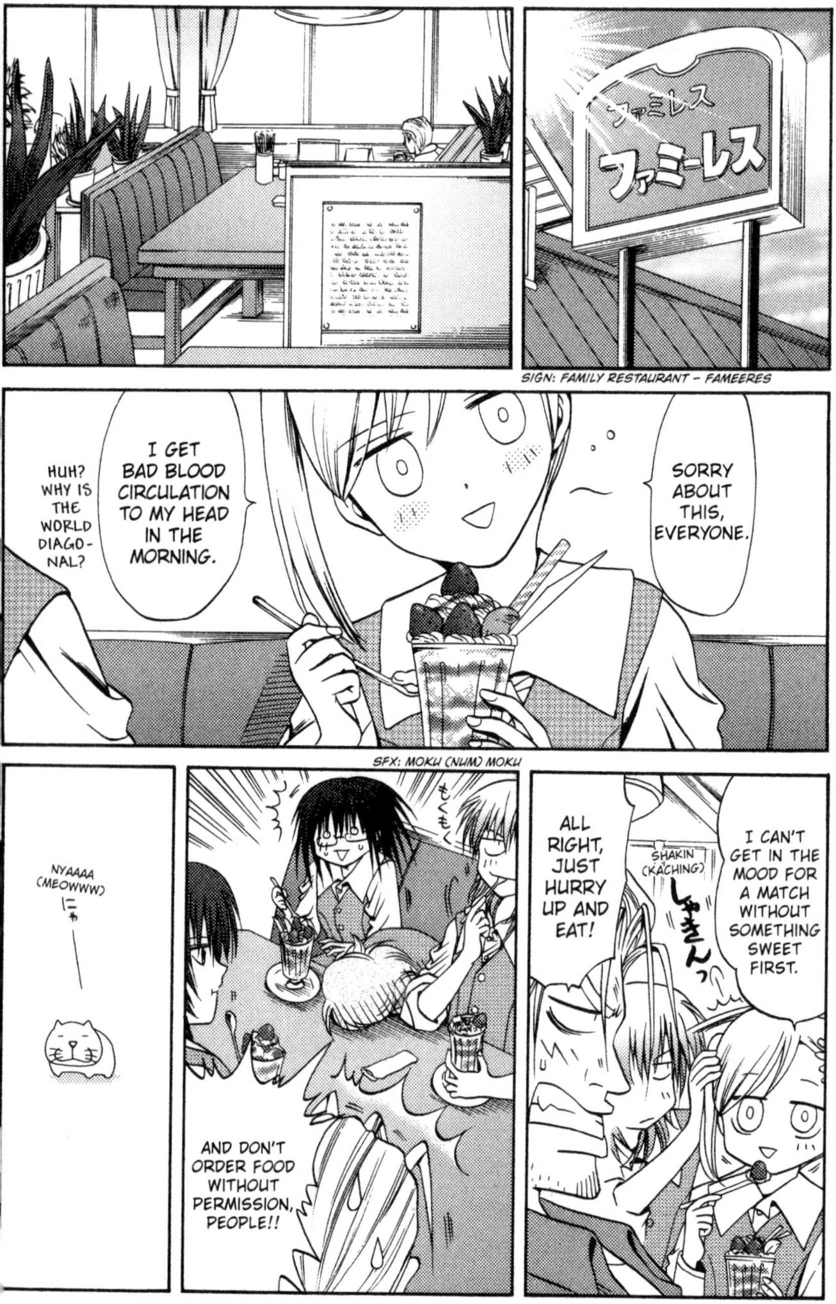
ファミレス
ファミーレス
SORRY ABOUT THIS, EVERYONE.
I GET BAD BLOOD CIRCULATION TO MY HEAD IN THE MORNING.
HUH? WHY IS THE WORLD DIAGONAL?
I CAN'T GET IN THE MOOD FOR A MATCH WITHOUT SOMETHING SWEET FIRST.
SHAKIN (KACHING)
しゃきんっ
ALL RIGHT, JUST HURRY UP AND EAT!
もくもく
AND DON'T ORDER FOOD WITHOUT PERMISSION, PEOPLE!!
NYAAAA (MEOWWW)
にゃー
SIGN: FAMILY RESTAURANT - FAMEERES

SFX: MOKU (NUM) MOKU

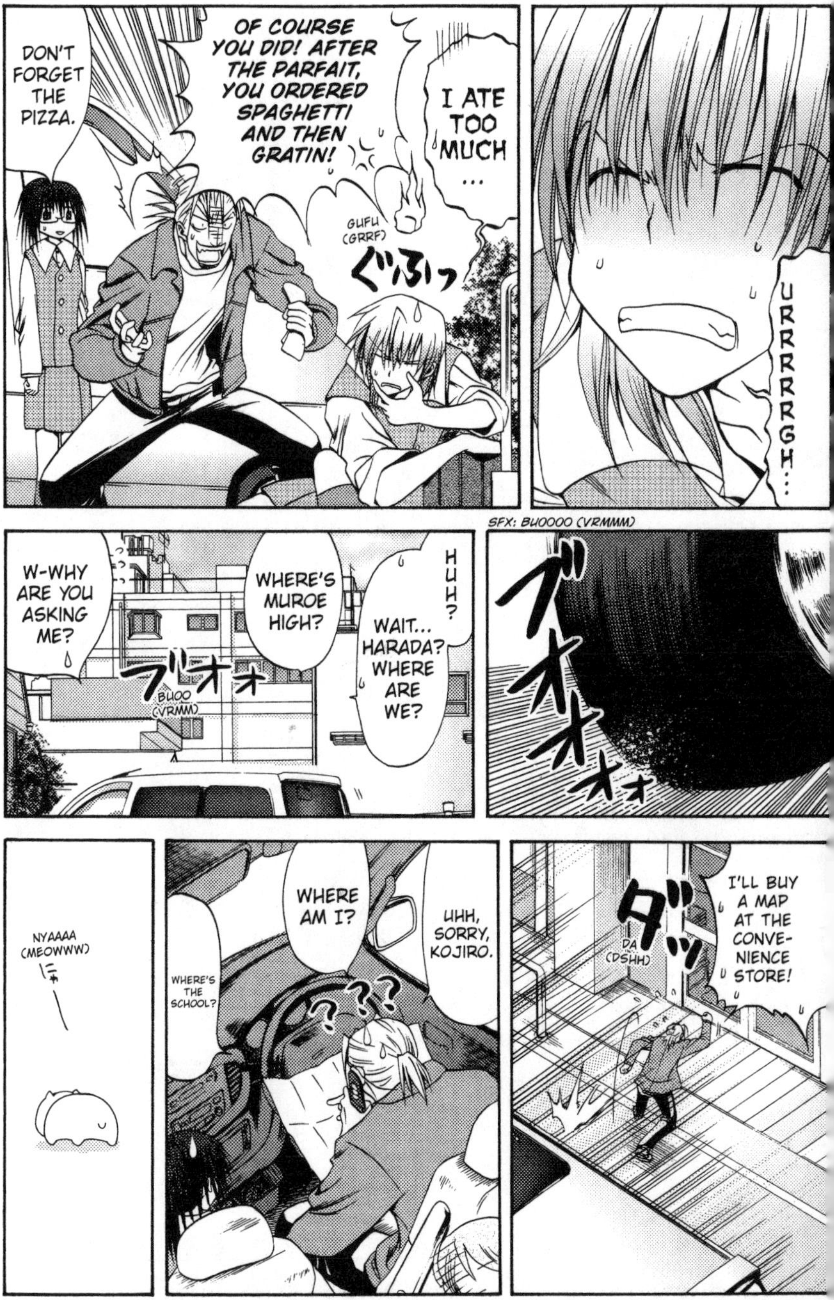
URRRRRGH...
I ATE TOO MUCH...
OF COURSE YOU DID! AFTER THE PARFAIT, YOU ORDERED SPAGHETTI AND THEN GRATIN!
GUFU (GRRF)
ぐふっ
DON'T FORGET THE PIZZA.
SFX: BUOOOO (VRMMM)
ブオオオォ
HUH?
WAIT... HARADA? WHERE ARE WE?
WHERE'S MUROE HIGH?
ブオオ
BUOO (VRMM)
W-WHY ARE YOU ASKING ME?
I'LL BUY A MAP AT THE CONVE-NIENCE STORE!
ダッ
DA (DSHH)
UHH, SORRY, KOJIRO.
WHERE AM I?
WHERE'S THE SCHOOL?
NYAAAA (MEOWWW)
にゃー

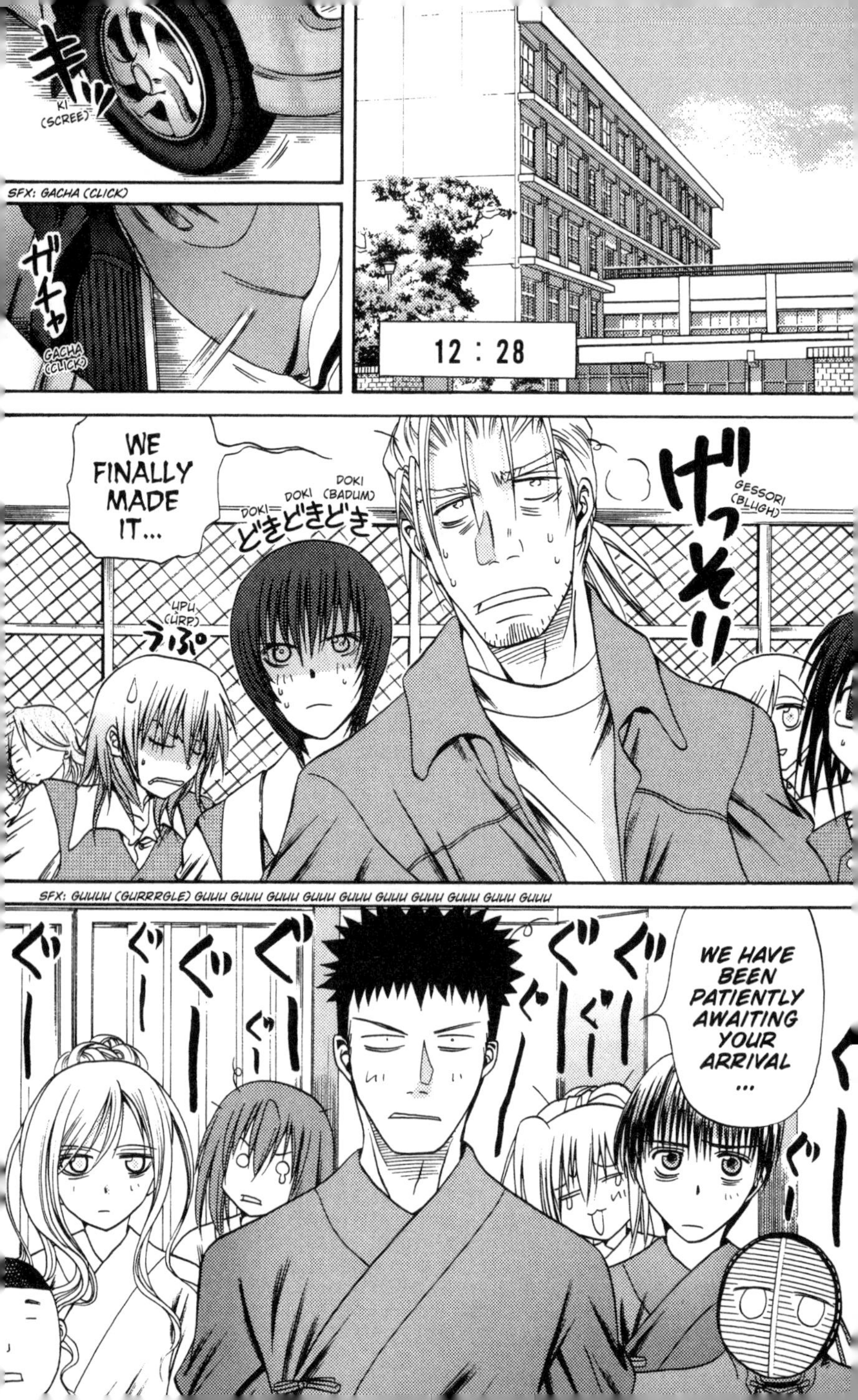
12 : 28
キッ
KI (SCREE)
SFX: GACHA (CLICK)
ガチャ
GACHA (CLICK)
げっそり
GESSORI (BLUGH)
WE FINALLY MADE IT...
DOKI DOKI DOKI (BADUM)
どきどきどき
UPU (URP)
うぷ
SFX: GUUUU (GURRRGLE) GUUU GUUU GUUU GUUU GUUU GUUU GUUU GUUU GUUU GUUU
WE HAVE BEEN PATIENTLY AWAITING YOUR ARRIVAL ...

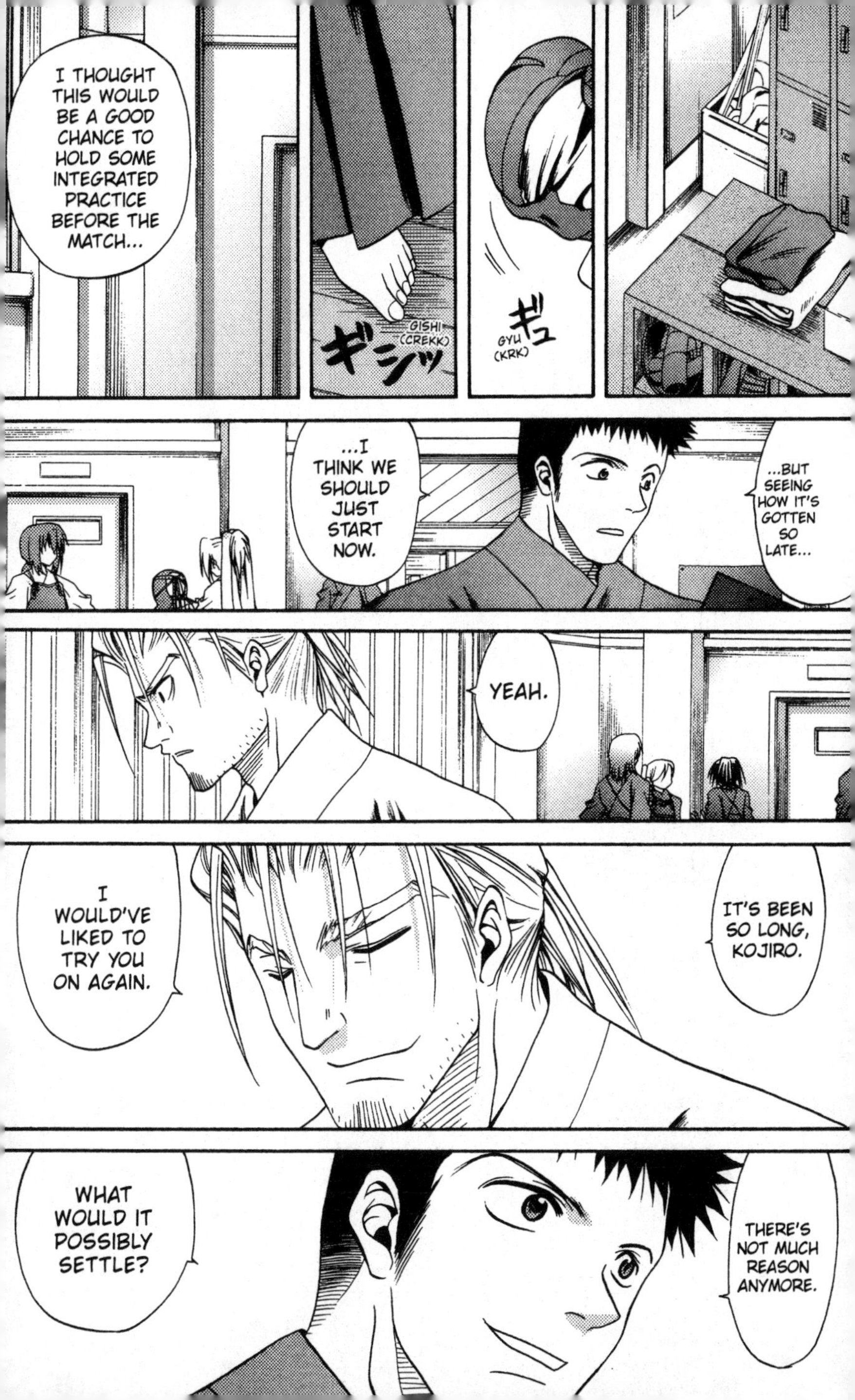
ギュ
GYU (KRK)
ギシッ
GISHI (CREKK)
I THOUGHT THIS WOULD BE A GOOD CHANCE TO HOLD SOME INTEGRATED PRACTICE BEFORE THE MATCH...
...BUT SEEING HOW IT'S GOTTEN SO LATE...
...I THINK WE SHOULD JUST START NOW.
YEAH.
IT'S BEEN SO LONG, KOJIRO.
I WOULD'VE LIKED TO TRY YOU ON AGAIN.
THERE'S NOT MUCH REASON ANYMORE.
WHAT WOULD IT POSSIBLY SETTLE?

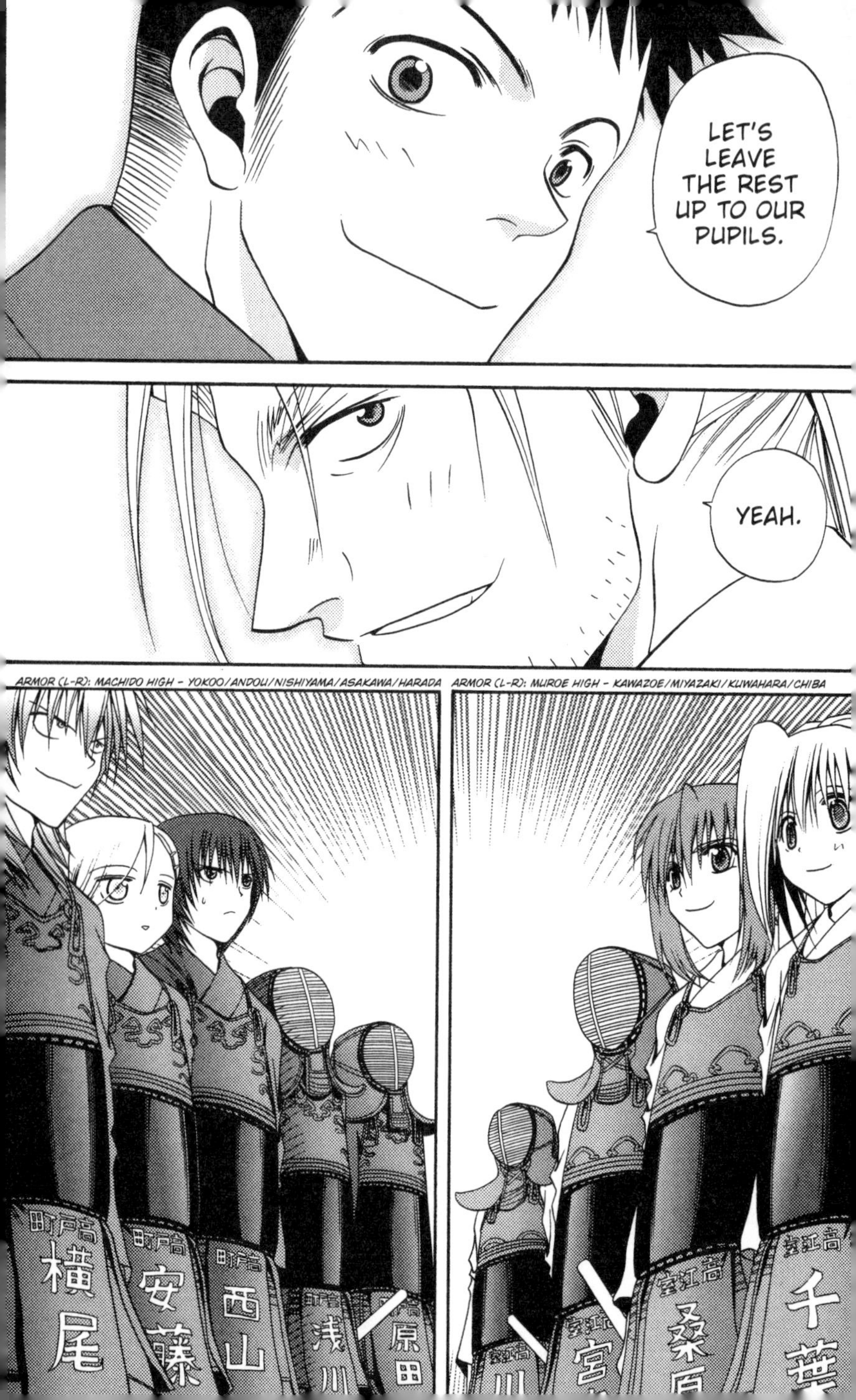
LET'S LEAVE THE REST UP TO OUR PUPILS.
YEAH.
ARMOR (L-R): MUROE HIGH - KAWAZOE/MIYAZAKI/KUWAHARA/CHIBA
ARMOR (L-R): MACHIDO HIGH - YOKOO/ANDOU/NISHIYAMA/ASAKAWA/HARADA

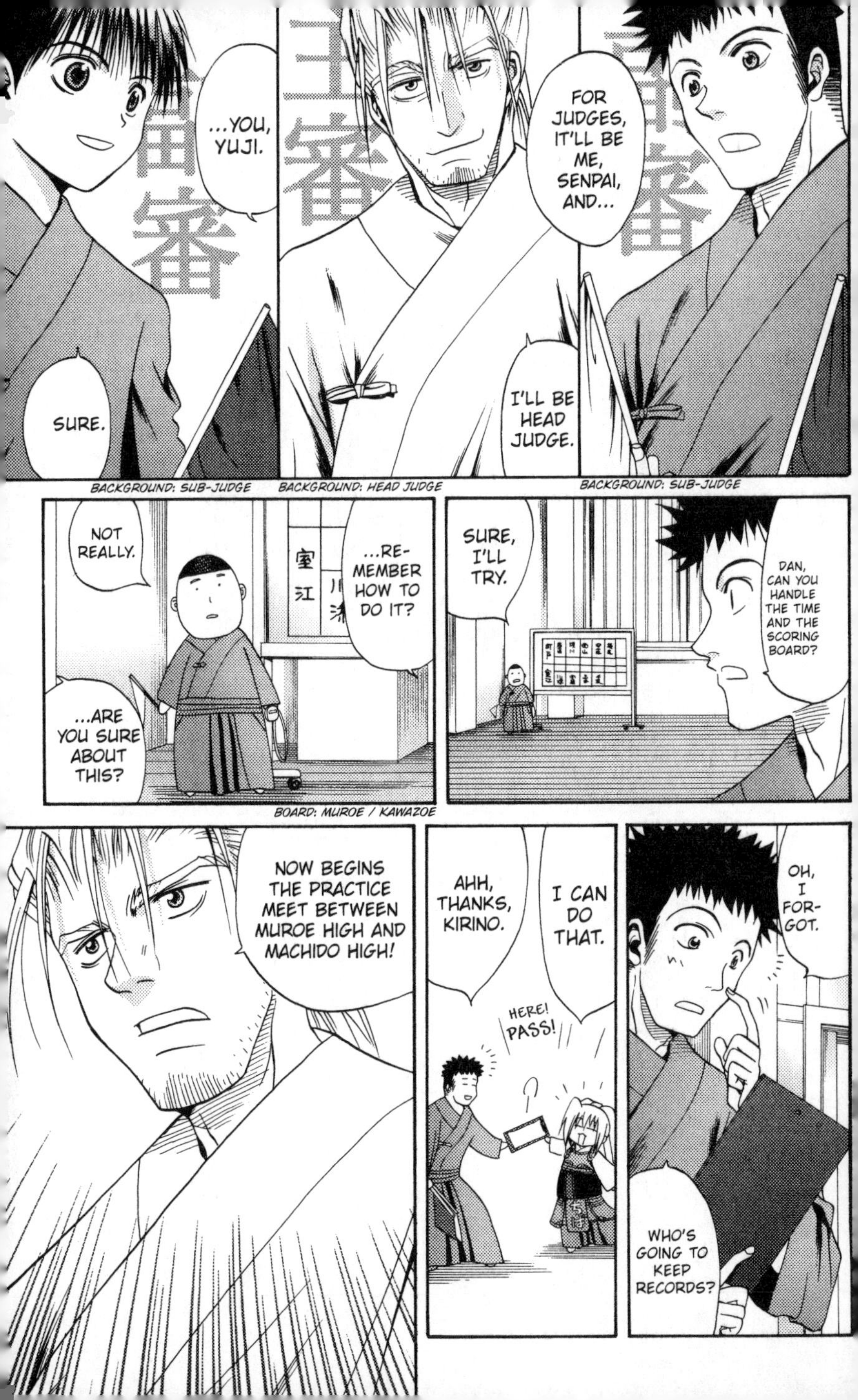
FOR JUDGES, IT'LL BE ME, SENPAI, AND...
BACKGROUND: SUB-JUDGE
I'LL BE HEAD JUDGE.
BACKGROUND: HEAD JUDGE
...YOU, YUJI.
SURE.
BACKGROUND: SUB-JUDGE
DAN, CAN YOU HANDLE THE TIME AND THE SCORING BOARD?
SURE, I'LL TRY.
...RE-MEMBER HOW TO DO IT?
NOT REALLY.
...ARE YOU SURE ABOUT THIS?
BOARD: MUROE / KAWAZOE
OH, I FOR-GOT.
WHO'S GOING TO KEEP RECORDS?
I CAN DO THAT.
AHH, THANKS, KIRINO.
HERE! PASS!
NOW BEGINS THE PRACTICE MEET BETWEEN MUROE HIGH AND MACHIDO HIGH!

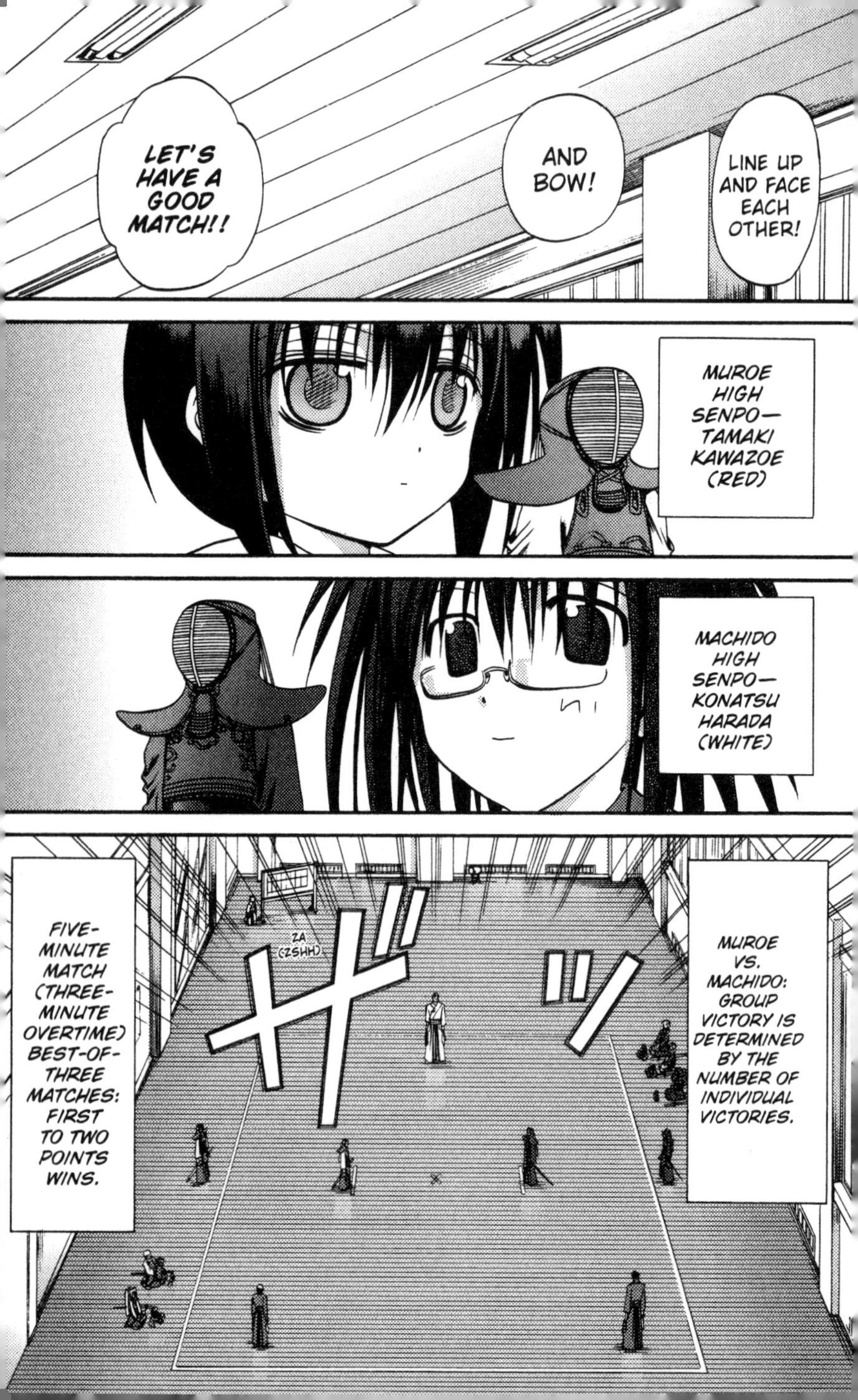
LINE UP AND FACE EACH OTHER!
AND BOW!
LET'S HAVE A GOOD MATCH!!
MUROE HIGH SENPO—TAMAKI KAWAZOE (RED)
MACHIDO HIGH SENPO—KONATSU HARADA (WHITE)
MUROE VS. MACHIDO: GROUP VICTORY IS DETERMINED BY THE NUMBER OF INDIVIDUAL VICTORIES.
ZA (ZSHH)
FIVE-MINUTE MATCH (THREE-MINUTE OVERTIME) BEST-OF-THREE MATCHES: FIRST TO TWO POINTS WINS.

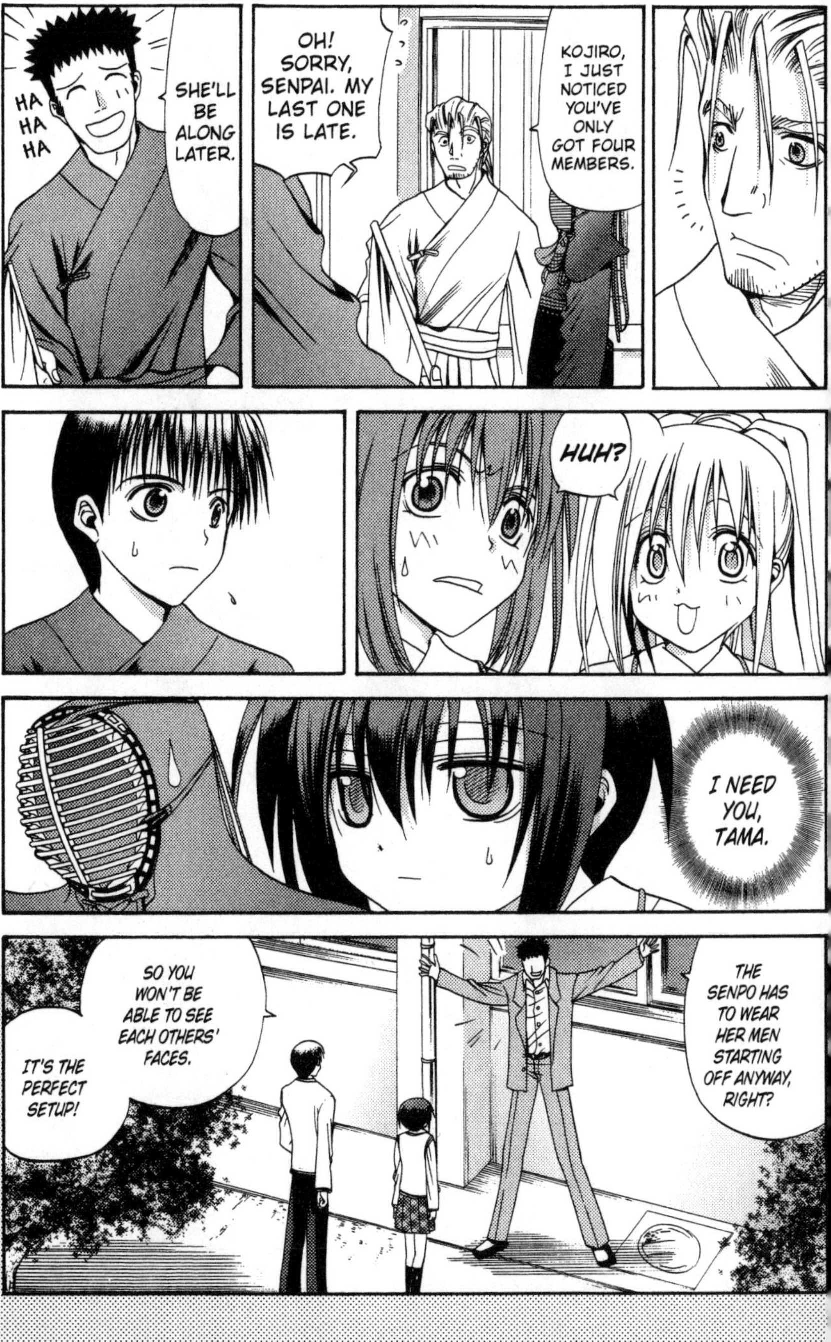
KOJIRO, I JUST NOTICED YOU'VE ONLY GOT FOUR MEMBERS.
OH! SORRY, SENPAI. MY LAST ONE IS LATE.
SHE'LL BE ALONG LATER.
HA HA HA
HUH?
I NEED YOU, TAMA.
THE SENPO HAS TO WEAR HER MEN STARTING OFF ANYWAY, RIGHT?
SO YOU WON'T BE ABLE TO SEE EACH OTHERS' FACES.
IT'S THE PERFECT SETUP!

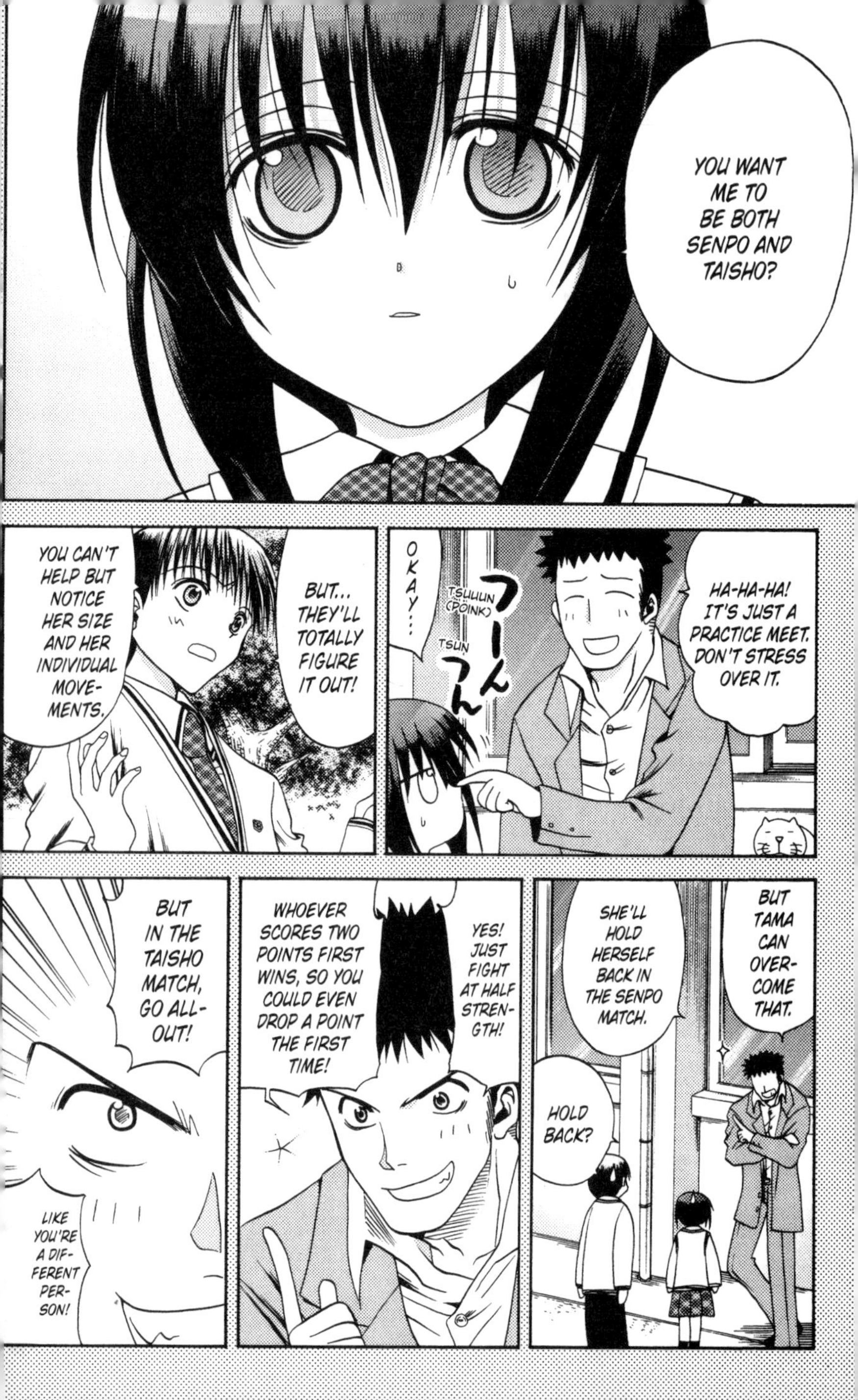
YOU WANT ME TO BE BOTH SENPO AND TAISHO?
HA-HA-HA! IT'S JUST A PRACTICE MEET. DON'T STRESS OVER IT.
TSUUUN (POINK)
TSUN
OKAY...
BUT... THEY'LL TOTALLY FIGURE IT OUT!
YOU CAN'T HELP BUT NOTICE HER SIZE AND HER INDIVIDUAL MOVE-MENTS.
BUT TAMA CAN OVER-COME THAT.
SHE'LL HOLD HERSELF BACK IN THE SENPO MATCH.
HOLD BACK?
YES! JUST FIGHT AT HALF STREN-GTH!
WHOEVER SCORES TWO POINTS FIRST WINS, SO YOU COULD EVEN DROP A POINT THE FIRST TIME!
BUT IN THE TAISHO MATCH, GO ALL-OUT!
LIKE YOU'RE A DIF-FERENT PER-SON!

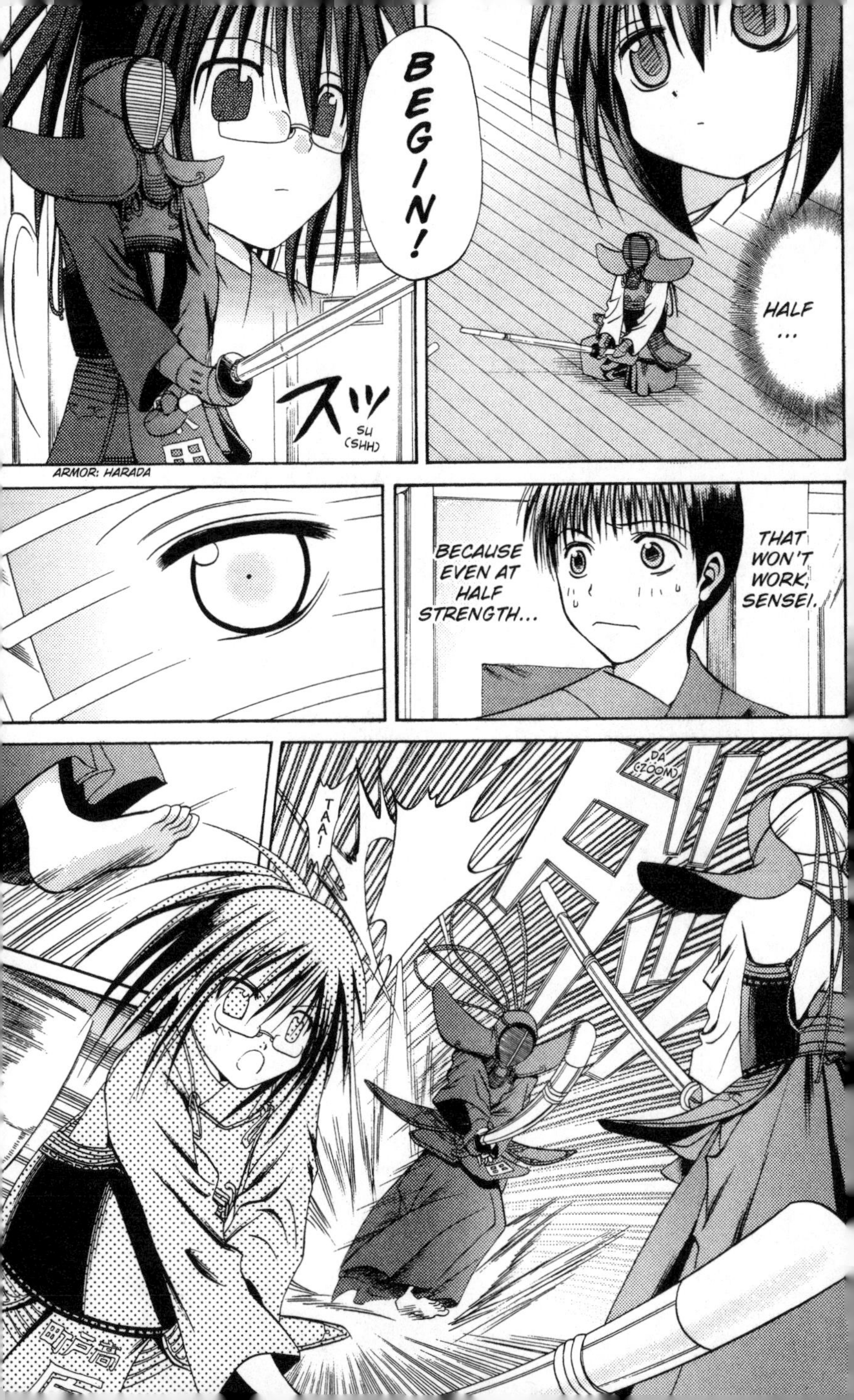
HALF ...
BEGIN!
スッ
SU (SHH)
ARMOR: HARADA
THAT WON'T WORK, SENSEI.
BECAUSE EVEN AT HALF STRENGTH...
DA (ZOOM)
TAA!

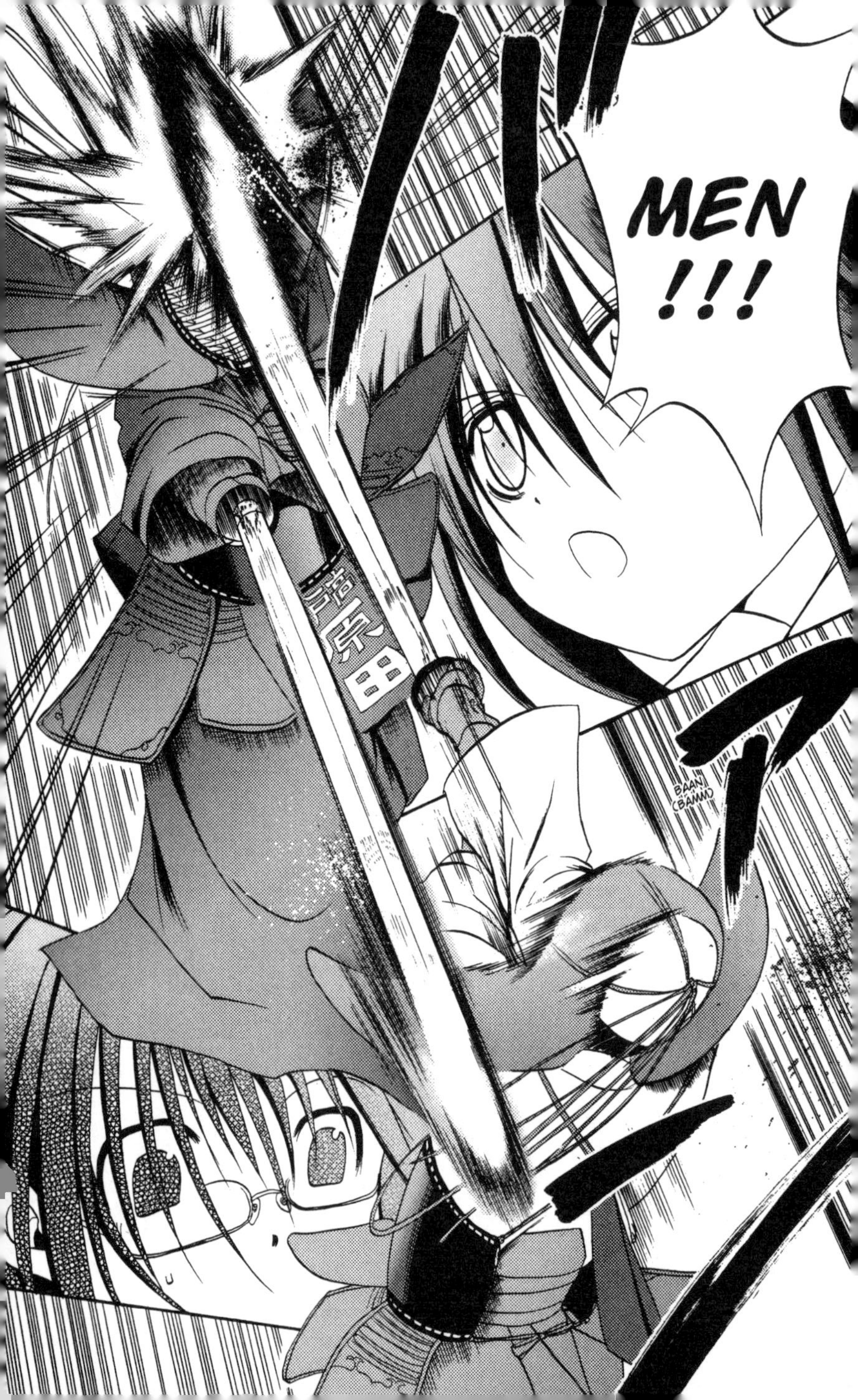
MEN !!!
BAAN (BAMM)

HUH?

MEN ARI!

ARMOR: HARADA

TAMA-CHAN'S NEVER SHOWN HER FULL STRENGTH AT PRACTICE.

SENSEI...

NOT EVEN HALF OF IT...

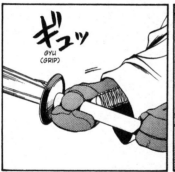

ギュッ
GYU
(GRIP)

UHHH, TAMA-CHAN?

ARMOR: KAWAZOE

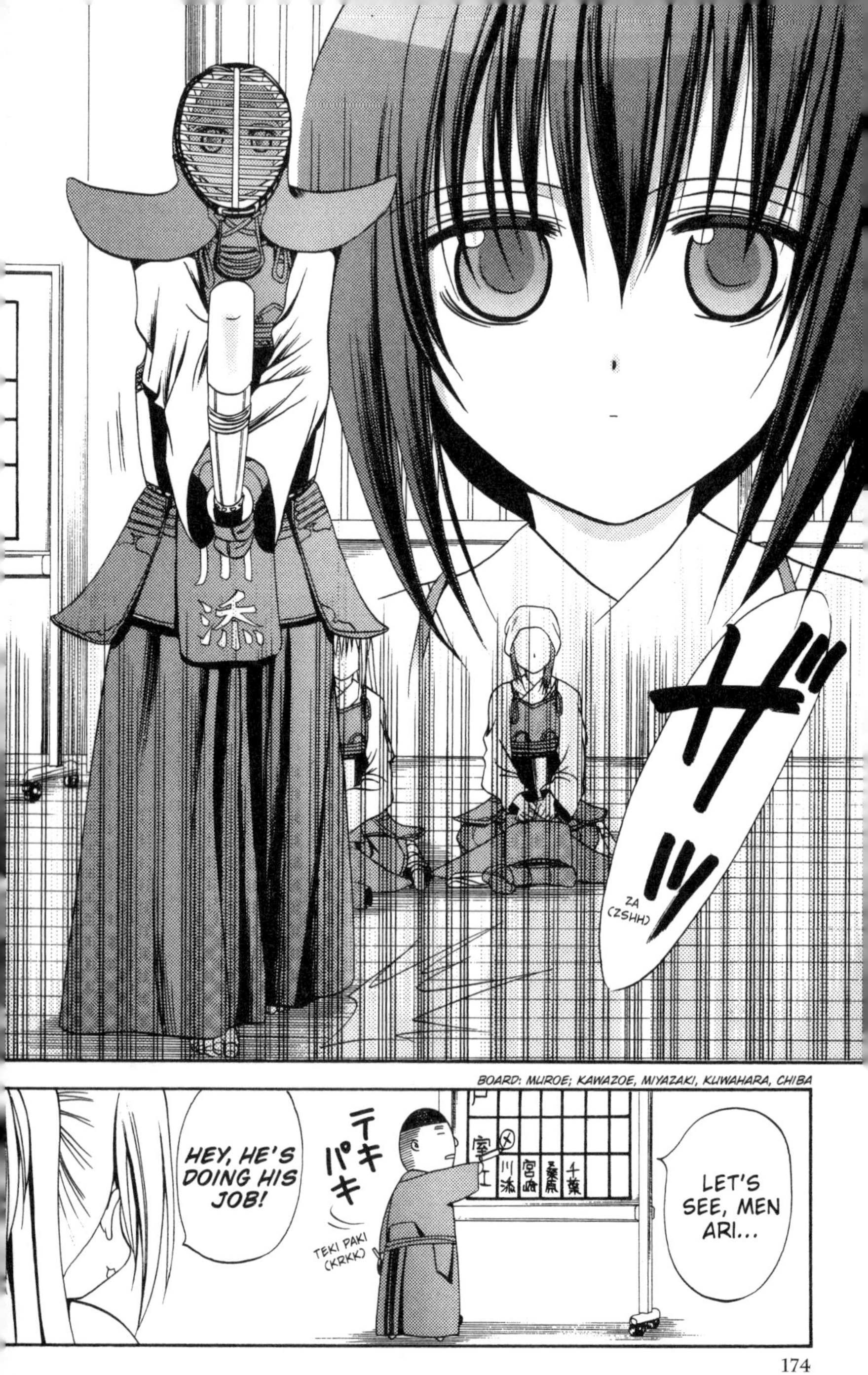
ザッ
ZA (ZSHH)
BOARD: MUROE; KAWAZOE, MIYAZAKI, KUWAHARA, CHIBA
LET'S SEE, MEN ARI...
テキパキ
TEKI PAKI (KRKK)
HEY, HE'S DOING HIS JOB!

BAMBOO BLADE

YOKOO-SAN AND ANDOU-SAN

SFX: GUDEEE (BLUGH)

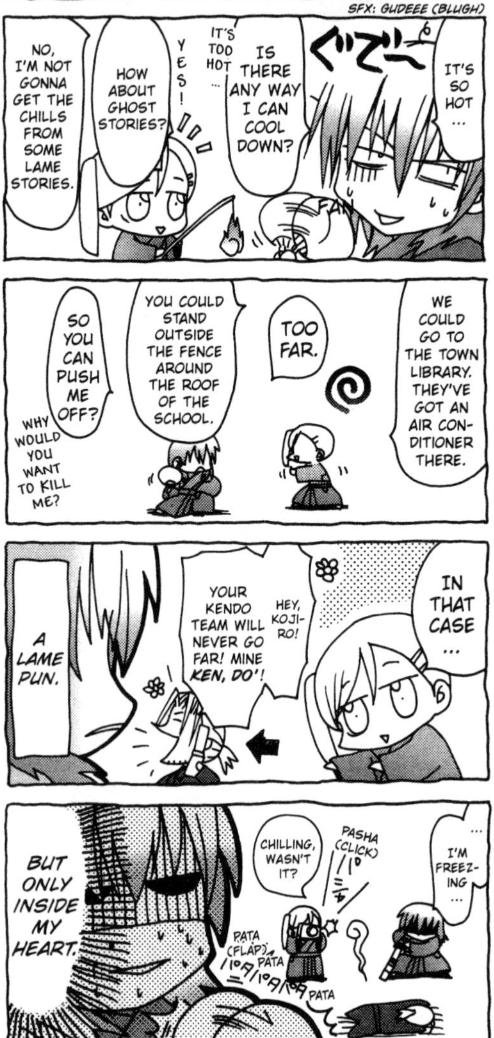
IT'S SO HOT ...
IS THERE ANY WAY I CAN COOL DOWN?
IT'S TOO HOT ...
FAN
YES!
HOW ABOUT GHOST STORIES?
NO, I'M NOT GONNA GET THE CHILLS FROM SOME LAME STORIES.
WE COULD GO TO THE TOWN LIBRARY. THEY'VE GOT AN AIR CONDITIONER THERE.
TOO FAR.
YOU COULD STAND OUTSIDE THE FENCE AROUND THE ROOF OF THE SCHOOL.
SO YOU CAN PUSH ME OFF?
WHY WOULD YOU WANT TO KILL ME?
IN THAT CASE ...
HEY, KOJI-RO!
YOUR KENDO TEAM WILL NEVER GO FAR! MINE *KEN, DO'*!
A LAME PUN.
... I'M FREEZ-ING ...
PASHA (CLICK)
CHILLING, WASN'T IT?
PATA (FLAP) PATA
PATA
BUT ONLY INSIDE MY HEART.

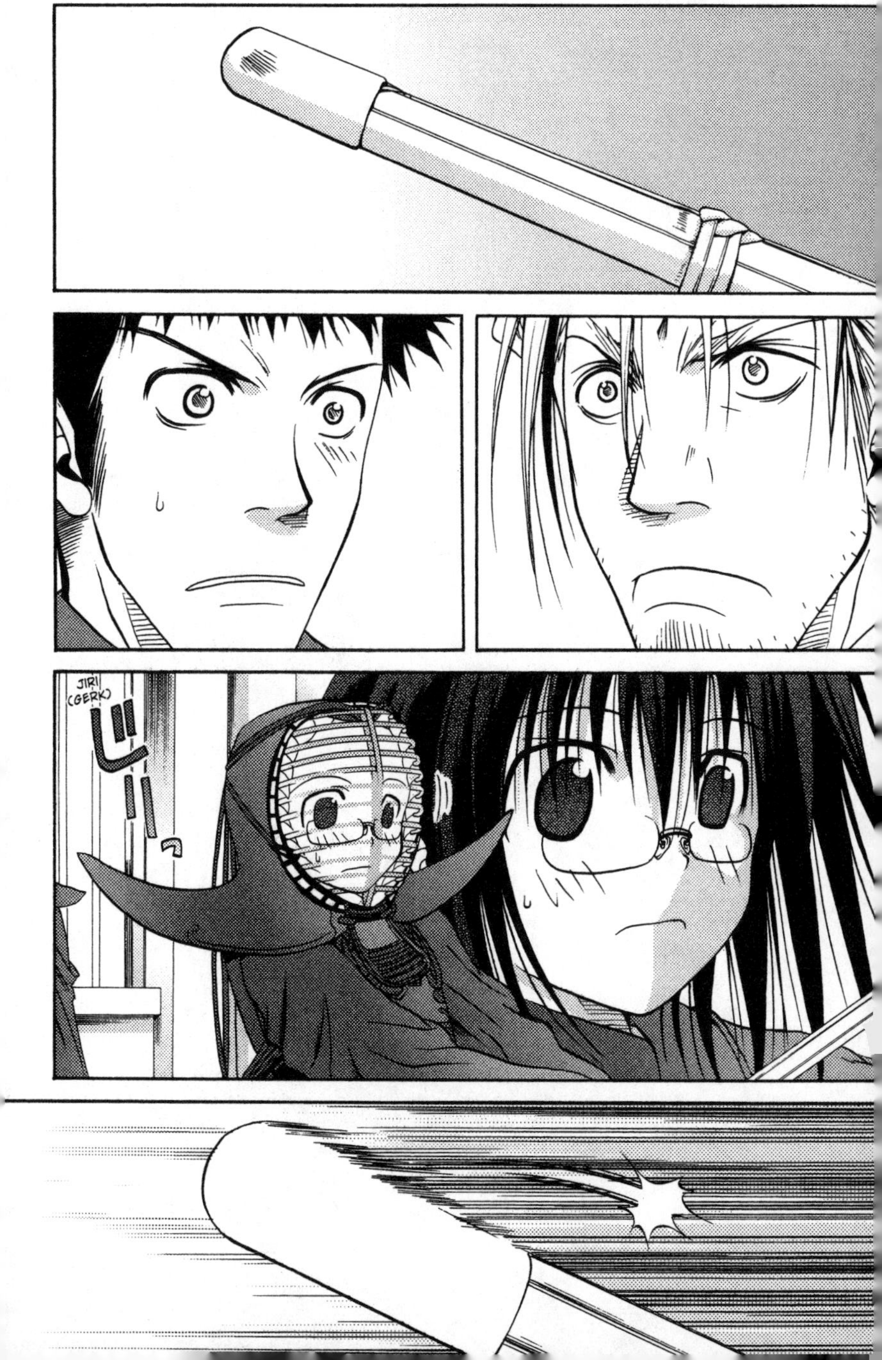
JIRI (GERK)
ジリ…ッ

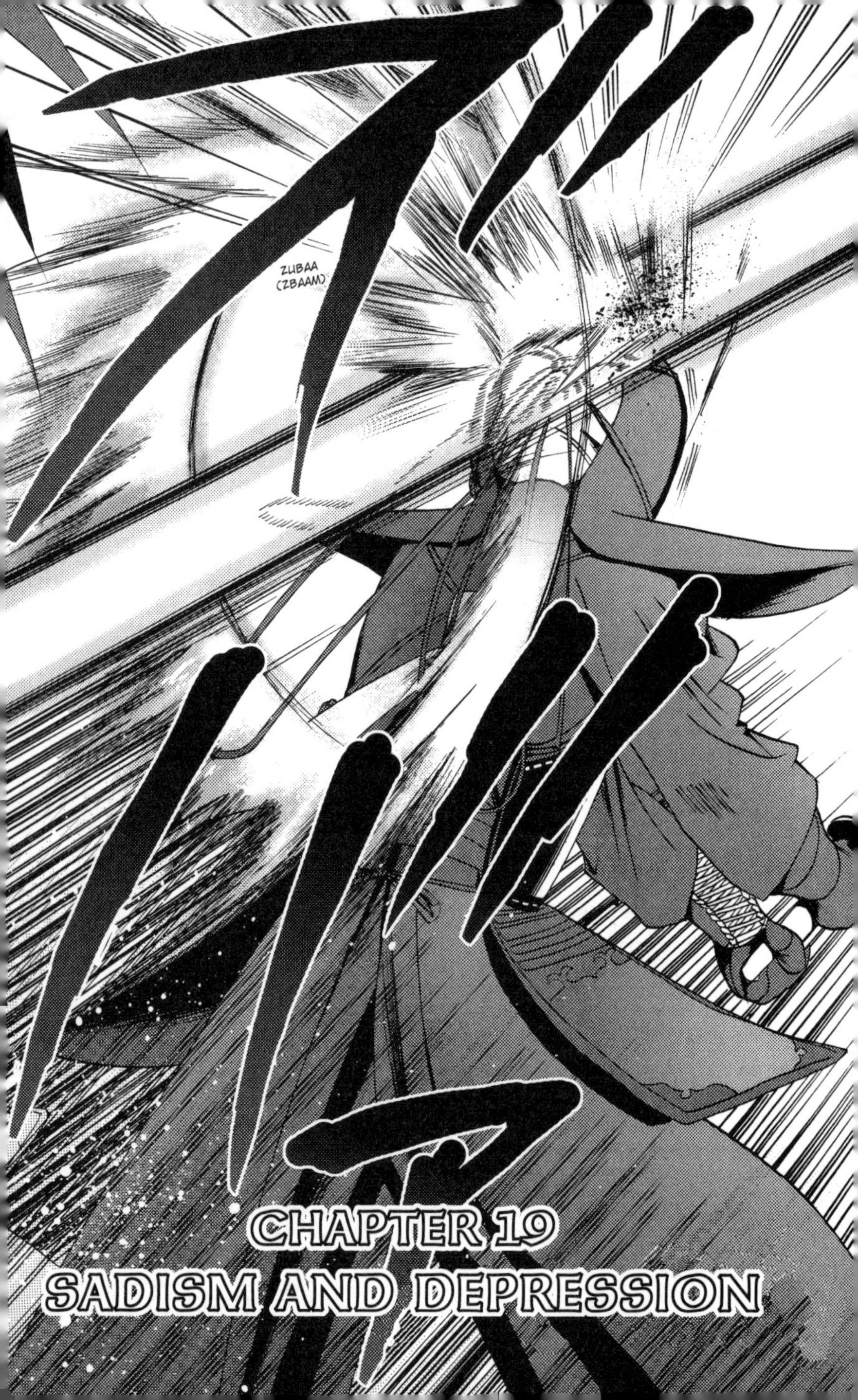
ZUBAA (ZBAAM)
CHAPTER 19
SADISM AND DEPRESSION

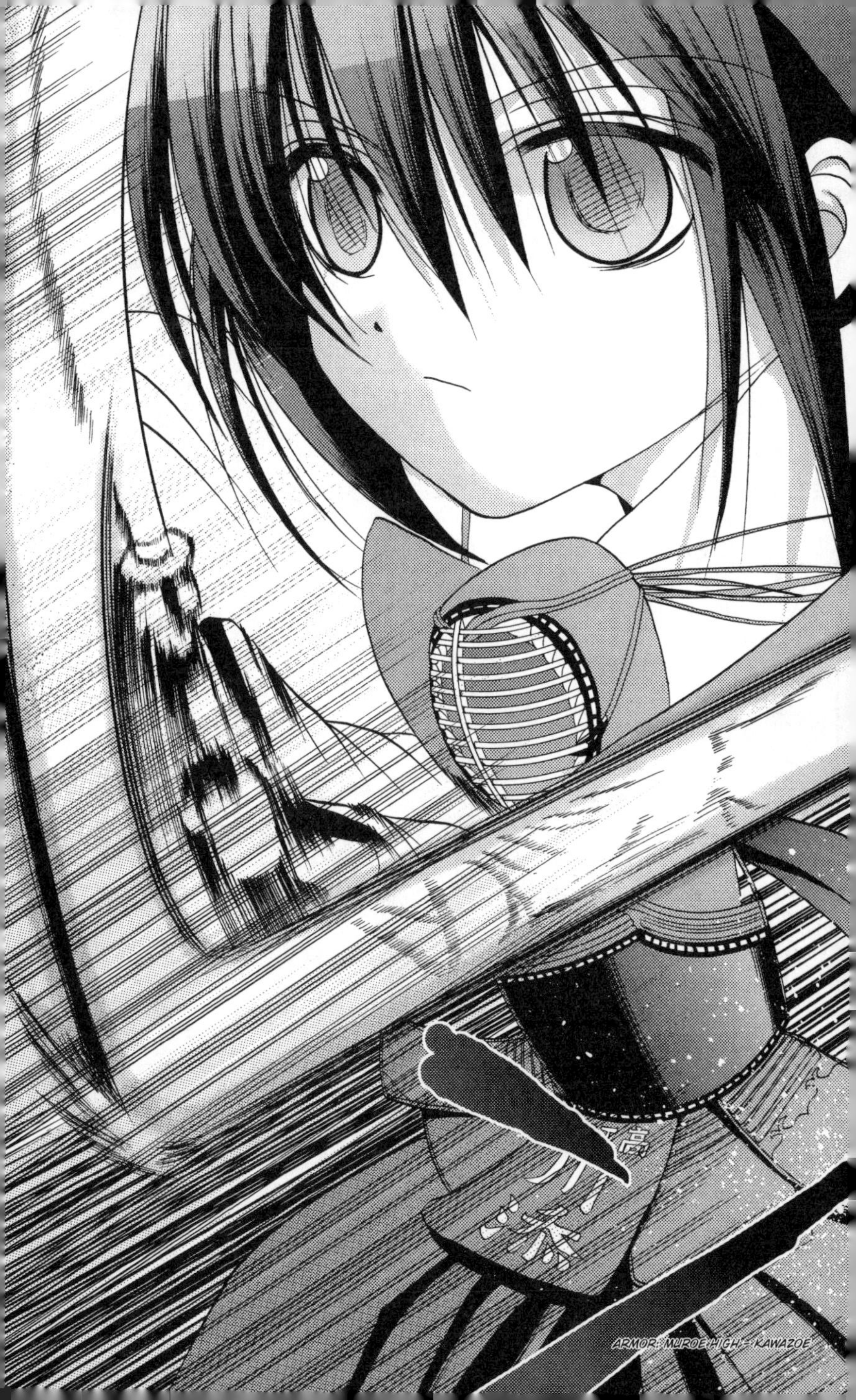
ARMOR: MUROE HIGH - KAWAZOE

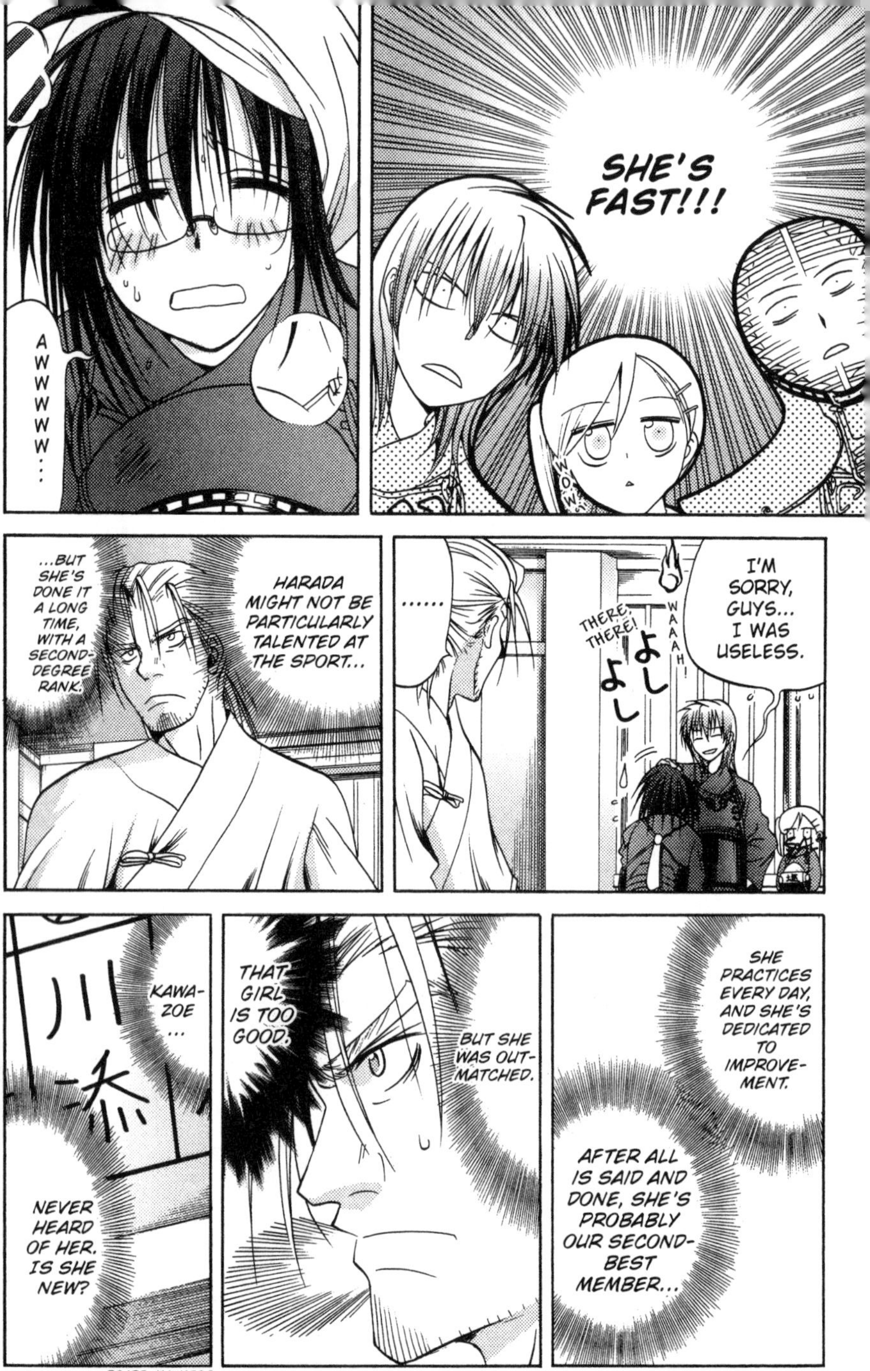
SHE'S FAST!!!
WOW
AWWWWWWW...
I'M SORRY, GUYS... I WAS USELESS.
WAAAH!
THERE, THERE!
よしよし
......
HARADA MIGHT NOT BE PARTICULARLY TALENTED AT THE SPORT...
...BUT SHE'S DONE IT A LONG TIME, WITH A SECOND-DEGREE RANK.
SHE PRACTICES EVERY DAY, AND SHE'S DEDICATED TO IMPROVEMENT.
AFTER ALL IS SAID AND DONE, SHE'S PROBABLY OUR SECOND-BEST MEMBER...
BUT SHE WAS OUT-MATCHED.
THAT GIRL IS TOO GOOD.
KAWA-ZOE...
川添
NEVER HEARD OF HER. IS SHE NEW?

BOARD: KAWAZOE

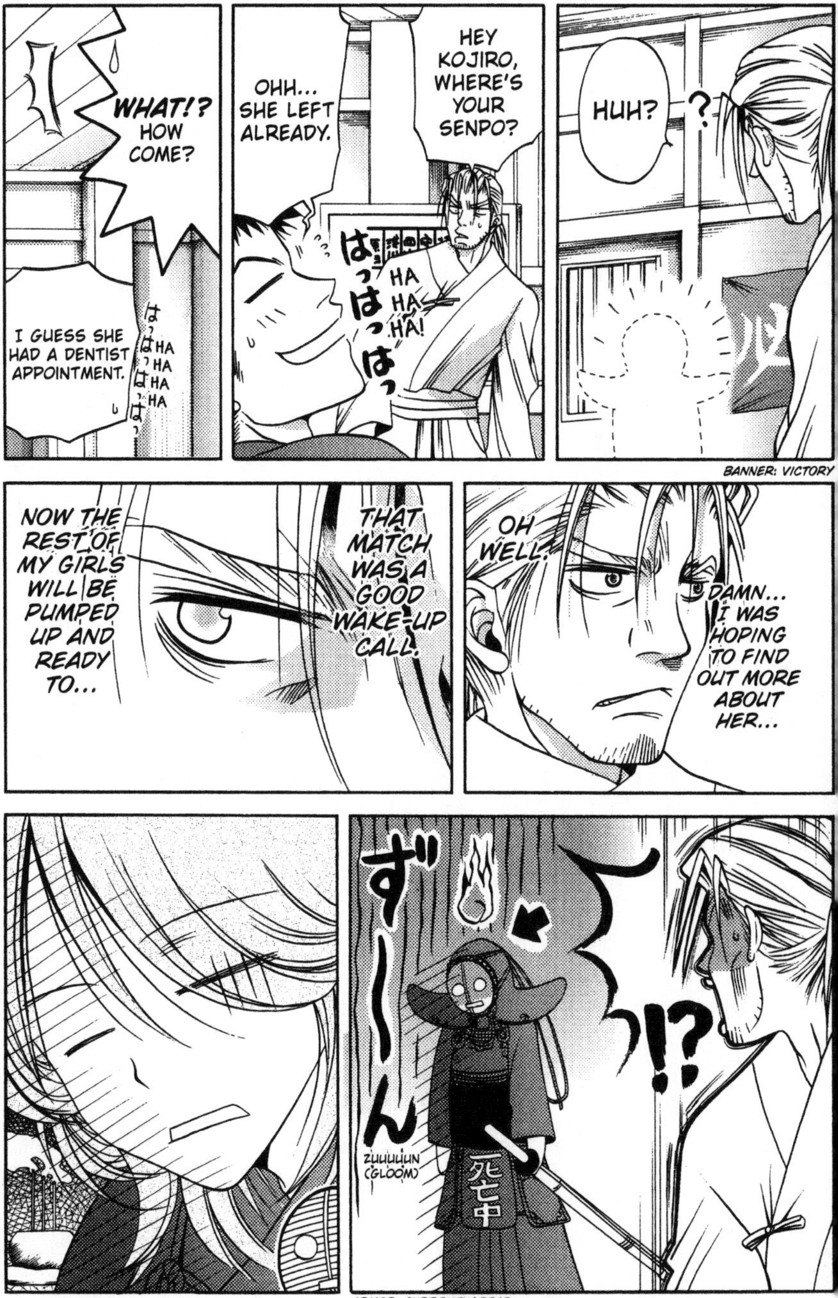
HUH?
?
HEY KOJIRO, WHERE'S YOUR SENPO?
OHH... SHE LEFT ALREADY.
はっはっはっ
HA HA HA!
WHAT!? HOW COME?
I GUESS SHE HAD A DENTIST APPOINTMENT.
ははははは
HA HA HA HA
BANNER: VICTORY
OH WELL.
DAMN... I WAS HOPING TO FIND OUT MORE ABOUT HER...
THAT MATCH WAS A GOOD WAKE-UP CALL.
NOW THE REST OF MY GIRLS WILL BE PUMPED UP AND READY TO...
!?
ずーん
ZUUUUUN (GLOOM)
死亡中
ARMOR: CURRENTLY DEAD

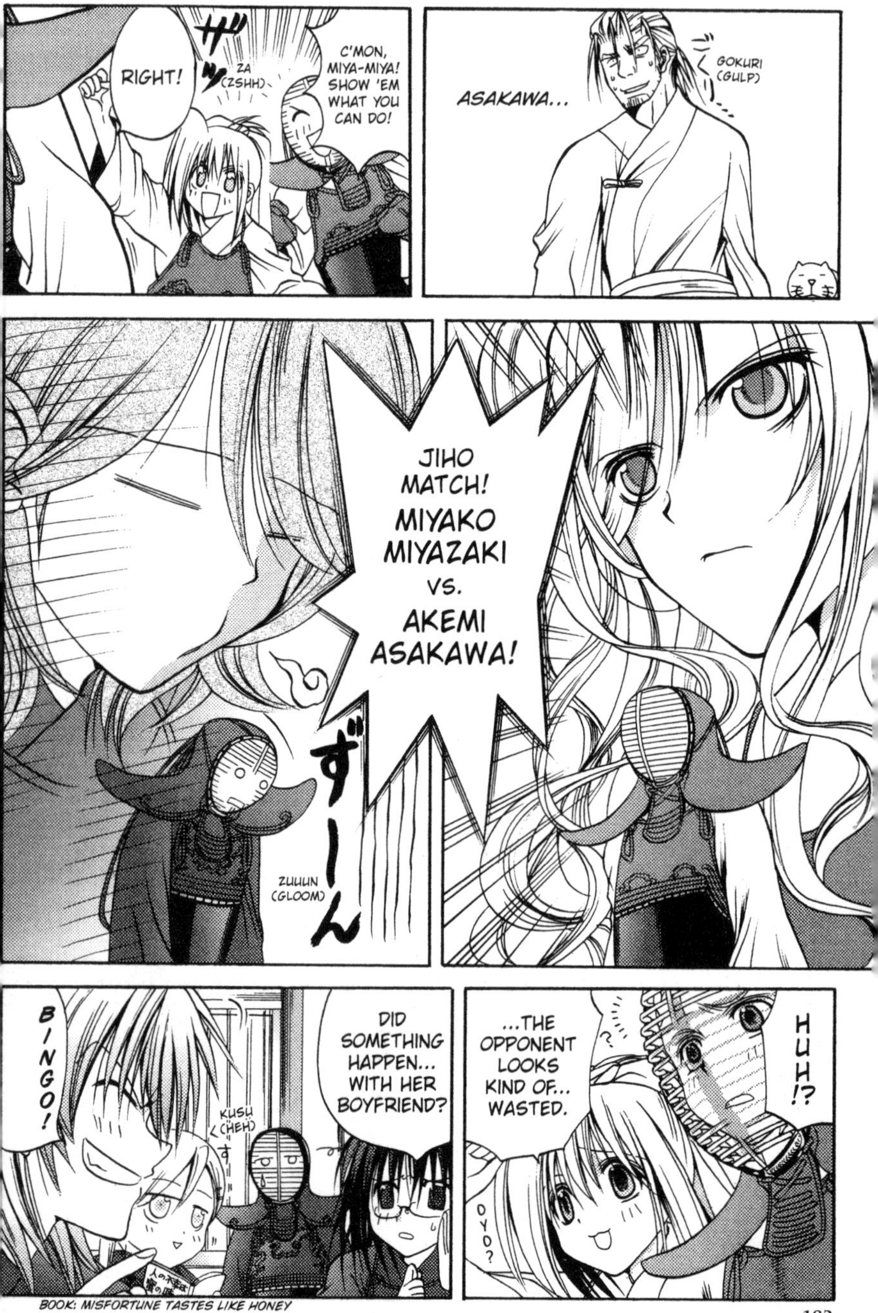
ASAKAWA...
GOKURI (GULP)
C'MON, MIYA-MIYA! SHOW 'EM WHAT YOU CAN DO!
ZA (ZSHH)
RIGHT!
JIHO MATCH! MIYAKO MIYAZAKI VS. AKEMI ASAKAWA!
ずーん
ZUUUN (GLOOM)
HUH!?
...THE OPPONENT LOOKS KIND OF... WASTED.
DYO?
DID SOMETHING HAPPEN... WITH HER BOYFRIEND?
KUSH (HEH)
BINGO!

BOOK: MISFORTUNE TASTES LIKE HONEY

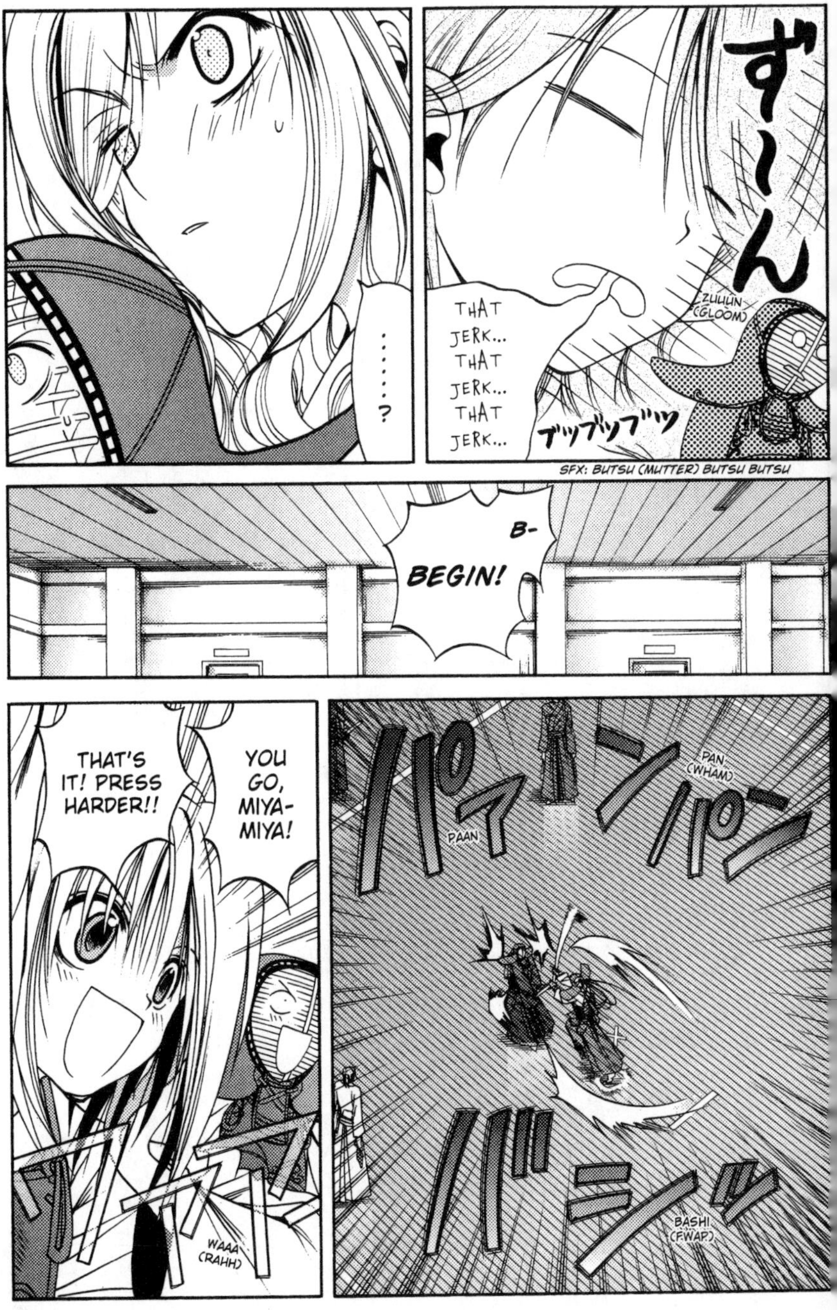
ずーん
ZUUUN (GLOOM)
THAT JERK... THAT JERK... THAT JERK...
ブツブツブツ
SFX: BUTSU (MUTTER) BUTSU BUTSU
......?
B- BEGIN!
パァーン
PAAN
パーン
PAN (WHAM)
バシーッ
BASHI (FWAP)
YOU GO, MIYA-MIYA!
THAT'S IT! PRESS HARDER!!
WAAA (RAHH)

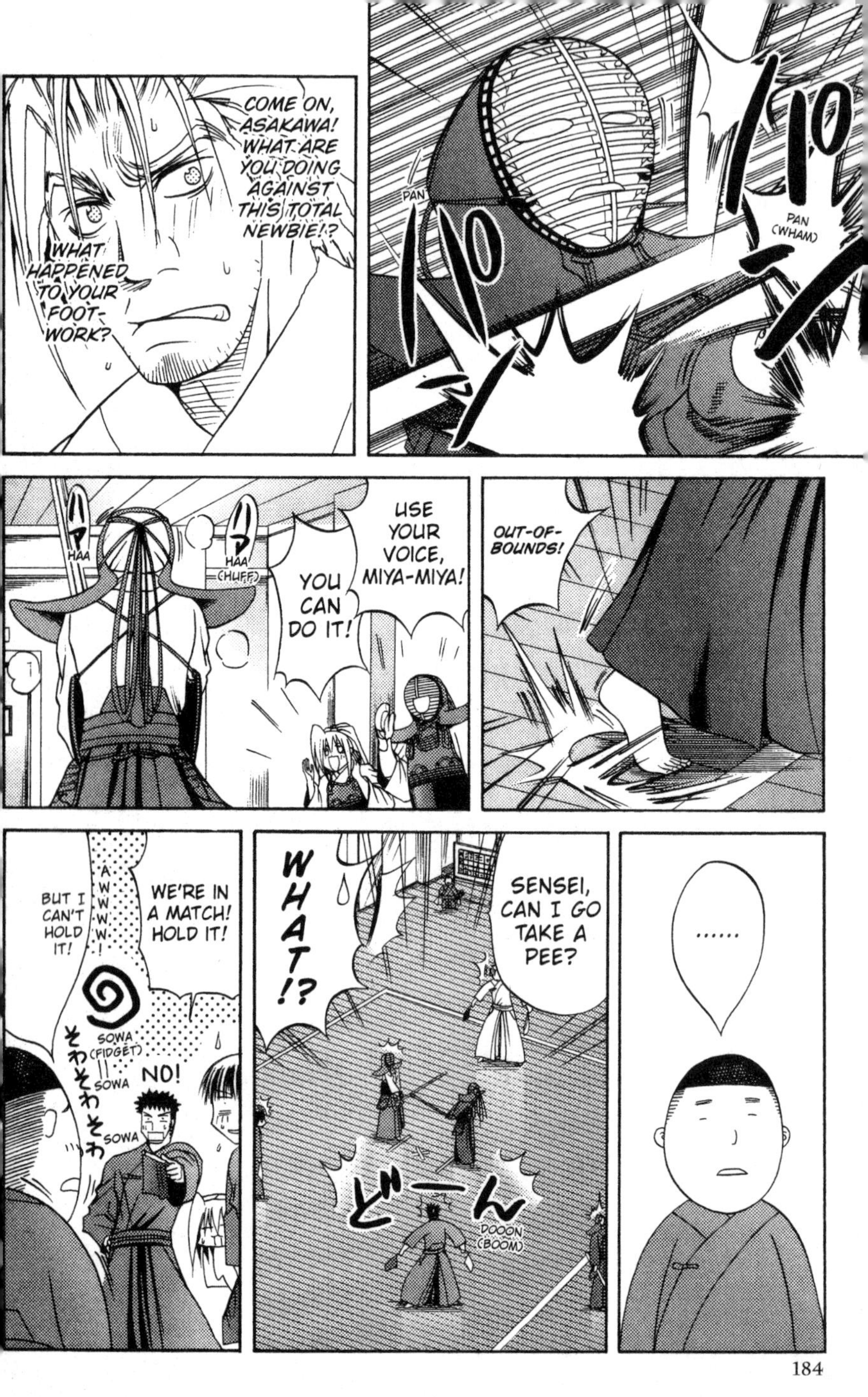
PAN
PAN (WHAM)
COME ON, ASAKAWA! WHAT ARE YOU DOING AGAINST THIS TOTAL NEWBIE!?
WHAT HAPPENED TO YOUR FOOT-WORK?
OUT-OF-BOUNDS!
USE YOUR VOICE, MIYA-MIYA!
YOU CAN DO IT!
ハァ
HAA
ハァ
HAA (HUFF)
......
SENSEI, CAN I GO TAKE A PEE?
WHAT!?
どーん
DOOON (BOOM)
WE'RE IN A MATCH! HOLD IT!
AWWWWW!
BUT I CAN'T HOLD IT!
NO!
そわそわ
SOWA (FIDGET) SOWA SOWA

ARMOR: MUROE HIGH - MIYAZAKI

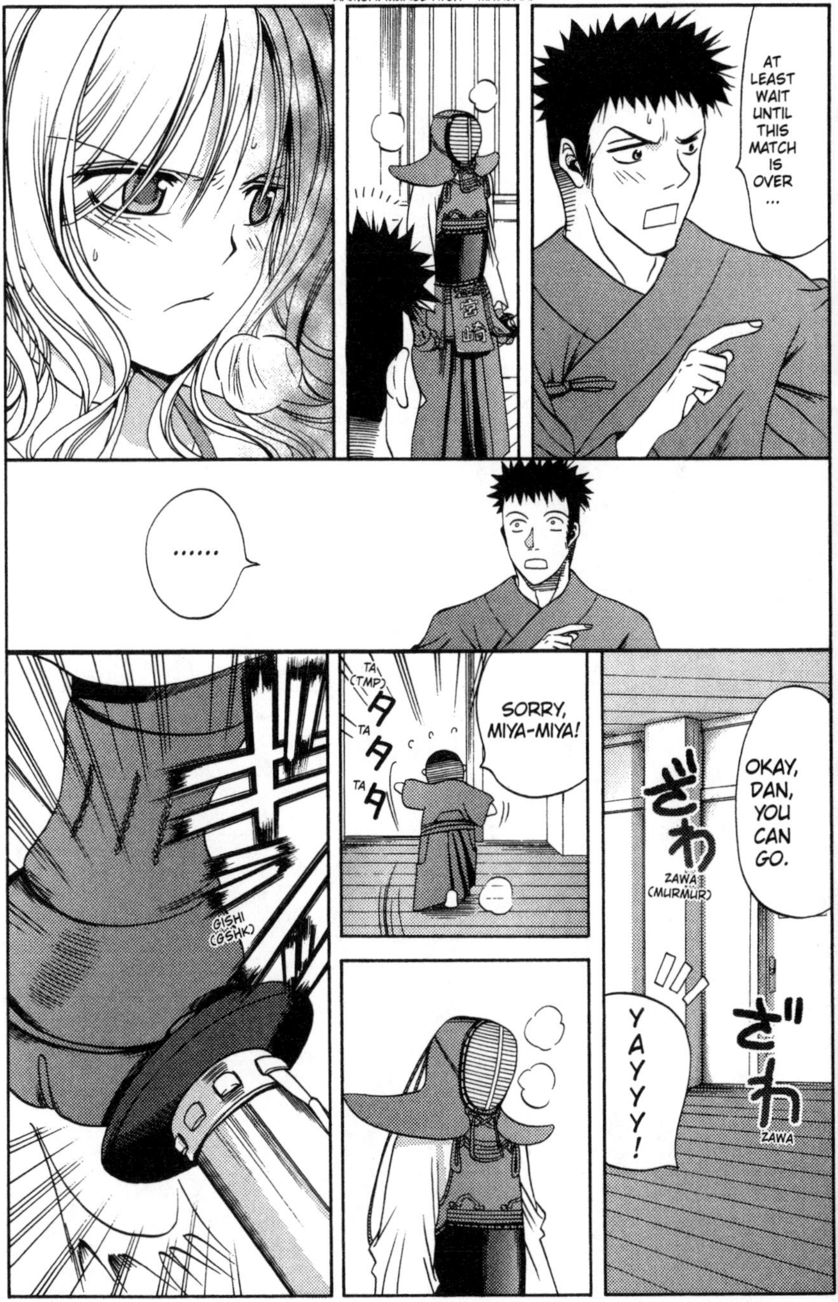
AT LEAST WAIT UNTIL THIS MATCH IS OVER...
......
OKAY, DAN, YOU CAN GO.
ざわ
ZAWA (MURMUR)
YAYYY!
ざわ
ZAWA
SORRY, MIYA-MIYA!
TA (TMP) タ
TA タ
TA タ
GISHI (GSHK)

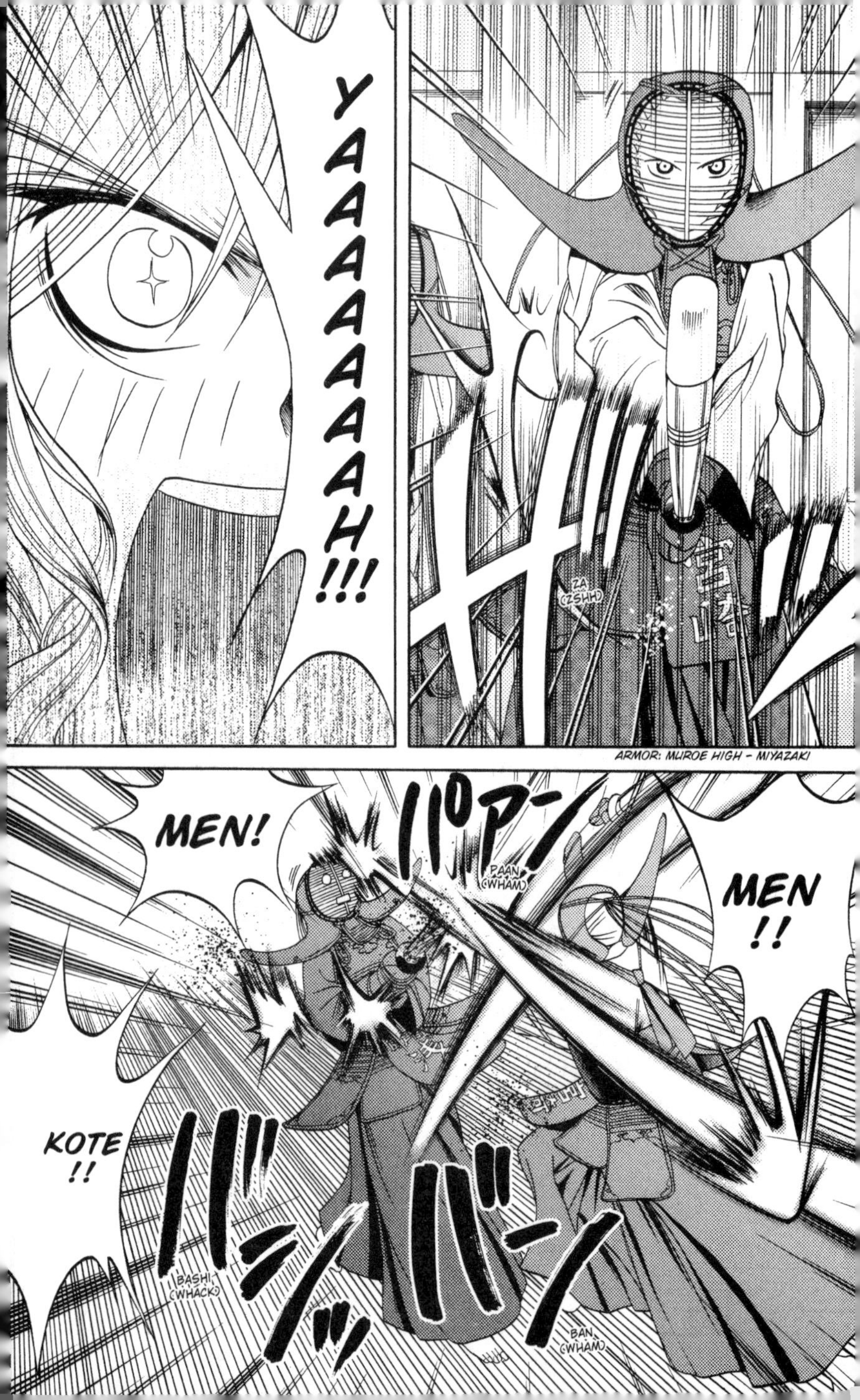

ZA (ZSHH)
ARMOR: MUROE HIGH - MIYAZAKI
YAAAAAAAAAH!!!
MEN !!
PAAN (WHAM)
MEN!
BAN (WHAM)
BASHI (WHACK)
KOTE !!

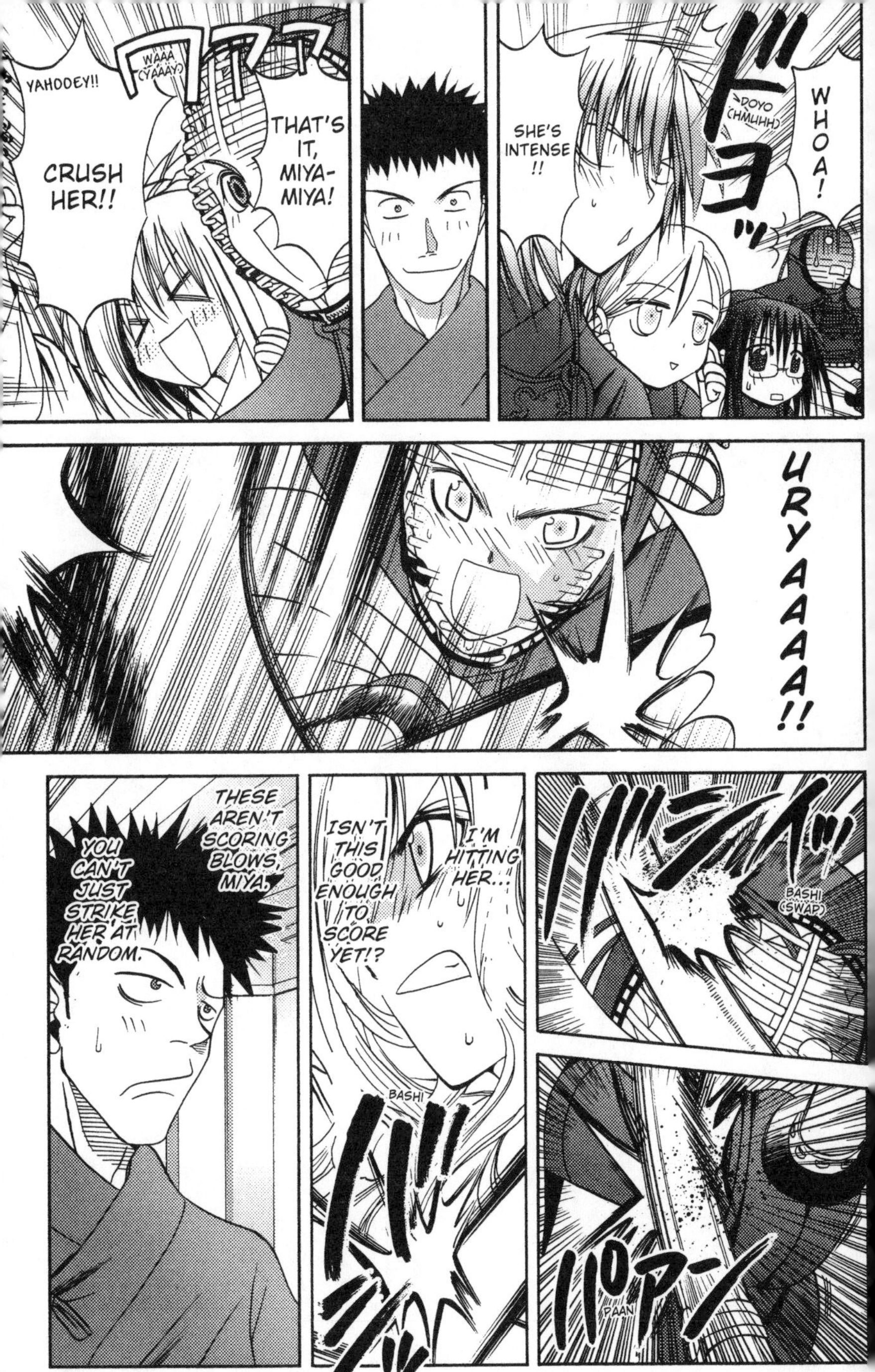
WHOA!
DOYO (CHMUHH)
SHE'S INTENSE!!
THAT'S IT, MIYA-MIYA!
WAAA (YAAAY)
YAHOODEY!!
CRUSH HER!!
URYAAAAAA!!
BASHI (SWAP)
PAAN
I'M HITTING HER...
ISN'T THIS GOOD ENOUGH TO SCORE YET!?
BASHI
THESE AREN'T SCORING BLOWS, MIYA.
YOU CAN'T JUST STRIKE HER AT RANDOM.

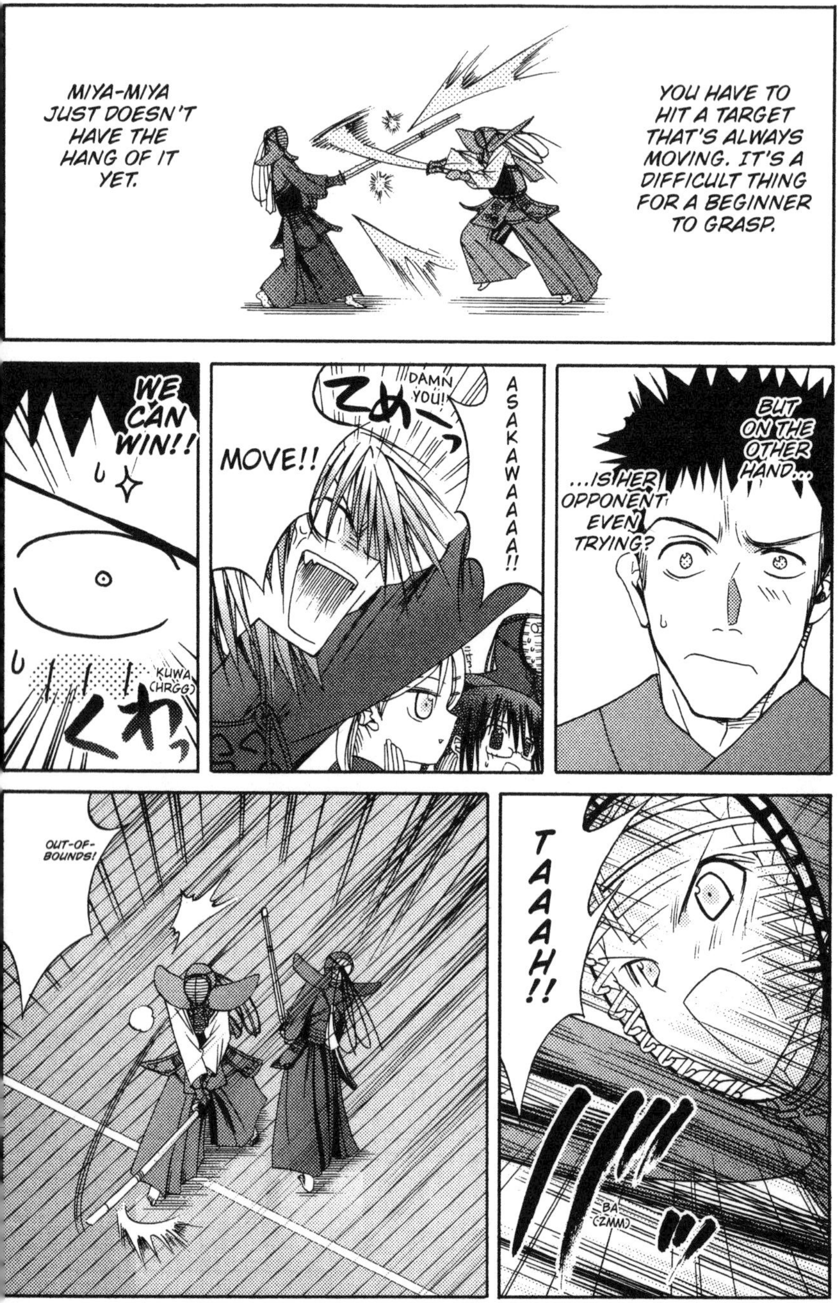

YOU HAVE TO HIT A TARGET THAT'S ALWAYS MOVING. IT'S A DIFFICULT THING FOR A BEGINNER TO GRASP.
MIYA-MIYA JUST DOESN'T HAVE THE HANG OF IT YET.
BUT ON THE OTHER HAND...
...IS HER OPPONENT EVEN TRYING?
ASAKAWAAAAAAA!!
てめーっ
DAMN YOU!
MOVE!!
WE CAN WIN!!
KUWA (HRGG)
くわっ
TAAAAH!!
BA (ZMM)
OUT-OF-BOUNDS!

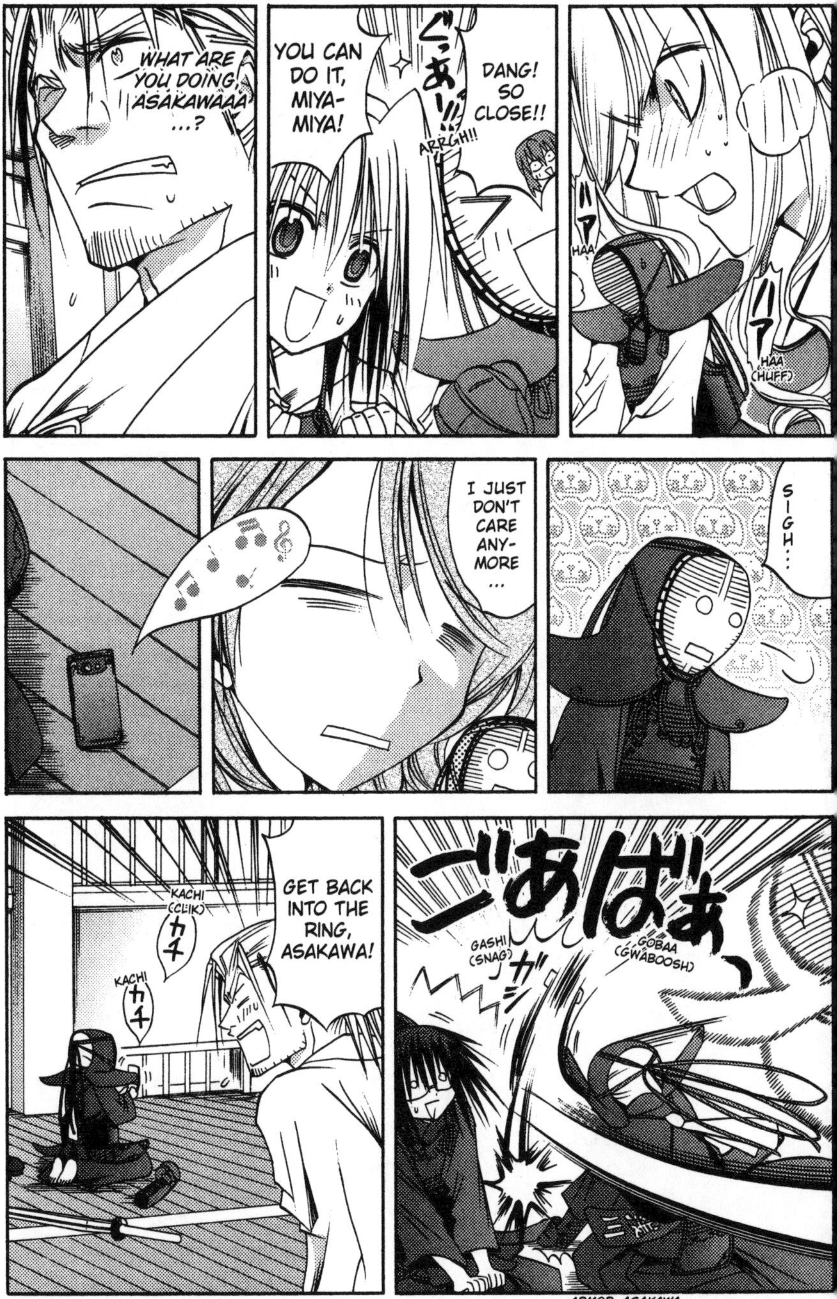
ハァ
HAA
ハァ
HAA (HUFF)
DANG! SO CLOSE!!
ぐっあー!!
ARRGH!!
YOU CAN DO IT, MIYA-MIYA!
WHAT ARE YOU DOING, ASAKAWAAA ...?
SIGH...
I JUST DON'T CARE ANYMORE ...
ごあばぁ
GOBAA (GWABOOSH)
ガッ
GASHI (SNAG)
GET BACK INTO THE RING, ASAKAWA!
KACHI (CLIK)
カチ
KACHI
カチ

ARMOR: ASAKAWA

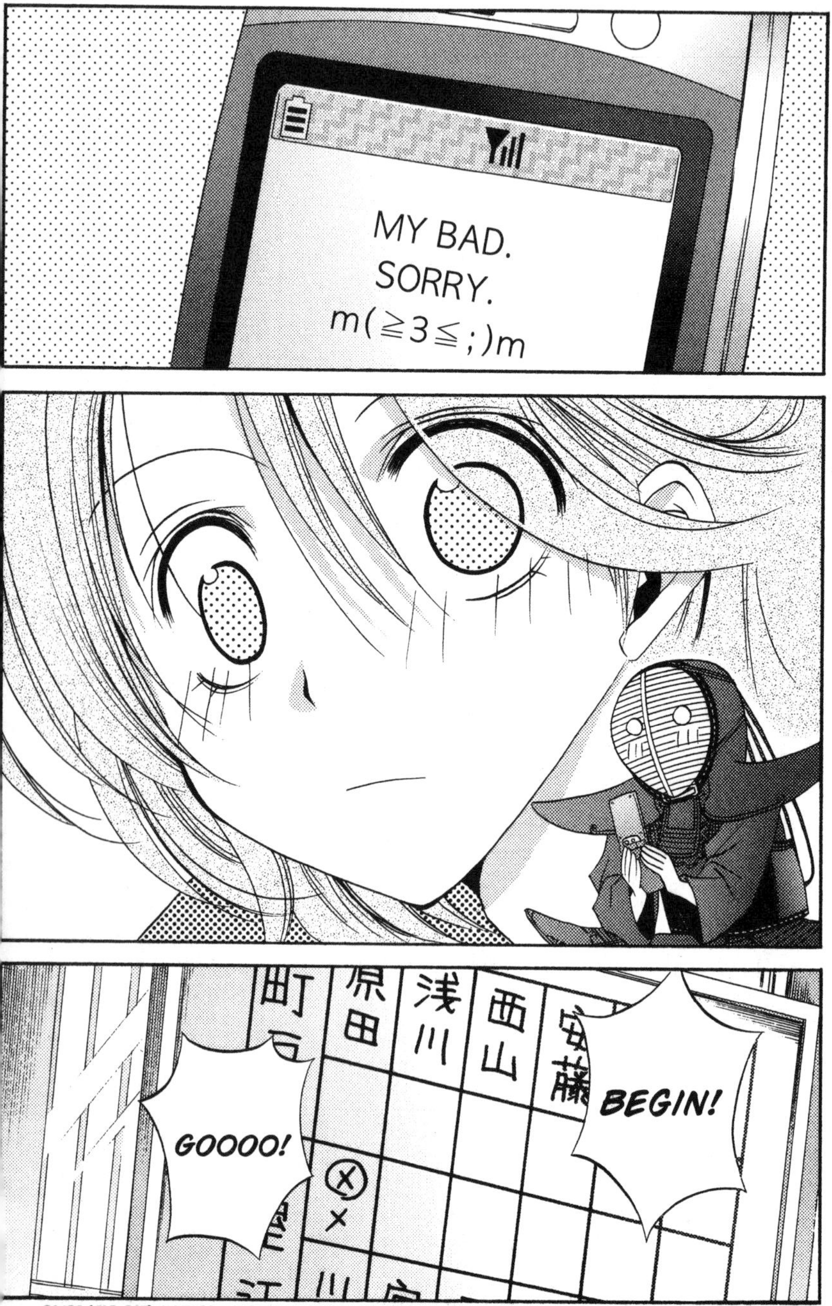
MY BAD.
SORRY.
m(≧3≦;)m
BEGIN!
GOOOO!
町
原田
浅川
西山

BOARD (TOP-BOT): MACHIDO - HARADA, ASAKAWA, NISHIYAMA, ANDOU / MUROE - KAWAZOE, MIYAZAKI, KUWAHARA

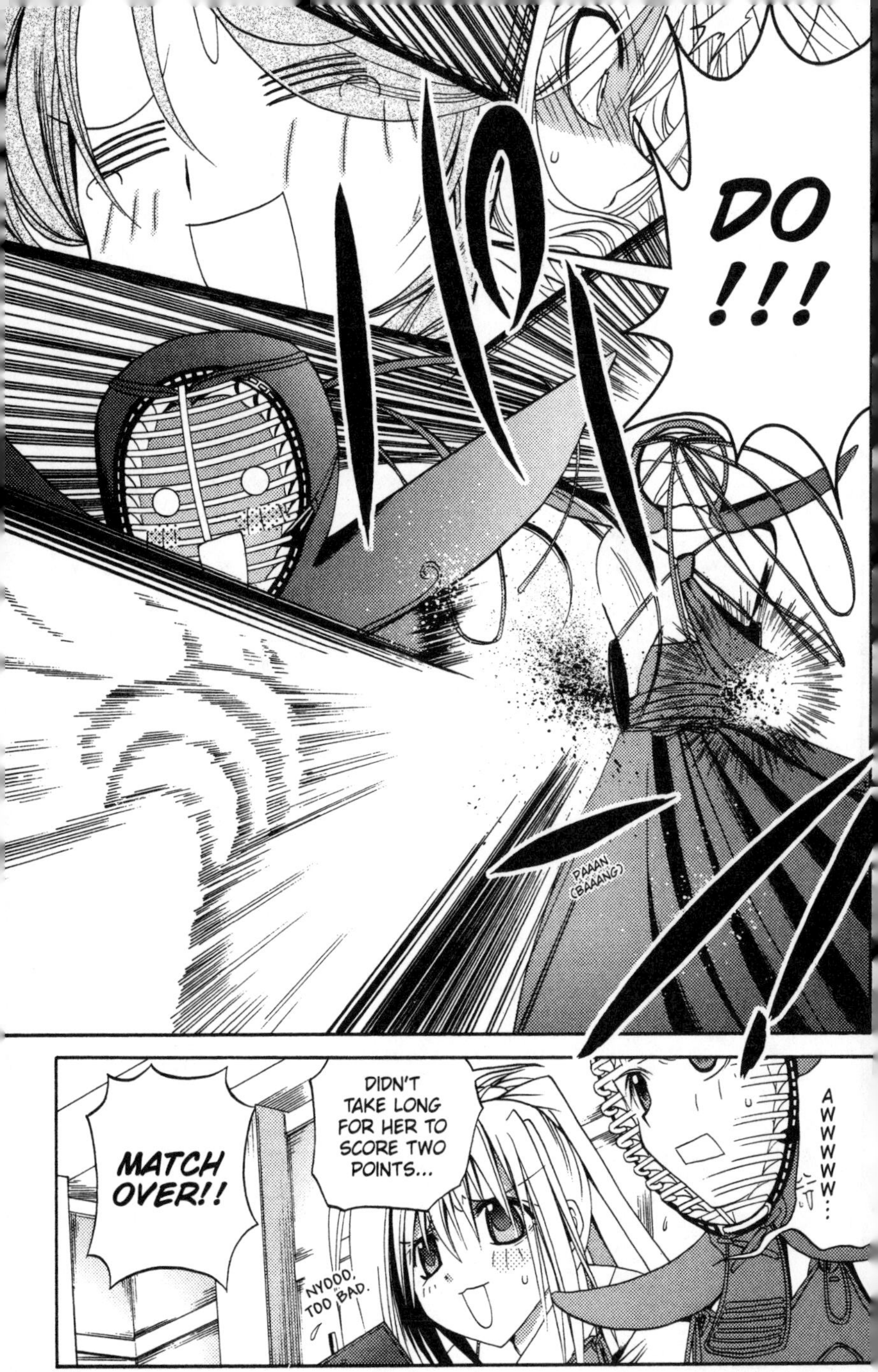
DO!!!
PAAAN (BAAANG)
AWWWWWW...
DIDN'T TAKE LONG FOR HER TO SCORE TWO POINTS...
MATCH OVER!!
NYOOO, TOO BAD.

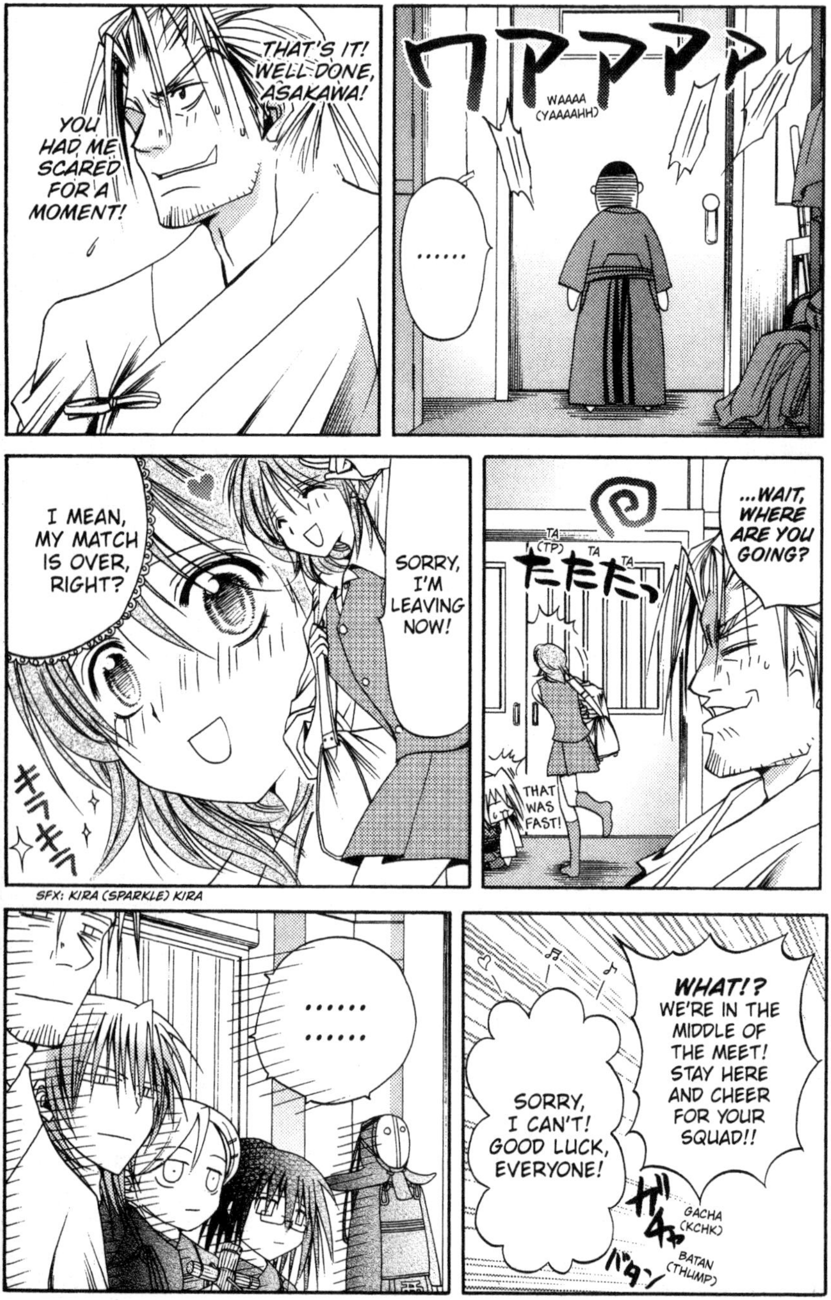
WAAAA (YAAAAHH)
......
THAT'S IT! WELL DONE, ASAKAWA!
YOU HAD ME SCARED FOR A MOMENT!
...WAIT, WHERE ARE YOU GOING?
TA (TP) TA TA
THAT WAS FAST!
SORRY, I'M LEAVING NOW!
I MEAN, MY MATCH IS OVER, RIGHT?
SFX: KIRA (SPARKLE) KIRA
WHAT!? WE'RE IN THE MIDDLE OF THE MEET! STAY HERE AND CHEER FOR YOUR SQUAD!!
SORRY, I CAN'T! GOOD LUCK, EVERYONE!
GACHA (KCHK)
BATAN (THUMP)
....

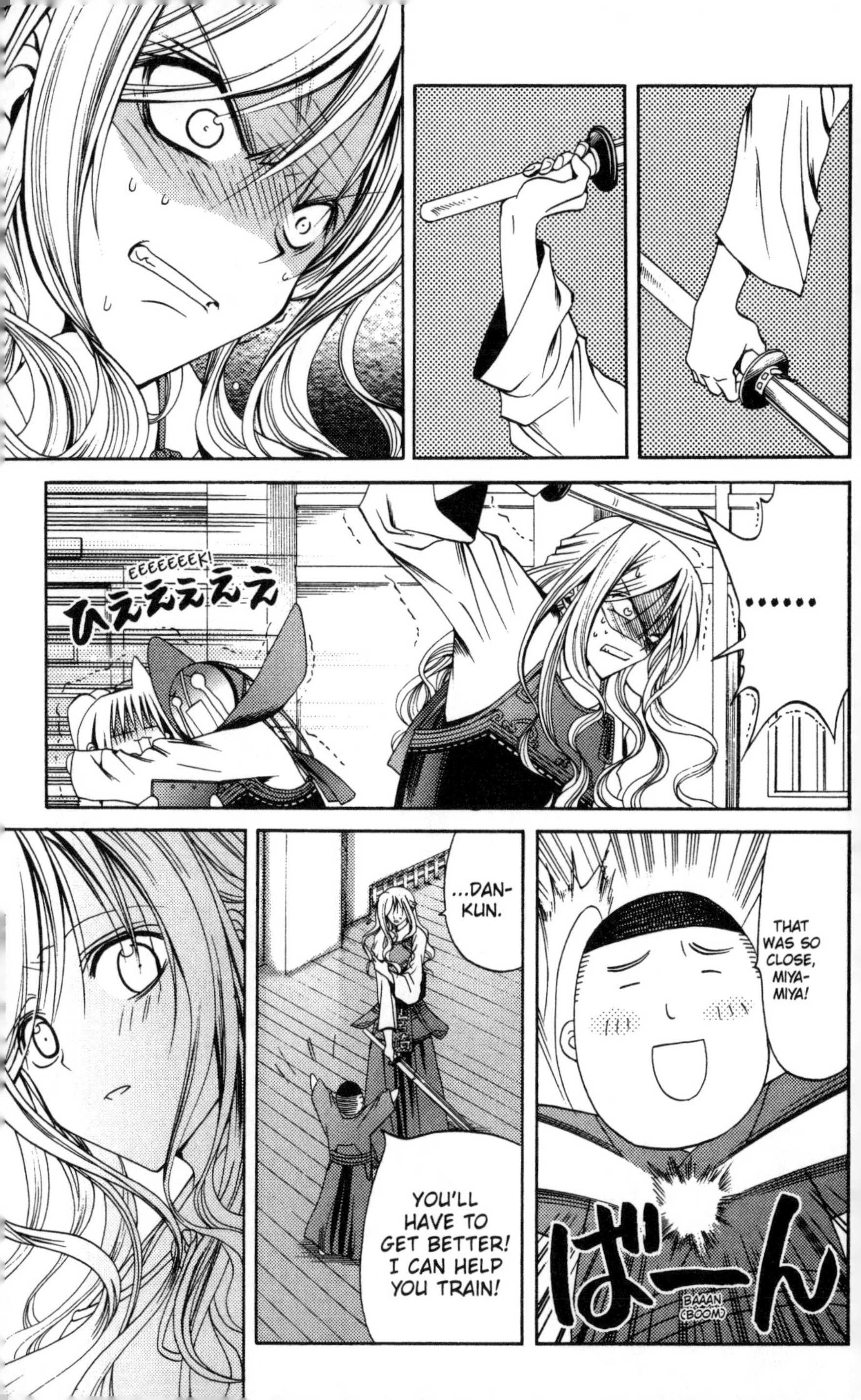
......
EEEEEEEK!
ひえええええ
THAT WAS SO CLOSE, MIYA-MIYA!
ばーん
BAAAN (BOOM)
...DAN-KUN.
YOU'LL HAVE TO GET BETTER! I CAN HELP YOU TRAIN!

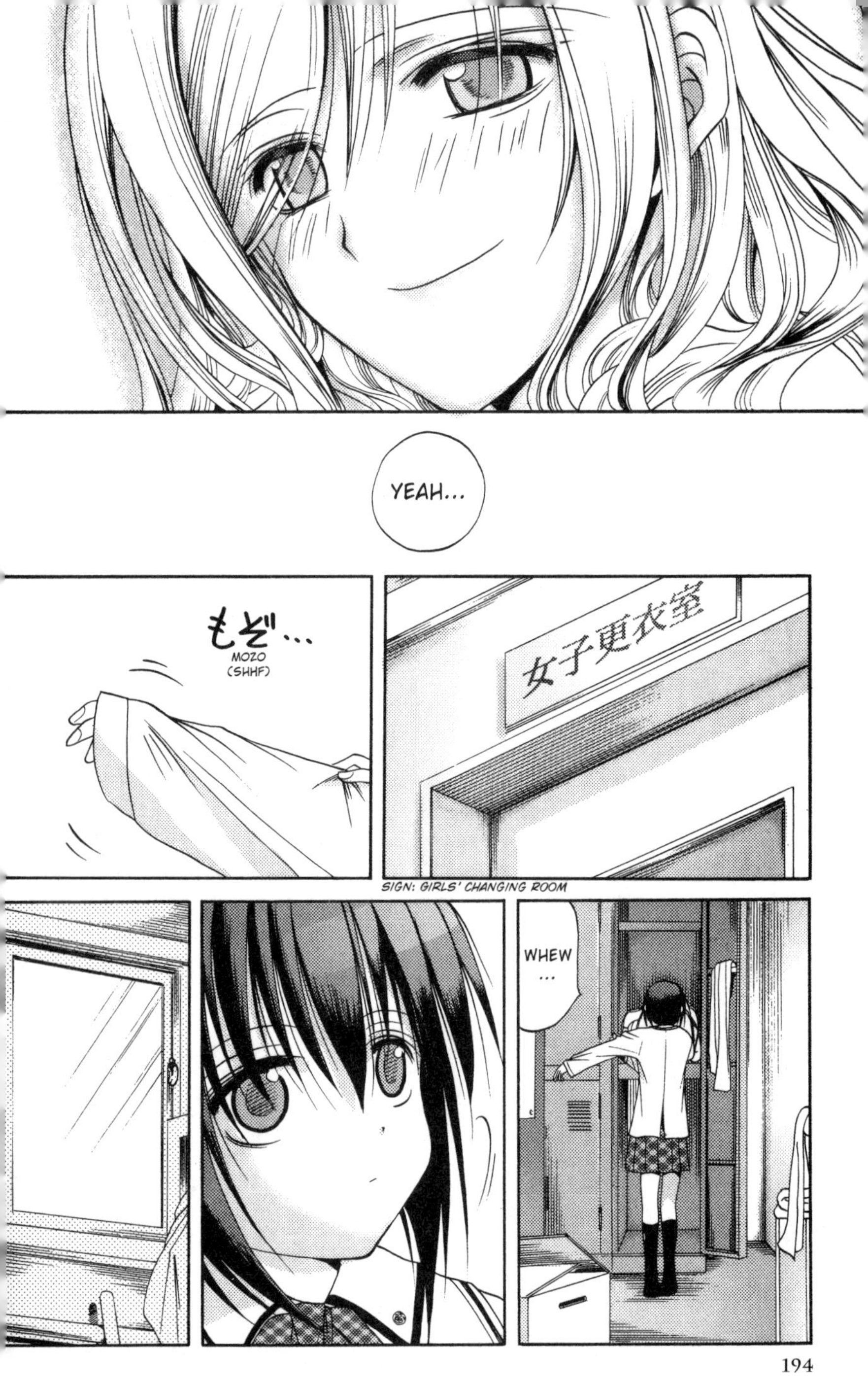
YEAH...
女子更衣室
SIGN: GIRLS' CHANGING ROOM
もぞ…
MOZO
(SHHF)
WHEW
...

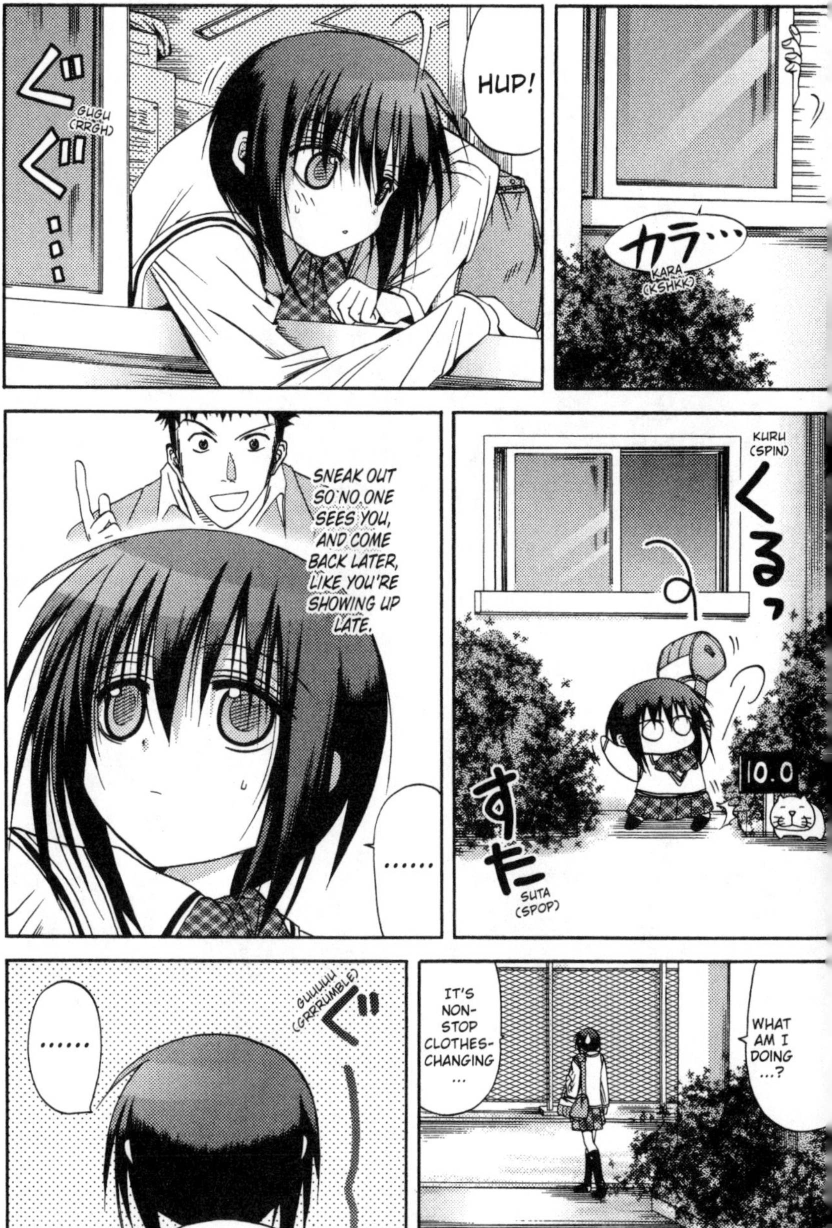
カラ…
KARA (KSHKK)
HUP!
ぐぐ…
GUGU (RRGH)
くるっ
KURU (SPIN)
すたっ
SUTA (SPOP)
10.0
SNEAK OUT SO NO ONE SEES YOU, AND COME BACK LATER, LIKE YOU'RE SHOWING UP LATE.
......
WHAT AM I DOING ...?
IT'S NON-STOP CLOTHES-CHANGING ...
ぐー
GUUUUU (GRRRUMBLE)
......

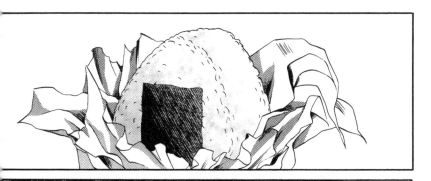

SORRY, EVERYONE.

I NEED TO FILL MY STOMACH ...

BAMBOO BLADE

YOKOO-SAN AND ANDOU-SAN (2)

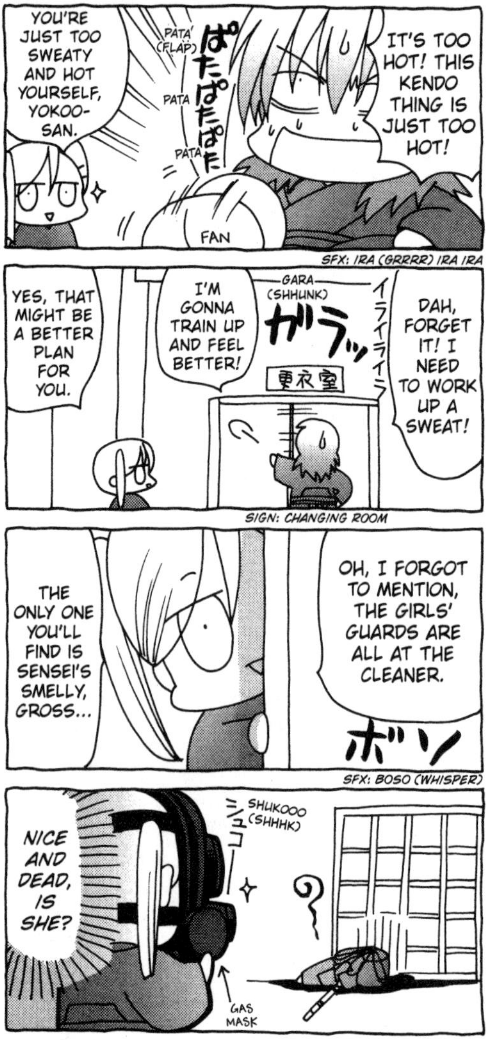
IT'S TOO HOT! THIS KENDO THING IS JUST TOO HOT!
PATA (FLAP)
PATA
PATA
ぱたぱたぱた
YOU'RE JUST TOO SWEATY AND HOT YOURSELF, YOKOO-SAN.
FAN
SFX: IRA (GRRRR) IRA IRA
DAH, FORGET IT! I NEED TO WORK UP A SWEAT!
イライライラ
GARA (SHHUNK)
ガラッ
更衣室
I'M GONNA TRAIN UP AND FEEL BETTER!
YES, THAT MIGHT BE A BETTER PLAN FOR YOU.
SIGN: CHANGING ROOM
OH, I FORGOT TO MENTION, THE GIRLS' GUARDS ARE ALL AT THE CLEANER.
ボソ
THE ONLY ONE YOU'LL FIND IS SENSEI'S SMELLY, GROSS...
SFX: BOSO (WHISPER)
SHUKOOO (SHHHK)
シュコー
NICE AND DEAD, IS SHE?
GAS MASK

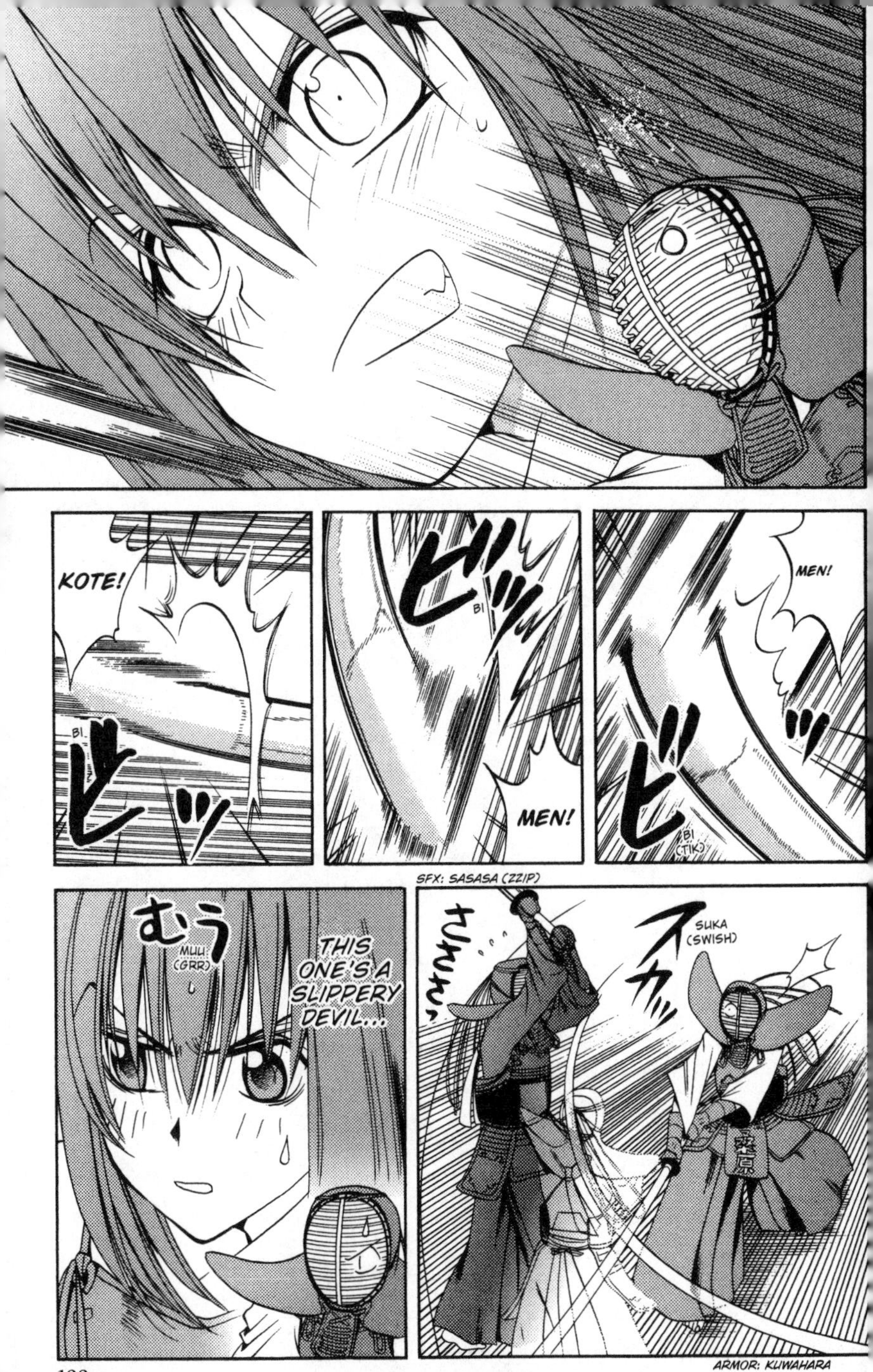
MEN!
BI
(TIK)
BI
MEN!
KOTE!
BI
SFX: SASASA (ZZIP)
SUKA
(SWISH)
MUU
(GRR)
THIS ONE'S A SLIPPERY DEVIL...
ARMOR: KUWAHARA

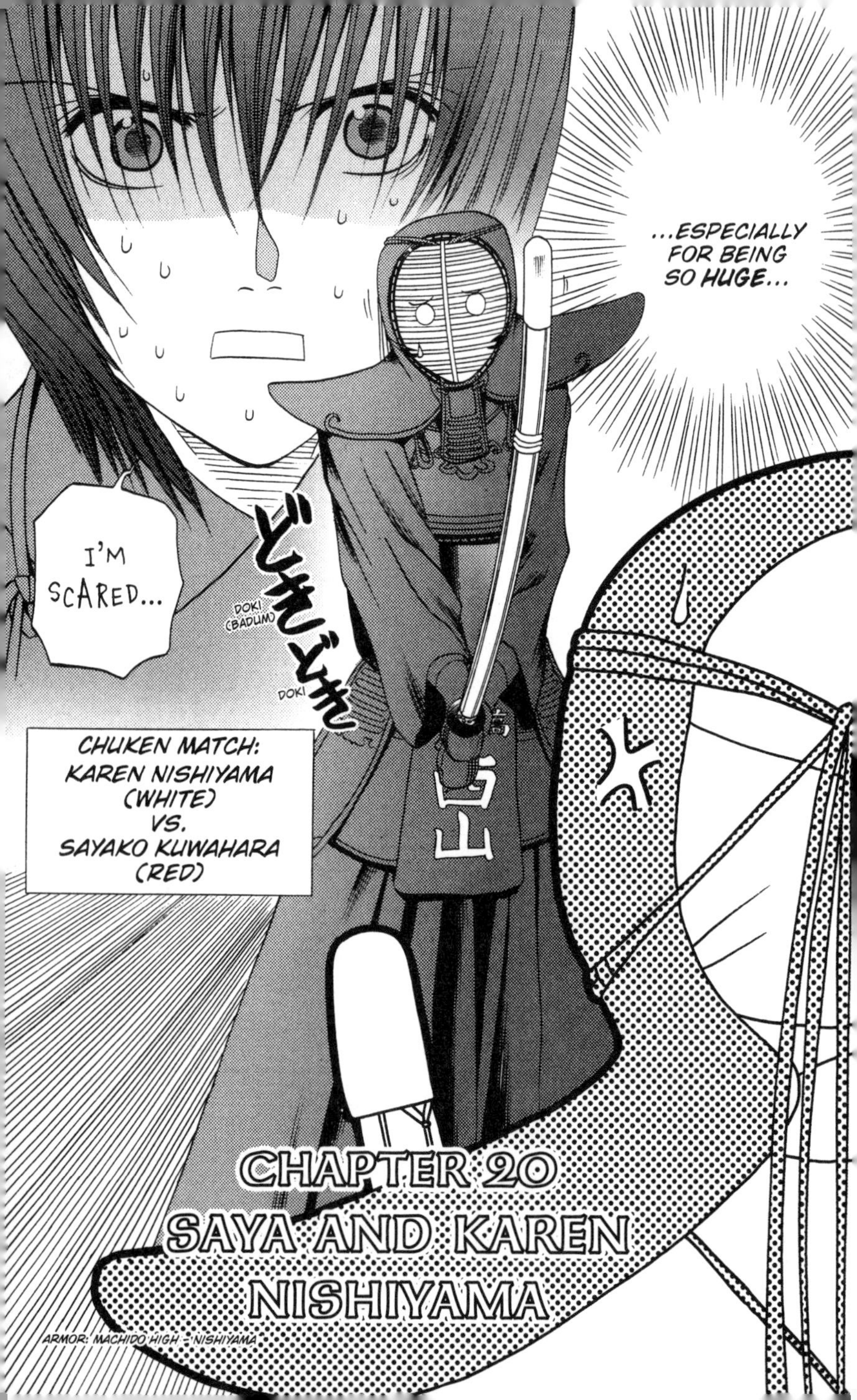
...ESPECIALLY FOR BEING SO HUGE...
I'M SCARED...
どきどき
DOKI (BADUM) DOKI
CHUKEN MATCH: KAREN NISHIYAMA (WHITE) VS. SAYAKO KUWAHARA (RED)
CHAPTER 20
SAYA AND KAREN NISHIYAMA
ARMOR: MACHIDO HIGH - NISHIYAMA

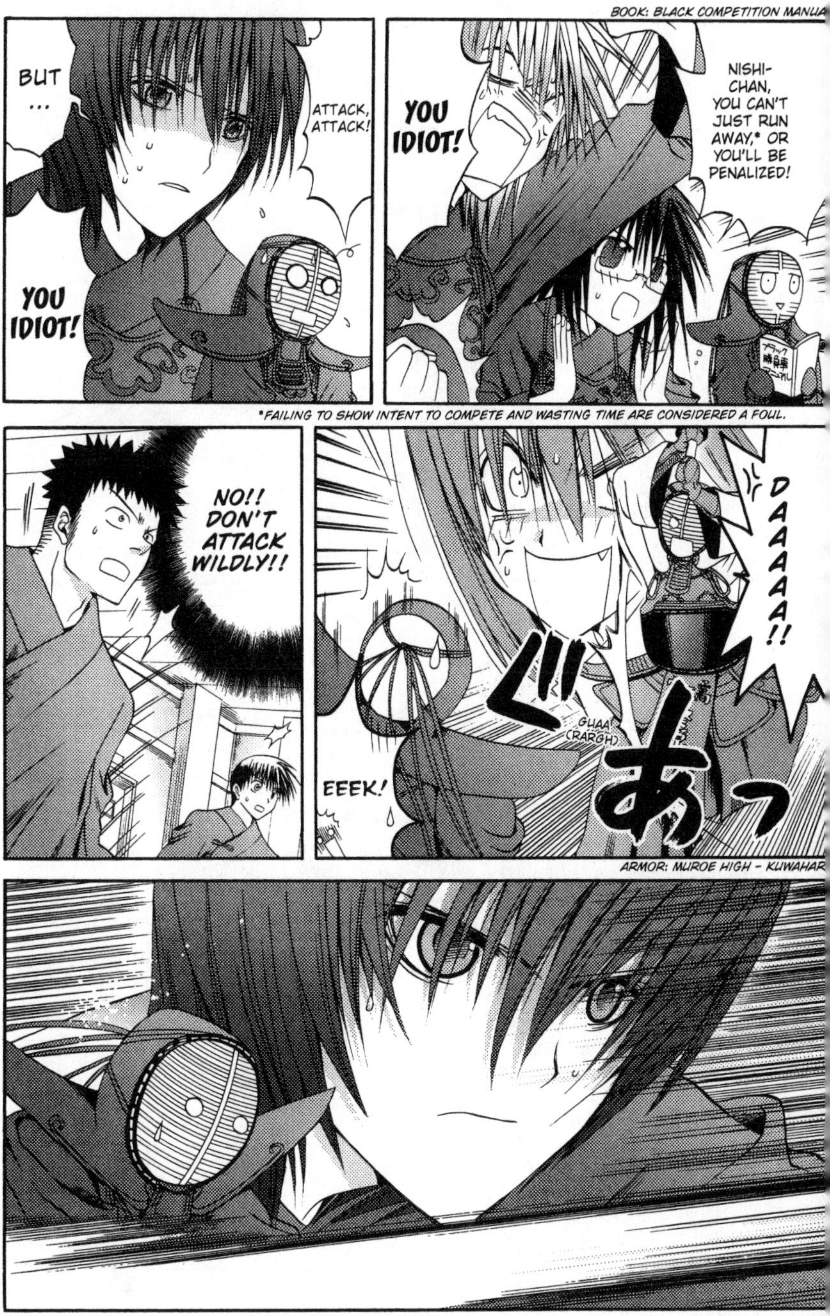
BOOK: BLACK COMPETITION MANUA
NISHI-CHAN, YOU CAN'T JUST RUN AWAY,* OR YOU'LL BE PENALIZED!
YOU IDIOT!
ATTACK, ATTACK!
BUT ...
YOU IDIOT!
*FAILING TO SHOW INTENT TO COMPETE AND WASTING TIME ARE CONSIDERED A FOUL.
DAAAAAAA!!
GUAA! (RARGH)
EEEK!
NO!! DON'T ATTACK WILDLY!!
ARMOR: MUROE HIGH - KUWAHAR

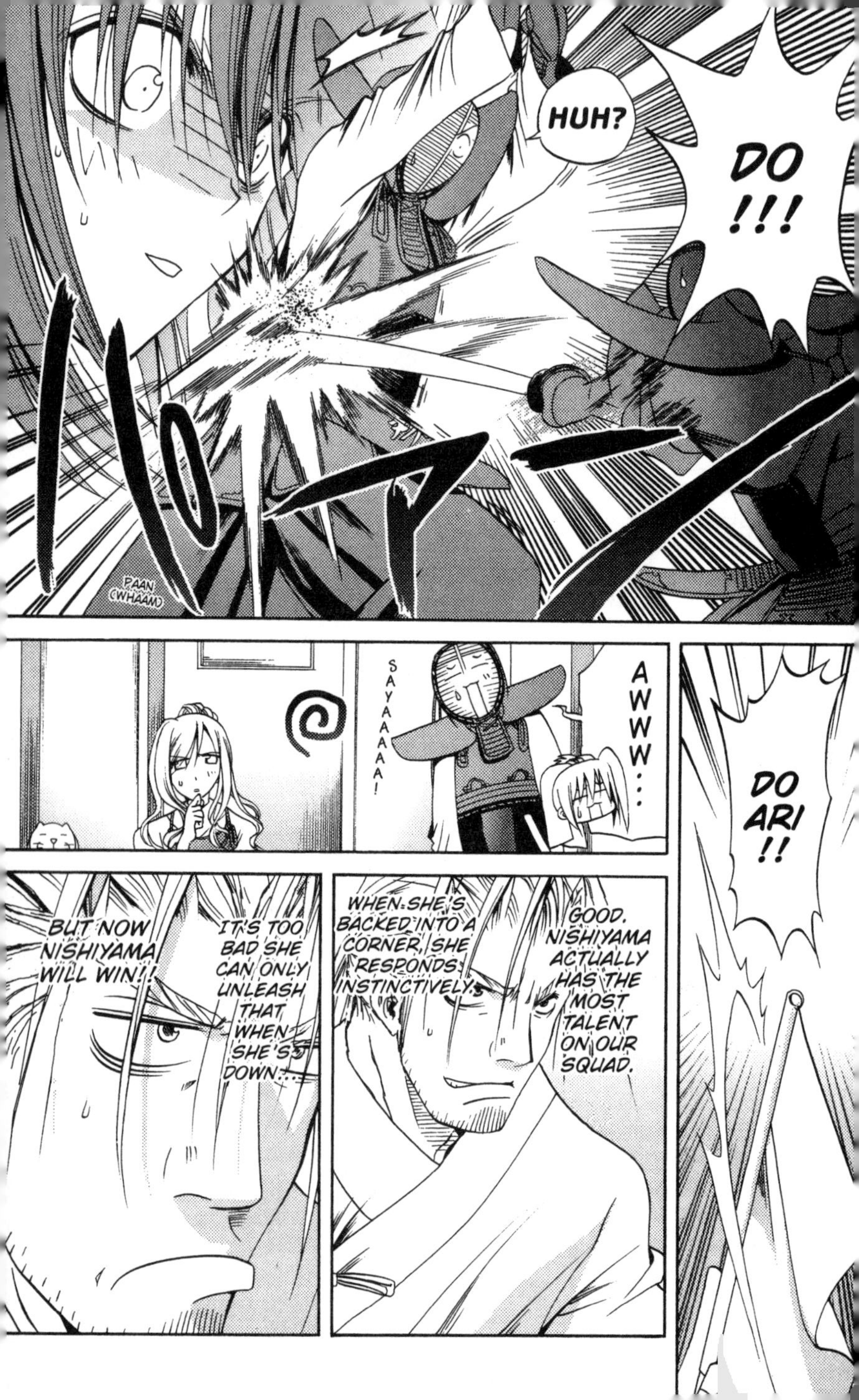
DO !!!
HUH?
PAAN (WHAAM)
DO ARI!!
AWWW...
SAYAAAAAA!
GOOD. NISHIYAMA ACTUALLY HAS THE MOST TALENT ON OUR SQUAD.
WHEN SHE'S BACKED INTO A CORNER, SHE RESPONDS INSTINCTIVELY.
IT'S TOO BAD SHE CAN ONLY UNLEASH THAT WHEN SHE'S DOWN...
BUT NOW NISHIYAMA WILL WIN!!

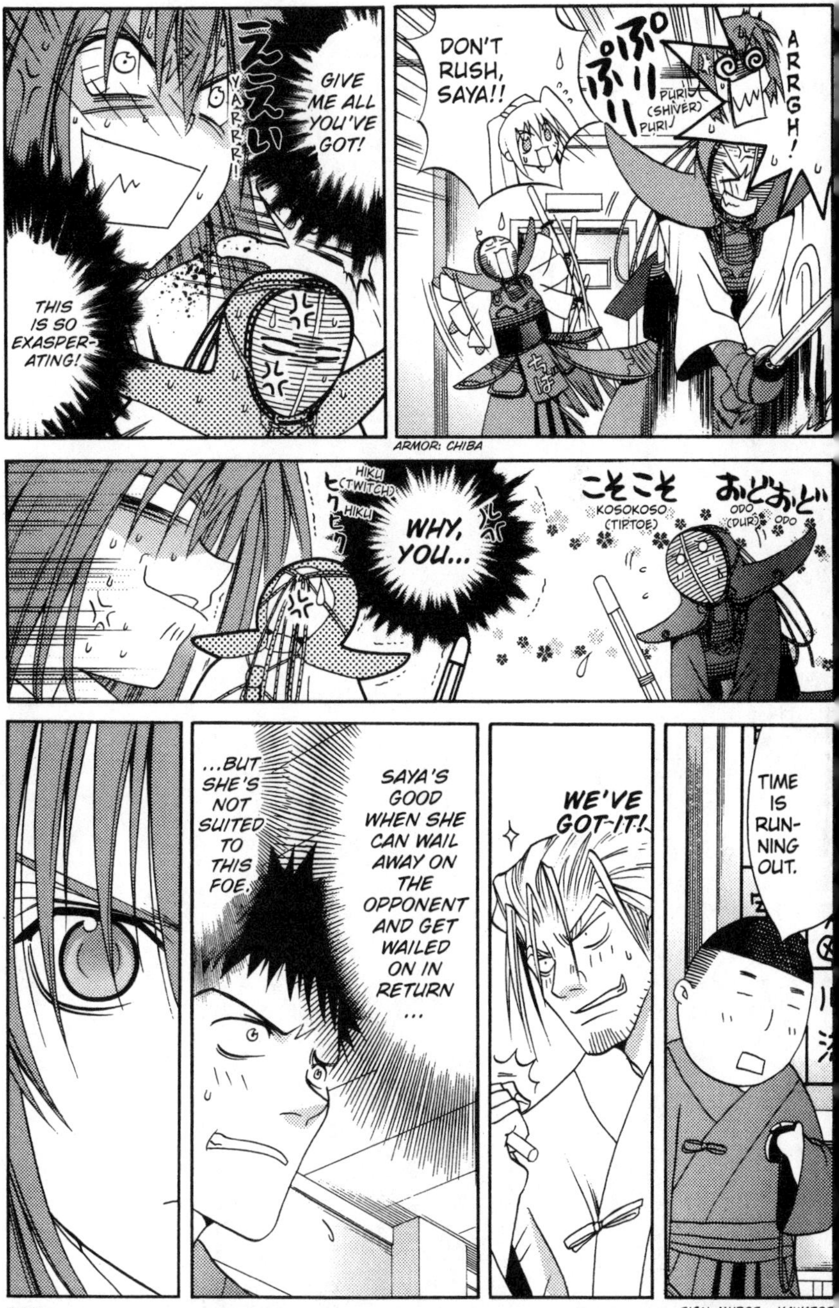
DON'T RUSH, SAYA!!
ぷりぷり
PURI (SHIVER) PURI
ARRGH!
ええい
YARR!
GIVE ME ALL YOU'VE GOT!
THIS IS SO EXASPERATING!
おどおど
ODO (DUR) ODO
こそこそ
KOSOKOSO (TIPTOE)
WHY, YOU...
ヒクヒク
HIKU (TWITCH) HIKU
TIME IS RUNNING OUT.
WE'VE GOT IT!
SAYA'S GOOD WHEN SHE CAN WAIL AWAY ON THE OPPONENT AND GET WAILED ON IN RETURN...
...BUT SHE'S NOT SUITED TO THIS FOE.
ARMOR: CHIBA

SIGN: MUROE - KAWAZOE

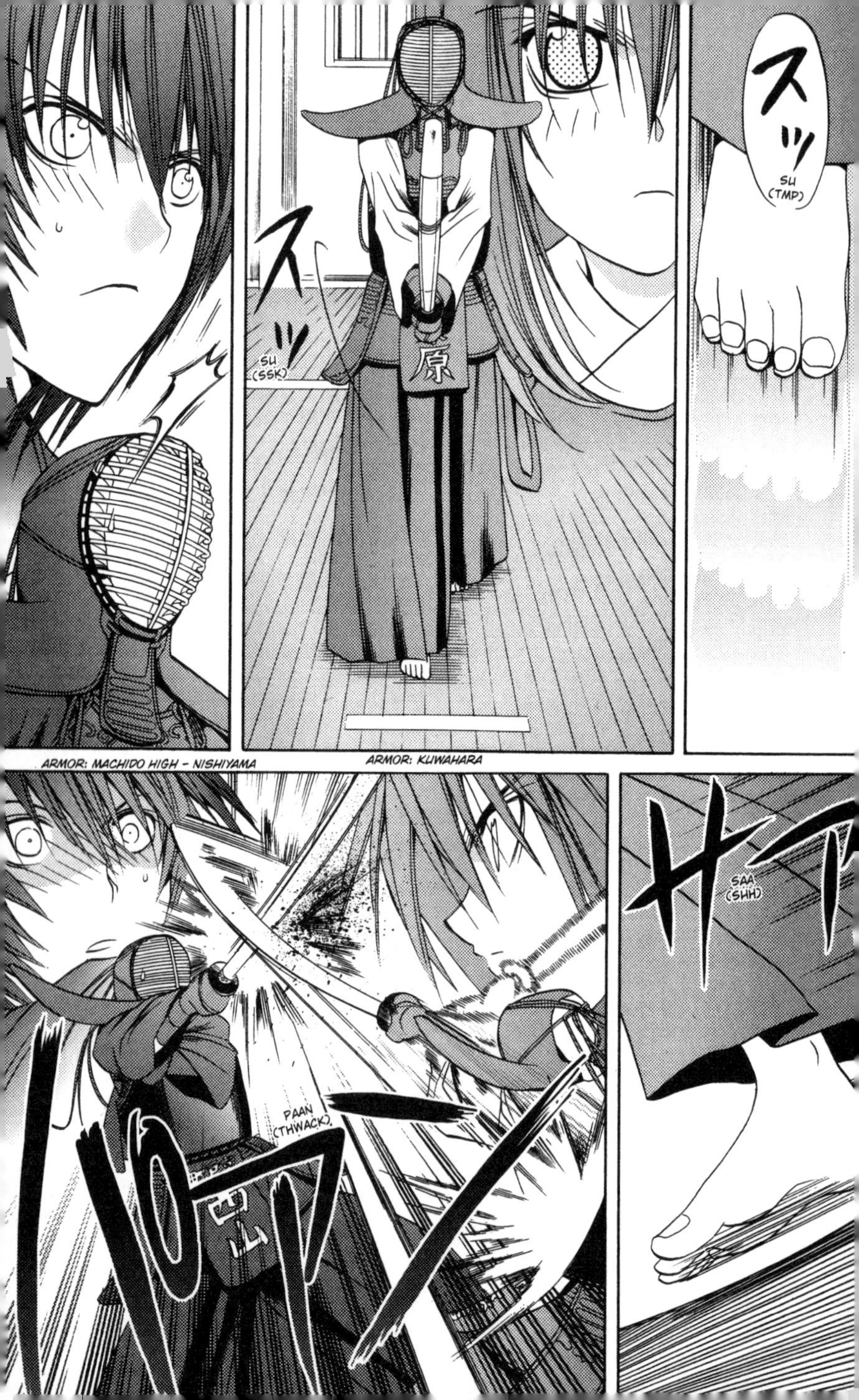
スッ
SU (TMP)
スッ
SU (SSK)
ARMOR: KUWAHARA
ARMOR: MACHIDO HIGH – NISHIYAMA
SAA (SHH)
PAAN (THWACK)

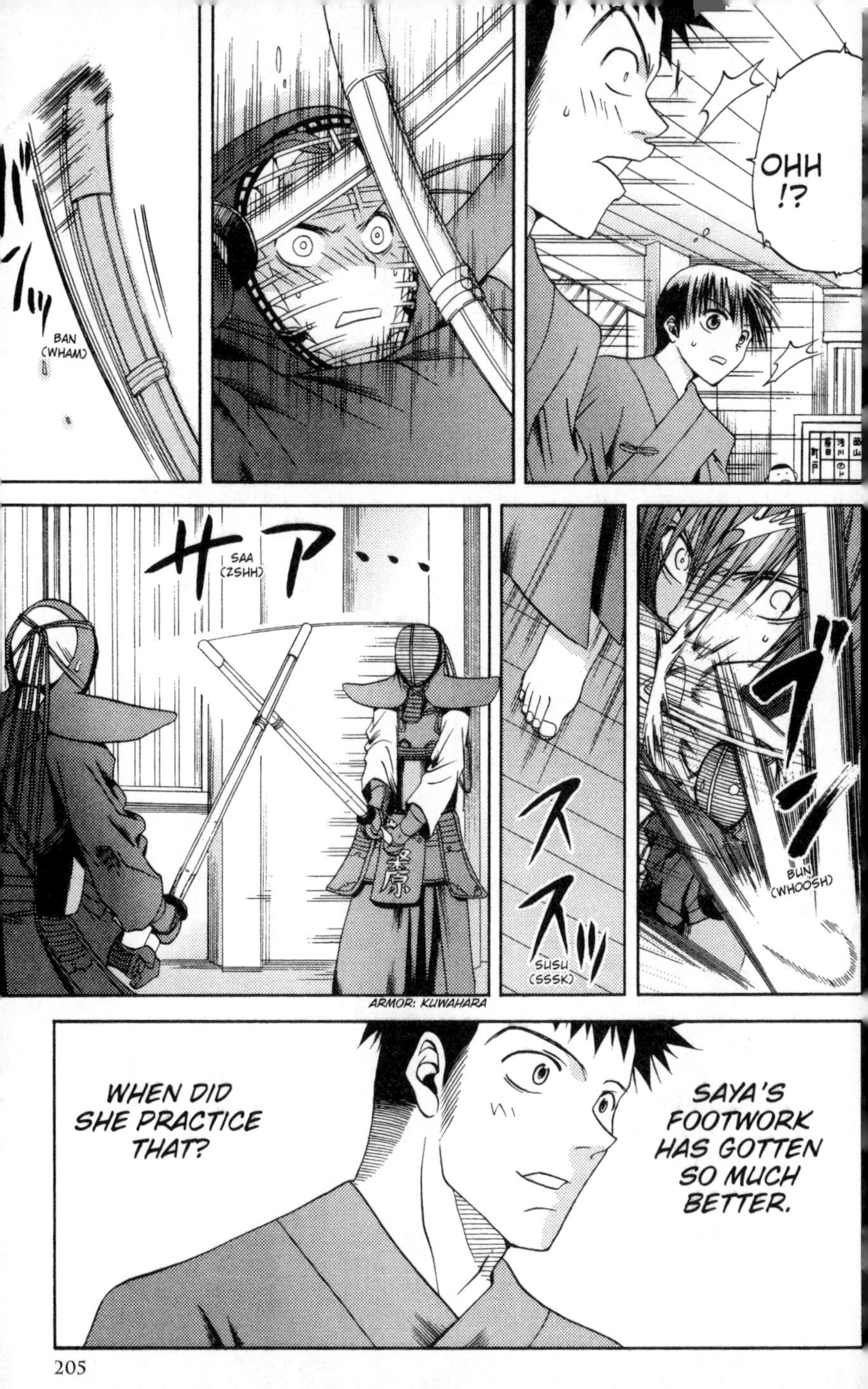
OHH !?
BAN (WHAM)
BUN (WHOOSH)
SUSU (SSSK)
SAA (ZSHH)
ARMOR: KUWAHARA
SAYA'S FOOTWORK HAS GOTTEN SO MUCH BETTER.
WHEN DID SHE PRACTICE THAT?

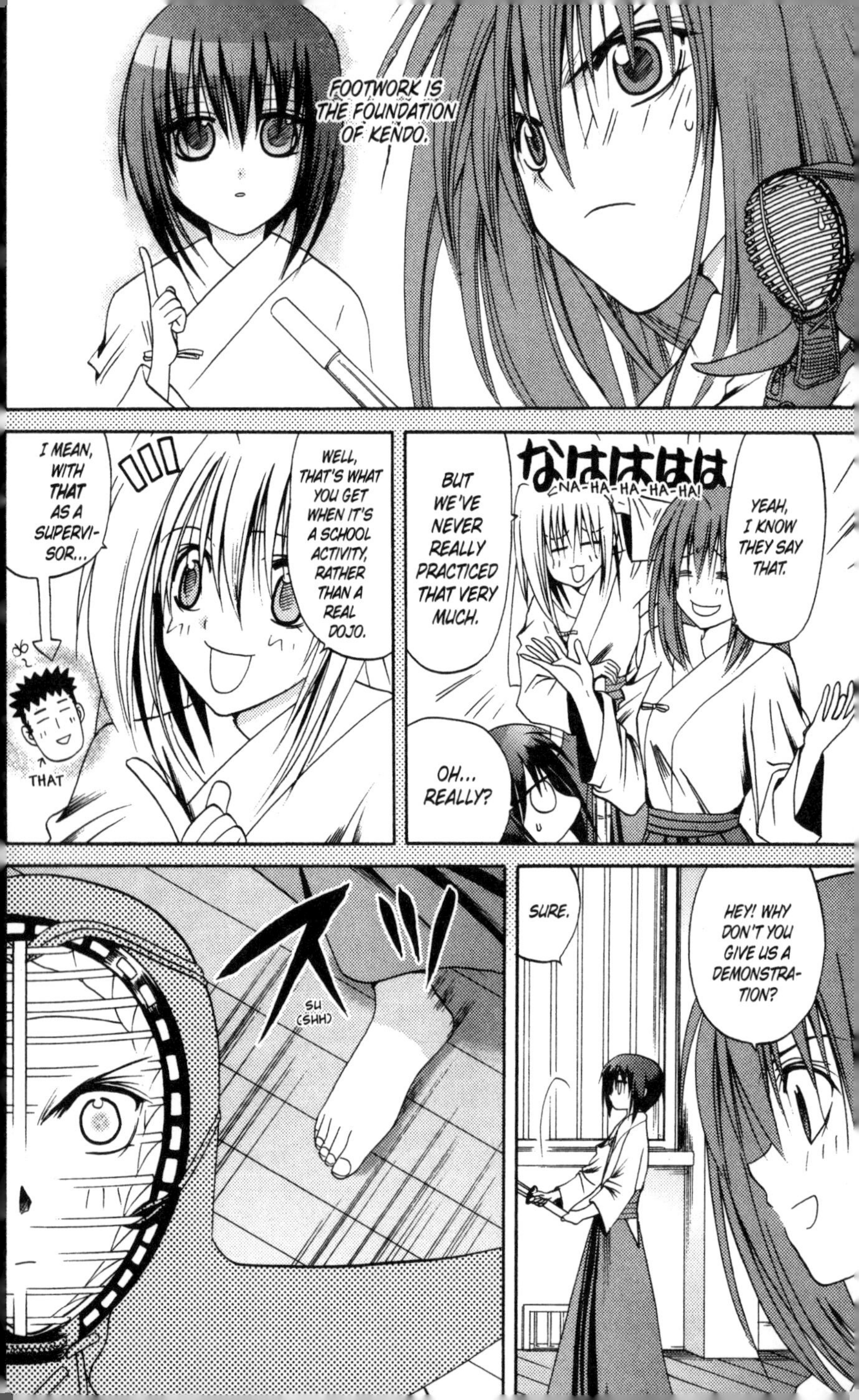
FOOTWORK IS THE FOUNDATION OF KENDO.
YEAH, I KNOW THEY SAY THAT.
なはははは
NA-HA-HA-HA-HA!
BUT WE'VE NEVER REALLY PRACTICED THAT VERY MUCH.
OH... REALLY?
WELL, THAT'S WHAT YOU GET WHEN IT'S A SCHOOL ACTIVITY, RATHER THAN A REAL DOJO.
I MEAN, WITH THAT AS A SUPERVISOR...
THAT
HEY! WHY DON'T YOU GIVE US A DEMONSTRATION?
SURE.
SU (SHH)

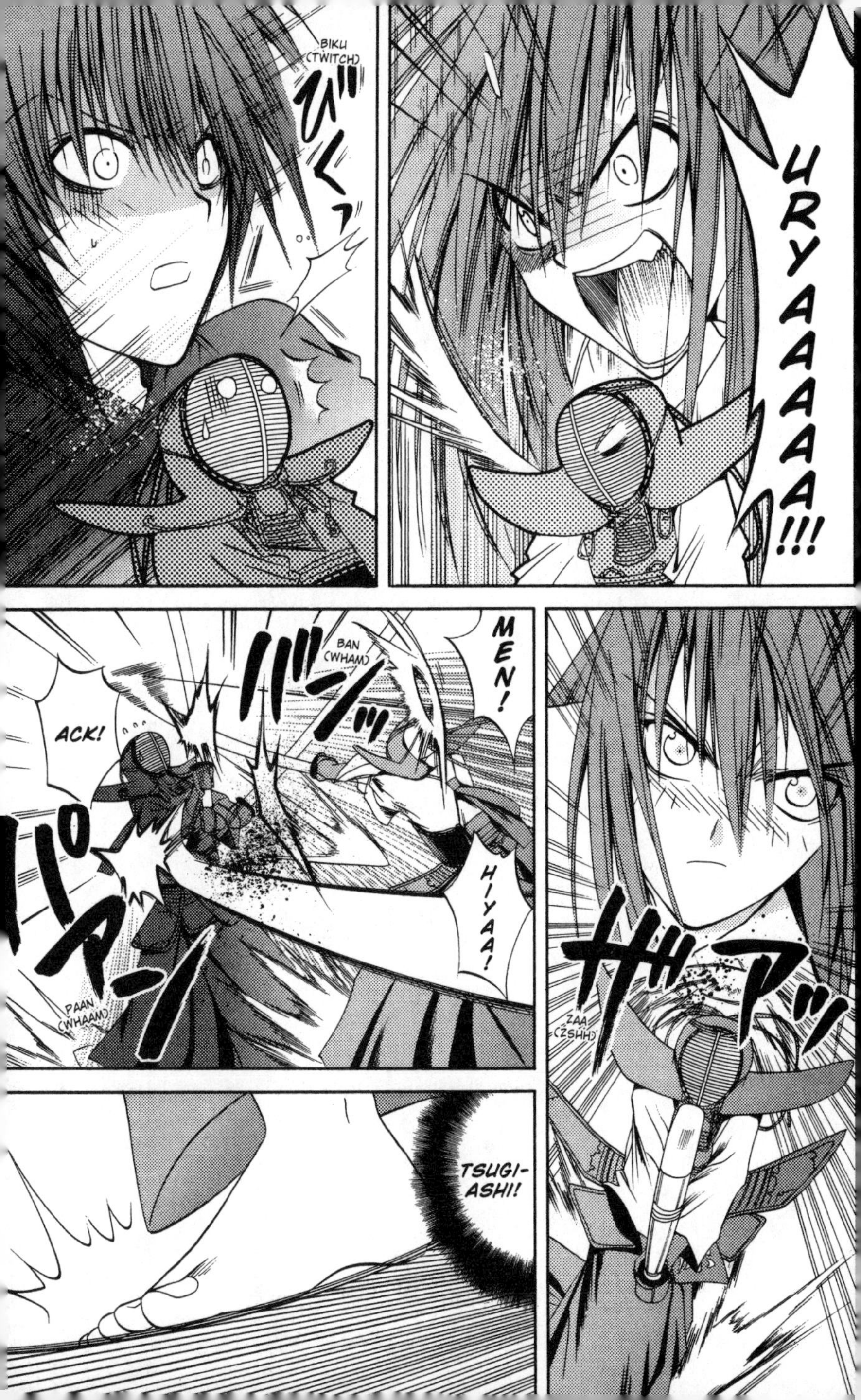
URYAAAAAAA!!!
BIKU (TWITCH)
びくっ
ザァッ
ZAA (ZSHH)
MEN!
BAN (WHAM)
バンッ
HIYAA!
ACK!
パァーン
PAAN (WHAAM)
TSUGI-ASHI!

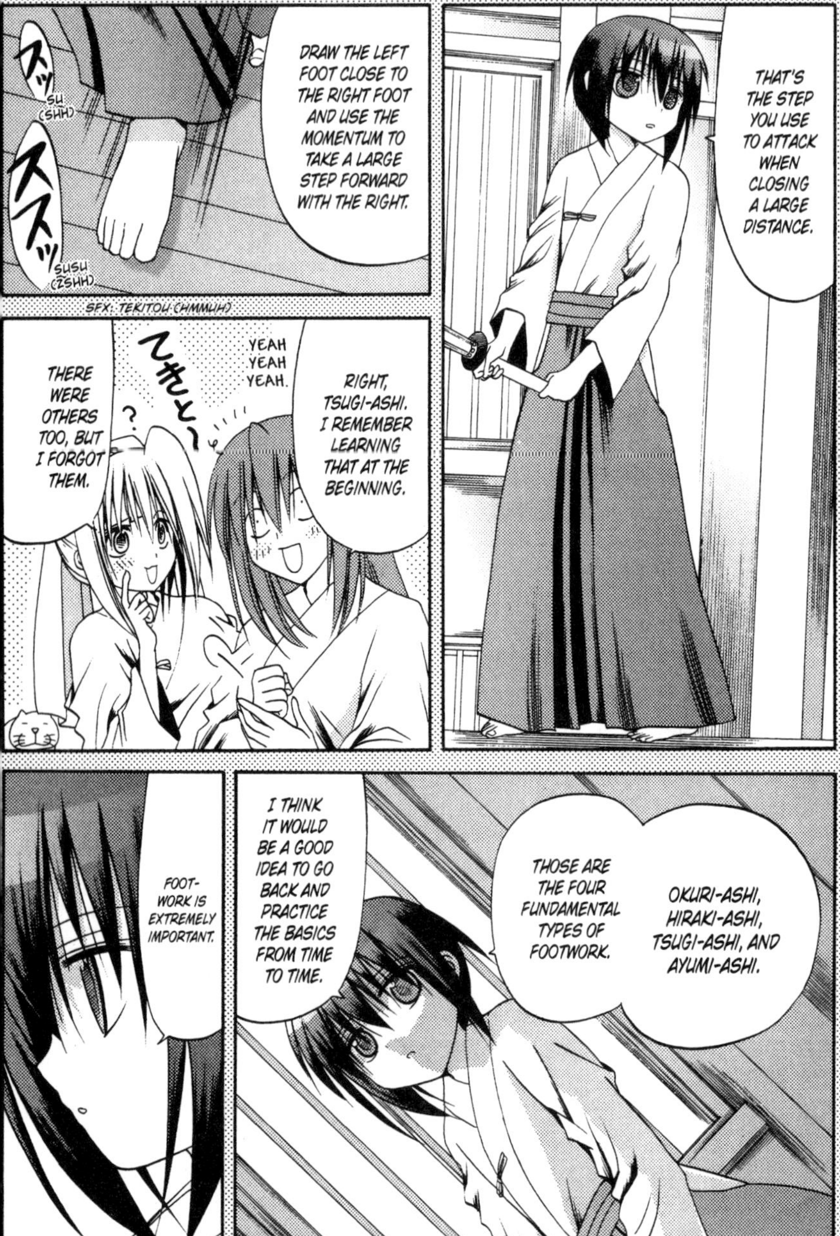
THAT'S THE STEP YOU USE TO ATTACK WHEN CLOSING A LARGE DISTANCE.
DRAW THE LEFT FOOT CLOSE TO THE RIGHT FOOT AND USE THE MOMENTUM TO TAKE A LARGE STEP FORWARD WITH THE RIGHT.
スッ
SU (SHH)
ススッ
SUSU (ZSHH)
SFX: TEKITOU (HMMUH)
RIGHT, TSUGI-ASHI. I REMEMBER LEARNING THAT AT THE BEGINNING.
YEAH YEAH YEAH.
てきと～
?
THERE WERE OTHERS TOO, BUT I FORGOT THEM.
OKURI-ASHI, HIRAKI-ASHI, TSUGI-ASHI, AND AYUMI-ASHI.
THOSE ARE THE FOUR FUNDAMENTAL TYPES OF FOOTWORK.
I THINK IT WOULD BE A GOOD IDEA TO GO BACK AND PRACTICE THE BASICS FROM TIME TO TIME.
FOOT-WORK IS EXTREMELY IMPORTANT.

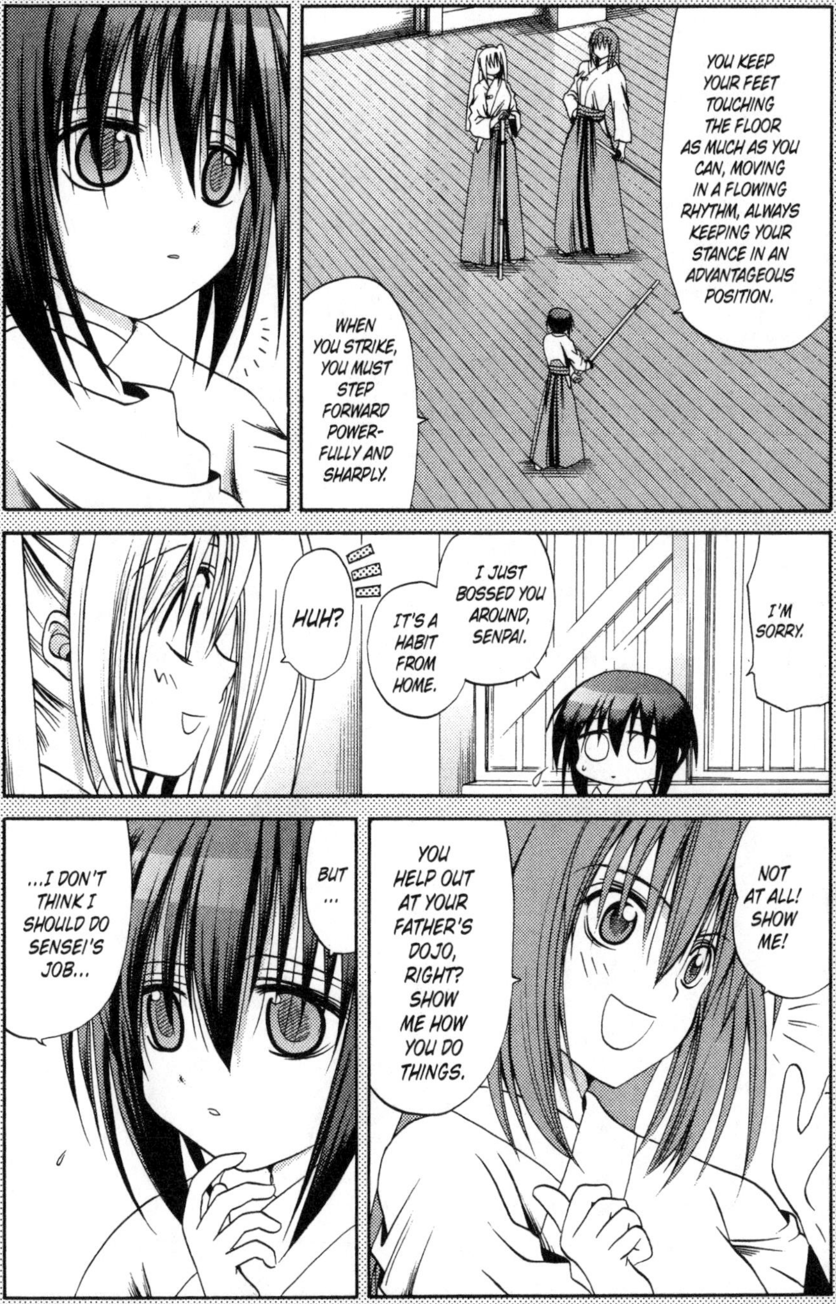
YOU KEEP YOUR FEET TOUCHING THE FLOOR AS MUCH AS YOU CAN, MOVING IN A FLOWING RHYTHM, ALWAYS KEEPING YOUR STANCE IN AN ADVANTAGEOUS POSITION.
WHEN YOU STRIKE, YOU MUST STEP FORWARD POWER-FULLY AND SHARPLY.
I'M SORRY.
I JUST BOSSED YOU AROUND, SENPAI.
IT'S A HABIT FROM HOME.
HUH?
NOT AT ALL! SHOW ME!
YOU HELP OUT AT YOUR FATHER'S DOJO, RIGHT? SHOW ME HOW YOU DO THINGS.
BUT ...
...I DON'T THINK I SHOULD DO SENSEI'S JOB...

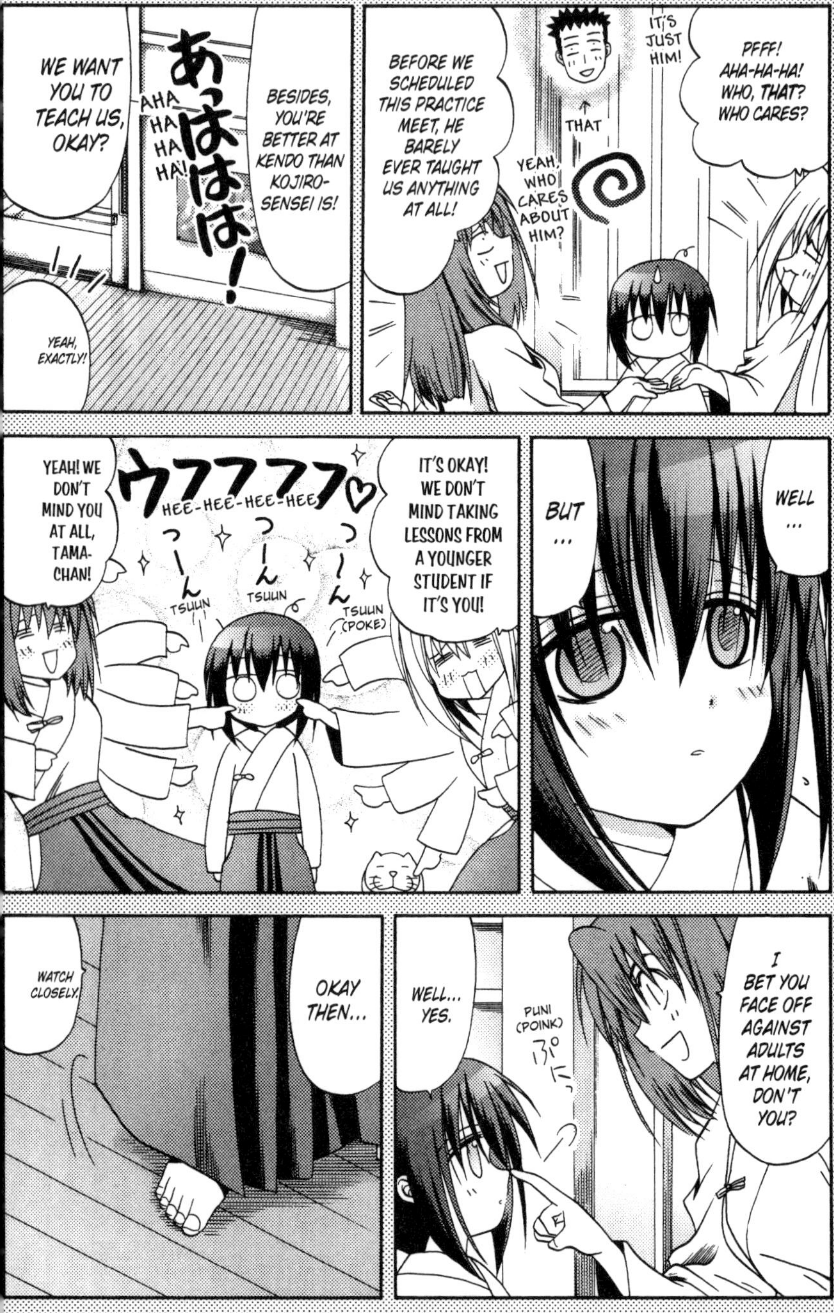
PFFF! AHA-HA-HA! WHO, THAT? WHO CARES?
IT'S JUST HIM!
THAT
YEAH, WHO CARES ABOUT HIM?
BEFORE WE SCHEDULED THIS PRACTICE MEET, HE BARELY EVER TAUGHT US ANYTHING AT ALL!
BESIDES, YOU'RE BETTER AT KENDO THAN KOJIRO-SENSEI IS!
あっははは!
AHA HA HA HA!
WE WANT YOU TO TEACH US, OKAY?
YEAH, EXACTLY!
WELL ...
BUT ...
IT'S OKAY! WE DON'T MIND TAKING LESSONS FROM A YOUNGER STUDENT IF IT'S YOU!
つーん
TSUUN (POKE)
ウフフフフ♡
HEE-HEE-HEE-HEE
つーん
TSUUN
つーん
TSUUN
YEAH! WE DON'T MIND YOU AT ALL, TAMA-CHAN!
I BET YOU FACE OFF AGAINST ADULTS AT HOME, DON'T YOU?
PUNI (POINK)
ぷにっ
WELL... YES.
OKAY THEN...
WATCH CLOSELY.

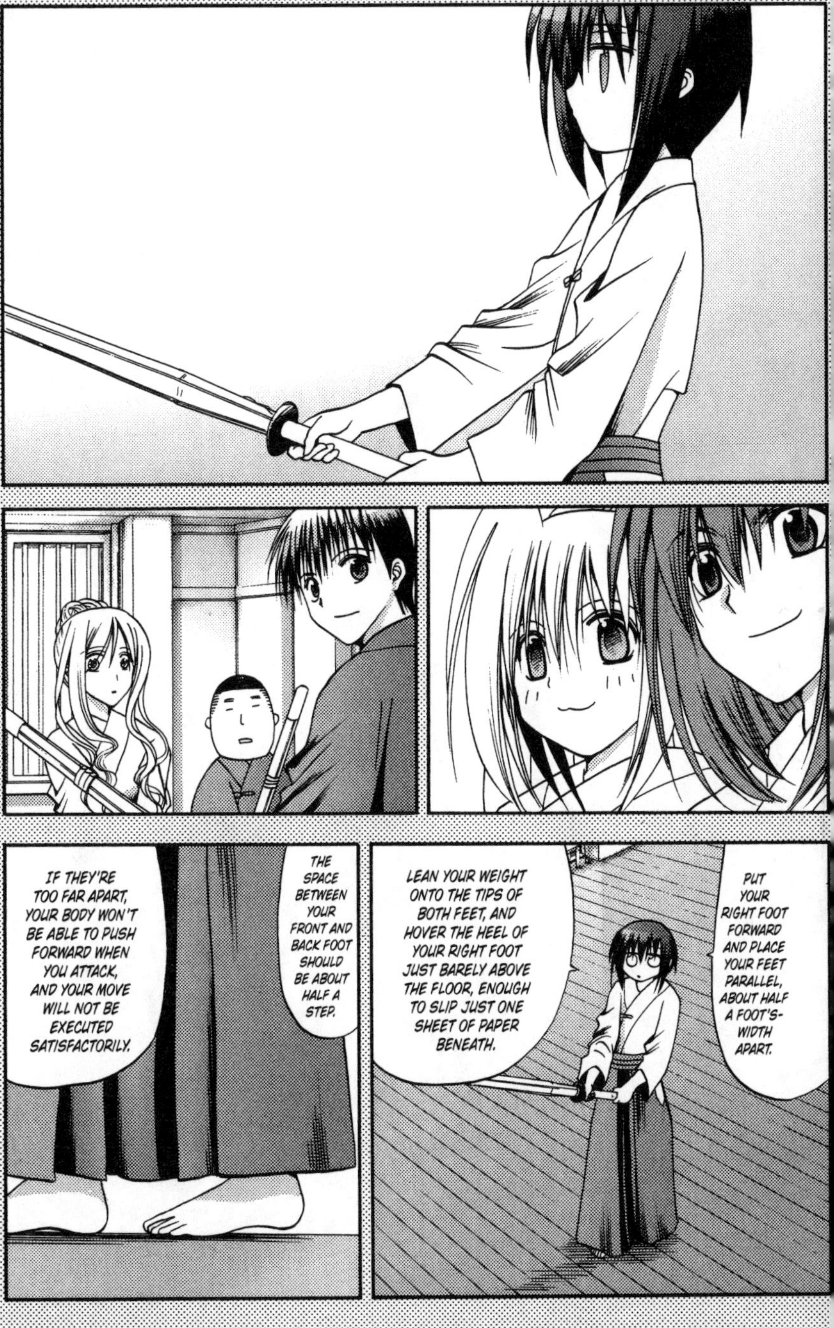
PUT YOUR RIGHT FOOT FORWARD AND PLACE YOUR FEET PARALLEL, ABOUT HALF A FOOT'S-WIDTH APART.
LEAN YOUR WEIGHT ONTO THE TIPS OF BOTH FEET, AND HOVER THE HEEL OF YOUR RIGHT FOOT JUST BARELY ABOVE THE FLOOR, ENOUGH TO SLIP JUST ONE SHEET OF PAPER BENEATH.
THE SPACE BETWEEN YOUR FRONT AND BACK FOOT SHOULD BE ABOUT HALF A STEP.
IF THEY'RE TOO FAR APART, YOUR BODY WON'T BE ABLE TO PUSH FORWARD WHEN YOU ATTACK, AND YOUR MOVE WILL NOT BE EXECUTED SATISFACTORILY.

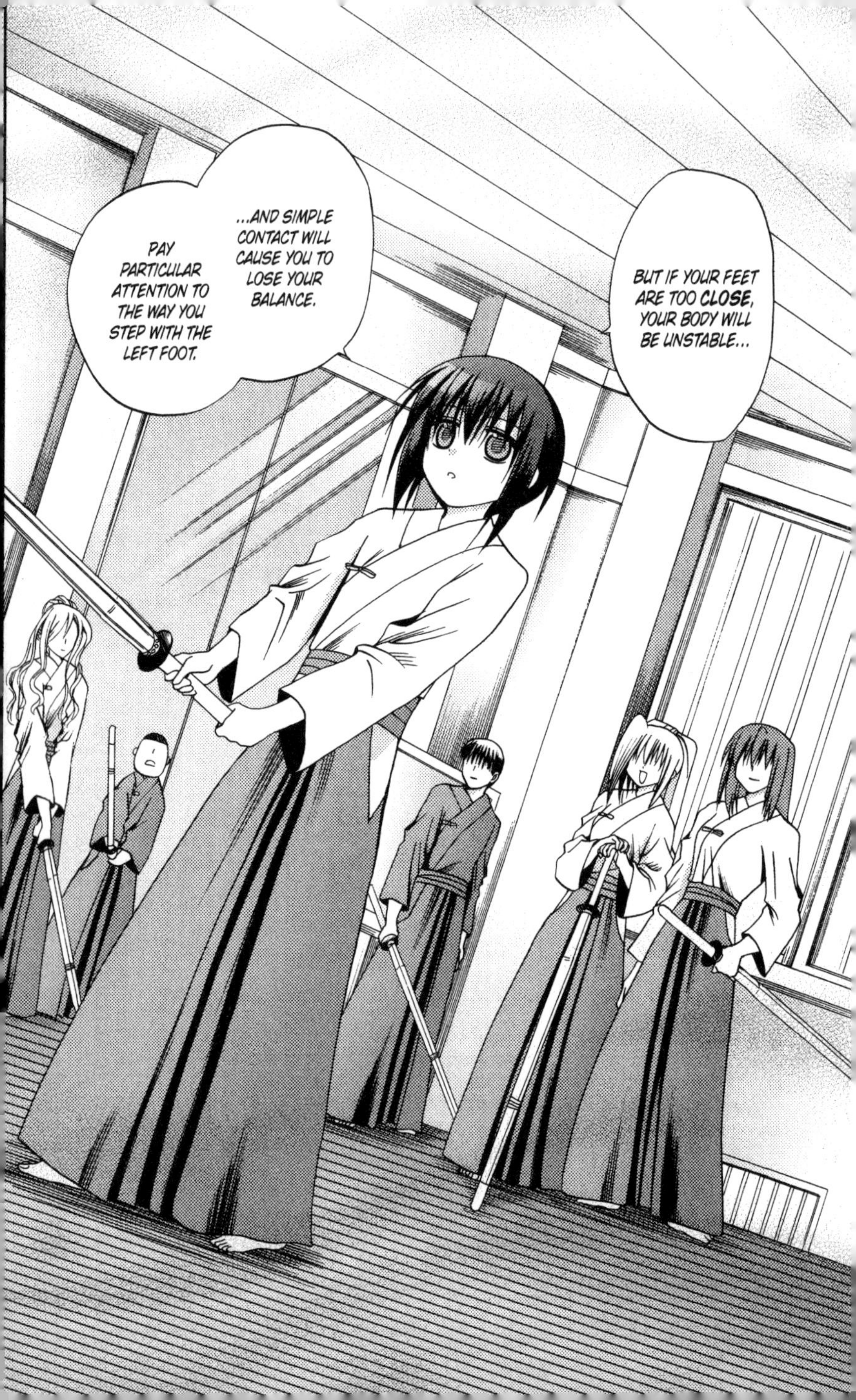
BUT IF YOUR FEET ARE TOO **CLOSE**, YOUR BODY WILL BE UNSTABLE...
...AND SIMPLE CONTACT WILL CAUSE YOU TO LOSE YOUR BALANCE.
PAY PARTICULAR ATTENTION TO THE WAY YOU STEP WITH THE LEFT FOOT.

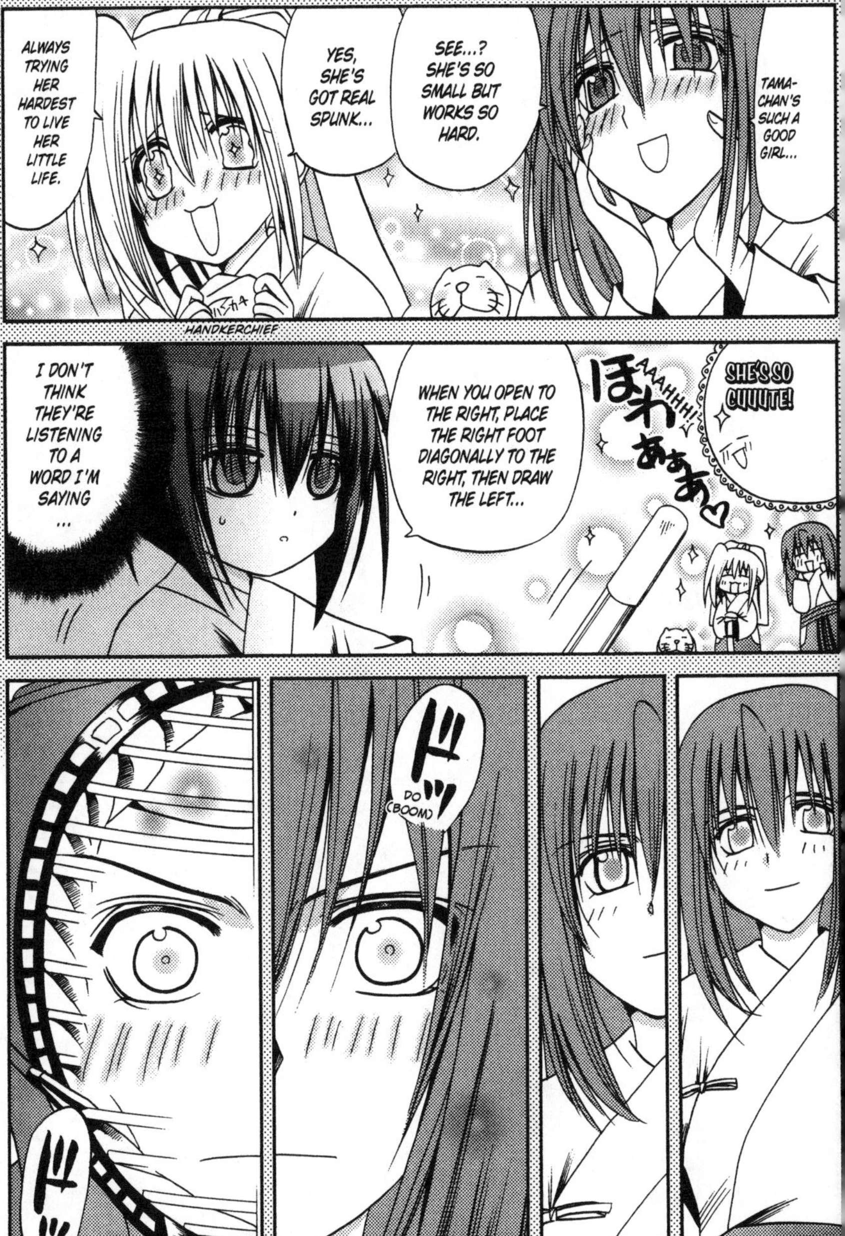
TAMA-CHAN'S SUCH A GOOD GIRL...
SEE...? SHE'S SO SMALL BUT WORKS SO HARD.
YES, SHE'S GOT REAL SPUNK...
ALWAYS TRYING HER HARDEST TO LIVE HER LITTLE LIFE.
ハンカチ
HANDKERCHIEF
SHE'S SO CUUUTE!
ほわぁぁぁ♥
AAAHHH!
WHEN YOU OPEN TO THE RIGHT, PLACE THE RIGHT FOOT DIAGONALLY TO THE RIGHT, THEN DRAW THE LEFT...
I DON'T THINK THEY'RE LISTENING TO A WORD I'M SAYING...
ドッ
DO (BOOM)
ドッ
DO

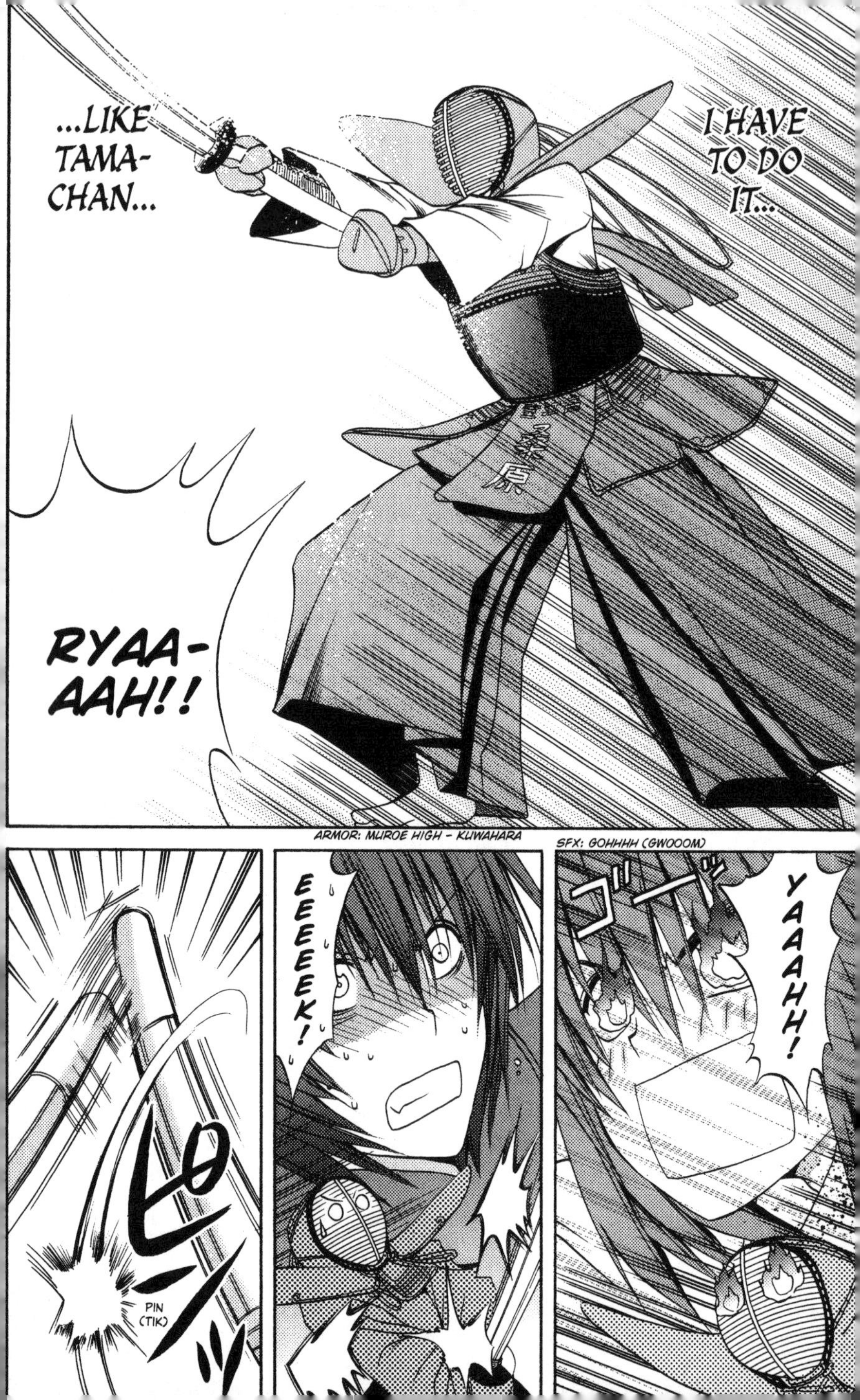
I HAVE TO DO IT...
...LIKE TAMA-CHAN...
RYAA-AAH!!
ARMOR: MUROE HIGH - KUWAHARA
SFX: GOHHHH (GWOOOM)
YAAAAHH!
EEEEEEK!
PIN (TIK)

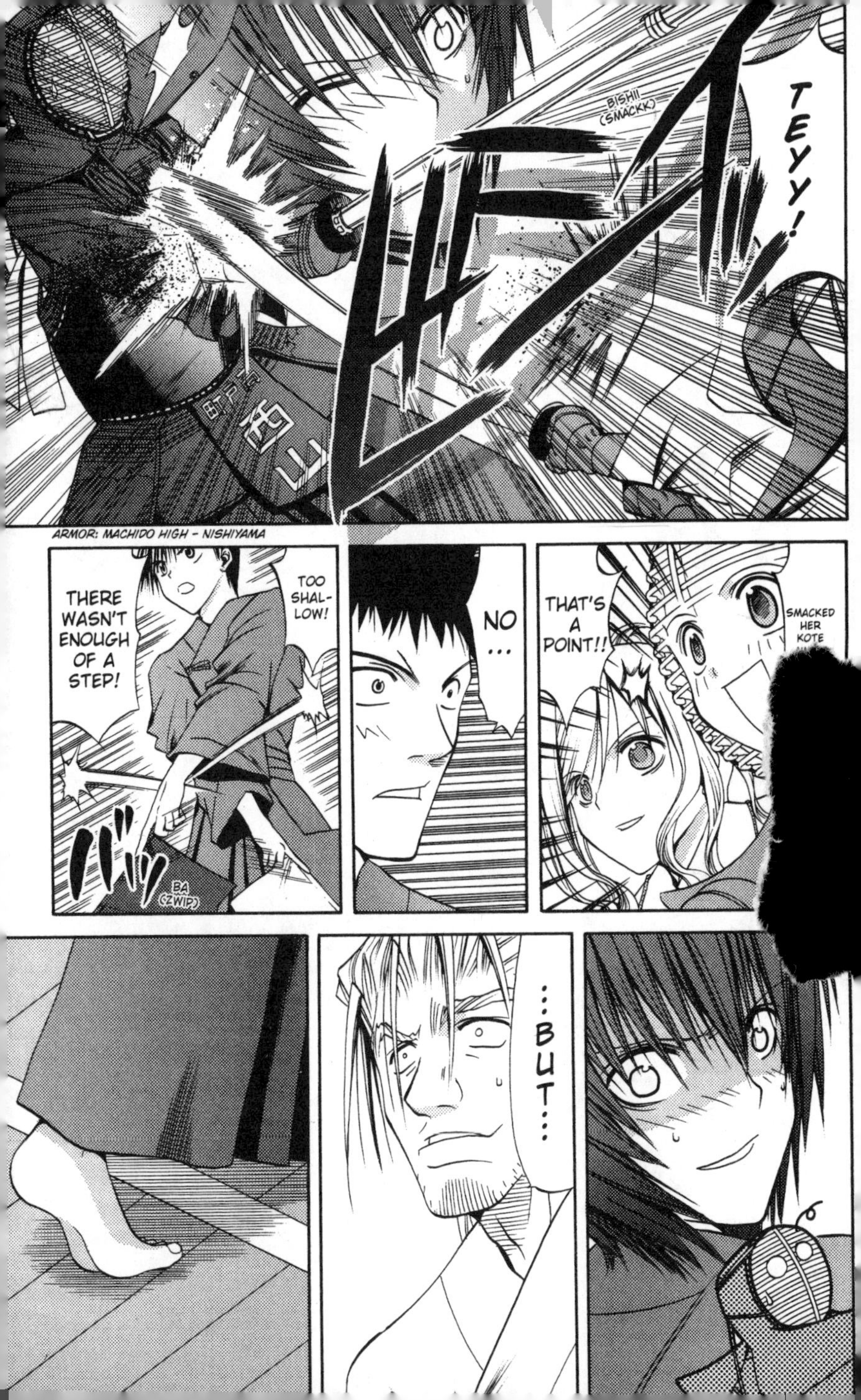
TEYY!
BISHI! (SMACKK)
ARMOR: MACHIDO HIGH - NISHIYAMA
SMACKED HER KOTE
THAT'S A POINT!!
NO ...
TOO SHAL-LOW!
THERE WASN'T ENOUGH OF A STEP!
BA (ZWIP)
...BUT...

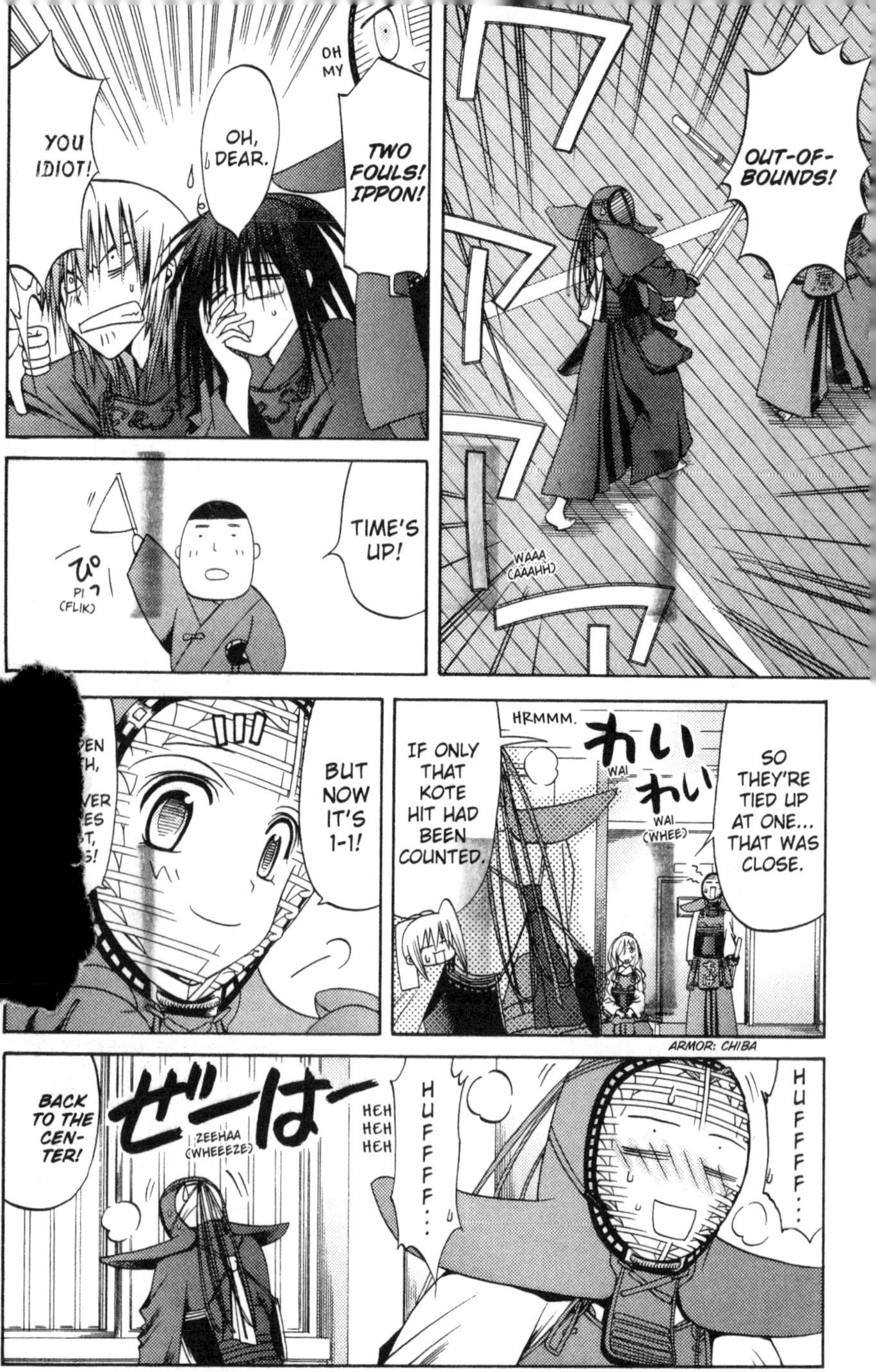
OUT-OF-BOUNDS!
WAAA (AAAHH)
OH MY
TWO FOULS! IPPON!
OH, DEAR.
YOU IDIOT!
TIME'S UP!
ぴっ PI (FLIK)
SO THEY'RE TIED UP AT ONE... THAT WAS CLOSE.
わい わい WAI WAI (WHEE)
HRMMM.
IF ONLY THAT KOTE HIT HAD BEEN COUNTED.
BUT NOW IT'S 1-1!
ARMOR: CHIBA
HUFFFF...
HEH HEH HEH
HUFFFF...
ぜーはー ZEEHAA (WHEEEZE)
BACK TO THE CENTER!

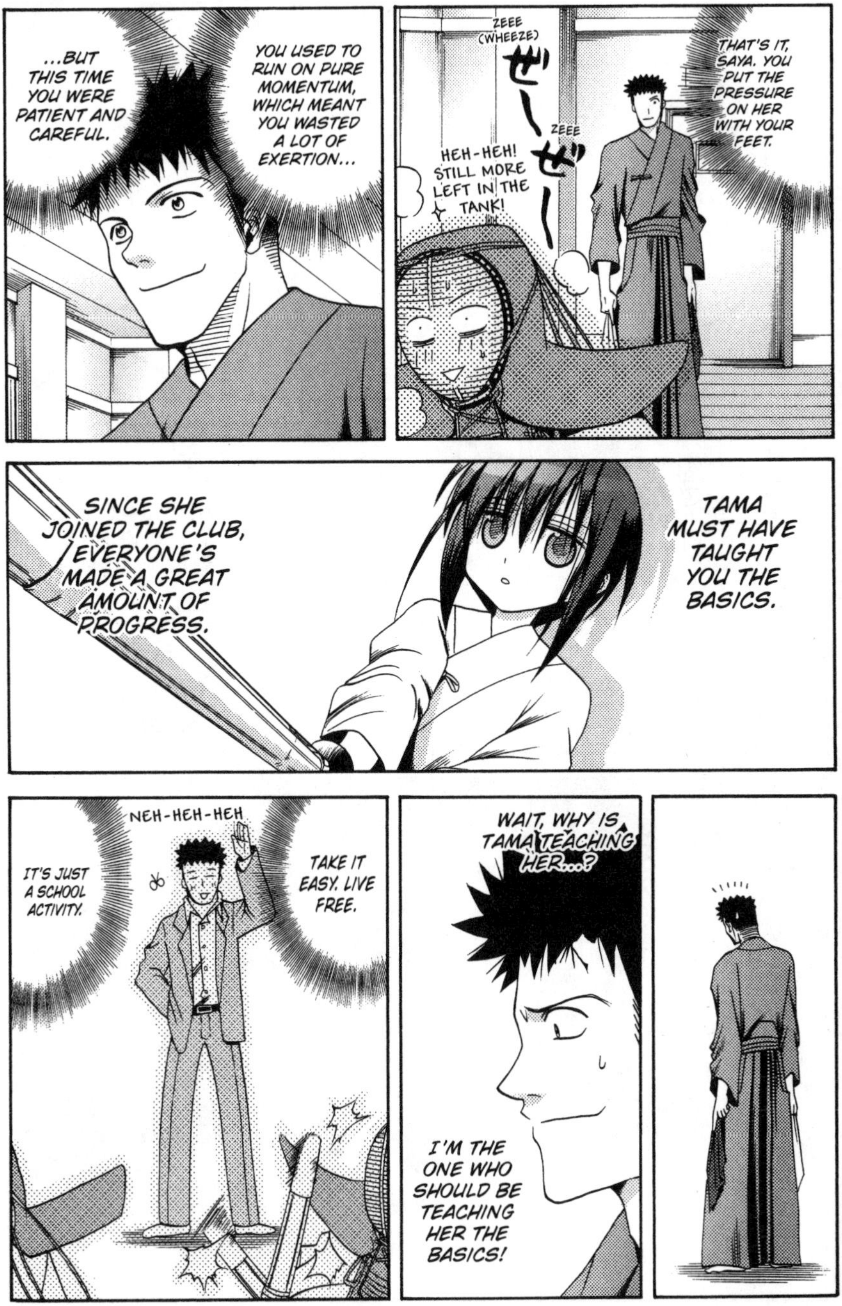
THAT'S IT, SAYA. YOU PUT THE PRESSURE ON HER WITH YOUR FEET.
ZEEE (WHEEZE)
ぜー
ZEEE
ぜー
HEH-HEH! STILL MORE LEFT IN THE TANK!
YOU USED TO RUN ON PURE MOMENTUM, WHICH MEANT YOU WASTED A LOT OF EXERTION...
...BUT THIS TIME YOU WERE PATIENT AND CAREFUL.
TAMA MUST HAVE TAUGHT YOU THE BASICS.
SINCE SHE JOINED THE CLUB, EVERYONE'S MADE A GREAT AMOUNT OF PROGRESS.
WAIT, WHY IS TAMA TEACHING HER...?
I'M THE ONE WHO SHOULD BE TEACHING HER THE BASICS!
NEH-HEH-HEH
TAKE IT EASY. LIVE FREE.
IT'S JUST A SCHOOL ACTIVITY.

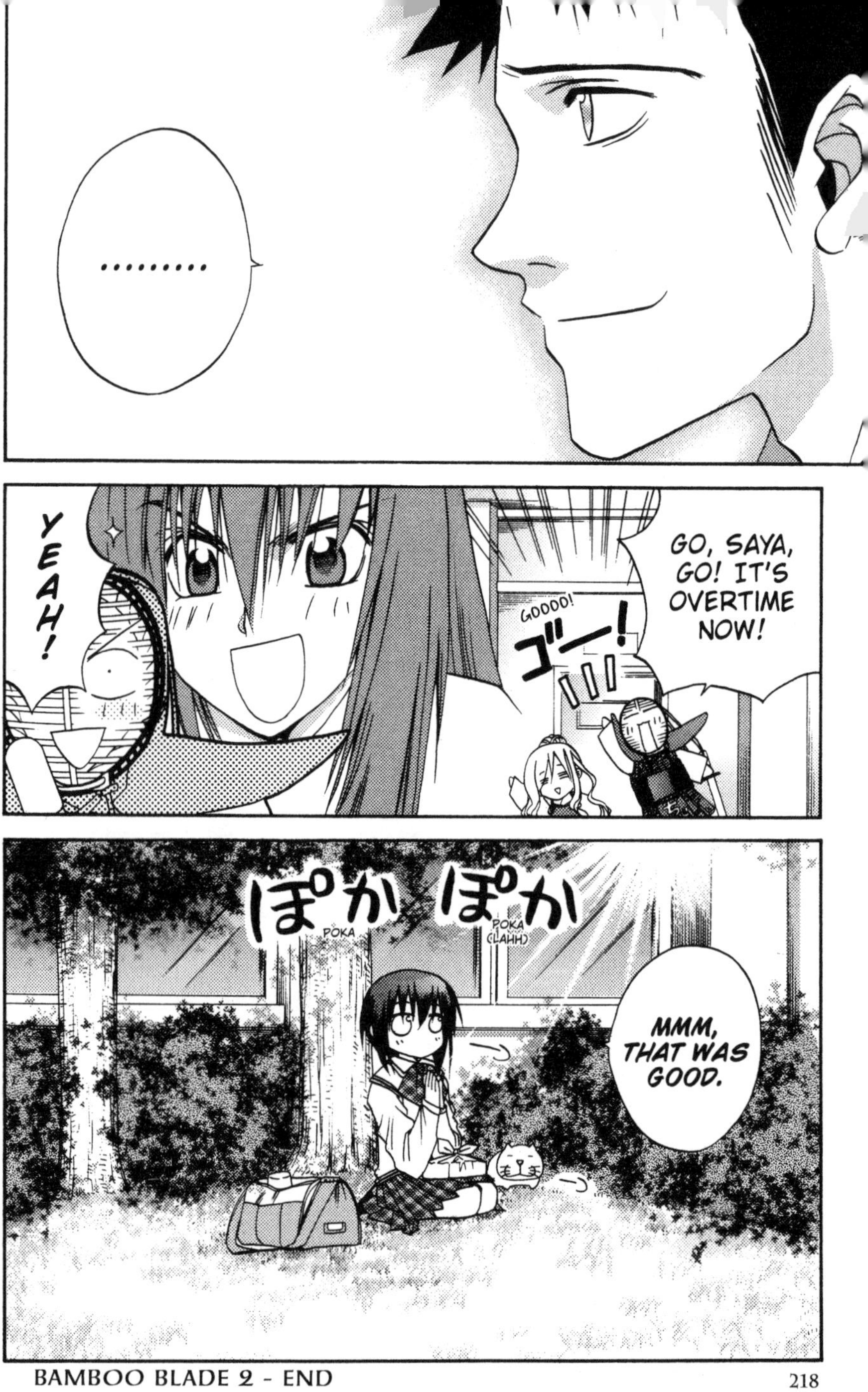
....
GO, SAYA, GO! IT'S OVERTIME NOW!
ゴー!
GOOOO!
YEAH!
ぽか ぽか
POKA
POKA (LAHH)
MMM, THAT WAS GOOD.

TRANSLATION NOTES

Page 6
Takeuchi: In this case, Kirino has misused the kanji for *shinai*, which literally reads "bamboo blade," the name of this very manga. Instead, she wrote "bamboo inside," which would normally be pronounced "*Takeuchi*," a fairly common Japanese surname. Naturally, the boys are confused.

Page 8
Armor: The guards, or *bogu*, all have their own names, which are mentioned in the dialogue. The *men* is the helmet and facemask that covers the head, the *do* is the breastplate that covers the chest, the *tare* refers to the hanging plates that are worn like a belt, and the *kote* are the gauntlets worn to protect the hands.

Shichi-go-san: The rite-of-passage day, observed in mid-November, for Japanese children. Literally meaning "seven-five-three," it's a festival day where seven-year-old girls, five-year-old boys, and three-year-old boys and girls are dressed up to go out to the nearest shrine. For many children, Shichi-go-san is the first time they are dressed in traditional kimonos, which is why Tamaki thinks of it when she sees everyone fussing over Dan's outfit.

Page 13
Eiko: There's just a slight visual difference between the kanji in Dan's last name, *Eiga* ("splendid flower") and the word *eikou* ("splendid light"), which means "glory."

Page 28
Men: As stated previously, this is the name for the helmet worn in kendo. It's common practice to call out "men!" when you strike at the head. The same goes for striking any other piece of armor—scoring a point in an official match requires you to vocalize the target area.

Page 37
Varcan: A parody of Varsan, a Japanese brand of canned bug repellent smoke.

Page 58
Kouhai: The opposite of *senpai*, i.e., one who is younger or newer within a group.

Page 127
Jagarico: A brand of crispy potato snacks that is sold in a cup.

Page 130
Visual-kei: Meaning "visual style," a type of rock music and its accompanying fashion, usually featuring extravagant costumes and makeup in a somewhat gothic, dark style with beautiful, androgynous performers.

Tongari Corn: A brand of corn snack that comes in a hollowed-out corn shape that is easy to slip onto the fingers, as shown here.

Page 131
Senpo, Jiho, Chuken, Fukusho, Taisho: These are the five ranks that make up a kendo team and determine the order in which the players appear. For more information on the formal rules and workings of kendo, see the bonus manga on pages 152-154!

Page 155
Toro, Ikura: *Toro* is tuna, and *ikura* is salmon roe (eggs). These are very popular sushi toppings.

Page 162
Fameeres: This name is a play on the Japanese term for "family restaurants," which is *famiresu*.

Page 173
Men ari: When a point has been scored, the judge will call out the area struck (*men*, *kote*, *do*, etc.) and then "*ari*," signifying that a point has been scored in the area named.

Page 208
Footwork: The meanings of the four types of footwork are as follows:
Okuri-ashi = "Sending steps"
Hiraki-ashi = "Opening steps"
Tsugi-ashi = "Connecting steps"
Ayumi-ashi = "Walking steps"

THANK YOU VERY MUCH FOR READING VOLUME 2. OUT OF EVERYTHING I'VE WRITTEN IN MY LIFE, *BAMBOO BLADE* IS BY THE FAR MOST "PLAIN" AND CONTAINS THE LEAST OF MY PERSONAL ECCENTRICITIES.

I AIM FOR A VERY BASIC FOUNDATION, THAT OF ENJOYING A WIDE CAST OF CHARACTERS ENJOYING THEIR EVERYDAY LIVES. I PUT AN APPRECIABLE—MAKE THAT CONSIDERABLE—AMOUNT OF CARE INTO THE STYLE OF THEIR DIALOGUE, BECAUSE I THINK THAT CAN SIGNIFICANTLY AFFECT THE WORLDVIEW CONTAINED WITHIN THE STORY. BY THE WAY, THE SMALLER, HANDWRITTEN LINES THAT APPEAR OUTSIDE OF THE BUBBLES ARE USUALLY ADDED BY IGARASHI-SENSEI TO THE STORYBOARDS I SEND HIM, SO PLEASE ENJOY THEM TOO.

THE SPECIAL OMAKE MANGA ON THE FOLLOWING PAGES WAS ALSO CREATED ENTIRELY BY IGARASHI-SENSEI. USUALLY I ASK HIM TO FOLLOW ALONG STRICTLY WITH THE STORYBOARD VERSION, BUT THESE ARE ENTIRELY HIS OWN CREATION. WILL THERE BE MORE IN VOLUME 3 TOO?

WELL, I REALLY HOPE YOU'RE ENJOYING THE RIDE SO FAR. WE'LL BE PUTTING PLENTY OF WORK INTO THIS GOING FORWARD, SO PLEASE STICK WITH US.

– MASAHIRO
*   TOTSUKA*

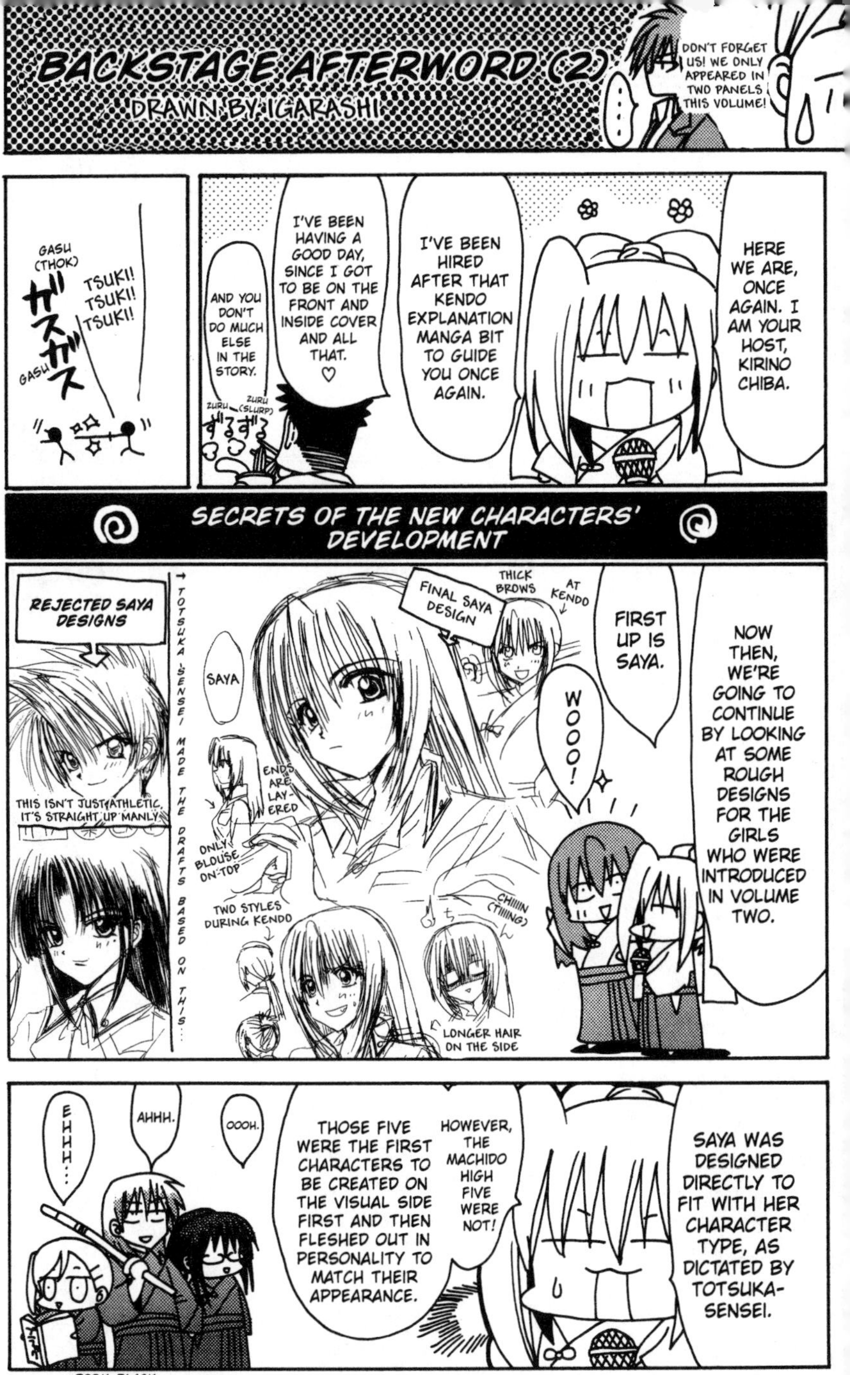
BACKSTAGE AFTERWORD (2)
DRAWN BY IGARASHI
DON'T FORGET US! WE ONLY APPEARED IN TWO PANELS THIS VOLUME!
...
HERE WE ARE, ONCE AGAIN. I AM YOUR HOST, KIRINO CHIBA.
I'VE BEEN HIRED AFTER THAT KENDO EXPLANATION MANGA BIT TO GUIDE YOU ONCE AGAIN.
I'VE BEEN HAVING A GOOD DAY, SINCE I GOT TO BE ON THE FRONT AND INSIDE COVER AND ALL THAT. ♡
AND YOU DON'T DO MUCH ELSE IN THE STORY.
ZURU ZURU (SLURP)
TSUKI! TSUKI! TSUKI!
GASU (THOK) GASU
SECRETS OF THE NEW CHARACTERS' DEVELOPMENT
NOW THEN, WE'RE GOING TO CONTINUE BY LOOKING AT SOME ROUGH DESIGNS FOR THE GIRLS WHO WERE INTRODUCED IN VOLUME TWO.
FIRST UP IS SAYA.
WOOOO!
FINAL SAYA DESIGN
THICK BROWS
AT KENDO
SAYA
ENDS ARE LAYERED
ONLY BLOUSE ON TOP
TWO STYLES DURING KENDO
CHIIIN (TIIIING)
LONGER HAIR ON THE SIDE
→ TOTSUKA-SENSEI MADE THE DRAFTS BASED ON THIS...
REJECTED SAYA DESIGNS
THIS ISN'T JUST ATHLETIC, IT'S STRAIGHT UP MANLY.
SAYA WAS DESIGNED DIRECTLY TO FIT WITH HER CHARACTER TYPE, AS DICTATED BY TOTSUKA-SENSEI.
HOWEVER, THE MACHIDO HIGH FIVE WERE NOT!
THOSE FIVE WERE THE FIRST CHARACTERS TO BE CREATED ON THE VISUAL SIDE FIRST AND THEN FLESHED OUT IN PERSONALITY TO MATCH THEIR APPEARANCE.
OOOH.
AHHH.
EHHH...
BOOK: BLACK

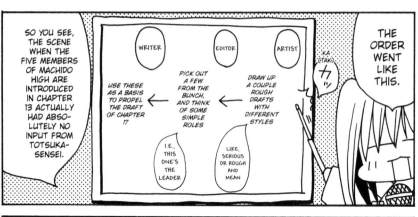

THE ORDER WENT LIKE THIS.
カッ KA (TAK)
ARTIST
DRAW UP A COUPLE ROUGH DRAFTS WITH DIFFERENT STYLES
LIKE, SERIOUS OR ROUGH AND MEAN
EDITOR
PICK OUT A FEW FROM THE BUNCH, AND THINK OF SOME SIMPLE ROLES
I.E., THIS ONE'S THE LEADER
WRITER
USE THESE AS A BASIS TO PROPEL THE DRAFT OF CHAPTER 17
SO YOU SEE, THE SCENE WHEN THE FIVE MEMBERS OF MACHIDO HIGH ARE INTRODUCED IN CHAPTER 13 ACTUALLY HAD ABSOLUTELY NO INPUT FROM TOTSUKA-SENSEI.
YOUR PROOF.
YOKOO.
HARADA.
14
OF COURSE, I WANT THE REST OF YOU TO PUT IN A STRONG EFFORT TOO!
BECAUSE LOSING TO KOJIRO IS THE LAST THING I CAN AFFORD!
PP.14-15 OF TOTSUKA-SENSEI'S STORYBOARD OF CHAPTER 13
WE'RE FACELESS ZOMBIES!!
WOOOOW
DURING THIS PROCESS, WE MADE ONE HUGE MISTAKE.
WHAT'S THAT?
THE CHARACTER THE ARTIST HAD ASSUMED WAS GOING TO PLAY THE "BOSS" ROLE TURNED OUT TO BE CAST AS A TOTAL WUSS.
...NISHI-YAMA...?
GOT IT IN ONE.
びくっ BIKU (TWITCH)
?

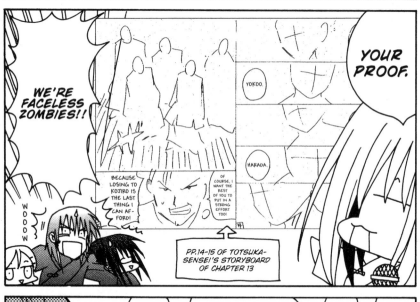

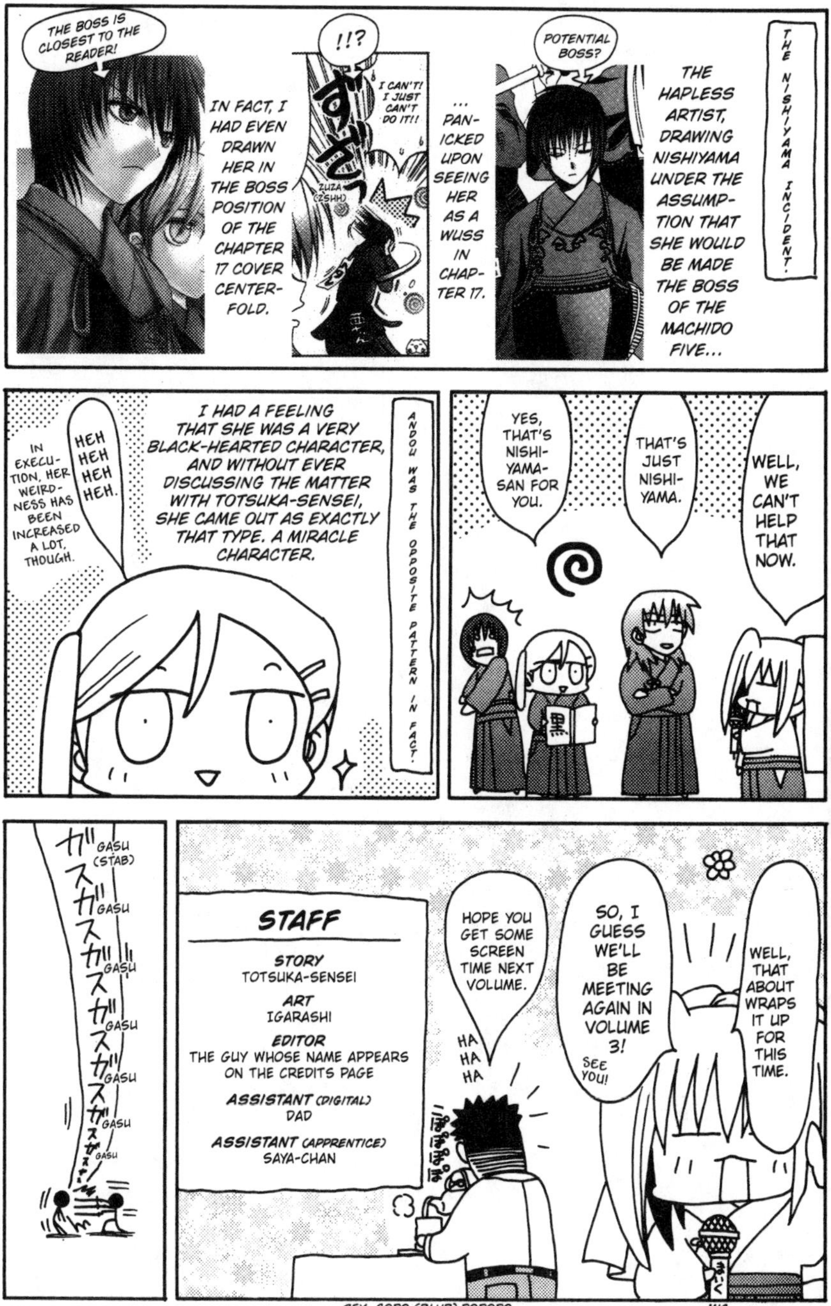
THE NISHIYAMA INCIDENT.
THE HAPLESS ARTIST, DRAWING NISHIYAMA UNDER THE ASSUMPTION THAT SHE WOULD BE MADE THE BOSS OF THE MACHIDO FIVE...
POTENTIAL BOSS?
...PANICKED UPON SEEING HER AS A WUSS IN CHAPTER 17.
!!?
I CAN'T! I JUST CAN'T DO IT!!
ZUZA (ZSHH)
IN FACT, I HAD EVEN DRAWN HER IN THE BOSS POSITION OF THE CHAPTER 17 COVER CENTERFOLD.
THE BOSS IS CLOSEST TO THE READER!
WELL, WE CAN'T HELP THAT NOW.
THAT'S JUST NISHIYAMA.
YES, THAT'S NISHIYAMA-SAN FOR YOU.
ANDOU WAS THE OPPOSITE PATTERN IN FACT.
I HAD A FEELING THAT SHE WAS A VERY BLACK-HEARTED CHARACTER, AND WITHOUT EVER DISCUSSING THE MATTER WITH TOTSUKA-SENSEI, SHE CAME OUT AS EXACTLY THAT TYPE. A MIRACLE CHARACTER.
HEH HEH HEH HEH.
IN EXECUTION, HER WEIRDNESS HAS BEEN INCREASED A LOT, THOUGH.
WELL, THAT ABOUT WRAPS IT UP FOR THIS TIME.
SO, I GUESS WE'LL BE MEETING AGAIN IN VOLUME 3!
SEE YOU!
HOPE YOU GET SOME SCREEN TIME NEXT VOLUME.
HA HA HA
STAFF
STORY
TOTSUKA-SENSEI
ART
IGARASHI
EDITOR
THE GUY WHOSE NAME APPEARS ON THE CREDITS PAGE
ASSISTANT (DIGITAL)
DAD
ASSISTANT (APPRENTICE)
SAYA-CHAN
GASU (STAB)
GASU
GASU
GASU
GASU
GASU
GASU

SFX: GOPO (BLUB) POPOPO MIC

NEXT VOLUME PREVIEW

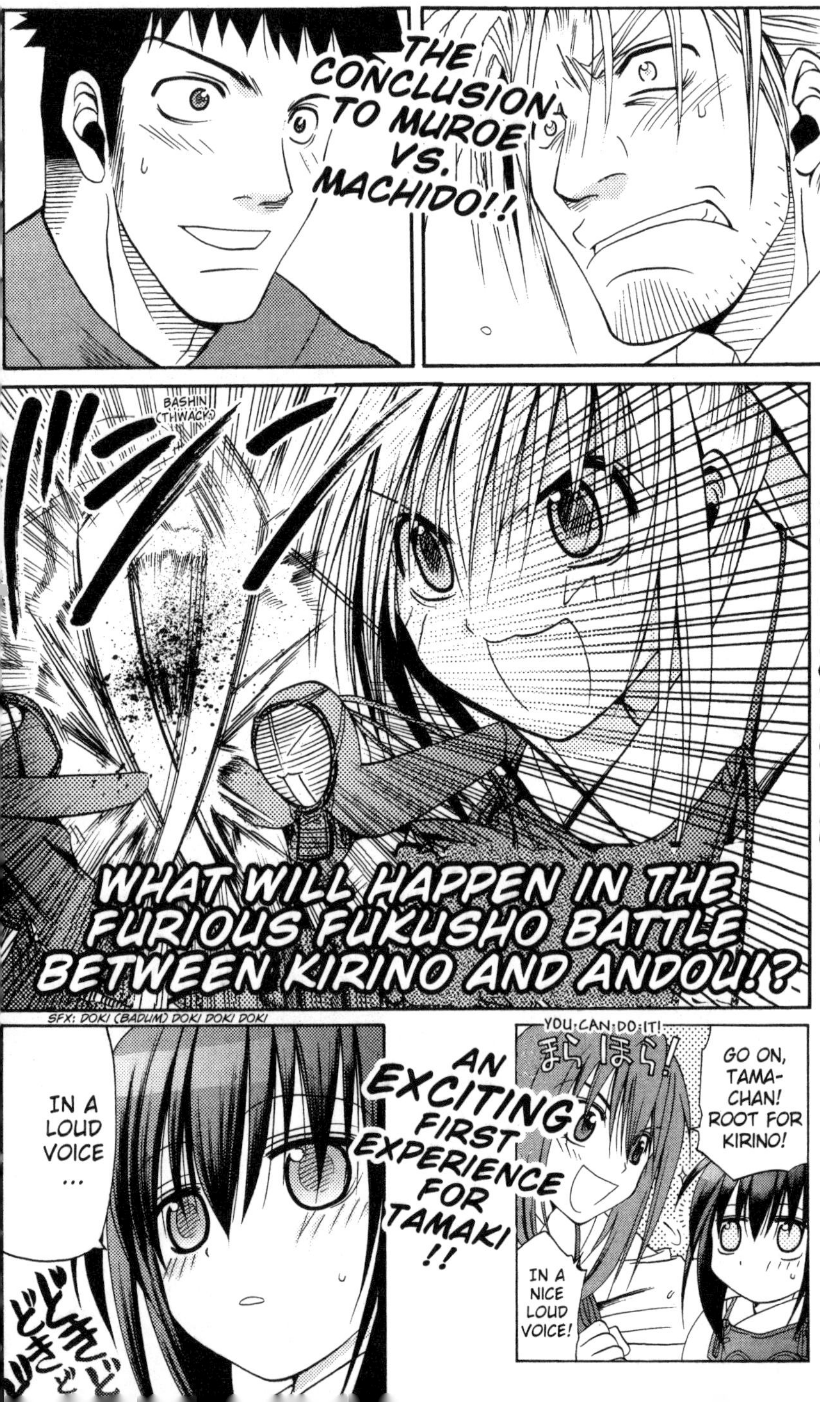
THE CONCLUSION TO MUROE VS. MACHIDO!!
BASHIN (THWACK)
WHAT WILL HAPPEN IN THE FURIOUS FUKUSHO BATTLE BETWEEN KIRINO AND ANDOU!?
SFX: DOKI (BADUM) DOKI DOKI DOKI
YOU CAN DO IT!
ほらほら!
GO ON, TAMA-CHAN! ROOT FOR KIRINO!
IN A NICE LOUD VOICE!
AN EXCITING FIRST EXPERIENCE FOR TAMAKI!!
IN A LOUD VOICE...
どきどき どきどき

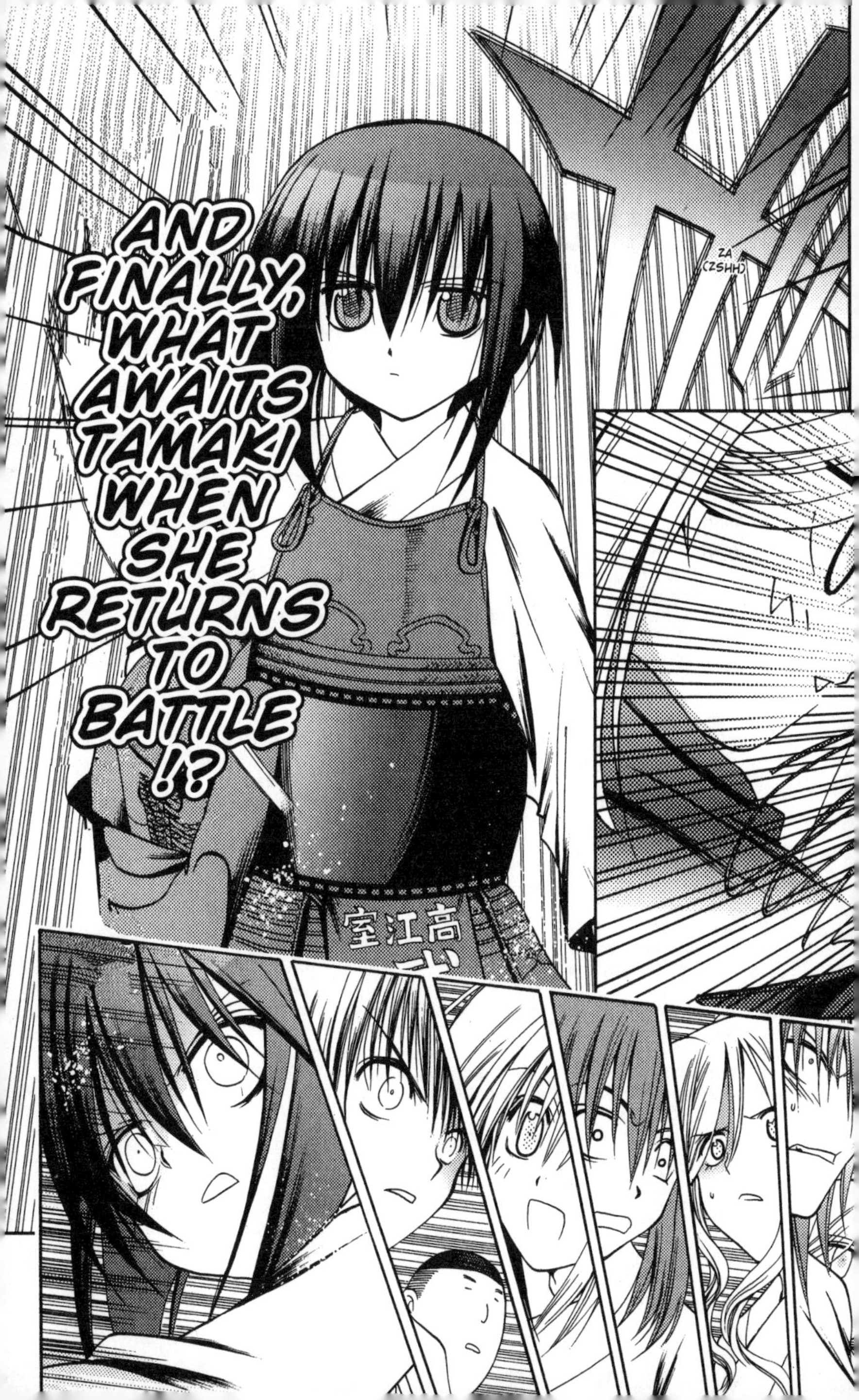
ZA (ZSHH)
AND FINALLY, WHAT AWAITS TAMAKI WHEN SHE RETURNS TO BATTLE !?
室江高

BAMBOO BLADE ②

MASAHIRO TOTSUKA
AGURI IGARASHI

Translation: Stephen Paul

Lettering: Terri Delgado

BAMBOO BLADE Vol. 2 © 2006 Masahiro Totsuka, Aguri Igarashi /
SQUARE ENIX CO., LTD. All rights reserved. First published in Japan in
2006 by SQUARE ENIX CO., LTD. English translation rights arranged
with SQUARE ENIX CO., LTD. and Hachette Book Group through Tuttle-
Mori Agency, Inc.

Translation © 2009 by SQUARE ENIX CO., LTD.

Yen Press
Hachette Book Group
237 Park Avenue, New York, NY 10017

Visit our Web sites at www.HachetteBookGroup.com and
www.YenPress.com.

Yen Press is an imprint of Hachette Book Group, Inc. The Yen Press name
and logo are trademarks of Hachette Book Group, Inc.

First Yen Press Edition: September 2009

ISBN: 978-0-7595-3046-1

10 9 8 7 6 5 4 3 2 1

BVG

Printed in the United States of America